# Fire Burn

"Double, double, toil and trouble,
Fire burn and cauldron bubble."

*Macbeth, IV, 1: The Witches' Song*

# *Fire Burn*

WORLD WAR II DIARIES

Irene Zarina White

Copyright © 2006 by Irene Zarina White.

Library of Congress Number:     2005907089
ISBN:          Hardcover        1-59926-349-1
               Softcover        1-59926-348-3

All rights reserved. No part of this book may be reproduced or transmitted in any form or by any means, electronic or mechanical, including photocopying, recording, or by any information storage and retrieval system, without permission in writing from the copyright owner.

This book was printed in the United States of America.

**To order additional copies of this book, contact:**
Xlibris Corporation
1-888-795-4274
www.Xlibris.com
Orders@Xlibris.com
27365

# CONTENTS

PREFACE .................................................................................................. 9

## PART 1: RED-WHITE-RED FLAG OF LATVIA

Chapter One: Latvia—Last Days of Freedom ............................. 13
Chapter Two: Under Gathering Clouds......................................... 38

## PART 2: HAMMER AND SICKLE

Chapter Three: The Soviet "Liberation" ....................................... 53
Chapter Four: The Sun of Stalin's Constitution ......................... 71

## PART 3: THE SWASTIKA

Chapter Five: Without a Country ..................................................... 91
Chapter Six: Buna, Bombs and Propaganda ............................. 115
Chapter Seven: Past and Present Meet ....................................... 144
Chapter Eight: Shadows of Death ................................................. 163
Chapter Nine: Love and Laughter versus Total War ............... 201
Chapter Ten: Terror ............................................................................ 237
Chapter Eleven: "To be or not to be" .......................................... 264
Chapter Twelve: Apocalypse ............................................................ 294
Chapter Thirteen: Götterdämmerung .......................................... 324

## PART 4: STARS AND STRIPES

Chapter Fourteen: Interregnum ...................................................... 345
Chapter Fifteen: Yankee Doodle Dandy ...................................... 381
Epilogue .................................................................................................. 411

To my daughters:
Mary White-Kaba, Ph.D.
Irene White Berwick, M.S.
Elizabeth White Randall, M.D.


And in memory of their father, Dr. Merit Penniman White,
Commonwealth Professor of Civil Engineering at the
University of Massachusetts at Amherst
(1908-1996)

# PREFACE

On June 17, 1940 the Soviet Union invaded my home country Latvia. The Red Army rolled over our borders straight to our ancient capital, Riga, and within a month we were annexed. Latvia became the fifteenth Soviet Socialist Republic against the will of its people. That conquest, however, was short-lived. In July of 1941 the German army was approaching the Baltic States and the Soviet occupation forces had to retreat. In their fury they began to destroy the old German parts of Riga, which had been founded in 1201 by colonists from northern Germany.

These included the seven hundred-year-old St. Peter's Church. Members of the Red Army threw canisters of burning gasoline into the church and shot the Latvian firemen who tried to save the building. The photograph on the front cover shows the steeple in flames. It was the highest wooden structure in Europe—134 meters. When it fell the bells rang for the last time and then there was silence. An ancient historic monument had been willfully destroyed in a fury of hatred and revenge.

I started writing these memoirs based on my diaries in 1950, shortly after coming to the USA, when the war years were still fresh in my mind. In the years following I was busily engaged in professional activities while also raising a family. In 1967 I again began to work on my memoirs whenever time permitted. This work is now completed.

The events and people described are genuine. All names, with the exception of historical personages, close relatives, and my lifelong friend Karen, have been fictionalized in order to protect the privacy of the individuals.

Irene Zarina White<br>
Westerly, Rhode Island<br>
August, 2004

# PART 1

## RED-WHITE-RED FLAG OF LATVIA

# CHAPTER ONE

## Latvia—Last Days of Freedom

*September 1, 1939, Mazsalaca* Another week and my summer vacation on Aunt Natalie's farm will be over! I am sitting under my favorite apple tree. I should be studying, but I am writing in my diary instead. I love the view from this place I call "Orchard Hill." The farmlands stretch all the way to the dark woods at the horizon. The sky is like a transparent dome rising high over the country. On a slight elevation above the fields and meadows, stands our old white country church—the only church for miles and miles around.

On Sunday mornings the farmers come from all directions in their horse-drawn carriages to attend church services. Then the bells ring in the high steeple, and on Orchard Hill we can hear the singing of the congregation. Familiar tunes of solemn anthems, sung for hundreds of years in Lutheran churches, come floating through the air. Church services and the daily evening train from Riga provide the only excitement in this little village. I find it the ideal spot to study for my finals.

I was still on Orchard Hill when I heard the 6:00 PM train from Riga approaching. Shortly thereafter, old Mr. Maximoff—the local Russian high-school teacher who is Aunt Natalie's year-round lodger—burst upon me. "Irene," he shouted in great agitation. "Irene, the war has started! This morning at dawn the German Army invaded Poland."

I should be alarmed, but I am not. I feel so safe in our remote little corner of the world. "Gottesländchen" the Baltic Germans used to call Latvia in former centuries—"God's own little country."

After supper, Aunt Natalie, Mr. Maximoff and I sat in front of the house near the flowerbeds. Dusk had clouded the countryside, and stars began to twinkle. Sweet fragrances of roses and reseda filled the air; windows in the village were lighted. Out of the darkness a bat appeared and began to circle above us. I watched its flight, no longer paying attention to the conversation. Suddenly Maximoff's voice reached my ear: "Today is a turning point. The short respite is over. This new war will change all our lives."

"You are seeing the situation too darkly, Mr. Maximoff," I protested. But he shook his head. "We are no longer in control of events, Irene. It is as though we unsuspectingly live on a volcano that might erupt at any moment and destroy us all!"

*September 2, 1939* Like every Saturday during my stay in Mazsalaca, this afternoon was again spent in the cemetery. The visit to the family plot once a week on Saturday afternoons is a sacred, time-honored institution for all villagers. From early spring till late fall, they will troop out to the graves of their departed. It is a time not only for reminiscing, but also for busy activity. The lawn covering the grave mounds needs trimming. This is done by hand with shears. Flowers growing on top and at the foot of graves need weeding and watering. Hedges surrounding the plot have to be cut. Marble and granite memorials need cleaning and polishing, so that names and dates carved into the stones will stand out clearly.

Aunt Natalie collected a big bunch of flowers growing in her garden: yellow roses, white carnations, golden-brown dahlias. Then we set out to the cemetery—I with a flowerpot of purple asters in one hand, while balancing a garden rake and watering can in the other.

Approaching, we could see the gold-painted tops of the black cast-iron fence. The fence enclosed our plot, glistening in the sun like a row of shiny sentinels standing watch over our family graves. I went to fetch some water from the cemetery well. Aunt Natalie removed last week's bouquets, and I carried them to the dump—a huge mound consisting of wilted and rotten flowers in a corner of the cemetery wall. From the dump emanated a strange odor of decay, conjuring in me memories of wakes and open coffins, and of gloomy, flower-laden funerals.

Upon returning, I helped Aunt Natalie groom our plot, doing all the tasks necessary. When things were in perfect order we finally decorated the graves with fresh flowers. Aunt Cecilia got the roses, Grandma Amalia the dahlias, great aunts Rosalie and Melitta the carnations. Grandpapa, Amalia's second husband, former state councilor in Czarist Russian times, was honored with the flowerpot of asters.

Then Aunt Natalie and I sat down on our dainty white garden bench in a corner near the fence. We rested while gazing at the surrounding plots, each of them a flower garden in miniature, each in perfect shape.

Before leaving, I took the garden rake and smoothed out the light colored sand between the green mounds, obliterating our footprints. As a final touch, I made designs with the rake in such a way as to form a parquet pattern on the ground. Locking the gate, we cast a last glance at our family plot. In the afternoon light, filtering through the branches of tall birches and poplars, our family's final resting-place looked very peaceful and very lovely—not a frightening, gloomy place at all!

*September 3, 1939* Aunt Natalie this morning asked me to accompany her to church. I complied. After the service was over, we again headed to the cemetery. So did everyone else in the congregation, as is the local custom. On Saturdays the graves are decorated, on Sundays it is family visiting hour at the plot. No grooming is done on Sundays. Family members just sit together in their "after-church outdoor parlor" and talk among themselves or carry on little conversations across the fences and hedges with friends on neighboring plots. Mental notes are made regarding the flower decorations "next door," with the purpose of coming up with an even nicer flower arrangement during the following week, so as to outdo the neighbors, if possible.

It is a friendly competition and I have the feeling that it is mainly stemming from the great reverence felt for the memory of our dead. By no means are they forgotten, even if they have been dead for half a century or more.

Rosalie and Melitta died long before my time, but I have heard a lot about their lives and their deaths, at a young age, of TB, in the 1890's. Two oval metal memorial boxes, with a glass window in front, are set up at the head of their graves. These boxes seem to have been very fashionable before and after the turn of the century. Many graves originating in those days are marked with such oval memorials. Inside are metal wreaths shaped in the form of laurel leaves intertwined with roses and forget-me-nots. Rosalie's and Melitta's wreaths are painted in bright colors, as an added decorative touch: the leaves are a vivid green, the roses a flaming pink and the forget-me-nots a piercing blue.

In the center of this metal flower splendor, the girls' photographs are displayed. Underneath each photograph, a silver cross hangs from a narrow black velvet ribbon. The girls used to wear these crosses around their necks during their lifetime. Judging from their pictures, Rosalie was a blonde, Melitta a brunette. Both were wearing the elaborate upswept hairdos of the nineties, their faces framed by ruffled and laced high collars.

Aunt Cecilia's grave is in the center of the plot. At the foot of it rises a massive black granite obelisk in memory of Cecilia de Dobroliuboff. On a marble square in front of Cecilia's grave is an inscription, a last loving message from her sorrowing husband, a Russian nobleman:

> "Spi mirno i spokoino.
> Vek i liuboff opatj soyedinayut nas."
> ("Sleep in peace and harmony.
> Time and love shall again unite us.")

Grandma Amalia rests on her daughter's left; Grandpapa is on Cecilia's right. Grandpapa, although younger than Amalia, preceded her in death. Grandma died last March. I can still see her image before me, a tiny figure with silvery white hair, a face with regular features showing traces of former beauty, blue eyes still sparkling with a youthful light. She was my friend and confidante, always willing to listen to me.

*September 4, 1939* Yesterday Great Britain and France declared war on Germany.

The visit to the cemetery brought back memories of Aunt Cecilia's last days. I was eight years old, visiting my grandparents:

Cecilia coming from Paris to visit her parents in Latvia; Cecilia arriving in a two-engine airplane in the airport of Riga, the airfield being nothing but a big meadow covered with green grass, strewn with daisies and buttercups; Aunt Cecilia emerging from the plane in a light gray knitted cape, long jade earrings dangling from under a highly puffed-up hairdo, decorated with a black velvet band around her forehead; Aunt Cecilia smiling and kissing me, then embracing my parents.

I remember the trip to Grandma Amalia's farm, first the four-hour train ride, then a twenty-kilometer trek by horse and wagon, where Grandma and Grandpa were waiting; a happy week in July filled with summer sunshine, berries in the orchard and fascinating farm animals: horses, cows, a mother sow with a dozen rosy piglets, dogs and kittens, rabbits and their soft-furred little bunnies; and not to forget the chickens, dozens of them, mother hens and their fluffy babies and one big, beautiful shiny, multi-colored rooster, who woke us every morning at dawn with a magnificent "Kikiri-kiki!" right under our bedroom windows.

Grandpa, Cecilia and I would go berrying in the woods or gather mushrooms, big baskets full. Grandma stayed at home, preparing meals and supervising the activities on the farm.

The summer was hot but the woods were always cool: only dim light could filter through the branches of huge pines and majestic centuries-old oaks. Once in a while we would come to a clearing that let in the sun and a glimpse of blue sky, where white stems of birches gleamed like silver and where big, red, juicy, over-ripe, wild strawberries could be found in the shade of tall green grasses. There we would sit down and take a rest. Cecelia was so beautiful, still young in her early thirties, reclining there in the green grass in her lace-trimmed, white Parisian dress. She was telling her father something about Uncle Volodya and how "the worst was over now." I didn't understand it then. Years later Grandma Amalia told me that Vladimir Michailovich, her husband, had finally managed after many lean years to get a teller's job at a bank in Paris and how happy Cecilia had been about this.

Dusk was falling as we walked home, our baskets filled to the brim. I stayed behind Cecilia, following her in my usual manner like an adoring puppy. Suddenly I perceived a most startling sight: a small copper-colored snake slithered out from behind a berry bush like a flash of lightning and wound itself around the heel of Aunt Cecilia's right shoe, instantly disappearing again.

"Aunt Cecilia, a snake, a snake!" I yelled in great agitation. Grandpa and Cecilia jumped, but the snake was gone.

"You surely frightened us, Irochka," Grandpa said sternly, "it must have been your imagination."

"Grandpa, it was a real snake: I saw it and I am scared!" I started to cry. Cecilia comforted me. The tears eventually dried, but the fear remained all evening long.

Grandma had prepared a most wonderful meal of mushrooms in a sour cream sauce served over boiled potatoes. The grownups chatted and laughed, sitting together by candlelight, enjoying freshly picked wild strawberries with sugar and cream for dessert, while I got more and more sleepy. Finally I was sent to bed.

I awoke in the dark of night from a horrible piercing scream. Jumping out of bed and running into Cecilia's room, I saw her standing in bright moonlight clad in a nightgown in front of the bed, clutching her side, her face contorted in pain. Grandpa and Grandma came rushing in, Grandma carrying a lighted kerosene lamp.

In the morning Cecilia was much worse and Grandpa sent one of his farmhands on a horse to fetch the doctor. There was no telephone in the farm country for miles and miles around. Our only physician was 20 Km away in Valmiera, the nearest town.

Hours of anxious waiting followed. I was not allowed to visit Cecilia. The farmhand returned about noon, saying that the doctor would be coming presently. At about 3:00 PM I heard a strange puffing and chugging noise and ran out to the road to see whether the doctor was finally arriving. A small black automobile was jouncing down the country road in an immense cloud of dust. Perched high on the seats in the open car were two figures: the doctor and his nurse. The nurse wore a white cap with a red cross on it.

I ran into the house shouting, "The doctor has come!" The physician and the nurse immediately were taken into Aunt Cecilia's room. I had to stay outside.

After a long, long wait the door opened, and Grandma came out crying. Cecilia is dying!" she sobbed. I quietly sneaked into the sickroom and timidly moved to Cecilia's bed. She was lying under the covers, motionless.

Grandpa stood at the foot of the bed and I heard him whisper with a hoarse, tear-filled voice: "Is there any hope, doctor?" The doctor shook his head. The nurse stood by silently.

Years later I heard from Grandma Amalia that Cecilia had suffered a violent attack of appendicitis, that the appendix had burst, and peritonitis had set in, that the doctor had come prepared to operate on the kitchen table, but that it was too late.

Standing there at Aunt Cecilia's bedside on that hot July, I had no conception of death or dying. She would surely recover and then we would again go berrying in the woods!

With these happy thoughts I skipped out of the room and decided to pick some flowers for Aunt Cecilia. I ran to the rye field not far from our house where I had seen blue cornflowers growing. I gathered a big bunch of these brightly colored, sweet smelling flowers and then dashed back to the house and tiptoed into Aunt Cecilia's room. The scene had changed. The doctor and the nurse were gone. Grandma was now standing at the foot of the bed. The afternoon sun was weaving golden patterns on the bedcover. I put my bunch of flowers right into the middle of those brightly colored sunny spots and circles and said, "I brought you some flowers, Aunt Cecilia!"

A weak smile crossed over Cecilia's face and she whispered, "Thank you Irochka . . . give my love to Volodya!" Exhausted she closed her eyes and said no more.

Evening came and I was sent to bed. I was fast asleep when a hand shook me awake at midnight: "Wake up, Irochka, your aunt is dying!"

I stumbled out of bed and was led into the death chamber.

Cecilia lay motionless, eyes closed, Grandpa and Grandma were at her side. At the other side of the bed stood three farm women in long, dark clothes and kerchiefs tied under the chin. They stood in a row silently, solemnly, waiting.

There was a strange tranquility in the room, no sobs, no words, no prayers, only stillness. Cecilia's breathing stopped.

At that moment the strangest thing happened. The three farmwomen approached the bed, lifted Aunt Cecilia's body and propped her up with her back against the headboard. Then they proceeded to wash her face and to comb her matted golden-brown hair, which was hanging in loose strands over her shoulders. "Grandma, what are they doing to Aunt Cecilia?" I asked in a state of shock.

"They are preparing her for burial!" said Grandma amidst sobs.

"What is burial?" I wanted to know, but got no answer.

Then Grandma tied a white silk handkerchief around Cecilia's lower jaw and fastened it in a knot above her forehead. Now Aunt Cecilia looked as though on top of all her other troubles she had a toothache too. I broke out in tears: "Poor, poor Aunt Cecilia," I sobbed, "what are they doing to you?" and I started to scream. I was hastily removed and put back to bed.

The day after Cecilia's death I peeked through the keyhole into the barn, where she was lying in state. I remember seeing candles flickering in the shadows filling the barn, and observing the multitude of flowers surrounding the coffin, and hidden among them buckets of ice to counteract the sizzling July temperatures.

*September 9, 1939, Riga* I am back home again in Riga, returning by train.

In front of the station, a row of horse-and-buggies was waiting. I hired one. My driver, in his dark blue uniform adorned with huge metal buttons, perching high on his elevated front seat, cracked his whip to start the horse. Leaning in the open back seat and listening to the rhythmic "clip-clop" of the horse's hooves, I watched the panorama of the city slide by: long alleys of trees by Wohrmann's Park, the Opera, the University, and the Esplanade—where Army parades are held. To the south of it the five onion-shaped cupolas of the Russian Orthodox Church glistened in the sun. A few blocks north we reached the Marksmen's Garden. One more turn, and I was finally home.

The dark, gloomy dignity of the apartment buildings on my street—row upon row of high stone fronts and heavy oak-paneled portals—depresses me. There is no tree, no sun, no grass on our street. The contrast between this dark solemnity and the open spaces in the country, illuminated by light and glowing colors, is almost too painful to bear.

*September 10, 1939* To my surprise, writing a diary has turned out to be a challenge. I am beginning to see my surroundings with a new awareness. I have lived in this town all my life. I have met people every day, some of them for many years. But my attention seemed directed inward: on my thoughts, my studies; on the books I read, the music I had heard.

Now suddenly a change has occurred within me. I see people and things as if they were on a stage—with a spotlight illuminating the actors and casting a sudden beam on a familiar street, an old house, a tree, a monument, a garden fence even, whose details I had never noticed before.

*September 11, 1939* Last night I thought about Grandma Amalia, who died just a few months ago. I remember how exciting it was for me to listen to her stories of her youth in old Russia, under the Czars.

Grandma Amalia claimed to be the natural daughter of a Baltic German nobleman. In those days the "jus primae noctis" was quite commonplace in our country—the right of the landowner to lie with the newly married peasant on the "first" night after the wedding. At any rate, she grew up in the nobleman's castles as the companion of his legitimate children.

At the age of 20, in 1872, she married Karl Zarin, whose ancestors had come across the Baltic Sea from Malmö in the 17$^{th}$ Century, when Livonia was part of Sweden. Their son, my father August Konstantin, was born in 1875.

I have always found Grandma Amalia fascinating. She was so sparkling and so full of life; old age had not affected her spirit. I wish I had her personality and her wit, but I don't. I am usually very, very quiet, very shy, dubbed the "introvert" by my fellow students. The only thing that I inherited from Grandma Amalia is her looks. However, I am an enlarged copy of the original. Grandma was only five feet tall, but I have her pale skin, her pale blonde hair, her long and narrow hands and feet. My only redeeming features are my eyes—they are dark blue and look enormous in my pale, thin face. They too are inherited from Grandma. Father had the same eyes.

*September 12, 1939* Here I am—a university student—and still losing myself in fancy, and escaping into old family memories. But I must return to reality. There is a war going on! I must not forget this. We listen to the broadcasts, and we read the papers, but it means so little to us. Nothing at all is happening here in our little country. Nothing has changed! Meanwhile the German Armies are stampeding through Poland and their "Führer" Adolf Hitler is triumphant.

I first heard of this man six years ago when I was still in the local German high school. The German students in my class were all very excited, because Hitler had just become Chancellor of the German Reich.

The German girls seemed to know a lot about Hitler. I had never heard of him before. An argument arose between some of the girls and our teacher of German Literature, Fräulein Josephine von Kolmer. In astonishment I heard the high-pitched voices of Gertrude and Eleanor and Gisela and a dozen others trying to convince our teacher, a dignified and strict middle-aged spinster, that Hitler was the salvation of Germany.

In reply, Fräulein von Kolmer shook her graying head exclaiming in a deep and sorrowful voice, "I am afraid for Germany, so very afraid!" I did not quite comprehend what she meant, but I have not forgotten her words.

*September 13, 1939* In a few days classes will start at the University. This is my last year—and by next spring I'll have earned my degree in Chemical Engineering. The going at times has been rough, the course load extremely heavy, with a majority of subjects considered traditionally more appropriate for men. (In fact my first year, I was the only girl out of 150 beginning students in the Chemistry Department.) Besides chemistry lectures and various chemistry labs, we have had courses in mechanics, engineering, physics, calculus, architecture, plant designing, chemical technologies, electrochemistry, and bookkeeping. All this has been completed, and my main job now is to finish up some special projects—among those a microscopy lab course—and to prepare for the finals.

This is just as well, because since starting to work full-time as a chemist last January, it is very hard to study at the same time. But I must not complain. I got the job upon recommendation of my professors, even before having earned my degree.

*September 14, 1939* Today I successfully passed the exam in Heat and Water Technology, for which I had been preparing during my stay at Aunt Natalie's.

As I stepped out of the Chemistry building I ran into Wolfgang Peters, my first love. I have not seen him in years, ever since that high school dance when I was sixteen and he a couple of years older.

The neighborhood children would gather in large groups and play exciting games of "Hide and Seek" or "Catch" in backyards, gardens and even in the gloomy high—ceilinged foyers of our apartment houses. Wolfgang lived around the corner from me. A multitude of languages were heard among the children; and this is how I acquired my first practice in Russian and even learned some Yiddish, besides speaking Latvian and German.

Wolfgang is a Baltic German whose family came from St. Petersburg in Russia. After we started going to elementary school, I to an all-girls' school, he to a boys' school, we didn't speak to each other again for years. Suddenly one Sunday I met Wolfgang in St. Peter's church. I had become a skinny, lanky teenager, and he was equally skinny and had grown quite tall. And, like me, he seemed forever puzzled about what to do with his arms and legs.

We recognized each other and exchanged a horribly embarrassed greeting. From then on we would occasionally meet in the mornings on the way to school. We walked together for three city blocks, where our ways parted because we went to different buildings of the German Gymnasium, he to the Boys' Section, I to the Girls' Department.

One day I realized that whenever Wolfgang was in sight, an alarming change seemed to come over me. I was happy and frightened at the same time, and these strange emotions made my head spin. About this time the date of the school dance was announced.

For several weeks, Mother and I were busy with preparations. Mother sewed my dress according to my own design. It was my first formal, and I planned the accessories, and even made myself an evening bag out of lace and glass beads over satin lining.

Father, an engineer working for the Government, chuckled whenever he observed these preparations. Since I was an only child, my ambitious mother had put all her hopes in me and had stamped me the "studious type."

My appearance must have surprised my parents when I finally was dressed, coifed, and ready to leave for the ball. I looked at myself in the mirror and saw a creature quite unknown to me. I was clothed in blue silk and white lace, with a wide skirt floating down to the tips of shiny silver slippers.

All this glory instead of the usual school outfit: narrow dark blue skirt and white blouse, long heavy cotton stockings and black leather flats. Instead of two braids, which dangled down to my hips or were wound around my head, there was a mass of curls piled high in back with graceful corkscrews falling gently to my shoulders.

I laughed in delight: what a change! All of my usual awkwardness and shyness had vanished! Now I knew how the ugly duckling must have felt when the miracle of his transformation came upon him.

My father hired a cab and took me to the ball. There I joined my classmates: the other girls all in their finery, and the boys, decked in dark coats and striped trousers. The boys stood by the opposite wall and stared at us. The teachers made some introductions.

Suddenly I spied Wolfgang coming into the auditorium. For the first time in my life feeling utterly irresistible, I floated up to him on a cloud of sky blue silk and started a conversation. To my surprise Wolfgang eagerly responded and soon we were both chatting away and dancing every dance together. Best of all I liked the Vienna waltz. To the lilting tunes of Johann Strauss we whirled faster and faster, the walls began to whirl with us; the other dancing couples became a blur. I looked up at the ceiling and saw the two huge chandeliers also whirl in rhythm with the music . . . one, two, three . . . one, two, three . . . while the lights were reflected in their vibrating crystals, set in motion by the music. I smiled at Wolfgang, his dark eyes smiled back at me. Even our usually stern teachers smiled at us!

And today I met Wolfgang again quite by accident. I had not seen him since that dance. That night he escorted me home and said goodbye with a handshake. Neither of us had enough courage to kiss the other goodnight, and the romance was over! We both made it a point to avoid each other. Why? I do not know!

Wolfgang told me today that he is preparing for a career in pharmacy and plans to graduate within a year or two. I have outgrown my puppy love for him, but I feel kindly toward him.

*September 15, 1939* This morning during microscopy lab I debated whether I should tell our professor Zemite that I am Cecilia's niece. I know all about his intentions of long ago to marry my Aunt Cecilia. Grandma Amalia had told me the story in great detail.

Professor Zemite is a medium-sized pudgy man with a shock of red hair and pale eyes disappearing in folds of freckled skin. When he knew Cecilia, he was a young student of Pharmacy at the University of Dorpat (Tartu) in Estonia. The year was 1912, and Grandpapa Ernest held a government job in that city in the service of the Czar. By imperial decree, Grandpapa had been made a "dvorianin"—a nobleman—for "services to the crown" and given the order of St. Ann. Ernest had started from humble beginnings, coming from a farm near Mazsalaca. Grandpa Ernest was the great-grandson of a French soldier in the Napoleonic army which invaded Russia in 1812. This military campaign ended in total disaster for the French. Hundreds of thousands of soldiers died in the icy winter of 1812. A few found refuge on Latvian farms. One of these was my step—grandpa's great—grandfather. Ernest rembered seeing the French military cap and cape, hanging on the wall of the farmhouse.

Grandpa Ernest decided that his only daughter Cecilia should marry no one but a Latvian. Janis Zemite was selected. Cecilia, then in her early twenties, intelligent and well educated, refused to take Janis Zemite for her wedded husband. She was in love with a Russian student of the Law. Handsome, dashing, high-spirited Vladimir Michailovich Dobroliuboff was a scion of an old, aristocratic and wealthy family then living in Moscow. Vladimir's oldest brother, Michail Michailovitch, was a poet and philosopher a close associate of Leo Tolstoy, the great Russian writer.

Zemite pressed his suit; and one morning, Grandma Amalia discovered to her great shock and dismay that Cecilia had disappeared without a trace. Cecilia had taken matters into her own hands and had eloped with Vladimir Michailovich. They settled in Moscow, where her husband's illustrious family received Cecilia with open arms, although she was not of noble birth, due to her charm, her beauty and her gentle ways. Aunt Cecilia soon became part of the noble circle surrounding the imperial family. Grandma Amalia told me that in 1916 Aunt Cecilia was one of a group of noblewomen invited to attend the court by the Czarina Alexandra Feodorovna, formerly a German princess and the granddaughter of Queen Victoria of England. The ladies entered the audience room all dressed in finery as required by court etiquette, with huge feathered hats, elaborate dresses and jewels. The Czarina appeared and addressed the women by saying, "My ladies, we must dress more simply. We are in the middle of a war." She wore a simple white blouse and a long black skirt, and no hat, not one piece of jewelry.

All this ran through my mind as I approached Professor Zemite. "Profesora kungs (Mr. Professor), do you remember Cecilia Zarina whom you used to know many years ago in Dorpat?"

"Yes, I do! What of it?"

"I am her niece, Profesora kungs."

A wistful smile crossed fleetingly over Zemite's face. "Poor Cecilia, she died so young. She was such a lovely girl when I knew her . . ." He seemed lost in thought. Then again turning his attention to me he said, "Thank you for making your identity known to me, Zarina jaunkundze (Miss Zarina). I hope all goes well for you. Good luck to you and your studies."

I returned to my seat in front of the microscope and continued to look at some bacteria embalmed in a blue dye solution between two glass slides. Maybe I should not have spoken to Professor Zemite? Maybe I should not have stirred up old memories?

*September 17, 1939* Forty-four German divisions have overrun practically all of Western Poland within the short period of a few weeks.

Today we heard over the radio that the Soviet Union also has started action. Soviet troops have begun to move into Eastern Poland.

*September 18, 1939* Every Monday night is sorority night. We have meetings every week, as well as literary and musical evenings, parties, and once a year our anniversary dinner dance.

Recently I was elected vice president of our sorority, which came as a surprise to me. With the exception of my good friends Elsa and Herta, most sorority sisters consider me a bookworm, and I cannot explain my sudden popularity. Maybe my new professional status as control and research chemist in a well-paying job has impressed them.

*September 22, 1939* I'm so involved with my studies and my work that I often seem to forget the war. What amazes me most is this peculiar friendship developing between Nazi Germany and Soviet Russia. From what little I had heard in high school from my Baltic German classmates, Hitler had earned his first laurels by fighting Communism, which won him the vote of millions of Germans. Now he is closely allied with his archenemy, Stalin, the world leader of Communism. Von Ribbentrop, Hitler's foreign minister, is a frequent visitor to Moscow, where a number of "trade" agreements have been ratified between the two countries within the last months. I wouldn't be surprised if a secret connection exists between these Nazi-Soviet talks and the recent division of Poland.

*September 27, 1939* Hitler's war with Poland has come to a rather rapid conclusion. It has taken the German Army less than four weeks to crush a nation of thirty-five million people. This sudden incredible defeat of a country to the southwest, separated from our territory only by about three hundred kilometers, has stunned the Latvian people. It seems strange that the military destruction of Poland has had no impact on our life here in Latvia.

The "volcano" on which we, according to Mr. Maximoff, are now supposedly living is very tranquil indeed. Are we to be spared for the first time in a tumultuous history of seven hundred years?

*September 28, 1939* Today one year ago was the twentieth anniversary of the founding of the Lativian University. (In Russian Times, under the rule of the Czars, this highest institution of learning in Latvia used to be the Polytechnic Institute of Riga. It produced such celebrities as Wilhelm Ostwald, the famous chemist who won the Nobel Prize in 1909, and Paul Walden who became well known for his work in stereochemistry. Both were natives of Latvia.) That morning last year, the anniversary festivities started with a solemn act in the newly built University auditorium. Our sorority had chosen me, the vice president, to be its representative at the commemoration exercises. I arrived in a black dress, wearing the wide tri-colored scarf of my sorority, which is donned only on important occasions. It covers the right shoulder and chest and is tied at the left hip. Representatives of other student organizations, similarly decked out in their colors, and I formed an honor guard, flanking the entrance to the auditorium. The President of Latvia, our popular Dr. Karlis Ulmanis, arrived accompanied by the president of the University, Dr. Primanis, who was clad in black academic robes wearing the heavy gold chain of office. As these two dignitaries walked by the honor guard, flashbulbs popped and I heard the clicking of cameras.

Early the next morning one of our neighbors came rushing to our door, "Irene, do you know that your picture is in the paper?"

When she showed me the latest edition of "Tevijas Sargs" ("The Country's Guardian"), I saw myself on the title page together with Dr. Ulmanis and Dr. Primanis. I had made the headlines! The newspaper photographers had snapped the picture at the exact moment when the state president was walking past me, as I was standing in the Honor Guard.

*September 30, 1939* This morning it was announced over the radio that a "mutual assistance pact" has been negotiated between the Soviet Union and Estonia. Our Baltic neighbor to the north has granted the USSR the use of naval and air bases on Estonian territory. This is the hand-writing on the wall. It can now be only days before similar pacts will be forced upon Latvia and Lithuania.

*October 2, 1939* We live in trepidation. When will the Soviets strike next?

*October 5, 1939* Today Latvia, as the second Baltic state, had to sign a "mutual assistance pact" with the Soviet Union. Red Army forces will be using military bases in our country.

Mother is in a state of shock. She already once before, in 1919, lived through a Soviet occupation of our country and she is frightened. The volcano has begun to rumble!

I myself have some memories of that time when I was very small. On my third birthday, my parents had just given me my first doll, clad in a red dress, with blond curls and blue eyes. While I was admiring her, we heard a very loud explosion. Father grabbed me holding the doll and shouted to my mother to follow him four flights down to the basement. I remember sitting on Father's lap in a very dark, cold room with other families from the apartment building, listening to explosions in the distance.

Another memory is the sudden arrival of armed men who forced their way into our apartment. I saw my parents standing motionless against a wall in the living room, while I hopped around joyfully shouting, "Visitors have come!" I could not understand why my parents were silent and did not move. The men disappeared into the adjoining rooms and came back laden with comforters, blankets, bed linen, and sweaters before leaving without a word. Years later Mother told me that she had been able to save her jewelry by hiding it under a loose piece in the parquet floor. Had the men been angered at us for any reason, they could have shot us all and no inquiry would have been made, in the interregnum of the brief Communist rule in our country.

Those were times of total insecurity and food shortage. I remember gnawing on a crust of hard black bread, sitting on a stool in the kitchen. Mother had given it to me, saying: "This is chocolate." I was chewing on it and saying happily to myself, "This is chocolate!" Suddenly Father appeared with two huge loaves of white bread, one under each arm. Mother's face lit up and I greeted him by dancing around him with joyous laughter.

These were tumultuous times of which I had no understanding. I remember Mother one day taking me by the hand for a walk through town. I saw a man lying on a street-corner with a red liquid oozing out of his head. I asked Mother in my childish vocabulary: "Why is this 'Uncle' sleeping there?"

Her answer was: "He has drunk too much tea."

Shortly thereafter, in front of a store, we came upon a woman lying on the sidewalk with a straw mat covering her head. A man stood nearby. Mother asked him what was going on. He said this was a female insurgent, and lifted the straw mat so that my mother could peek under it. Mother remained motionless and calm.

Later I understood that this was the aftermath of May 22, 1919, the day when the Soviet occupation forces had been defeated by Latvian patriots with the aid of the Baltic German defense forces, allowing Latvia to remain an independent state. What I cannot understand is why Mother would take me, a small child, to witness such horrors.

*October 7, 1939* I still can't believe it! I can't believe it! It is incredible! The so called "Führer" of the "Third Reich" has issued a manifesto requesting all people of German origin, in the three Baltic States, Estonia, Latvia and Lithuania, to come "home to the Reich."

What an absurdity! Many of the families, in particular the German nobility, have been here for hundreds of years, since the time of the Teutonic Knights who conquered the Baltic Territory in the thirteenth and fourteenth centuries. With them came the first German settlers, merchants, craftsmen and their families. In later centuries this stream of settlers steadily increased. The major cities were integrated into the medieval trading network of the Hanseatic League. Until conquest by Ivan the Terrible in 1560 the territory was part of the medieval German Empire, and under the succeeding Swedish and Russian rulers the Baltic Germans continued to play the dominant role in the Baltic Territory—much to the discomfort of the native population.

After the end of the World War, in 1918, the three Baltic countries became independent, and with the ensuing land reform the German supremacy ended. The new governments of the three states confiscated the estates of the German gentry and distributed the land equally between the native Latvian, Lithuanian and Estonian farmers, who in former centuries had worked as serfs on this same soil. The German landlords were allowed to keep a share with the rest of the new owners, but most titled families refused to stay in the country and moved to the city instead. There they eked out a comparatively meager living in different professions. Many of my high school teachers came from these families. These people know no other home; Latvia is their home too. It is where their roots are. All my German friends in Riga are in an uproar. All conversations deal with one subject only: Repatriation—the pros and cons, the hopes and fears evoked by such a move. I can't imagine that many local Germans will follow the "Führer's" call! After all, who would be crazy enough to leave home, peaceful home, and move into a country at war?

*October 16, 1939* Today at the university I met a young German who asked me whether I planned to obey the "Führer's" call and return home to the Reich. He did not realize that although I have attended German schools, I am an international mixture of a Latvian father and an Estonian mother, with German and Swedish dating back to earlier centuries.

It was Mother's idea to send me to German school, I guess, because my parents' language of communication was German. It was a good school: besides knowing German I also became fluent in Russian and English. I'm grateful for that, but I also suffered a lot during my school years. I was looked upon as "undeutsch," a derogatory term used for all non-Germans by my conceited schoolmates, many of whom were children of the impoverished Baltic German nobility. They formed a tightly knit clique and I was excluded, rejected, frequently ridiculed and once even slapped across the face by a very thin, very bony, very likely inbred hand, belonging to Gertrude, a horse-faced, narrow-shouldered bore. I have never forgiven her. Even today, six years later, deep resentment is burning within me just remembering the insult. I retaliated by fighting Baltic German haughtiness with intellect. I became the top student in my class and graduated at the head of my class.

Out of curiosity I asked the young German, "What would I be doing in Germany? Could I complete my studies there and get my degree?"

"Of course not," he replied in a stern voice. "We will put you to work for the greater glory of the Reich. Whether you complete your studies or not is of no consequence whatsoever! Only the Reich matters! Heil Hitler!" He saluted me with his right arm outstretched. What a peculiar salute! I have never seen anything like it.

There is no doubt in my mind that Mother and I will be staying in Latvia!

*October 18, 1939* The repatriation action is in full swing! The older generation at first seemed most reluctant to go, but the propaganda from the Reich won them over along with the mounting excitement of the local young Germans, who have been duly stirred up into a frenzy of devotion to the "Führer."

Practically all my German friends are leaving. Among them are Wolfgang and my oldest and dearest friend Karen. My German fellow students from high school are going, and all my former German teachers. All German professional people: lawyers, clergymen, doctors and dentists, chemists and pharmacists are leaving, as well as all German merchants, landlords, and craftsmen.

They have been promised compensation in the Reich for property left behind, and they are expecting to be resettled in their old professions. It is a mass exodus!

*October 19, 1939* This morning Frau Lubbe, an old German lady who lived next door to us—rich widow of a pharmacist, and owner of the huge corner drugstore in our immediate vicinity—was found dead. She had taken an overdose of sleeping pills. She chose this way out rather than leave her home country where she had lived for more than 70 years. She was found lying on her bed, beautifully clothed. Her dyed mahogany red hair was immaculately coiffed, her nails brightly polished, her hands bedecked with precious rings, and a diamond broach glittered at her throat.

*October 21, 1939* There have been a number of suicides among the older people. The younger ones are rushing into marriage. The young couples suddenly all want to get married in the old country, before setting out for the new and unknown land of their future.

This morning I attended a wedding at St. Peter's. My former classmate in high school, Veronica, married Baron von Stierna. She is in nurse's training at the local German hospital, and he is an intern there.

The bridal couple walked the incredibly long aisle to the carved marble altar, where tall white candles flickered, casting lights and shadows on the medieval painting of the crucifixion above. Organ music thundered through the high Gothic vaults. The Lutheran minister in black robes and a narrow white collar solemnly intoned the marriage service. Vows and rings were exchanged, and the brief ceremony was over. The bridegroom kissed the bride's hand, and then both turned and walked away from the altar. There were no attendants, no bridesmaids, no ushers. Only the immediate families and friends were present. At the foot of the steps leading to the choir loft, the bride suddenly stopped, and with tears streaming down her face, looked back at the altar. The tall, blond bridegroom put his arm around his frail, dark-haired young bride and led her out of the church.

*October 25, 1939* This evening I visited my friend Karen, playmate of happy childhood days, in the German hospital where a few days ago she gave birth to her first baby: a little boy. She, Erich, and their tiny son Bernd are scheduled to leave for Germany within a week.

Karen and I met in elementary school and have been friends ever since. Her marriage to Erich never interfered with our friendship. Today

I went to see Karen's baby and also to take leave of her. The nurse brought in baby Bernd sleeping sweetly in a brown wicker basket. He is adorable! I can't imagine that in a few days such a tiny baby will go on such a long trip.

After little Bernd had been taken back to the nursery, Karen and I began to reminisce about our childhood adventures together: "Remember, Irene, how you almost set our house on fire by overturning the burning kerosene lamp?"

"Remember, Karen, how we went sledding in the woods, and had a snow-fight with a bunch of boys?"

"Remember, Irene . . ." and as Karen talked, I was back again at her parents' old country house at the outskirts of Riga. It was equipped with a spacious garden, outhouse, and no electric lights. It was so different from our modern apartment building in the city, but it was paradise to me. There I could run and jump and climb and shout and forget about behaving like a young lady of nine or ten. At home I had to keep my dress and my behavior immaculate and had to practice the piano daily. For recreation I was allowed to play with my dolls. No wild games were tolerated. Little girlfriends were permitted to visit me only at Christmas and on my birthday.

I must have acted like a wildcat in Karen's home because her very authoritative Grandma, Madame Vishnevsky, disliked me intensely. Grandma began to feel much friendlier toward me as I grew up into a rather quiet, well-mannered university girl. She used to sigh, "If I had only known then, how someday you would change for the better . . . ." Sweet, stern old Madame Vishnevsky. She too is leaving for Germany with her family.

*October 28, 1939* My birthday.

Although eight months have already passed since Father's death, I am still in deep mourning. There will be no party for me. I wear mostly black: black dresses, black shoes, black stockings. Only once in a while will Mother allow me to put on a print in black and white or a dark gray dress. Mother herself is swathed entirely in widow attire. She wears a long black veil covering her face and flopping around her tiny figure down to her knees. Mother plays the role of the grieving widow to perfection: no entertainment is possible, no music in the house, no visits to the movies or theater are allowed. It is to church every Sunday morning, followed by a visit to Father's grave, and another church sermon in the afternoon. I have occasionally rebelled, but without success.

The irony of this all is that as long as Father was alive, Mother nagged and tormented him with words as sharp as razor blades. She found nothing good in him. But when he died, she suddenly began to display insurmountable grief. I begin to suspect that she rather enjoys the drama of it all. I have a feeling that my always cheerful and loving father, who enjoyed life and who was a born optimist, would not want me to waste months and months in senseless mourning. I want to live according to his code: make the best of life, of every golden moment.

So tonight I went out on some pretext and met Ingmar, my wonderful Ingmar, my love! I am so glad that he has finally decided to continue his architecture studies. He was gifted but lazy, because his parents handed everything to him on a silver platter. He won't listen to them, but he does to me. I give him pep talks, argue with him, have persuaded him to learn German and English, have given him books to read, taken him to concerts, operas and plays. When he gazes at me with his radiant green eyes my heart melts in happiness. How lucky I am that Ingmar came into my quiet dull life. To me he is my Prince Charming. Mother, of course, dislikes him intensely.

Ingmar and I had dinner in Riga's famous Dairy Restaurant, where butter can be ordered as a main course. Our president, Dr. Ulmanis, did just that. He ordered a dish of butter at the opening ceremonies of this Dairy Restaurant several years ago.

Ingmar and I, however, did not celebrate my birthday with a dish of butter. We ordered dark bread soup with raisins and whipped cream, peas and cubed ham, in a sweet and sour hot dressing, and cranberry jello with vanilla sauce on the side. The beverage was a yogurt shake. These were all Latvian specialties of the Dairy Restaurant. Thanks to Ingmar, I had a nice birthday party after all!

*November 11, 1939* Saint Martin's Day!

This means masquerades and fun. Children and young adults alike dress up in costumes, don masks, and visit their friends' and neighbors' homes. High school and university students usually attend St. Martin's Day parties with their organizations. Our sorority has arranged a party in our elegant headquarters located near the University. In spite of Mother's protestations I have decided to attend. I find myself more and more at odds with Mother. Ever since Father's death she is focusing her sole attention on me, trying to force her will upon me continuously. I hate to be an only child . . . I am so young. I too want to be merry and happy, and sing and laugh with my friends.

I have dressed up as Frederic Chopin. Father's tailcoat fits me admirably, since all his life he had cut a very slim and elegant figure. I needed tight fitting knee pants and white silk stockings for the rest of my costume. Mother's pearl gray, knit woolen knee-length underpants are just the thing. White rayon knee socks, and Grandma's old blouse with lacy ruffles at the front and the wrists, complete the outfit. I have painted on melancholy eyebrows, romantic sideburns and covered my face with pale powder. My shoulder length hair is caught in back with a black velvet ribbon, copying men's hair styles of the early nineteenth Century.

*November 12, 1939* Last night an icy wind swept through the streets as I hurried to the party at our sorority headquarters. I appeared: a slim, sad, silent and romantic figure to a loud and laughing crowd. I went over to the grand piano. I sat down, arranged my coattails, and began to play Chopin's Revolutionary Etude with drama, pathos and deep feeling, all exaggerated, of course. My Sorority sisters realized whom I meant to portray. They crowded around me, and laughed and shouted in delight. All of the sudden a hush fell on the assembly. The wide double doors leading to the entrance hall had opened and there stood the image of George Sand—French author and Chopin's lady friend. The girl wore a black gentlemen's outfit with white vest and high hat. The appearance of "George Sand" came as a complete surprise to this latter-day Frederic Chopin; but, true to form, I jumped up from the piano and fell into "Sand's" arms, while flashbulbs flashed and cameras clicked.

*November 18, 1939* Twenty-one years ago today the Latvian Republic was founded. I remember that as a child this anniversary date always had such a joyful meaning—for one reason only—it was the one day in the year with special illumination displays in town.

Father used to take me out for a walk as soon as it grew dark. Hanging on to his hand I watched in admiration how hundreds of lights flared up in the streets of Riga, outlining the facades of government buildings, the old castle, our theaters and the Opera House. Floodlights brought historic monuments out of the darkness of the night: the cathedral, St. Peter's, and nearby the House of the Black Heads, our merchants' guild built in the thirteenth century. Opposite it, on the other side of our center square, the white columns of City Hall shone in the light. In the middle of the quadrangle, the stone carved figure of Roland, legendary hero of Charlemagne's Circle, kept watch over our town with his sword and his horn, as he had done for many centuries.

On the streets leading to the Center Square, "ploshki" had been set out in rows on the sidewalks. These little oil lamps were merrily burning with a faint hissing noise. In fascination, I watched the reddish flickering flames rising from small metal pots. Shop windows displaying pictures of the Latvian president and his cabinet ministers were decorated with national flags. Crowds of people pushed their way through the streets. Everybody was out admiring the illumination.

As I've grown up, I've come to understand what it means for a small nation that had been in bondage for seven hundred years finally to be free—to have its own government.

As always on this day, sorority members met in the morning at their headquarters, and then marched with the other University student organizations to "Brālu Kapi"—the "Cemetery of the Brethren" or War Cemetery. It was a splendid procession. The students were wearing their various multicolored fraternity and sorority caps, and the presiding members wore their colorful scarves slung over the shoulder and tied at the hip. We marched in rows of eight, in a solemn and orderly fashion.

Every building in town today is displaying the National Flag. As we walked through the streets we saw red-white-red banners blowing from housetops on both sides. The symbolic meaning of our National Flag came to my mind:

"Ar sarkanām asinīm izpirktā baltā zeme" ("White country ransomed with red blood."—"White" here has the meaning of "precious," "noble," "good.")

The five-kilometer trek to the cemetery took us over an hour. We entered the impressive stone-carved cemetary entrance that depict battle scenes, and wounded and dying soldiers. This burial ground has been dedicated to the Latvian soldiers who were killed during the War of 1914-1918 and during the fight for independence against the Soviet occupation in 1918-1919. It has become a national shrine.

We gathered on a large platform around a stone pedestal where an eternal flame burns in memory of the dead. From there we could see row upon row of graves, each marked with a simple white wooden cross, giving the name and dates of the soldier buried there. In the background rises the huge statue of a sorrowing woman, symbolizing Mother Latvia weeping for her dead sons.

We stood silent for a moment and then we sang our National Anthem:

"Dievs, svētī Latviju
Mūs' dārgo tēviju,
Svētī jel Latviju
Ak, svētī jel to!
Kur Latviju meitas zied,
Kur Latviju dēli dzied,
Laid murns tur laimē died,
Mūs' Latvijā!"

("God bless Latvia,
Our dear fatherland.
Bless our Latvia,
Oh, give us Thy grace!
Where Latvian daughters bloom,
Where Latvian sons are singing,
There let us dwell in happiness,
In our Latvia!")

Father's grave is nearby in the civilian section of "Mezha Kapi" ("the Woodland Cemetery") but I couldn't visit it because, immediately after the singing of the anthem, we went back into formation and returned to town.

*November 20, 1939* All my German friends have left by now. They went to Germany by boat. German ships came to the harbor of Riga, twelve Kilometers up the river Daugava from the Baltic Sea, and collected the repatriates and their belongings. They went home to the "Reich." To be more specific, they are being resettled in the Polish territory around Posnan, called "Posen" by the Germans. It was occupied last September by Hitler's troops and is now renamed "Warthegau." I understand that Karen and her husband are now in Posen, and so are Wolfgang and his family.

*November 22, 1939* By now Russian military bases have been set up in strategic places all over the three Baltic States. Lithuania was the last one to accept the "mutual assistance pact." This was supposedly done for "protection purposes." Protection for what and from whom? The population doesn't know much about these bases. Rumors are flying. All we know is that some Soviet troops are stationed there and that pictures of Stalin have been seen in buildings on the bases, decorating the walls along with red flags and the hammer and sickle. Stalin is a Georgian; his real name is Dzhugashvili. He wears a long hanging black mustache, and rather resembles an old walrus.

What does he want in our country? We are not Russians; we are Latvians. We are not Slavic; we belong to the Baltic group of people: the Latvians, the Lithuanians, and the now extinct Prussians. Remnants of Prussians survived until the seventeenth century in the territory that is now Prussia, and since has become part of Germany. The original Prussians were Balts, not Germans. They had their own language, akin to Lithuanian and Latvian. It is dead now. Only some old documents in this language still exist.

Since 1198, the Baltic people—who settled two thousand years ago at the southern and eastern shores of the Baltic Sea in the north of Europe—have struggled for survival as wave upon wave of foreign armies rolled over their land. These armies include the Teutonic Knights from the West, the Russian hordes from the East, and the Swedish forces of Gustav Adolf and Charles XII from the North. Livonia, which is the medieval name given to Latvia and Estonia, in former centuries was called poetically "the much-wooed bride." The native population had to pay for this courtship in blood.

*November 30, 1939* The Soviets have attacked Finland. The Finns refused to lease their naval bases in the Gulf of Finland to the Russian Forces. Now a heavy military campaign is going on against the small Finnish Army.

*December 3, 1939* The first Sunday in Advent. I went to church early in the morning. The streets were dark and empty. Some snow had fallen.

On my way I passed the Powder Tower, whose massive brick structure loomed through the gray mist. The tower is part of the ancient city wall; its remnants are still standing in the oldest part of town. In medieval times the tower was used as a storage house for ammunition and arms, for the defense of the city whenever the enemy attacked.

A curved, very narrow cobblestone street without sidewalks runs from the tower along the old foundations of the wall. It is called Alarm Street, because whenever the lookouts, stationed on the then intact wall, saw the enemy approaching, they sounded the alarm. They did this by sending special messengers through Alarm Street, which in those times ran along the inside wall in full circle, who would make a lot of noise and warn the population. Nowadays, the Powder Tower serves as War Museum.

Following Alarm Street, I soon came to St. Peter's Church. As I entered, I saw far away on the altar a single candle burning. The church was not lighted. The first scant gray rays of a winter morning began to filter through the multicolored windows; the faces of the churchgoers present were not yet discernible in the darkness. I moved down the aisle toward the lonely light that began to shine brighter and brighter. Ancient coats-of-arms of noble families, hanging on walls and pillars in memory of deceased members of long ago, appeared out of the dark shadows and disappeared again, as I walked closer to the altar where the flickering flame was beckoning. The words of the Bible came to my mind: "And a light shone in the darkness . . ."

The single lighted candle is a symbol of the first Sunday in Advent. Next Sunday two candles will be lit, and then three and four, and then—after the Advent light will have prepared the way for the coming of the Lord—Christmas Day will be upon us.

*December 16, 1939* The Finnish will to resist the Soviet invasion is incredible. They fight like fierce devils; against all odds, a small nation totally alone against a giant. Not a single country in Europe has come to the military aid of Finland. While a war is raging in the north, it is "all quiet on the Western front," to quote the title of Erich Maria Remarque's book.

The French sit behind their Maginot Line; and the Germans behind their Siegfried Line, also called the West-Wall.

*December 24, 1939* Holy Night—my first Christmas without Father!

In the afternoon it started to snow: large flakes slowly descended from a gray sky, and soon the streets were covered with a white blanket. Mother and I visited Father's grave. We brought a small Christmas tree decorated with wax candles, and placed it on the snow-covered mound. We lit the candles; and with the falling of dusk, their light began to shine more brightly and was reflected in the myriad of snow crystals covering the grave. There was no wind; the candles burned very quietly, each flame forming its own golden halo. It was so peaceful, so truly a holy night.

# CHAPTER TWO

## Under Gathering Clouds

*January 1, 1940* Last night was my saddest New Year's Eve ever. We first attended church, then sat at home and heard the clock towers strike midnight. I felt utterly alone, suspended in a vacuum somewhere between past and future. The past is gone and the future is not yet, and a nameless fear seems to be lurking in the shadows of my mind.

*January 8, 1940* This morning, my technician Andris and I went to our plant's steam boiler room to take some water samples for water hardness testing. We saw a man there shoveling coal into the furnaces. As we approached, the man stopped, straightened out, and with shovel in hand stared at us with strangely gleaming eyes. He was tall, gaunt and sinister. Andris said a few words to him, and he answered with a Slavic accent, while scrutinizing me most carefully in my white lab coat. I felt rather uneasy under his penetrating stare, and left in a hurry followed by Andris.

"Who is this strange character?" I demanded to know.

"His name is Petkevich," Andris replied, "and he is a Communist. He was in prison for fifteen years for subversive activities and has just been recently released. He could not find work until our director Dinbergs gave him a job at our plant, because he feels sorry for Petkevich and his family. Petkevich's wife also works here; she is in the bicycle tire department."

I have never met a Communist before. The Communist Party is illegal in Latvia. No doubt, there are people here with leftist leanings, but they know better than to publicize their opinions. They would lose their friends, their jobs and their social standing. Latvians have not forgotten the wave of Red terror that swept over our country in 1919. The Soviets invaded our newly established Latvian Republic, looting, robbing, murdering and burning. Besides imprisoning thousands of innocent people, the Reds committed dreadful atrocities, torturing and massacring innocent men, women and children.

*January 20, 1940* Our next-door neighbors in the apartment house have a visitor from the provinces—a Mr. Fabergé. Today I met him; he is an elderly slender man with a sad and gentle expression. He told me his story: he is stateless and wishes to emigrate to Germany. He has come to Riga in order to personally apply at the local German Embassy for an entrance visa to the Reich. This was refused him, in spite of many entreaties. Mr. Fabergé appeared nervous and rather frightened.

"Why is it so important for you to leave Latvia, Mr. Fabergé?" I asked him.

"My dear young lady, my father was the famous jeweler to the Imperial Court of the Czars. Have you never heard of the House of Fabergé?"

"Of course, I have heard of Fabergé, the court jeweler. He fashioned the fabulous Easter eggs made of gold and precious stones, which the last Czar used to give to his Czarina on Easter Day."

"This is correct, Miss Irene."

"But what has that to do with your urge to leave this country, Mr. Fabergé?"

"Don't you understand that as soon as the Soviets come to Latvia I am lost!" Mr. Fabergé exclaimed.

I looked at him in surprise. "But the Soviets aren't coming to Latvia? Where did you get that idea?"

"Mark my words, young lady, it won't be long now," Mr. Fabergé sighed. And then he grew agitated again, overcome by fear. I felt sorry for him, so I promised to speak in his behalf with Walter Seebeck, who is consular attaché in the German Embassy, and who greatly admires me.

*January 26, 1940* Mr. Fabergé has his visa. I got it for him, but it was quite some job to persuade Walter to give poor, frightened, old Mr. Fabergé permission to enter Germany. "The German Reich frowns on stateless persons," Walter explained. Besides, being old and poor, Mr. Fabergé would be no great asset as a resident or citizen of Germany. But I overcame Walter's objections by counter-arguments and even tears—I felt so sorry for poor Mr. Fabergé. Walter finally gave in: "Well, send your protégé to my office, I'll give him his visas." I hurried home with the good news.

Today Mr. Fabergé came to our apartment and thanked me with tears in his eyes. He kissed my hand and seemed greatly moved. Then he took his leave; he is traveling tomorrow morning by train, straight to Germany.

*February 5, 1940* One year ago today, Father died of pneumonia after an illness of nine days. I had been working in my chemist's job for only a month and was extremely busy setting up the new control lab when Father took sick. The last days were agony. Right after work I would hurry to the hospital and sit at his bed. Father was delirious most of the time, and did not recognize Mother or me. He talked in disrupted sentences mostly of his work, his machines, his inventions. The night before his death a change seemed to come into his face, strange shadows were under his eyes and around his mouth. His straight nose all of a sudden seemed more pointed, longer.

He died alone at 2 AM, with only a nurse in attendance. We were notified the next morning. Mother collapsed and I realized that it would be up to me to make the funeral arrangements. So I set out for the hospital to find out what steps to take first. In the hospital I met Alfred Pakalns, who is now an intern there.

I told Alfred the sad news and mentioned that I would have to buy the coffin. Alfred, whose father lived for many years in America, informed me that other countries, and particularly America, have undertakers whose job it is to help the bereaved family with preparations for burial. Here in Latvia the family members themselves make all funeral arrangements.

First I talked to the hospital authorities and gave permission for an autopsy, then I went to a coffin store—one of those dreadful places on "Brivibas Iela—Liberty Street" which exhibit coffins in their display windows. I chose a coffin of polished brown oak. The worst moment came when I had to select a pair of black velvet slippers for my dead father. I stood there in the store surrounded by coffins, and looked at a display of black slippers and white satin-covered pillows for the dead. Suddenly I felt the presence of death and shuddered in fear. I somewhat recovered on the way home.

I found Mother still in the same state of collapse as in the morning and unable to make any decisions. I set out again, this time to the cemetery, where I selected a lot under a group of pines for Father's final resting place.

By this time, I was in a state of physical and emotional exhaustion and the following days until the funeral are just a blur in my memory. Mother's younger brother, Uncle Adi, finally came to my assistance, helping to make arrangements for funeral services in the hospital chapel and for burial in the Woodland Cemetery.

At the funeral, the Lutheran minister officiated a choir sang and then the coffin was closed and carried outside to the hearse, which was pulled by two black horses. The horses were covered with heavy black netting fringed with pompons around the edges. The horses' head-gear was adorned with black ostrich feathers and as they moved nodding their heads in rhythm with their steps, the ostrich feathers rose and fell . . .

rose and fell . . . creating a strange spectacle at the front of the funeral cortege. Six hired pallbearers walked along with the hearse, three on each side. They were clad in long black capes, trimmed with white edging. On their heads they wore three-cornered black hats, also edged with white.

The street before the chapel was sprinkled with sawdust on which cut pine branches had been scattered. The funeral cortege began to move. All mourners made the long trek to the cemetery on foot. I was at the head of the group, right behind the coffin. Uncle Adi escorted me. Mother rode with the minister in a motorcar. As the cortege slowly moved through the streets all passers-by stopped: men removed their hats in greeting, ladies bowed, soldiers and policemen saluted. To me, this was an endless walk through a reverent, silent, saluting crowd that had come to a standstill. It was like a pantomime.

The scenes at the burial site are again hazy in my memory. I remember the choir, and the hollow sound when Mother and I threw three handfuls of soil onto the coffin as a final farewell. It was getting dark, and rather chilly, but we stayed till the very end, till the grave was closed and a small mound rose above the snow-covered ground.

*February 12, 1940* My job at the plant is going nicely. I got an increase in salary, after having successfully analyzed and quantitatively determined the chemical contents of a rubber stopper. This was to be the supreme test of my abilities as chemist, which one of our directors had dreamed up for me. The trick was that he knew what the rubber stopper contained, because we manufacture these items in our plant.

I like working at "Varonis" ("The Hero") where I am in charge of the Analytical Lab. I have acquired three more assistants. Andris and the new girls are all very nice young people. I am friendly also with the different department heads, the plant technicians, and the secretaries. I usually meet them at lunch, which always turns out to be a very pleasant meal. Luncheon becomes a high-spirited affair whenever my part-time colleague Captain Ancans attends. He is always full of smiles and jokes; an army officer aged thirty-six and working for a degree in chemical engineering. At present, he has a chemical consultant's job at the plant.

*February 20, 1940* Extremely cold winter weather had put a halt to it, but now fighting between Soviets and Finns has started anew. The number of Finnish casualties is tremendous, but the Russians also are suffering extremely high losses. We Latvians deeply admire the fierce Finnish determination to protect their freedom at all costs.

*March 3, 1940* Alfred, my intern friend, had sent me an invitation to attend a party at his parents' home, which took place last night. Since my year of mourning is over, I was able to accept. There I met a number of Alfred's fraternity brothers and their girlfriends. Old Mr. Pakains, who I hear made a fortune in America, has done all in his power to further his children's careers. Alfred has completed medical school and is currently preparing to set up his own practice. He is a member of one of the most elegant student fraternities in Riga. Alfred's sister Ann is likewise well taken care of. She is still a student at the university. We had a very nice time and I danced a lot with Alfred. Some years ago I had a crush on him, but he can't compare with Ingmar.

Later in the evening a strange incident occurred. I had wandered off from the party into one of the adjoining rooms. From the medical books on the shelves I gathered that it was Alfred's study. And then I saw it—the skull. It was sitting on Alfred's desk, staring at me with hollow eyes and displaying a set of immaculate white teeth. I shuddered at this unexpected sight, when suddenly I heard Alfred's laughter behind my back.

"Did Johnny frighten you? Don't worry, he is quite harmless."

"Where did you get it?"

"Quite simply, I dug him out."

"Dug him out? Where?"

"Dug him out of his soldier's grave. Johnny was killed in the last war and was buried in a lonely grave in the woods near our summer home."

I stared at Alfred in disbelief. "And you disturbed his rest?"

"Don't be silly, Irene. Dead is dead, and I needed a skull!"

"For what?"

"For study and display."

"What did you do with the skull after you dug it up?"

"I cleaned it . . ." and Alfred started to go into detail. I wanted to hear no more and rushed out of the room.

Alfred seems like such a nice, honest, dependable fellow. Why did he do such a bizarre thing, verging on criminal? Alfred, a grave robber? But maybe medical men reason differently about matters of life and death?

*March 12, 1940* Today a peace treaty was signed between Finland and the Soviet Union. The Finns have lost Karelia but have preserved their independence.

*March 14, 1940* For a number of days now, Captain Ancans' behavior has been puzzling me. Contrary to his usual jovial self, he appears very quiet and withdrawn, and there is a frightened and mournful expression in his dark eyes. Today I finally asked him, "What is the matter with you, Captain? Is something wrong?"

"Oh it is terrible, just terrible," he groaned.

"Is something wrong with your family?"

"It isn't that at all; it is something entirely different. At Army headquarters I have heard the most terrible news."

"What news? What is going on, Captain?"

Another groan. "I can't tell you, I am not allowed to talk about it." He would say no more. I can't make sense out of it.

*March 23, 1940, Tallin* Here I am in the capital of Estonia on the eve of cousin Elra's wedding. She will be married tomorrow, on Easter Sunday.

I came to Tallin with Uncle Adi and his new bride Erika. Although I have been in Tallin before, I joined them on their sightseeing tour. Tallin or Reval (the old German name) is frequently called the "Nuremberg of the North," because like Nuremberg Tallin's city walls are still intact, displaying towers of various shapes and sizes. The citizens of long ago nicknamed them, and the names have stuck to this day. My favorite towers are "Long Herman," "Fat Margaret" and "Kiek in die Kök ('Kitchen Watcher") the latter tower named so because it rose high above the old houses of former centuries, and was thus able to "look through the chimneys down into the kitchens."

Like Riga, Reval has lovely old churches: the Cathedral, St. Olav's, St. Nicolaus, the church of the Holy Ghost, the Swedish Church . . . . Most of them were built in the Thirteenth Century. My favorite is St. Olav's. On a clear day, from the high needle-sharp steeple, one can see the coast of Sweden across the Baltic Sea. St. Nicolaus church is remarkable for its sixteenth-century copy of the "Totentanz," a famous medieval painting in St. Mary's in Lübeck, Germany. The painting depicts the Dance of Death of emperors, popes and beggars—who, regardless of their former station in life, are all being whirled away by skeletons.

Most of all I enjoyed visiting Katherinental, a small resort place near Reval, which was named after the Czarina Katherine I of Russia, second wife of Peter the Great.

I am fascinated by the lives and times of historical personages. I want to know how they lived, how they acted, what decisions they made, what they looked like, and how they dressed. That's why I love to read biographies and history.

Katherine I started life as Martha Skavronska, born a Lithuanian serf in 1684. She was a servant in the household of Pastor Glück, a Baltic German Lutheran minister in Aluksne, Latvia. In 1711 Peter made Martha his Czarina. Chosen his successor in 1725, Martha ruled Russia ably as Katherine I.

Peter, seven feet tall and of bear-like constitution, shied away from the elegance of castles. He built himself a small house near Katherine's palace in Katharinental. It contains only one bedroom, a long narrow dining room, and a huge kitchen, where whole oxen could be roasted on a spit over the fire under a huge hood. I stepped under the hood and looked up through the chimney. I saw the stars in the sky above, although it was daylight outside. This was due to the dark and high chimney. The bedroom contains Peter's bed made of wooden planks, and covered with faded green silk. Under the bed are Peter's wooden shoes, which he had carved himself to be at least 15 inches long.

As the story goes, Peter himself also made the narrow oak dining-room table and twelve carved matching chairs. This is quite plausible because between 1697 and 1698, Peter visited Holland where he learned the carpenter's trade.

After sightseeing all day, we joined the large family gathering in Uncle Karl's and Aunt Meralda's spacious villa in the suburbs of Reval. Aunt Esmeralda is Mother's younger sister, but I had never met her. Some silly feud instigated by Mother has kept the families apart for twenty years or more. Mother has not come to the wedding. Meralda is lovely, very high-spirited and handsome, and very kind to me. Her only child Elra will be tomorrow's bride.

*March 24, 1940, Reval* Easter Day, and morning of Elra's wedding:
I didn't believe my eyes as I looked out of the living room window, where I had slept on a couch. It is winter again; a heavy snow has fallen and covered the bushes and pine trees in front of the house with white furry caps.

The wedding will be a candlelight ceremony. We are spending a leisurely day in the villa preparing for the festivities.

Luncheon was delightful, with family members talking in four different languages. Since I don't speak Estonian, although Mother is Estonian, and the Estonians don't speak Latvian, we must converse in either German or Russian. In the innocence of his heart, little cousin Sven from Tartu apparently made remarks about cousin Elra being an heiress and therefore having no trouble catching the most eligible, most handsome bachelor in town—a young lawyer. Probably these were bits of information that he had garnered from his parents' conversations. Sven spoke Estonian and I could not understand his words, but I saw the poor bride-to-be blush, and Sven's parents Arno and Meta exchange embarrassed glances. My neighbor at the table, a retired colonel, explained to me in Russian the joke "out of the mouth of babes."

It is already 2 P.M. and time for me to change into my party gown. I'll wear the emblem of my sorority: the tri-colored woven silk ribbon fastened across my chest. I will be the only Latvian student among the bridesmaids and ushers, many of whom are students at the Estonian University in Tartu. They too will be wearing their organization emblems.

*March 25, 1940* Elra's wedding was the most elaborate ceremony I have ever witnessed. As dusk was falling, candles were lighted, and soon the church was aglow in white and gold: white woodwork edged in gold, white pews, white marble altar and gilded lacy framework. The wedding march sounded and in walked twelve ushers in pairs, clad in black tailcoats and white tie, each carrying a six-armed silver candelabrum with burning candles. They were followed by twelve bridesmaids, also in pairs. They wore white, like the bride. Then came the bride and groom. Elra's white-gloved hand rested on Jan's arm. In her right hand she carried a bouquet of Easter lilies. The couple approached through the aisle, as we watched from the choir loft. Elra was radiantly beautiful with her immaculate complexion, her huge blue eyes and her silver-blond hair. A lacy veil framed her face and cascaded in rich folds down to the train of her heavy white satin wedding gown.

After the church ceremony, we all drove to Jan's fraternity house, where the reception was held.

*March 26, 1940* We are on the train back to Riga. Elmer, my escort of yesterday's wedding reception, came to the railroad station in Reval to say goodbye. As a farewell he brought me a bouquet of red roses and kissed my hand in parting. He is the son of a high Estonian government official.

*March 29, 1940* Spring is in the air. Cold winds are still blowing, but the sun is climbing higher and higher daily, and the snow is beginning to melt. Ingmar waited for me at the gates of the plant to take me home. He does that often. We walked down "Brivibas Iela" ("Liberty Street") to the very center of town. I wonder what Riga will look like 50 years from now? Will our "Brivibas Piemineklis" ("Statue of Liberty") still be standing in the center of town? The center on one side is flanked by the Opera house with adjoining gardens, and on the other side by one of the city parks where the "Snail Hill" is located. This artificial elevation was created about two centuries ago, when the town magistrate decided to raze the city wall and fortifications, and fill in the ditches around the wall. With the development of modern firearms, the ancient defenses had outlived their usefulness. The resulting debris and excess soil was dumped in one spot until it rose to the height of a small hill. Winding paths resembling the convolutions of a snail's shell have given it its name.

Ingmar invited me to have a cup of hot chocolate at Cafe Schwartz, Riga's most elegant coffee house. We had a delightful time watching people and traffic in the Opera Plaza. Through the huge windows of the Cafe we saw street lights go on, saw multicolored ads flare up, saw the gleaming white facade of our Opera house suddenly emerge out of the darkness, as floodlights began to play on its neoclassic columns and triangular roof.

*April 10, 1940* Yesterday German forces started a massive surprise attack on Denmark and Norway.

*April 16, 1940* Denmark surrendered without fighting. Norway and her coastal waters have become the main battle territory for the British and the Germans.

*April 22, 1940* I am extremely busy preparing for my finals. Most nights are spent at home studying. Once in a while I attend an opera or a theater performance with Ingmar.

*April 30, 1940* Today Mother accused me of having forgotten Father. "How can you study so hard and be so cheerful, when your father is in his grave, Irene?"

I looked at her in surprise. "What a strange thing to say, Mother. Life goes on. Father wouldn't want me to stagnate and mourn everlastingly. He had a happy nature and he enjoyed life."

"Yes, in a happy-go-lucky way, but he lacked ambitions."

"He was so loving and so kind and utterly devoted to you and me, Mother."

Mother did not reply. I noticed with surprise that she has finally given up wearing her long black widow's veil.

*May 2, 1940* Graduation is in June, and I still have a lot to do. Fortunately, I have passed all my finals But I must now finish my special project in the ceramics lab. Professor Kocins gave me a piece of white glazed tile, and asked me to make a quantitative analysis of the glaze.

I have done so. Now I am supposed to use my analysis results as a recipe for glazing a piece of earthenware.

*May 8, 1940* The glaze which I concocted, based on my analytical findings, appears to have been successful. It covered my earthenware tile well and did not crack in the kiln; Professor Kocins seemed pleased.

The next and last project is an evaluation of the efficiency of a heating plant, with special emphasis on calculations of energy input in form of the heating material—coal, as compared to useful energy output in form of steam. The percent efficiency of such a system has to be determined.

*May 10, 1940* German tanks today rolled into Belgium and the Netherlands.

*May 11, 1940* Yesterday, a new National Government was formed in England under the leadership of a new premier. His name is Winston

Churchill. He replaces Chamberlain, who in 1938 tried in vain at the ill-fated conference of Munich, to prevent Hitler from occupying the Sudeten territory of Czechoslovakia.

*May 12, 1940, Sunday.* I worked all day on the graphs for my thesis. In the evening, Ingmar and I went for a stroll through the former Imperial Gardens near my home, renamed "Viestura Darzs" after one of our Latvian heroes. The swans are out on the pond and the ancient linden tree, which Peter the Great planted in 1721, has begun to sprout tiny leaves. In our parts spring comes late.

*May 14, 1940* Today I ran into Kreina, my little Jewish playmate of kindergarten days. She is now a saleslady at Feitelbergs, the largest and most elegant department store in Riga. I hadn't seen her in years. She told me that Karlitis, a Latvian boy who used to be our neighbor, is now her boyfriend. Kreina seemed very happy: she has the same smile as when she was six years old.

*May 15, 1940* On this date in 1934, Dr. Karlis Ulmanis crushed a Communist uprising that was about to explode and sweep away our democratic form of government. It had been prepared by the Communist underground, which had collected huge arsenals of weapons with the secret help of the Soviet Union. Ulmanis was able to save our country from becoming a Soviet satellite. He took over the reins as State President and formed a National Unity government. He has guided our country through six prosperous years. Ulmanis is a brilliant man who received his university education in America. He is very much liked by the population. High school and university students adore him.

Tonight, members of University student organizations will serenade our president.

*May 16, 1940* Last night, as darkness fell, student groups assembled at the University and marched in formation to the castle of Riga. Male students flanking the procession carried flaming torches. Floodlights played on the castle walls. The torchbearers formed a circle around the main body of the students, who had gathered in front of the castle. We sang Latvian folksongs and student songs. The president, white-haired and smiling, appeared at a window and waved at us. The boys, while shouting greetings to the president, took off their fraternity caps and started whirling them into the air, catching them as they fell. In the floodlights it looked as though many bright-colored flowers were rising and falling in the darkness. I will never forget that sight.

*May 17, 1940* The Dutch Army capitulated two days ago. The Belgians are still fighting the Nazi invasion.

*May 20, 1940* German Forces have reached the English Channel after driving their tanks through the Ardennes forest and into Northern France.

*May 24, 1940* I spent a whole morning in our plant's boiler room, assisted by Andris, taking measurements for my heating plant project. Petkevich watched us noncommittally.

*May 28, 1940* The Belgians have capitulated.

*June 1, 1940* A terrible battle is raging at the French port of Dunkirk on the English Channel. The British and the French are the losers, and their troops are being evacuated from the beaches of Dunkirk across the Channel to England.

*June 4, 1940* The battle of Dunkirk has ended. The Germans are the victors.

*June 10, 1940* Listening to the radio broadcasts from the Western front, I have the irrational feeling as though all this terror and bloodshed should not concern us here in Latvia. We seem to be living in peace and safety in spite of the Soviet bases. No Soviet troops are in evidence, no changes have occurred.

*June 13, 1940* Paris has fallen to the Germans.

*June 14, 1940* The last weeks have been rather hectic for me. I've had to put the finishing touches on my thesis, and finally its successful defense. Besides that, the heating plant efficiency calculations had to be presented, as well as the last preparations made for graduation exercises. But now all is done.
   Tomorrow I graduate!

*June 15, 1940* Commencement day. Exercises began at 11:00 A.M. in the library of the Chemistry Department. I wore a black dress decorated with my sorority ribbon. The dean addressed us, and then Boris, one of the graduates, spoke. He was rather nervous and kept shifting his feet about every thirty seconds: right foot forward, left foot forward, right foot forward . . . Soon the professors as well as the candidates for a degree were staring in fascination at his shifting feet. I wonder if any one present ever heard the rest of Boris' speech?

My mind went back to our freshmen days. The program at the Chemical Engineering Department had seemed formidable, almost unconquerable. Today we had made it: three of us were girls. Now I could relax. The degree of Chemical Engineer "First Class" (comparable to *summa cum laude*) was conferred upon me. But I was so exhausted that I felt no elation.

Mother, still in mourning, but no longer wrapped in a black veil, waited outside for me with a bunch of roses. I walked home with her, carrying the roses.

That night, the new university graduates held a dance at our fashionable Officers' Club. Most chemistry professors attended. A band provided the music, and I will never forget the pianist. He played Strauss waltzes with the greatest of ease and skill, while reading the newspaper spread out before him on the music stand. I wore a white gown decorated with a sprinkling of artificial violets. A transparent shawl in a color matching the violets was draped around my neckline.

My favorite professor, white-haired old Dr. Keshans, in formal attire, courteously offered me his arm and led me into the ballroom. While we danced he asked me what my future plans were. We talked about my work at the Varonis plant. Then he offered some advice:

"Irene, should you ever plan to get married, choose your husband with care. None of these young fellows here in attendance tonight is right for you."

I assured Professor Keshans that I had no interest in any of the young men, but wanted to know what was wrong with them.

"Nothing is wrong with them. They are just not intellectual enough for you, not polished enough. You should find yourself a man of high social and educational standings." I laughed in amusement; nothing is further from my mind.

The professors retired about midnight, but we continued dancing. Dawn comes early in June, and as the first rays of the sun began to peep through the windows, we all filed out into the open and danced a polonaise around the building. The dew, still on the grass, wet the hem of my white gown. The linden trees were in bloom, white petals formed lacy patterns on jasmine bushes. A giant chestnut tree had put out its flower candles, whose pink little blossoms burned like tiny flames in the rising sun.

I was at the head of the polonaise; the group followed. Suddenly a big black tomcat appeared out of green shadows and marched ahead in front of me—head high and tail proudly uplifted.

A black tomcat has led me out of my university years into the new life to come.

# PART 2

## HAMMER AND SICKLE

# CHAPTER THREE

## The Soviet "Liberation"

*June 16, 1940, Majori* Early this morning, as the sun was rising, I danced in the park in my white ball gown; and now I'm here at the seashore in my blue swimsuit in the noonday heat. My thoughts are sailing with the gleaming clouds. The sea below is as blue as the heavens above; once in a while a silvery ripple will travel over the calm waters. There is no surf in the Bay of Riga—incoming and outgoing tides are hardly perceptible at this Baltic shore and at this time of year. How I love this landscape: the endless expanse of the sea, the high dunes, the pine trees, the white soft sand of the beaches forming an arch around the southern shore of the bay.

I am alone in the dunes; it is so tranquil here. A soft rustling noise is coming from the breeze in the pine trees. A dragonfly just landed on my arm. His transparent wings fluoresce in the sunlight.

I came here to relax from the tensions of the last week. Only now do I begin to realize how exhausted I really am—relieved too—that I have done what I set out to do when I was seventeen.

What next? I'll go on working, at Varonis, marry Ingmar, have a family . . . . Is this really what I want? I had always hoped to see part of the world before I settle down.

How strange that the war has passed us by. At this moment, it seems like an exciting, dreadful story that one reads in safety.

Life is so peaceful. I couldn't be calmer, happier, more content on this Sunday afternoon in the midst of sand and sea and sky sparkling with sunshine and color.

*June 17, 1940, Riga* This Monday morning, as usual, I arrived at eight o'clock at the plant. I had just put on my laboratory coat and was adjusting a distillation apparatus when the door suddenly burst open. In stormed one of our secretaries, Mirdza Darzina, in a great state of excitement. She shouted, "Miss Zarina, the Russians are crossing our borders!"

I was so stunned that I remained quite calm: my first reaction was one of utter disbelief. "Who told you such nonsense? It's impossible!"

"We heard the announcement on the radio just now, Miss Zarina."

Still, all morning long I couldn't bring myself to accept the incredible news. I went about in a daze, did my work as though nothing had happened, but in the back of my mind was the horrifying fear of the Soviet military machine breaking into our country.

Hour upon hour we followed the movements of the Red Army as they were announced over the radio. By three o'clock in the afternoon, outposts of the Soviet military forces had already reached Riga. I left the plant at 4 P.M., and started to walk home on Liberty Street. Suddenly, three tanks appeared at the far end of the street. They loomed larger and larger as they kept rolling slowly uptown in my direction. My first impression was that the tanks and soldiers were inferior to those of our Latvian Army. The tanks were rusty and beat-up, and cranked along heavily with creaking noises. The soldiers' uniforms were shabby and torn. On this hot summer day they were wearing quilted jackets and winter caps with lamb's fur. There is such a vast difference between these short, squat, bedraggled-looking Soviets, and our own trim Latvian soldiers in their neat uniforms.

People who happened to be on Liberty Street watched the troop movements in silence. Fear and depression were written on every face.

When I came to Elizabeth Street, crowds had suddenly emerged. From the heated conversation, I realized that they were Jewish émigrés from Germany, who had found refuge from Hitler's persecution in our hospitable little country. They actually acted as though they were pleased to have the Soviets in our capital. They waved and shouted at the tanks, ran into the street and greeted the Red soldiers with happy countenances. It hurt me badly to see these demonstrations of joy at this moment.

I walked along, winding my way through these throngs of foreigners. A couple of times I was pushed in the ribs as I tried to pass rows of six or seven persons, who had hooked arms and were occupying the whole width of the sidewalk. Belligerence was in the air. Suddenly I heard a faint hissing noise that puzzled me. When I got home I found spit on the back of my blue summer dress. Someone had spit at me. Why? Out of hatred, because I am a Latvian and obviously professed no joy in the presence of the Red Army. How terrible!

Late afternoon . . . .
The newspapers have printed the Soviet explanation of their takeover. Yesterday, Molotov sent a note to the Latvian Ambassador in Moscow declaring that "the existing military alliance, which is aimed against the Soviet Union, between the three Baltic States—Latvia, Estonia and Lithuania—is considered by the Soviet government not only to be completely inadmissible, but also highly dangerous to the security of the borders of the Soviet Union."

We are more than startled, because no Latvian has ever heard anything about a "military alliance between the three Baltic States." In fact, no such alliance exists. It is all a lie. What a ridiculous idea—that three such small countries, with a total of seven million inhabitants, could ever endanger the security of the Soviet Union with her two hundred million people.

Mother and I are in a state of shock. Yesterday our world was full of summer sun and peace and hope, and today we have been thrown into an abyss of uncertainty.

*June 18, 1940* This morning I went to work as usual. From my laboratory assistants, I heard that disorders had started last night in a few strategic places in town: at the Main Railroad Station and at the Main Police Station. There, apparently, mobs had gathered consisting of Communists from the underground and agitators. Our policemen, who tried to stop the fighting and control the rabble-rousers, were attacked with guns and paving stones. Sixty-two policemen have been wounded.

In the plant today, I noticed no difference at first. Everyone—the director, engineers, technicians, office and factory workers—continued with their work. But after lunch, things began to change. All of a sudden, a fellow appeared whom I least of all expected to emerge from his secluded working place. It was Petkevich, the worker in charge of our steam boilers. There he stood, his tall, gaunt frame covered with coal dust, black smudges on his emaciated face. A fanatical fire burned in his green eyes as he began to shout Communist slogans—in between informing us, with his heavy Slavic accent, that he had just been made General Manager of our plant by orders from Moscow.

I couldn't believe my ears! This totally uneducated man, with no inkling of business administration, engineering or chemistry, is suddenly to be our highest administrator? He is reaping his due rewards. This is the only explanation I can think of.

Our factory workers were just as flabbergasted as I about Petkevich's sudden rise to the very top. They stared at him in total silence, openmouthed. Petkevich, however, immediately started his new managerial activities by organizing a demonstration of our workers in the streets of Riga. Somewhere he had obtained red silk kerchiefs, which he distributed to our women-workers with orders to wear them on their heads. To my great relief, the professional staff was not invited to join the demonstration. Then he instructed the workers to raise their right clenched fists and to shout: "Long Live Stalin! Long Live the Communist Party! Long Live the Red Army! Long Live the Soviet Union!" After a bit of rehearsing, the volume of the shouts seemed satisfactory to Petkevich, and he led his demonstration out in triumph through the factory gates.

Three hours later the demonstrators came back. I heard that they had marched through the streets of our capital with Petkevich in the lead, shouting what they had been taught. The singing of the "Internationale" however, was a total failure because none of the workers knew either the text or the tune.

*June 19, 1940* Work continues in a haphazard way. It is hard to concentrate on everyday duties when such an upheaval is taking place. I talked to some of the workers, asking their opinion about all these startling developments. I have the impression that most of them are rather reluctant to accept the changes, but are very afraid to say anything against the new order. Andris, however, thinks that the unexpected activities of the last days are lots of fun and very exciting. In his defense, I should remember that he is barely eighteen.

On June 16—on my peaceful Sunday—Molotov had demanded that the legal Latvian government resign. Their place has immediately been taken over by puppets of the Soviets: Kirchensteins, Blaus, and Lacis, who seem unable to express an opinion other than the one prescribed by Moscow. I am surprised that Kirchensteins, who is a professor at the University of Latvia and a well-known scientist, would be willing to take over the role of traitor to his native land.

*June 20, 1940* The mobs have demanded that the Latvian Communist Party be legalized. Today, the new government promptly granted this.

*June 21, 1940* By order of Moscow, all prisoners, political as well as criminal, have been set free. Today, mobs led by agitators gathered before the

Central Prison of Riga with Red flags and pictures of Stalin and Lenin; they received the liberated prisoners with the usual slogans. They were then marched in triumph through town.

Ingmar came to take me home from work. We are both very depressed.

*June 22, 1940* This morning, Petkevich organized another demonstration. This time, I too was forced to go and march along the streets of Riga, shouting slogans at regular intervals, accompanied by a lot of fist-raising activity. I was so furious I could have exploded, but I had to check myself for my own safety's sake. I find it very hard to control myself in the face of such abuse.

Petkevich led us straight to the Soviet Embassy located near the Marksmen's Garden. The Embassy has become the center of all political demonstrations and agitations. As soon as our factory group arrived at the Embassy, after a trek of several kilometers, a man appeared on the steps of the building and delivered a fiery speech, in which he expressed the "will of the persecuted and depressed people of Latvia" to become part of the "happy" Union of the Soviet Socialist Republics. At the conclusion of his speech, the agitator expressed the "deepest gratitude" of the Latvian nation to "Father Stalin" (hateful old walrus) that the latter had liberated the "enslaved" Latvian workers with the help of the "Glorious Red Army" (glorious indeed, with their rusty tanks, torn quilted uniforms and dirty lamb-fur caps) from the "exploitation of their capitalist employers."

All this is presented to the world as the "Voice of the Latvian Nation." What about the real voice of the Latvian Nation—a chorus of despair!

*June 23, 1940* France has fallen.

According to news reports, Hitler literally "danced with glee."

Yesterday an armistice was signed. Under its terms German forces will occupy all of Northern France.

*June 24, 1940, Sigulda* Today we celebrate St. John's Day!

A few days ago I received a note from Ingmar's mother inviting me to spend the Ligo Festival and St. John's Day at their country estate.

I'm sitting in a clearing at the edge of the woods. A bee is buzzing from flower to flower busily collecting honey. Ingmar, who is looking over my shoulder, thinks that writing a diary is old-fashioned and downright useless. In his opinion I am the "silliest chemical engineer that ever existed." The sun is shining brightly, it is very warm and I feel a bit drowsy, particularly since we were up until dawn celebrating the Ligo Festival.

Ligo, goddess of beauty, love and youth—our Baltic Venus—for thousands of years Latvians have sung praises to you at the time of the summer solstice! The Catholic Church could never quite destroy your wild and passionate image. You still rule supreme on June 23, the night before St. John's Day. Even the Soviet occupation forces have not dared to eliminate your celebration.

Last night I arrived at the Sigulda Railroad Station. Ingmar was waiting for me. He took me to his parents' home. After supper we walked to a meadow near the river Gauya, where the Ligo celebration was to take place. A crowd of young people had already gathered. In the middle of the meadow a wood fire was burning. Its orange flames leaped high into the silvery skies. The "white nights" of our Northern Hemisphere are upon us, where the sun hardly sets before rising again.

Ingmar looked into my face, and I looked back at him—at his large liquid eyes, his straight nose and his soft young mouth—and I realized how much I love him.

It is considered good luck to jump through the flames on Ligo night. Ingmar and I joined hands, took aim, ran and jumped over the fire. This is expected of all couples in love. After that, we were supposed to go looking for the "miraculous flower" that blossoms only on Ligo night. If you find it, you will be happy for the rest of your life.

We did not find the flower; nevertheless we know that we love each other. We went down to the river and watched it flowing along with swift little waves. Fireflies swarmed around us. High above us rose the dark ruins of the Sigulda castle, built in the Thirteenth century by Teutonic knights. One year ago last summer, Ingmar and I danced there all alone in the inner court of the castle under a full moon.

We walked and walked. We came through fields covered with daisies. The flowers looked like little stars shining in the strange white night competing with the stars above. We walked into a pine grove. It was very dark there, but at the end of the path a silvery light was beckoning—the entrance to a forest clearing. We came to the edge of a rye-field, where green stalks gently waved in the early morning breeze. At that moment the sun rose again. We were overwhelmed by the beauty of it—and by our feelings for each other. Ingmar fell on his knees and pressed his lips against my hands. I dug my fingers into the heavy crop of his wheat-colored hair.

I love you, Ingmar Gunarsons, my "brother" and my idol. I want to have sons like you—by you—my love . . .

*June 26, 1940, Riga* The Latvian Army has been incorporated into the Soviet forces. It was announced on the radio that Russian political commissars, so called "politruks," will immediately start to reeducate Latvian soldiers and officers so to make them into "worthy" members of the "glorious" Red Army. Poor Captain Ancans, he is still with Varonis, but is beside himself with fear and loathing. As a member of the Officers' Corps, he knew all along what was in store for Latvia, but was not allowed to divulge this tragic secret.

*June 27, 1940* Today Vishinsky, vice-chairman of the Council of Comissars for the Nations of the Soviet Union—what a title—visited our capital. He delivered a speech in which he expressed his hope that "the flags of the Soviet Union and of Latvia will fly in friendship side by side as a symbol of the friendly cooperation between both countries."

*July 1, 1940* A new Latvian Parliament ("Saeima") is to be elected. Election date is July 16. A big campaign has sprung up. Signs in the streets and on house-fronts, huge ads in the newspapers carry slogans like these: "Vote for the Block of the Workers' List #1." "No parties are truly democratic except the 'Block of the Workers' List #1.'" "Workers, in your own interest, ignore all other parties—vote only for List #1."

Loudspeakers are blaring these same and similar slogans out into the streets. The local radio station broadcasts them every hour on the hour. There is feverish excitement in town, augmented by a multitude of red streaming banners, Soviet flags, and huge pictures of Lenin, Stalin and Kirchensteins decorating the spaces in the streets that have not yet been taken up by election slogans. What bedlam!

In contrast to all this the Latvian citizens show no elation whatsoever. We are depressed and miserable.

*July 2, 1940* We at Varonis, today at lunch were asking ourselves: "What of the other parties for Parliament? Whom do they represent?"

No one has an answer. There is a rumor that General Balodis, our recently deposed Minister of War, has attempted to form a Farmers' Party in order to represent the interests of the Latvian rural population. No details are known.

*July 5, 1940* This afternoon on "Dzirnavas Iela" ("Mill Street") on my way home from work, I caught sight of an election slogan actually written in German: "Wir politische Emigranten marschieren mit der Kompartei." ("We political emigrants march with the Communist Party.")

I stared in disbelief—but there they were: German Jewish refugees, carrying a long sign with the above inscription written in huge red letters, briskly marching along, keeping in step, as the demonstration wound its way through town. There was an expression of something akin to triumphant joy in many of their faces. They were smiling and I noticed the sunlight being reflected in the gold tooth of one woman. Her eyes seemed to flash just as much as her gold tooth. How could these people to whom our country gave refuge support our enemies? Maybe they feel they have no choice.

*July 6, 1940* Last night I dreamed of Gabriel, my first partner in dancing classes for secondary school students. In my dream I walked with Gabriel through a green meadow dotted with blue flowers, just as blue as his eyes.

I remember being fourteen with blond braids down to my waist. I was very shy. The dance master intoned, "The gentlemen invite the ladies to dance!" I stood next to a pillar in the school hall and stared at the floor. Suddenly two big feet, clad in black shoes, appeared in front of me. I looked up right into a pair of very blue eyes under dark bushy brows and a head full of black curls.

That's how I met Gabriel, who was one year older than I. Not having any brothers or male cousins I was at a loss as to how to talk to a boy. At first our conversation was awkward, but in the course of following lessons we began to talk to each other. Gabriel told me that his family had emigrated from Poland to Riga, where his father held a professorship at the University of Latvia; the family had converted from Judaism to Christianity. Gabriel and his brother were confirmed in the Lutheran Church.

During dancing classes Gabriel always stuck with me. Once in a while we would meet in friends' houses at parties and also on the ice skating rink, where Gabriel would pull me behind him as he raced around the rink.

After finishing secondary school I lost track of Gabriel. I heard that he had gone to study Engineering at the University of Zürich.

Four years ago, when I was already a University student in Riga, I quite accidentally met Gabriel again at a streetcar stop. He had returned from Switzerland to visit his parents.

During the following summer months we would occasionally go out together, to a movie or a dance, and then it was time for Gabriel to return to Zürich. He wrote me a farewell letter from the Riga railroad station. I have not heard from him since, and now this dream has brought back his memory.

*July 8, 1940* Our beloved state President, Dr. Karlis Ulmanis, has been arrested and has disappeared. We at Varonis are quite certain that he has been deported to Siberia.

The same fate has apparently befallen General Balodis. He too, has disappeared. The Farmers' Party has come to nothing. There are no other parties for whom one could vote. It is all a big lie and a trick to create the illusion, as though these were free democratic elections with a choice of parties. There exists only one party—the Communist Party—List #1.

*July 16, 1940* The big day! The workers of Varonis including the office and professional staff were marched in groups of twenty or so to the polls. Near the entrance, the ballots were distributed. I looked at my ballot: it was a single piece of paper folded once, containing the names of the candidates of List #1. There was no other list. No marking was required to make the ballot valid. We were ordered to move along a counter on which stood the ballot box. Behind the counter were several members of the Communist Party who watched us closely, as we slipped our ballots into the box. Then one of the Communists stamped our passports to indicate that we had obeyed Moscow's orders and could no longer be considered "enemies of the people."

I noticed several voting booths that had obviously been set up for show. Under these circumstances nobody dared to use them, for his name could easily be taken from his passport. For the same reason, it would, no doubt, be dangerous to put any marks on the ballot.

*July 17, 1940* Late last night, the election results were announced over the radio with triumphant blares and ovations: 99.67% of the Latvian population has given their vote to the "Workers' Block," alias the Communist Party.

According to our radio commentators, these results made headlines in the international press, convincing all the nations, which are still "enslaved" in the "grip of capitalism and imperialism," that the Latvian people are overjoyed to have been "liberated" by the military-might of their only "true friend"—the Soviet Union. Therefore, the Latvians have happily, and unanimously with all their hearts, embraced the blessings of true democracy, made possible only under the "Sun of

Stalin's Constitution": Liberty, equality, brotherhood . . . and so on and so forth.

I wonder what effect these manufactured election results may have on the Western nations. Could the English or the French or the Americans actually believe that the votes were the "free will of the Latvian people?"

*July 21, 1940* The inevitable has come to pass. Today, our newly elected Latvian Parliament proclaimed the foundation of the Latvian Socialist Republic. In the streets we had the usual demonstrations with pictures of Lenin and Stalin, red flags, hammer and sickle emblems, slogans, fist clenching and shouting. By now, due to enforced rehearsals, the singing of the "Internationale" has taken on more volume.

*July 23, 1940* The families of the Soviet occupation forces have begun to arrive. We meet more and more Russian women and children in the streets, easily recognizable by their shabby clothing and coarse hairdos. The women all wear the same style of dark gray coats and printed cotton dresses, mostly in pink and white, and narrow beige-colored shoes. These outfits are usually complemented with a white "bublichka"—a kind of French-style beret—or by a gray wool head shawl, worn in the middle of our July heat.

The children are noisy and destructive. I saw one boy, about ten years old, dig out a cobblestone from the pavement and hurl it at a passing horse and buggy. A couple of days later I observed another Soviet child prodding a horse with a stick. The animal was standing harnessed to its buggy, in front of the railroad station while its driver had gone off for a glass of vodka.

*July 27, 1940* The Soviet soldiers and their womenfolk are invading our department stores, buying all they can get. The exchange rate of rubles to Latvian money is very favorable. Today I saw a Soviet soldier in our most fashionable shoe shop buying eight pairs of women's shoes of all colors, and half a dozen pairs of men's shoes. He paid the sizable bill unhesitatingly, and haughtily ordered the women's shoes shipped to Moscow. This fellow wasn't even an officer.

*July 28, 1940* This morning on my way to church I saw three Soviet ladies out for a stroll in the Esplanade Gardens. I didn't believe my eyes: they were wearing quilted bed-jackets fashioned in a multi-colored flowery print with pink ribbons and ruffled laces at the throat and cuffs. These women, no doubt, are of the opinion that their pretty cover-ups are for street wear.

Services are held as usual at St. Peter's every Sunday; but since the departure of the Baltic Germans, they are now conducted in Latvian. Latvian or German—it doesn't matter. St. Peter's is still my church, where I was confirmed, where I belong.

*August 1, 1940* Our enthusiastic Communist demagogues continue daily to express the "will of the people," by demanding that Soviet Latvia be incorporated into the Union of all the other Soviet Republics.

Our own "Saeima"—obedient instrument of Moscow—decided to give in to the "unanimous and justified demands" of the Latvian nation, and has sent the appropriate petition to the Kremlin.

*August 2, 1940* Professor Kirchensteins has left for Moscow in order to prepare and ratify the incorporation of Soviet Latvia into the S.S.S.R.— Soyuz Sovietskikh Socialisticheskikh Respublik.

What a farce! There is no doubt now that long before the Latvians ever had an inkling, the Kremlin had already decided to swallow up the Baltic States. Now our puppet regime has to go through the motion of humbly petitioning for the honor of being swallowed up.

*August 5, 1940* Free Latvia is no more. Today Moscow proclaimed Latvia to be a full-fledged member of the Soviet Union. As of today, it is forbidden by punishment of arrest, to display our red-white-red striped flag. It flew in freedom for such a short time only—from 1918 to 1940. I still can hear Vyshinsky's words: "The flags of the Soviet Union and of Latvia will fly in friendship side by side . . . ."

*August 6, 1940* Today the Soviet newspaper "Isvestiya" announced the incorporation of Latvia in glaring headlines: "Long live Soviet Latvia, an equal in the fraternal confederacy of the nations of the Soviet Union!"

Lithuania and Estonia are undergoing the same fate—strictly according to plan.

*August 8, 1940* Moscow, it seems, is bent upon introducing to the Latvian people the blessings of "Sovietskaya kultura." We can enjoy matinee or nightly performances of the "Soviet Soldier's Show," free of charge. These shows take place in the open, weather permitting, in parks or even in the streets, with dancing, singing, and accordion-playing members of the Red Army performing.

These shows are nice to watch, the Russian folk-songs are beautiful, and the soldiers really can dance the "kazachok" to perfection: kicking their legs from a squatting position to the rapid beat of the fiery tunes of the accordion, or leaping high up into the air. But I hate their marching songs because of the sentiments they express: "There exists no other country where a man can breathe as freely, as happily as in our Soviet-land . . ."

The amateur shows, on the other hand, prepared by "cultural" groups of factory workers, are quite a different story. In my estimation they are a total failure. These amateur singers and players, without training or talent, are herded every Sunday morning into large trucks and taken all over the country to perform in the provinces.

Petkevich, naturally, has also formed one of these "cultural" entertainment groups from our workers. Today he came storming into my laboratory: "Comrade Zarina, I hear that you are a good pianist!"

"What of it?" I hardly ever bring myself to use the hateful title "Comrade" when addressing a person. The terms "Mister," "Mrs.," or "Miss" are strictly forbidden. The only way out is not to address anyone by name, and thus be impolite!

"Comrade Zarina, I have come to ask you to join our Varonis cultural group as piano player." There was arrogance in his face, but did I detect a hint of pleading in his strange eyes?

I pulled myself up, "No, I can't do it!"

He stared at me for a long moment, then turned without a word and left the lab.

I am truly frightened. I am in this strange man's power; we all are at Varonis. What will his reaction be?

*August 10, 1940* So far Petkevich has left me alone. Very likely he is too busy preparing the plant for nationalization.

Banks, factories, warehouses and all other private enterprises are being nationalized. Last night I went to the movies. The newsreel showed scenes of the "wonderful and prosperous" life in Latvia under the new government. One part showed the nationalization of a jewelry store. All of the goods, jewelry, crystal and silverware were displayed on long counters as government agents took inventory. The speaker explained the goings-on, and then announced in an impressive voice, ". . . and now all this belongs to the Latvian people." The reaction of the audience was a loud, scornful laugh. Disorders started and a policeman was called in to quiet the people down.

*August 15, 1940* Today Petkevich called a meeting for all employees in a former assembly hall, which by now has been converted into our new

"Worker's Club." He delivered another of his fiery speeches. "The plant is now the workers' own property," he shouted. "Therefore you all have to take good care of the machines and equipment and do your best to increase production. Overtime is no longer a chore, but a welcome opportunity to contribute your own free time, your enthusiasm, and your energy to the common goals. Therefore there will no longer be any compensation for overtime. Also, as of today, it has become the duty of you all, who are now the new plant owners, to safeguard your own property. For this purpose, we will immediately establish a Red Factory Guard!"

Petkevich chose workers on the spot, including women. The duty and "honor" was conferred upon them to take turns patrolling the factory grounds day and night with rifles, to guard the plant against robbery and sabotage by the enemy of the people.

*August 19, 1940* Ever since our "Workers' Club" was established, all Varonis employees are forced to assemble there every noon. A stage has been built at one end of the hall, decorated with red flags, pictures of Lenin and Stalin and the other usual attributes: Red Star, Hammer and Sickle. And above all this, the inscription: "Workers of the World, Unite!"

From this stage, every day Petkevich delivers his speeches praising Communism and the leaders in Moscow, never forgetting to point out how tremendously life has improved, in comparison with pre-Soviet times, all the while urging us to show our gratitude to "Father Stalin" by producing more and better rubber articles than before. He then talks about the daily happenings in our factory, mostly berating our white-collar workers.

Today, all of a sudden, he started to attack me. Maybe it was an act of retaliation on his part for my refusal to join his "cultural" group. Turning his gaze upon me he shouted, "And now, I want to ask our laboratory supervisor, Comrade Zarina, why she still keeps on sending her laboratory reports to Comrade Dinbergs instead of me? Doesn't Comrade Zarina realize that times have changed? Comrade Dinbergs was dismissed from his General Manager's post because his capitalistic background makes him totally unsuitable to be a leader of workers. I am now in charge here. We have been lenient with Comrade Dinbergs and have allowed him to remain at Varonis as a chemical engineer. That, however, does not give Comrade Zarina the right to show her reports to him."

I felt a tremendous urge to jump up from my seat and challenge the new General Manager by asking him whether he would be capable of understanding chemical formulas or reports. I wanted to yell in his face that the only reason why Dinbergs has not yet been arrested or fired was the fact, plain and simple, that his professional knowledge and advice were vital in keeping the plant going in the midst of incredible incompetence and confusion.

Fortunately, I controlled my furious resentment, which would have endangered not only myself but Dinbergs also. I must at no time forget that it is utterly senseless to express one's true opinion. I must keep my mouth shut, no matter what!

At the end of this memorable noon-hour meeting we all, as usual, had to sing the "Internationale," simultaneously raising our clenched fists. Then came the usual three shouts: "Long Live Lenin! Long Live Stalin! Long Live the Soviet Union!" Then we were released and told to go back to work.

*September 2, 1940* The nationalization wave continues. By now, even small items of personal property are being nationalized.

This afternoon, upon my return from work, I found two men standing on the landing in front of my flat. I felt most apprehensive when they introduced themselves as government agents, sent to inspect my apartment. After the inspection, they announced that my piano and my sewing machine had been nationalized. Furthermore, according to Soviet regulations, my mother and I occupied much too much living space. Each person is entitled to no more than nine square yards of living area. Our apartment is therefore much too large for two people. I have the choice either to take in tenants (most likely a Soviet family belonging to the Occupation Forces—no thank you!) or to pay three times as much rent. I decided instantaneously on the higher rent. In my case, nationalization means that I am no longer allowed to move or to sell my piano or my sewing machine.

*September 12, 1940* It no longer comes as a surprise that farms are also being nationalized, in spite of the declaration of our Soviet Latvian Agriculture Minister Vanags: "Peasants, farmers and all tillers of the soil! Don't lose your faith! Believe and follow the directions of our people's government . . . The Communist Party has guaranteed that the farmland, cattle and moveable goods of the farmer-workers will not be subject to expropriation. Collectivization will not be enforced . . ."

And now expropriation of farmland is in full swing. All nationalized large farms are divided into 25-acre plots. The former owner—if he is lucky—may keep 75 acres. The small 25-acre plots are being leased to individuals who have no land of their own.

We at Varonis feel very strongly that this is being done to prepare the country speedily for the collective farming system of Soviet Russia. Meanwhile, Minister Vanags goes on spouting grand phrases: "Working peasants! After long years of slavery and mental darkness we are free again. We shall never forget that our freedom was given to us by the strong and heroic Red Army. Therefore, the friendship between the workers and the working peasants and the Soviet Union will be eternal, because the Red Army is a reliable pledge of our freedom . . ."

I can't help feel the hidden threat: "The Red Army will make sure that Moscow's orders are obeyed"—what Vanags really meant.

*September 15, 1940* With new troubles brewing daily in Latvia, the Western Front is almost forgotten. All summer long battles in the air have been fought between the German Luftwaffe and the British Royal Air Force. Hitler apparently is preparing for the invasion of England by trying to destroy as many English airplanes as possible. The English are retaliating by shooting down scores of German planes.

Here, we have no air raids, no bombings and no ferocious battles raging, but we have other horrors to cope with.

*September 18, 1940* The first excitement over the Red Guard has diminished. It has become a duty loathed by the workers. They have to donate their free time without compensation. This morning as I entered the factory gates I saw a woman worker who had been on guard all night, being led away by two men. She had been overcome either by fatigue or vodka. The woman was unable to walk, stumbling at every step, the rifle still dangling from her shoulder.

Very likely she was drunk. Alcohol in Soviet Latvia is about the only thing one can buy cheaply and in unlimited quantities. Never before have I seen so many drunks lying in the gutter as in these last few months. In Latvian times the police would take drunkards to the police station or to the hospital, nowadays apparently nobody bothers. I wonder what will happen when the cold weather starts.

*September 20, 1940* Our life is now completely dominated by Communist doctrines and slogans, which day after day blare from loudspeakers into the streets and flash in huge red letters from house-fronts.

The newspapers are bragging daily about the new principles being taught in elementary and high schools, based on communist ideology.

Two days ago the fall semester started at my Alma Mater. The University's educational system has been completely reorganized according to Communist standards. The theology and philosophy departments have been closed; logic as a branch of study has been eliminated. Its place has been taken by a new discipline: Communist doctrine, consisting of the theories and principles of Marx, Engels, Lenin and Stalin, obligatory to all university students, and taught by professors imported from the Soviet Union.

I am so glad that I have graduated. Today I went to the secretarial offices of the University to pick up my diploma, the printing of which had been delayed due to all the upheavals. I was very much afraid that the name of the University might have been changed on my diploma from "University of Latvia" to the "Polytechnical Institute of Soviet Latvia." Fortunately, my fears were unfounded.

At the University too, it appeared that a kind of Red Guard has been established. A girl student patrolled the entrance hall, wearing a wide red band around her right sleeve and a revolver in a holster on her hip. She sternly asked me what my business was. I had to produce my passport in order to identify myself. My name was registered in a visitors' book, arrival and leaving times were marked down.

I must say, I greatly resented this ridiculous procedure. That girl seemed determined to demonstrate her newly found power in a totally unwarranted, hostile attitude.

*September 30, 1940* In the past week, great changes have taken place at Varonis. A number of employees, who in the opinion of Petkevich did not seem loyal to the Communist cause, have been fired. Every day, I too expect to be fired, but so far nothing has happened. Petkevich, passing me at the noon hour rally, will cast sidelong-glances at me. But since his attack on me, he seems to ignore me completely. However, I don't trust him!

The most important change has been the recent installation of a new technical director, Comrade Jacob Lemke of German Jewish origin. He actually is a chemical engineer and he has been assigned, it seems, to relieve Petkevich of plant engineering duties (which the latter was totally unable to carry out in the first place). Dinbergs has not been fired, and I am very glad of it. All the old employees, including the staff and me, are very devoted to him because of his kind and gentle attitude and his fatherly concern for us.

Lemke is a tall, rather thin man in his early thirties. He is timid, and seems overwhelmed by the enormity of the honor bestowed upon him by the Communist Party.

"Why me? Actually becoming technical director of the large plant! For a long time after graduating from the Latvian University, I couldn't even find a chemist's job!" He told me a couple of days ago.

He at least is honest, and I like him for that.

Lemke has even been given an assistant named Chaim Reshin. As far as looks are concerned, Comrade Reshin is a smaller version of Lemke: equally skinny, equally timid, but about one head shorter. Reshin is in charge of rubber mixing and vulcanizing procedures. Lemke oversees the entire plant operation. Dinbergs apparently is kept as a safety measure, whenever Lemke and Reshin are unable to make any kind of decision. Neither Lemke nor Reshin have much of an idea about the operations of a rubber plant. Both got the jobs because they are good Communists.

*October 4, 1940* This morning I had a chat with Reshin, who seems a friendly little fellow. "You know, Comrade Zarina," he said to me, "if I had wanted to, I could also have gotten a director's job like my friend Lemke."

"Why didn't you, then?" I asked him. His surprising reply was:

"Directors' posts are usually dangerous. If anything goes wrong, they get at the top man first."

*October 7, 1940* For a number of weeks now, I have been forced to partly neglect my chemist's duties in favor of the "Wall Gazette." This typical Soviet invention was installed when our new "Worker's Club" first opened up. It is a kind of bulletin board, carrying not only announcements of political meetings or other important events, but also short compositions, written mostly by Petkevich, expressing various aspects of Communist ideology, as well as criticisms in connection with our work. The production charts of our departments also have a permanent place in the Wall Gazette. The rest of the space is used for gossip and denunciation. All workers are encouraged to send in contributions. These are usually unsigned letters dealing with the personal life and morals of individuals in the plant, mostly the workers' superiors.

I, of all people, have been appointed by Petkevich to be editor of this abominable Wall Gazette—which involves collecting and arranging the material. I couldn't dare to eliminate even the worst gossip, because I would immediately be accused of disloyalty to the workers. Andris, on the other hand, takes great delight in assisting me with the job. He decorates the Wall Gazette with his own free-hand paintings and with the usual Soviet emblems.

A new Wall Gazette comes whenever we have enough new material. The Wall Gazette is placed in the so-called "Red Corner" of the plant. Red Corners have been established in every conceivable place, in every factory, large office, school, institute or club. Besides the Wall Gazette, they also contain pictures of Lenin and Stalin, Soviet emblems, red flags and the usual slogans.

The Red Corner in our Worker's Clubhouse is a popular spot. During our daily noon rally, people are always seen studying the Wall Gazette, especially the gossip column.

*October 8, 1940* This evening I quite unexpectedly met my former classmate Monika on "Kalku Iela." Monika gave me some news about long-lost Gabriel. Shortly after I last saw him he had gotten married in Switzerland, but had soon lost his bride. She died in childbirth together with the baby. Now poor Gabriel is alone in this war-torn world.

# CHAPTER FOUR

## The Sun of Stalin's Constitution

*October 10, 1940* Today a Workers' Committee was formed with Petkevich as chairman representing the highest administrative power. Due to the formation of the Committee and also due to Lemke's arrival, Petkevich's responsibilities—supervising all and everything—have become somewhat more limited. He now has to share his activities with director Lemke. At this point Petkevich is handling only administrative and personnel problems. He is also our political supervisor, making sure that all directions given by the Communist Party are carefully carried out.

Because of his new position, the former boiler operator now has his own office. He now has achieved the same coveted position that the hated capitalist director had when Petkevich was still shoveling coals. He struts about his new office, or sits majestically behind his mahogany desk, and gives orders in a ringing voice.

Every morning he arrives at the plant in his chauffeur-driven car; sometimes accompanied by his wife, a tiny woman, who until recently had been on the assembly line in our plant. We have nicknamed her "the Director's lady."

Petkevich, I must admit, is quite successful in achieving the air and the bearing of a person in power. He does a good job in copying his former bosses, the capitalists and the imperialists, as he calls them. Now he feels that he has become their equal. But, at the same time he is most careful to emphasize that he is still a proletarian, a "comrade." He comes to the office dressed more shabbily than ever, usually wearing an old Russian shirt, faded breeches and scuffed high boots. To complete his proletarian appearance, he seems to shave only once a week.

*October 12, 1940* Last night Ingmar and I attended a performance of Bizet's "Carmen" at the National Opera House. The singers and the music were splendid. I particularly enjoyed Don José's aria "Take This Flower" sung by our most famous opera tenor, Arturs Priedniecks-Cavarra.

During the intermission, Ingmar and I went strolling to the lounge where, to our surprise, we met two Soviet ladies in nightgowns. One was wearing a pink taffeta creation with tiny shoulder straps, covered with ruffles and bows; the other, a light blue, sheer, batiste concoction with short puffed sleeves, gathered under the bosom and decorated with laces and thin velvet ribbons. Fortunately the second lady had enough sense to wear a slip under her sheer gown.

Ingmar and I almost burst out laughing—so did many others—upon realizing that these Soviet officers' wives had assumed that they were buying evening gowns when in fact they had selected nightgowns.

I suspect that our newly arrived Soviet citizens have never before in their lives seen most of the fashionable items sold in the stores and boutiques of Riga.

*October 15, 1940* This morning I had another chat with Reshin. I met him at one of the rubber mixing machines. He seemed greatly agitated because he had soiled his clothes with black carbon powder. I asked him what the matter was and he broke out complaining, "Oh Comrade, I spoiled the only suit I have. What kind of life is this anyway! Before this I had nothing and now I still have nothing!"

I couldn't help replying with faint mockery, "But Comrade Rashin, don't forget, now you live under the 'Sun of Stalin's Constitution.' Isn't that of greater value than anything else?"

Chaim Reshin looked at me with a rather doubtful eye, but as he could not make out whether I was serious or not, he decided not to continue our discussion any longer.

*October 17, 1940* I wonder if ever before in history a plague has been known called "production charts?" These charts tie in with the Stackanov system which Petkevich introduced to our factory last month. "Every one of you," he shouted, "can become a 'hero of work,' just like Stackanov and many other distinguished workers in our beloved Soviet Union." But our workers are not at all enthusiastic. This just means longer working hours and harder work without adequate increase in wages. Now there is constant nerve-wracking urging by the supervisors to do more and more. No limit, apparently, is ever set.

In order to record the increase of output, production charts have been set up. It is one of my jobs, on top of all my chemical duties, to prepare them for all departments of the factory. Andris and I are forced to spend a great deal of our time on this.

The trouble is that Petkevich demands and expects a steady increase of production. This goal of his is doomed to failure because we are using our pre-Soviet production, which is already at a high level, as the standard.

Mine is the horrendous task of trying to make the best out of the long list of figures sent weekly to my desk. Somehow the department supervisors seen to feel that it is all my fault if the charts do not show the desired increases. In the back of my mind is the fear that eventually I might become the scapegoat and be accused of sabotage. No wonder that Logic has been eliminated from the University program.

*October 21, 1940* It is getting cold and I need a new winter coat. Today, right after work, I went shopping at Feitelbergs, which is still one of our most elegant clothing stores. Prices have gone up tremendously, but they still have a nice selection. As I was trying on coats, I watched a Soviet woman come into the store accompanied by her soldier husband. She selected a very expensive black velvet creation with a silver fox collar, which she began to model in front of a huge three-part mirror. On her feet the woman wore the inevitable "Valienki" felt boots; and around her head a shabby grey wool shawl. Her husband stood by in rapt admiration, urging her to buy the coat. But Madame pouted and wanted something else, something better.

*October 28, 1940* My birthday! Ingmar took me to Tchaikovsky's opera "Eugene Onegin." I was enchanted. The scenes from Pushkin's masterpiece, which we had read in Russian high school classes, came to life accompanied by beautiful music.

*November 9, 1940* The anniversary of the Russian Revolution of 1917. Petkevich has arranged a great celebration, which will take place tonight at our Meeting Hall. The large room and the stage have been decorated with nothing but Soviet emblems. The Red Star with Hammer and Sickle in all sizes covers the walls, hangs from the ceiling, and flashes above the stage. A piano has been set up on stage, and I have been ordered to play tonight. I'm wearing a Latvian national costume: a long, wide, dark blue wool skirt; a dark blue spencer; and a white, full-sleeved linen blouse with red cross-stitching embroidered in the sleeves, cuffs, and collar. My hair is in two long braids; and on my head is a wreath made of multicolored ribbons with streamers falling to my back. Only unmarried girls may wear the wreath; married women must don a white cap.

*November 10, 1940* At the party last night, Petkevich first, as was to be expected, made a fiery speech praising the revolution. Then the musical program started. A worker's chorus sang Soviet songs. Two particularly are still echoing in my mind. One describes the immenseness of the Soviet Union and the happy life of its citizens. The other is a soldier's song with the following refrain: "And Marshall Voroshiloff goes with us to war, to war!"

Then I played the piano. I had been ordered to play Russian composers only, so I played Tchaikovsky. Next a young worker (in normal life, a maker of rubber boots) played the violin while I accompanied him. He was so excited that he started the second piece first, while I, as planned, started with the first piece. Somehow I managed to change the music and catch up with him. Fortunately, our audience was not too critical and the mishap went by almost unnoticed.

During the following dance, Petkevich—oh horror—did me the "honor" of dancing a Polka with me. He even tried his hand at polite conversation. Since I was most unresponsive, not much came of it and the "old firebrand" soon departed from my side. Shortly thereafter I managed to slip out and get home.

*November 11, 1940* I heard at work that last night Communists broke into one of our cemeteries and damaged a number of graves, toppling their crosses. Then the vandals triumphantly carried the crosses to the town dump. Stalin's constitution supposedly guarantees freedom of religion; but everyone, including young schoolchildren, is encouraged to attack the church and its teachings.

*November 12, 1940* On my way home today I noticed a lovely aqua-blue wool dress in a display window at Feitelbergs. The price is fifty Lats. I can't get it out of my mind. I think I'm going to buy it in spite of its high price. It is just lovely!

*November 15, 1940* Today the newspaper boasted how "free-spirited youths" had destroyed a "reactionary" monument in Rositten, one of our predominantly Catholic towns in the south of Latvia. The monument showed a Latvian girl in national garb, holding a cross up into the sky, as if to ask God's blessing upon our country. Last night the statue was pulled down with the help of heavy trucks. According to the papers, two Protestant churches have recently been changed into warehouses, and four Catholic churches into dance halls.

We Latvians are constantly being accused over the radio of being a culturally very backward people, because we continue going to church.

*November 18, 1940* Today is our State Holiday, except that we are forbidden to celebrate it. It is forbidden to sing the Latvian anthem, it is forbidden to display our red-white-red Latvian flag.

But this morning thousands of bouquets were found placed on the pedestal of the Monument of Liberty in the center of Riga.

Thousands more flowers were brought to the War Cemetery at the outskirts of Riga. They were laid on the graves of the soldiers, and before the monument of our "Sorrowing Mother Latvia" dedicated to the war dead of the war of 1914 and the fight for independence. I, too, brought flowers. When dusk fell, the crowd, which had assembled in the cemetery before the monument, began to light candles and to place them on the soldiers' graves. I was doing the same when suddenly a short stocky fellow appeared before me and asked in broken Latvian with a heavy Russian accent, "What are you doing here, comrade?"

I answered tersely, "What do you think? I lit a candle?"

"What do you do that for?"

"This soldier gave his life for our country, that's why."

The crowd behind me, consisting mostly of University students wearing their fraternity caps, repeated in low angered voices: "He gave his life for our country!"

The Russian started and looked around. It was a scene as dramatic as any on stage: the villain and the heroine in the center, before the huge monument from which daylight was fading rapidly, while the students in the background murmured scornfully like an ancient Greek chorus. The Russian suddenly extinguishing my candle hissed at me: "Go away if you don't want to get into trouble or I will arrest you." Then, raising his voice he shouted: "Yes, I will arrest you all" and disappeared into the dark. But I lit my candle again.

*November 19, 1940* This morning has brought another heavy blow. Our Latvian money has been devalued to one tenth of its former value. Up to this date, one Lat had been equal to ten Soviet rubles; now overnight, one Lat is only one ruble. We have lost nine tenths of our savings. Although salaries have remained the same, prices for nearly all kinds of merchandise including food, have gone up ten times. Strangely enough, only the prices for alcoholic beverages have remained the same.

My lovely aqua-blue dress in Feitelberg's window now has a new price tag: 500 rubles. Alas, I can no longer afford it!!

*November 25, 1940* This afternoon some of my women friends in the plant came to my laboratory office. They seemed very depressed and complained heavily of their disappointment in the Communist promises of a better and happier life for the working classes. The situation can actually be expressed in figures. By now I would have to work for an entire month in order to buy my aqua-blue dream dress.

*November 27, 1940* We live in constant terror of the Secret Police. By word of mouth we daily hear of sudden arrests on the streets, investigations and cross-examinations out of the blue, and mysterious disappearances of innocent people. Who will be next?

*November 28, 1940* This morning I called supervisor Kocins of the Technical Department into my office. I showed him his department's production charts: there had been a 14% increase in September, a drop to 9% in October, and a rise again to 14.5% in November.

Comrade Kocins was terrified. It is exactly as Chaim Reshin has put it—if anything goes wrong they get at the top man first. Kocins implored me not to consider the results for October when preparing the final quarterly chart for Petkevich. I decided to do just that. I have omitted the 9% for October, thereby getting a nice, slowly but steadily increasing production curve. This chart can now be sent safely to the government exhibition of plant production charts, which is on continuous display in the Town Hall of Riga. Maybe I should go and take a look at the exhibit.

*December 1, 1940* I did go! I went to the plant production exhibition today. And lo and behold! I am thoroughly impressed by the tremendous efficiency of the new Soviet working methods. I did not see a single chart that showed any irregularities or drops. All curves rose steadily and uniformly. This has indeed convinced me that the other plants in Latvia are solving their difficulties with production charts the same way we do.

*December 3, 1940* On one hand we have production charts, on the other hand we have "Sovietskaya Kultura." Part of the efforts to bring some enlightenment to us backward Latvians are Soviet moving pictures. We are entertained by films about Ivan the Terrible, Peter the Great and other historic personages suitable to the Communist cause, and also by films of the new Soviet life. Last night I saw a story of a Russian girl who works in an auto repair shop as a mechanic. After all kinds of adventures, she becomes a famous singer. This film, made in 1938, i.e. in "peace time," has given me some definite ideas about daily life in Soviet Russia. It shows working men and women in factories and shops—the women doing work totally unfit for their sex, like lifting heavy construction parts by hand, welding metal with acetylene torches or crawling under cars on their backs. It shows the uniformity of clothing and the terribly crowded apartments of Moscow.

Rooms are shared by several large families. In the hall of a flat, half a dozen little kerosene stoves have been set up all in a row, and women are seen preparing their respective families' breakfasts. Meanwhile the menfolk stand in line before the bathroom door patiently awaiting their turn. It seems so unwise to show scenes like that to us—who, all our lives, have been used to a normal amount of living space in our homes.

The heroine lives in that flat and part of her adventures consist of struggling with all those daily inconveniences and with the hostility of her fellow tenants. At the same time, she has to go through many hardships at her working place, the repair shop. But finally she emerges happily smiling on stage, wearing women's clothes for the first time (so far she had only been seen in overalls) and singing a jubilant song. She has made it; she is now a singer. Her lover, a famous actor who once also had been a working man, appears. They hold hands and sing a duet.

*December 6, 1940* St. Nicholas' Day! Today, according to legend, Santa Claus fills the shoes of good little children with sweets and leaves a switch for the naughty ones. I'm afraid our kids at present have other problems. All young school children are forced to become members of the Communist youth organizations "Pioneer" or "Komsomol." This is usually against the will of their parents, but if a parent dares to object, he is arrested and often disappears. Our historic castle of Riga, built in the thirteenth century, has been turned over to the Pioneers and is now a kind of clubhouse for the kids. This is hailed by the press as a highly social deed.

High school and university students' extra-curricular activities are street demonstrations with the usual slogans, shouting, fist-clenching, and marching songs. By now all this has become such a bore and utterly meaningless!

Our University fraternities and sororities have been accused of representing the spirit of the capitalistic upper classes and are now in the process of being dissolved. The property and belongings of our sorority—the furniture, silverware, china, crystal, books, and all recordings—have been confiscated and will be shipped to Russia.

*December 11, 1940* The tension is growing daily. Our people in the plant are tired of working overtime without additional pay, of listening to the same old slogans and of the constant urgings to increase production. An employee is not even allowed to stay at home in case of sickness, unless he can get approval from a special government doctor. Since these doctors are quite scarce and have strict orders not to declare a person sick unless he is already half dead, the situation has become rather difficult for us.

I have a bad cold, but it is literally a crime to stay at home without written permission. My temperature is up to 102 degrees. I'm risking it and not going to work today. But every instant I could expect to be arrested by the Red Guard or the Secret Police as a saboteur, an "enemy of the people," and I would be accused of intending to lower the plant's production by refusing to do my daily work.

*December 13, 1940* I'm back at work. Strangely enough, there were no repercussions in the wake of my unauthorized sick leave. Maybe my absence has not been recorded due to a great new excitement that has stirred up our plant. A group of Soviet engineers and chemists from Moscow is visiting us. They are swarming all over the place, claiming that they have orders to analyze and improve our techniques with the goal of production increase according to Soviet pattern.

Among the Soviets there is a woman, a chemical engineer like myself. I can't help but regard her with great mistrust and antipathy. She seems to feel the same towards me and we make it a point to avoid each other. She is a short, stout person with short straight yellow hair and a plump face. She is always wearing a brown leather jacket over a cheap pink print dress, and the inevitable white felt "bublichka" is perched squarely on her head. Her feet are adorned by "valienki" felt boots, in spite of the fact that she works in a rubber plant in Moscow. This is giving us cause for endless speculations and jokes: "Why doesn't Comrade Masha Petrovna wear rubber boots? Doesn't she trust the quality?"

*December 20, 1940* During our noon hour meeting today Petkevich suggested that we ignore Christmas as a holiday because it is "just one of those senseless old-fashioned church festivals." He exclaimed enthusiastically, "Let us make a resolution that we are going to work on Christmas Day and send a telegram to Father Stalin announcing our intention. Raise your hands, those who agree with me!" Expectantly he looked around; a few hands rose, but that was all. Petkevich urged, "Comrades, come on, what's the matter?" A few more hands rose. He counted them and shouted, "Not enough, nowhere near enough! Let's count once more!"' And so by constant urging and threatening and counting hands over and over again, he finally got the necessary majority and could wire to "Father Stalin" that the workers of the Varonis Rubber Plant in Riga had "enthusiastically and unanimously resolved to work on Christmas Day."

*December 29, 1940* Christmas was a sad day for the people in Latvia and all the other Soviet-occupied countries, but so it was for Western Europe, especially England. The German Luftwaffe is flying massive bombing attacks against English cities almost daily. Yesterday I picked up a brash German fighting song on our short-wave radio: "Wir fliegen gegen Engelland!" ("We are flying against England!") was the refrain.

The manufacturing town of Coventry was almost completely destroyed by German bombs last month. Just now terrible fires are raging in the center of London caused by German incendiary bombs.

*January 1, 1941* Last night I lived through another sad New Year's Eve. We live in constant fear now. To make matters worse, we were told by Erika that Uncle Adi has terminal cancer and that he only has a few weeks to live, and that she herself is expecting her first child in spring. The poor child will never know its father.

This morning Ingmar brought me a good luck present—a chocolate piglet, wrapped in pink aluminum foil with a big pink bow around its neck. I had to smile in spite of the sadness in my heart. What will become of our dream—Ingmar's and mine?

*January 6, 1941* The New Year has brought some changes for Petkevich. He has been promoted. So far he had only been functioning as chairman of the Soviet Committee for our plant, but now he has been elevated to chairman of the newly established "Committee for Increasing Production of the Soviet-Latvian Chemical Industry." This means that all thirty-nine chemical factories in Riga are under his direct supervision. He still keeps his office in our plant, but most of his time now is spent racing through Riga from one factory to the next, haughtily reclining in the back seat of his chauffeur-driven limousine.

*January 7, 1941* This morning "old Firebrand" quite unexpectedly appeared in my laboratory and ordered me to prepare and conduct a chemistry course for our factory workers. The course is to be started within a few days. Petkevich explained that he has arranged such courses in all of his thirty-nine plants.

I got busy setting up some simple experiments in inorganic chemistry, and preparing an introductory talk geared to the level of my expected audience. I consider this idea the only sensible plan that has so far come out of our new administration. It is certainly a lot more rewarding than the making of production charts and wall gazettes.

*January 10, 1941* I have made the headlines! The newspaper "The Young Communar" on its front page today ran a picture of me teaching chemistry class to our plant people. The article states that the reason for this educational plan is to ". . . create well-qualified and valuable workers for the Soviet industry. Out of these new and highly trained groups will come our best workers and followers of Stackanov."

*January 13, 1941* This afternoon Petkevich again showed up in my office—he always comes galloping in, always out of breath, always barking commands—and shouted in a stern voice, "Comrade Zarina, you are ordered to appear tonight at eight o'clock before the Committee for Increasing Production."

I parried in surprise: "What for?"

Petkevich shot me a fierce and scornful glance and growled, "You will be elected secretary of the committee."

I am stunned and frightened. What am I to do? Shall I ignore the summons? I'm liable to be arrested for sabotage, for not obeying party command. Shall I go? I'm liable to be scorned and mocked and abused, because I am determined to refuse that job. There is no way out, I *must* venture into the lion's den and leave the outcome to my guardian angel.

I am still in a state of shock. I have just returned from the meeting and I am worse off than ever.

Tonight, as I arrived at the designated place, I found myself in the midst of tough-looking men and women. Both sexes wore leather jackets and knee-high leather boots. All women had red scarves around their heads and carried rifles over their shoulders. These are true Communist fashions, and there I was in my "capitalistic" garments: gray Persian lamb fur coat, black felt hat, black dress, purple chiffon scarf, silk stockings, and patent leather shoes. The women looked me up and down and bristled with ill-will and distrust. The men eyed me speculatively. As much as I hate Petkevich, I was glad to see him come storming in. He at least would protect me, I hoped, from the hostile crowd.

Petkevich in turn seemed highly pleased that I had come. Without much ado he opened the meeting. "Comrades, today we meet here in order to elect a secretary for our committee. I wish to introduce Comrade Zarina. I propose her for the job."

Loud murmurs of disapproval were instantaneously heard and phrases that might be roughly expressed as, "We don't want that fancy dame. Who is this capitalistic female anyway?"

As much as I was scared, this group resistance nevertheless gave me some hope and enough courage to stand up and join in the protest. "The honorable members of the committee are absolutely right," I stated. "I am totally unfit for such a great responsibility since I have neither the experience nor the training for it. I can't even type!" The complaining growls died down and I felt relieved, but only for a moment. Petkevich jumped up and eyes blazing shouted at me, "Comrade, I am here in command. You *can* do it. Your intelligence and your energy will carry you through. Now, go ahead and give us a brief account of yourself, your education and experience." I started to protest once more, but he shouted me down, this time addressing the group. "As you can see, Comrade Zarina is perfectly fit for the position. I'm sure, you are all convinced of this by now, and so I declare Comrade Zarina unanimously elected secretary of the Committee!"

No one, including me, thought it wise to make any more protests and so the session was closed, and I have just walked home with a new title: Secretary of the Committee for Increasing Production in the Soviet-Latvian Chemical Industry. In spite of my perturbed state of mind I cannot help but marvel at the Soviet fondness for long and complicated titles. I wonder what would be a fitting contraction: SECCOMINPROSOVLATCHEMIND, maybe?

*January 14, 1941* Once more I've made the headlines, this time in the newspaper "Cina" ("The Battle"). This morning "Cina" brought my picture together with this wonderful long title for my new responsibility.

I have not slept all night. It has become quite clear to me that Petkevich is weaving a net around me in ever-tightening spirals. He wants to recruit me for the Communist Party—what a feather in his cap that would be! Petkevich—the Black Spider! I must break out before I am helplessly trapped.

During the night a bold idea has formed in my mind. I'll take a chance!

*January 15, 1941* Yesterday morning, rather than going to my laboratory I went straight to Comrade Director Lemke's office. He and Chaim Reshin greeted me with fervent exclamations, "Oh, Comrade, what an honor for our plant! Receive our congratulations, we are proud of you!"

Resolutely, I cut them short, "I'm going to resign from my chemist's post in this plant, because you obviously no longer need a chemist here!"

"But Comrade, what makes you think so?" Lemke protested.

"If you cared for my work you wouldn't have agreed to my election as secretary of Petkevich's committee."

"But Comrade, this secretarial work is honorary; you are expected to do it after working hours. The production figures of thirty-nine chemical plants will be sent to your desk and you will have to prepare production charts and compare them. The results of these comparisons will then have to be put into new general charts to be sent to Moscow."

All this was news to me because Petkevich had not bothered to explain my future duties. I retorted, "That is even worse! How can I possibly manage two full-time jobs, one chemical and one secretarial, in one working day?"

Lemke seemed impressed by that argument and said he would telephone Petkevich about it immediately. When Petkevich heard about my objections he became so enraged that even I, who was standing at a distance from the telephone, could hear his shouts. But finally Lemke managed to persuade Petkevich that he would have to find himself someone else for his committee.

I have a respite, but for how long?

*January 27, 1941* Two weeks have gone by and there has been no further move from the Black Spider. But I can sense danger. A fanatic like Petkevich never gives up. My time is running out. My guardian angel must be most efficient to have kept me safe for so long in such adversity.

Mother is no help at all. I have mentioned leaving the country. It would be possible right now because Germany and Soviet Russia, keeping up their facade of political friendship, have recently signed an agreement whereby Latvian, Estonian, and Lithuanian citizens who can lay claims to any kind of German ethnic origin, are allowed to leave the country and emigrate to Germany. Mother wants no part of it. She is afraid to give up her place to live, her material possessions, and her daily routine. In vain am I pointing out to her that forced deportation to Siberia is happening daily to many people in our country. "I cannot imagine anything more horrible, Mother, than being dragged off to a slave labor camp to icy Siberia—there to be beaten, abused and starved. It would be the end of all hope."

"Would you prefer living in Nazi Germany, Irene, in a country at war, with bombs raining down from heaven daily, where every moment might be your last? And where innocent people are being persecuted because of their religion?"

"I know, Mother, we are caught between two evils. It is hard to decide which might be the lesser."

"I prefer to stay where I am. I'd rather die at home than in a foreign country."

"Mother, don't talk like that. It is not a matter of death; it is a matter of life We want to live, and I believe that with luck we have a better chance to survive in Germany."

Mother turned a deaf ear.

*January 29, 1941* The final blow fell today! And it did not come from Petkevich. I started to walk out of the main gate on my way home when one of our Red Guards suddenly stopped me by holding his rifle horizontally in front of me, sternly inquiring, "Did you go through the control booth?" I was utterly surprised. "What? Me? It is not customary to inspect professional personnel."

"We have new orders from the director."

I turned around and rushed back to the main building into Lemke's office. "Did you give orders that I be searched?" I demanded. Lemke was greatly embarrassed; he hemmed and hawed and tried to explain things: "You see, Comrade, the workers are mad that we suspect only them of stealing and concealing rubber articles in their clothing, whereas the professionals and staff may go home undisturbed. Therefore, I have ordered that everyone be checked, and (here his tone became conspiratorially confidential) furthermore, I plan to introduce a system where everyone secretly observes everyone else and reports their findings to me!"

Speechless for once, I stared at him for a long moment: what a miserable creature he is, what a miserable system this is. Then I caught myself, "If that is so, was comrade Reshin inspected on his way out?" Lemke actually was honest enough to admit, although reluctantly, that Reshin had not been searched. "In that case," I declared, "I won't be searched either!"

Lemke finally agreed and I went back to the main gate, but the guard, one of the fanatics, became furious and would not let me pass. With gleaming eyes and a voice filled with hatred he shouted, "Who do you think you are? You probably still consider yourself a classy, educated young lady, one step above us common workers! Well, sister, those days are over. We now live under the Sun of Stalin's Constitution, which makes us all equals. We have no more ladies in Soviet Latvia, you conceited female, and your whole education isn't worth a Kopeck to me!"

With rage rising in me I stepped forward trying to force my way through. But the man lifted his rifle and screamed livid in the face, "One more step and I'll shoot you."

That indeed was too much. No longer able or caring to control my temper, I shouted back at the brute, looking straight into those green, glittering, hate-filled eyes of his. "Yes, indeed, you are right. I *am* a lady and I don't give a damn for Stalin's Constitution as long as his followers are such brainless fools as you and your gang!" The man's face turned white. He did not move and neither did I. Our stares met and locked. Fortunately, at that moment the chief of the Red Guards appeared and inquired about the disturbance. Full of self-righteous fury the guard demanded, "What shall I do with this citizen? She does not follow orders! Shall I arrest her or shall I shoot her?" The chief seemed to have some sense of humor. He began to laugh, waved his hand and told the man to let me go.

Once safely outside the factory gates, I decided that I would leave the country. I cannot take this oppression.

Then, instead of going home, I hurried to the German Embassy to see Walter. I explained what had happened and asked for advice. Walter's answer was "Germany needs professional people like you and will accept you, but will the Soviets let you out? That is the question!" He gave me a note with the German Consular seal on it. Tomorrow morning I am to take it to the joint German-Soviet Repatriation Commission headquarters. They have set up office in my former high school building.

The excitements of the day have utterly drained me. I have no fighting spirit left to argue my decision with Mother. I will simply inform her that tomorrow we are opting for Germany.

*January 30, 1941* Mother has accepted my decision . . .

This morning we arrived in front of the Repatriation Commission's Offices, and found there a milling crowd of hundreds of people, all wanting to depart to Germany. It was impossible to even get near the doors of the building. On the steps leading up to the entrance, two German soldiers from the Reich stood guard, clad in greenish-blue uniforms decorated with swastikas, directing the onslaught of people. I tried to get their attention by waving my consular note. One of the soldiers noticed me, recognized the seal, pushed an opening into the crowd on the steps before him, came down, took me by the hand and pulled me up to the entrance. I, in turn, hung on to Mother, thereby managing to get her in too.

Once inside the building, it took only a short time to get the permission to leave Latvia and to enter Germany. Since Mother and I both speak fluent German, and since I have attended German schools, it was relatively easy for me to convince the joint Commission—consisting of one German from the Reich, one Soviet from Moscow and one interpreter between the two—that we should be let go. We got an official document to that effect and could depart. We will be notified soon of our departure date.

On our way out, once more passing through the crowd, I heard a Latvian tell his friend how a minister had forged his baptismal certificate, so that the latter could pass as a German.

It is 10 a.m., and I have not shown up at the plant. I must go there now and inform them of my act.

*January 31, 1941* Yesterday morning I was really scared in what manner Lemke, Reshin, and particularly Petkevich would react to the news. Amazingly enough, they all took it calmly, although at first they tried to persuade me to stay: "In Soviet Russia a fine career as a professional woman would await you, Comrade Zarina, if you were willing to join the Communist Party. Educated women like you are sorely needed," Lemke exclaimed.

These dreams of female glory in a Soviet paradise made me shudder. I stood my ground, refusing any further negotiations. I took my leave, hopefully never to have to encounter this particular trio of comrades again.

I am afraid. There is no guarantee, no protection from arrest by Soviet agents and subsequent deportation to Siberia. All we can do is hope that the Soviets do not wish to aggravate the German government by abusing the persons who have opted for Germany. If only our luck holds until we cross the borders!

*February 3, 1941* Second anniversary of Father's death . . .

On the way to the cemetery, Mother and I talked about the fact that Father left this world just before big trouble started. He died in peace, and within two years we, the survivors, have lived through many upheavals and great anxiety. Mother laments, she wished she too were dead; but knowing her fascination with dramatic carryings-on, I am not very worried. Her spirit will pull her through. She is still a young woman although she loves to refer to herself as "old and feeble." What nonsense!

Father is no longer alone in his peaceful spot under the big pine trees. Many a new grave has been dug in those two years since Father's funeral.

"*Saldu dusu, Tevs!*—Sweet dreams, Father!" We will no longer be able to come and visit you.

*February 10, 1941* We have been notified that we are allowed to take some household goods and personal property with us. So today I ordered a container built, in which our belongings can be transported to Germany. A lively trade in the manufacturing of containers seems to have sprung up. I had to try three different places before I could find a company that was still willing to take my order. The price is prohibitive, and what's left of my money will be spent on it. But what does it matter! I can't take Russian rubles with me across the border anyway. Will I ever visit Grandma Amalia's country estate again?

I remember the night she died. She was eighty-seven, a frail tiny figure lying on her bed, covered with a lace shawl. Heavy bed covers bothered her. She had gone blind, but her mind was still clear. We were alone in her house in Mazsalaca. The nurse had gone for the night.

A lonely candle on her nightstand gave a flickering glow. I had turned off all electric lights. I found them too bright.

Grandma held my hand. We talked about Father. She knew that he had died just six weeks earlier. She whispered, "I will soon follow him." And she did, that same night.

*February 21, 1941* The container is ready. Today the piano was loaded into the van. It was an incredibly difficult job getting the heavy piece lowered over the winding stairs. But by now all the belongings that we plan to take with us have been safely taken away. The apartment looks quite empty. We still have our bedroom furniture, though.

*February 24, 1941* Villis Zvaigznite, who last year graduated with me from the Chemistry Department, was arrested on the street, and has been deported.

Poor little Villis! He was a country boy, the kindest, gentlest, sweetest of all my fellow students. I shared a laboratory desk space with him for two semesters, and he was most helpful and considerate, merrily smiling up at me from his short height with blue eyes twinkling under an unruly bush of blond hair.

We took the University entrance exams together, since his last name was in alphabetical order right after mine. We were both seventeen at the time and both scared. Villis' hands trembled badly as he was busily engaged in solving a calculus problem for the exam. "Zvaigznite" ("Little Star")—that's what your name means in Latvian, and that's what you were.

*February 27, 1941* Dreadful rumors are spreading about brutal Secret Police activities and about torture cells in the basement of our former Latvian Ministry of the Interior. The cells are described as so small and narrow, that the occupants can neither stretch nor move, nor sit, nor stand. The temperature in others can be raised until the prisoner faints. Then he might be revived by flooding him with freezing water. I pray that we may get out alive before it is too late!

*March 1, 1941* Tonight we said farewell to Uncle Adi. He is dying, but since he is under heavy sedation, he doesn't seem to realize it. His face looks like a skull, with yellow skin pulled tightly over his high cheekbones, which gives him the look of an old Chinese man. He is only forty-five years old.

Aunt Erika, big with child, was in tears most of the time. What could I say to comfort her? At 8:00 PM my good friend Dr. Alfred Pakalns arrived to give Uncle Adi another morphine shot. I talked to Alfred briefly in the living room, saying good-bye to him also. He made me promise to write to him from Germany. A last handshake and he was gone.

*March 4, 1941* We have been notified that our train to Germany is leaving on the evening of March 7. By now we are sleeping on the floor. We have given the rest of our furniture away to Anna Schmidt, the woman who lives in an attic of our big apartment building with her illegitimate child, seven-year-old Kurtchen. Anna is truly of German descent, but is determined to stay here. Maybe she is still hoping that the boy's father, a Latvian fellow, will marry her.

*March 6, 1941* Tonight I said goodbye to Ingmar. Incredibly enough, instead of spending my last evening at home with final preparations, I went to the Russian Theater with Ingmar and saw Gogol's "The Inspector." I had also read this play in Russian classes in high school. I was amazed that Ingmar and I did not feel sad or depressed; on the contrary, we laughed and had a wonderful time.

Ingmar escorted me home. Fully aware of Mother's dislike for Ingmar, I did not invite him upstairs. I did not want to spoil our last moments together. I kissed him and stroked his face and felt tears on his cheek. I took off my red ruby signet ring—one of our family heirlooms—and put it on Ingmar's little finger. Thus we parted.

*March 7, 1941* This morning I took a walk to say farewell to Riga, city of my birth. Kurtchen accompanied me, hanging on to my hand. He chatted gaily in his thin little child's voice about the things that attracted his interest on the street: horses and buggies, doggies, other children . . . . But I was lost in memories and pretty close to tears.

Tonight we leave.

# PART 3

## THE SWASTIKA

# CHAPTER FIVE

## Without a Country

*March 8, 1941* On a train—somewhere in Germany

We have now been traveling for a night and a day. The compartments are crowded; the wooden benches are hard. Sleep is not possible, except perhaps in a sitting position. I am very tired, but am trying to scribble notes into this book.

Last night Kurtchen saw us off. He accompanied us to the train, and rode with us and our bags in a horse-and-buggy to the station. I kissed the poor little child's thin face in parting and gave him all the remaining cash I had, which was not much. I am so sorry now, that I never before paid any attention to this boy. Kurtchen standing on the platform—a lonely little figure—started to cry as the train pulled out. Soon afterwards, Russian soldiers entered the train and confiscated our Latvian passports. Now we are stateless, without home or country or money. Our only possessions are four bags containing clothes, some bed linen and valuables. All night long I listened to the monotonous rattling of the wheels, felt the swaying motion of the car, as we were riding through Latvia, Lithuania and Poland toward the German border.

Shortly after dawn, the train came to a stop. I looked out the window and saw a heavy barrier painted in stripes of red and white looming through the early morning mist. Nearby stood a Russian soldier wearing the gray uniform of the Soviet Army, the Red Star gleaming on his military cap. After a little while the train started up again, I opened the window and leaned out. As we passed the soldier I saw him give me the Soviet salute by raising his arm and making a fist.

Thus we crossed into Germany. On the other side of the border we again received a military salute, this time from a German soldier in green uniform. He also raised his arm in greeting, but it was a stiffly streamlined arm and hand, and he shouted, "Heil Hitler!" Once well inside the border, we were ordered to disembark and were led to barracks with primitive washing facilities. Breakfast, consisting of dry dark rye bread and "Ersatz" coffee, no milk or sugar, was laid out for us on long bare wooden tables. Hardly any of the Latvians partook of this. We have our own copious food supplies with us: white bread, butter, ham and cheese, boiled eggs, fried chicken.

Pretty soon, three men in gold-brown uniforms with red badges and swastika signs on their sleeves made an appearance. I was told that these are SA men—civilian members of the National Socialist Party. One of them made a speech urging us to be grateful to the Reich, because it is giving us shelter from political persecution and we must, therefore, obey all orders and regulations. Then he mentioned the war situation, ending with: "Germany will surely be victorious under the leadership of our beloved Führer!" No sooner was this statement uttered than the three men began to sing the German Anthem and the Horst Wessel song: "Die Fahne hoch," raising their arms and giving the "Heil Hitler" salute. We were asked to join in the songs and in the salute. Hardly anyone knew the words or the tune. Many of the refugees did not even know enough German to understand the speeches, not to mention the songs. However, all of us were forced to raise our arms in this pompous salute.

This afternoon, our train stopped in Thorn, a town that formerly belonged to Poland. Now it is on territory occupied by Germany in the so-called "Warthegau." Many of the Baltic Germans who left their homes in 1939, following the "Führer's" call, are now settled here.

*March 9, 1941* Our trek continues. This morning at some station we met a train heading eastward filled with children and it was a very strange sight. I saw many pale faces pressed against the windows looking at us with large wistful eyes. I questioned our train attendant, a big husky man, who these children were and where they were being taken. He responded in an angry voice, "Never mind, they are being sent to a place where they will be taken care of properly! The damned little mongrels!" There was hatred showing in the man's face.

Scared, but also greatly puzzled, I persisted, "Are these children perhaps being transported to safety in the country, away from bombing attacks in the big cities?" "Safety? Ha, ha!" the man laughed jeeringly. "Safety indeed!" And then turning a burning stare at me he hissed, "What business is it of yours, young woman? Go back to your compartment and stop asking foolish questions."

We are travelling for the third day. My feet are swollen and I'm utterly exhausted. I wonder where they will finally take us. Last night our train stopped at a big station but we were in darkness due to the "blackout." I raised a window and looked out over the platform. A nurse came along with some drinking water and I asked her where we were. She answered, "In Halle an der Saale." So, now I know that we are in Thuringia. We were told that tomorrow we will arrive in Schwarzburg, a small village where a refugee camp has been set up for us.

*March 12, 1941, Schwarzburg* I like the landscape here. A brook, the "Schwarza," flows through the little village, which is surrounded by high pine-covered hills. From one of these hills, an old castle, the Schwarzburg, looks down into the valley. A local man told me that the "Führer" has visited the castle several times and there is a rumor that he intends to declare it his property. We refugees have been settled in two local inns. Most of our people live in dormitories but some have been lucky enough to get single rooms. Mother and I share a room. It is better than most, although it is up in the attic, unheated and dreadfully cold.

*March 13, 1941* Our meals are served to us in a big dining hall. This is also the place where one meets the other refugees. We have people from all walks of life: professors, businessmen, farmers one opera singer, a man without a profession, and their respective families. Also, there is a former office manager, who is a bachelor, and a Miss Nina Keller, until very recently a student of languages at the Latvian University. Nina and I are the only two single young girls here and we are fast becoming friends.

*March 15, 1941* The bachelor, Herr Luckas, has been elected to act as representative of our group. The first thing he did, was to order Nina and me into permanent kitchen and house-cleaning services, which means washing dishes three times a day for about 30 people and cleaning the dining room, the halls, the stairs, and the toilets once a day. The reason he gave us this order is that we are the only unmarried girls in the group and "therefore have superfluous time" on our hands.

*March 18, 1941* This afternoon, a travelling movie theater came to our little village and gave a show. The film, called "Jud Süss," is directed by Veit Harlan, with Kristina Söderbaum and Ferdinand Merian in the starring roles. It is a story about the German Jews, who in the middle ages were forced to live in ghettos but who in due course, managed to get out of their confinement and acquired wealth and power.

Jud Süss is characterized as a pretty bad and unappealing character chasing a blond beauty and finally seducing her and abandoning her to her fate. The local people started to shout curses and shake their fists in the face of the screen image. It seems that Soviet Russia is not the only country where public opinion is manufactured.

*March 20, 1941* The daily dishwashing and house-cleaning service slowly gets on our nerves. It is also very unpleasant to sit around here without a single penny. I am trying to get out of this camp as soon as possible. I have written to a number of big chemical companies, applying for a job.

*March 22, 1941* Today, Nina and I made friends with the retired postmaster of Schwarzburg. He told us, among other things, that the now reigning Queen of Holland, Wilhelmina, when still a young crown princess, met her future husband here during a summer vacation.

*March 23, 1941* Except for the food, which is quite poor as compared with Latvian standards, and the nightly blackouts, there are no signs of war here.

*March 24, 1941* Today two letters came, expressing interest in hiring me, one from Düsseldorf and one from Hamburg. I phoned the rubber plant in Hamburg that had contacted me and arranged for me to go by train to Hamburg for an interview. The company will be sending me some money for travel expenses.

*March 27, 1941, Hamburg* This morning I left for Hamburg. I had to change trains four times before I finally arrived. The passengers were all quite talkative and all were very sure that Germany would win the war. That was the general theme. I, in turn, told them about the Soviet Russian Regime in Latvia and about the Red Terror; but nobody seemed to believe me. Well, I must not forget that Germany and Russia are friends and it is obvious that the German Department of Propaganda in Berlin tries, apparently quite successfully, to create an atmosphere of sympathy for Soviet Russia.

The Germans have strange ideas about the Northeastern European countries. One woman, after having watched me for a while, suddenly remarked, "I never knew that people who live somewhere behind Poland could be so nicely dressed and have such good manners!" This remark annoyed me. "Madame," I said, "you probably don't know either that Latvia's pre-Soviet standard of education was one of the highest in Europe!"

I arrived in Hamburg in the late afternoon and was received by a representative of the rubber company. He took me to the hotel "Die Vier Jahreszeiten—the Four Seasons." On the way, I noticed that Hamburg, a beautiful and interesting old town, resembles Riga somewhat. When we came to the famous alley called "Jungfernsteg," one thing baffled me. I saw an immense pond, all covered with wooden planks. My escort explained that this was the so-called "Binnenalster," which had been covered in order to camouflage it in case of air raids by the enemy. He also pointed out a phony bridge which had been built at a distance of several hundred meters from the real bridge crossing the Alster. This had been done for the same purpose, hoping that the English bombers would get confused and hit the phony bridge instead. It sounds a bit naive! So far, I have not seen a single bomb-damaged building, though there are several in Hamburg.

*March 28, 1941, Hamburg* In the morning, the owner of the company, Herr Burg, took me in his car to the plant and showed me around. In one workroom I saw a big heap of small transparent cylindrical rubber articles. I asked naively what they were. After a moment of hesitation Herr Burg replied: "These are condoms. Our 'Führer' has ordered that all birth control devices be destroyed. Germany needs more offspring. Therefore, this rubber material will be used to fashion other articles." I blushed in embarrassment.

We had lunch together with Frau Burg, whom we met in a famous downtown restaurant, the "Ratskeller." The food was certainly much better than at our camp in Schwarzburg. Again I noticed that I was being watched carefully, this time by Frau Burg—a young, pretty and well-dressed woman who smoked incessantly. Again, the remark that followed her scrutiny annoyed me: "I didn't know that people from the East could have such good table manners." This also acutely embarrassed her more diplomatic husband who was trying very hard to persuade me to take the job. In turn, the wife became more annoyed and she suddenly interrupted him: "Why all that fuss about her? I too had a job before I was married, but nobody ever made such a fuss about me."

I asked her politely what kind of job she had held. Upon hearing that she had been a secretary, my smile may have been a bit malicious as I commented, "Couldn't the reason for all this fuss be that there aren't as many lady chemists around as there are secretaries?" This put an end to her comments but also to her husband's hopes of interesting me in the job.

In the afternoon, I went for a walk. In the oldest part of town, small houses are standing closely together at the edge of narrow canals, which form a network through the old city. Medieval churches reach high into the sky with their Gothic spires. The modern department stores are quite a contrast to the old buildings, but most of their merchandise is just junk: cheap costume jewelry, plastic combs, powder, lipstick and worthless pictures in cheap frames. Dresses and shoes are strictly rationed. I have neither ration cards nor money anyway. On the way back to my hotel, I saw a house that had been destroyed by an English bomb. Nothing is left but a heap of rubble. Three people were killed there.

*March 29, 1941, Schwarzburg* Nina and I have dreamed up a great idea. In order to brighten the monotony of our life in camp and to revenge ourselves for having been pressed into this exclusive dishwashing and house-cleaning service, we have decided to play tricks on our fellow refugees on April Fool's Day.

*March 31, 1941* We went to our friend the old postmaster and typed a number of letters on his typewriter to all of our outstanding camp people. Each got a different letter: The bachelor received a marriage proposal from an anonymous beauty; the professor, an offer to teach higher mathematics at a nursery school; the man without a profession, an offer to play the star role in a movie entitled, "The Ghost on the Cemetery Wall." In addition, Nina set up new "House Rules" consisting of ten points, with the purpose of ridiculing some of the disadvantages of our camp life. Point 7, for instance, reads: "Camp members are requested to overlook that the oranges sent to us for general consumption are hoarded by the innkeeper and used for her own family. As they can't eat them up fast enough, a large percentage is rotting away." We discovered this during our house-cleaning duties. Tomorrow we surely will have fun and liven up the day.

*April 1, 1941* We livened up the day all right, but there was no merriment at all. Everyone who received a letter was mad at us. Of course, they all immediately suspected Nina and me, and we did not deny it. Worst of all was the moment when our innkeeper discovered the new "House Rules" tacked on a door by Nina. Madame was blazing with indignation and she withdrew, together with our camp nurse—an unintelligent, German woman—to hold a secret council. The result was that they called in two Nazi party officials of the Schwarzburg section, and a trial was held on the spot Nina and I, the two black sheep, were ordered into an office room and bombarded with a barrage of questions: "Why have you written the new 'House Rules'? Do you intend to create misgivings and slander in town? Are you planning to undermine the unity of the 'home front?'" The SA-men, clad in brown shirts decorated with swastikas, then expressed the suspicion that we might be spies infiltrated from Russia to create trouble.

The ignorant nurse started to call me names until I lost my patience and protested, "Your accusations are completely unfounded. Our only intention was to play tricks on April Fool's Day, as is the custom in our country. We never intended to hurt anybody. We were sure that our jokes would cause much laughter!" The Nazi men thought this over, and one replied with a stern face, "There is no fun and laughter in the Third Reich!" But finally they let us go with a strict warning: "If anything like this happens again, you both will end up in concentration camp." Once out of the room, I whispered to Nina, "It seems we did indeed jump from the frying pan into the fire." She nodded in agreement.

*April 8, 1941* After the incident on April 1, life in camp has become more unpleasant than ever. The innkeeper and the nurse hate me, and that is one more reason for getting out of here as fast as possible. In a few days, I will go to Frankfurt, to visit I.G. Farben, the largest conglomerate ("Interessengemeinschaft") of German chemical industries (including Bayer and BASF), from whom I also have received an expression of interest in hiring me.

*April 11, 1941, Höchst* Right now I am in my hotel room in Frankfurt-on-Main-Höchst, a small town where the main I.G. Farben Plant—Höchst Farbwerke—is located. I arrived in Frankfurt at about 4:00 PM. Stepping out of the railroad station, I saw before me a large square with streets going in all directions. The square is surrounded by high buildings with many stores. Frankfurt looks like a very busy place with lots of people in a big hurry.

I made the trip to Höchst—about 8 kilometers—by streetcar. In the personnel office of I. G. Farben, I was told that the chief technical director would receive me tomorrow morning at 10:00 AM. As I have this evening to myself, I will go to a play in Frankfurt.

*April 12, 1941* Last night, I saw "Caesar and Cleopatra" by Bernard Shaw, played at the Schauspielhaus in Frankfurt. I find it interesting that in spite of one and a half years of war with England, the Germans still keep the play of an Irish author on their program. Could it be because the

Irish also are at odds with England? In the middle of the night, I was frightened out of my sleep by a rhythmically increasing and decreasing howl. I realized that this must be an alert signal announcing enemy planes. Everyone is supposed to go down into the basement air-raid shelter of the hotel, but being very tired I stayed in bed. Nothing happened anyway, and after a while the sirens began to sound a long drawn-out howl announcing the end of the alert.

In the morning, I was introduced to Dr. Kron, one of the executive directors of I.G. Farben, and after discussing details, I agreed to accept a position as Research Chemist in their Technical Applications Department. I will be in charge of the Analytical Laboratory testing new synthetic rubber products. The necessary papers are being prepared, and tomorrow I will sign the contract.

*April 13, 1941* Right now, I'm on the train going back to Schwarzburg to get Mother and our four bags. This morning I rented a room in Höchst—apartments are not to be had.

*April 15, 1941* The innkeeper and the nurse are terribly annoyed that I got a job so quickly. I am the first to leave camp, and the first out from under their control.

*April 18, 1941, Frankfurt* Today, Mother and I arrived in Frankfurt. Mother is depressed, because compared with our apartment in Riga, one room is not very comfortable.

*April 21, 1941* I started my new job as a chemical engineer. My boss, Dr. Haller, in charge of the Technical Applications Department, seems to be a polite, amiable man. I have to test synthetic rubber products just as I tested natural rubber products in my laboratory in Riga; determining their physical properties with the help of instruments: tensile strength, elongation, elasticity, resilience, abrasion, hysteresis. I have to calculate results and hand in weekly reports to the organic chemists next door who synthesize the test materials.

I have an assistant, Herr Fersen, a man from Aachen, about 45 years old. He told me that he was badly injured in World War I. He was buried under a collapsing building after a mine close by detonated. His nervous system seems to be in a rather poor state. He is jumpy, restless and easily upset.

*April 30, 1941* My fellow chemists in our department are all very nice. They keep on asking me a lot of questions about life in Latvia before and after the Soviet occupation. I have a feeling that many of them do not at all agree with the regime in their own country. But, of course, I must realize that it is dangerous to say anything openly against the Hitler government. One of the chemists gave me a riddle to solve: "What is the difference between Germany and Russia?" I gave him all kinds of answers, but nothing satisfied him. Finally he supplied the answer: "In Russia, it is colder!" We all laughed, but silently I agree with him.

*May 5, 1941* Springtime is wonderful here. It is much warmer than it is this time of year in Latvia. The fruit trees are already in bloom. In a few days, I am scheduled to go to Schkopau near Halle an der Saale to visit the new synthetic rubber plant which was recently built there by I. G. Farben.

*May 10, 1941* It's Saturday. There is great excitement throughout Germany! Rudolf Hess, the Deputy "Führer," flew a plane from Augsburg to England all by himself, with the intention of starting peace negotiations between Germany and England. The newspapers and the radio announced the story today. The official explanation is that Hess is a romantic, a dreamer, who had lately come under the influence of astrologers and clairvoyants, and who undertook the trip by himself without permission from the "Führer." But the Germans do not seem to believe this official version. In a country with so much military discipline, it is nearly impossible that a German official with so many responsibilities—Deputy Führer, Reich Minister without Portfolio, Member of the Council for the Defense of the Reich, Member of the Secret Cabinet Council for Germany, Leader of the Nazi Party, etc.—would dare to act without permission. My neighbors and fellow workers are all convinced that it was the Führer's own plan, that he gave his consent to this unusual undertaking. But since the plan ended in failure, Hitler is renouncing all responsibility and has declared his closest friend a lunatic.

*May 15, 1941, Halle* Last night, my boss Dr. Haller and I arrived in Halle by train. This morning, we went to the Schkopau plant. I was introduced to a number of chemists. Their spacious laboratories are equipped with the most modern rubber-testing instruments. There is also a large-scale pilot plant. I will remain here for a week to learn their testing procedures. I will then introduce them to our laboratory in Höchst.

*May 16, 1941, Halle* During lunch today, Dr. Wingart the Research Director here, told me a strange story. Ten years ago, while a student at the University of Tubingen, he attended a party at his fraternity house.

Suddenly, the door opened and in walked an alumnus of the fraternity, now a famous judge. The old gentleman asked in a grave voice if any of the boys would like to act as witnesses to an execution that was scheduled to take place in the vicinity at midnight. He needed three witnesses. Wingart, being in a tipsy mood, volunteered to go along with two others. When they arrived at the place of execution, they saw a scaffold. The clock struck midnight and the condemned man was led in. The executioner appeared clad in a red robe with a hood over his face and holes for eyes. He carried a huge sword. The condemned man was made to kneel in front of the block. The judge broke a wooden stick in two, and addressed the executioner: "Do your duty!" The executioner raised his sword and cut the condemned man's head off in one stroke. Then he seized the cut-off head by the hair, held it up in front of the judge and asked, in solemn tones: "Judge, did I do this man justice?" The judge replied, "You did him justice." Poor Wingart almost went out of his mind watching this terrible scene and still has nightmares about it. He told me that even now executions in Germany are carried out in the medieval pattern, although in some places a guillotine is used.

Now I realize what the blood-red posters really mean, which I saw the other day in Frankfurt, plastered on walls and fences. The posters read: "Sentenced by the sword were the following enemies of the people . . . ." (What a familiar term!) And then followed the names of the executed.

What kind of barbarian government is this, that maintains gruesome relics of the Middle Ages?

*May 18, 1941, Halle* Yesterday afternoon, I went by train from Halle to Leipzig in order to do some sightseeing. I did not have much time, only a few hours, before it became dark. The railroad station is very large; it is said to be the largest in Europe. From there, I walked to the old part of town. On my way, I passed the Augustus Square where the building of the famous "Universitas Lipsiensis" stands. The town hall is also very old. Next to it is a little square called "Naschmarkt" ("Candy Market") with a monument of Germany's greatest poet Goethe, depicting him as a young student, in memory of his stay at the Leipzig University from 1765 to 1768. Right across from his monument is the famous old tavern, Auerbachs Keller. I had dinner there and dutifully consumed some wine with my meal, which entitled me to inspect the old tavern. A waiter showed me the chamber where, according to legend, Dr. Faustus, with the assistance of Mephistopheles, rode out of the premises on a wine barrel. The wine barrel is still to be seen in a corner and a huge wooden candelabrum in the form of a barrel hangs from the ceiling carrying Faustus and the devil, two witches, and several fat naked little boys on a merry flight.

The walls are decorated with framed original letters written by Goethe and his Leipzig friends and with old silhouettes of those friends.

*May 23, 1941, Frankfurt* Last night I returned to Frankfurt, and on the train I had a rather strange encounter. The train was, as usual, overcrowded and no seats were available. So, I sat down on my bag in the aisle. Beside me in the crowd stood a bespectacled young man wearing a green Tirolean hat with feathers. After a while, he made a remark about the inconveniences of travelling on crowded trains. We started a conversation in the course of which he asked me what my profession was. I told him about my work and then I, in turn, asked him about his job. He smiled and a mysterious expression crossed his face, "I can't tell you that. You and the people around us would be frightened!" Remembering Dr. Wingart's story, I asked, "Why, are you maybe the executioner?"

"What an idea! Of course not, but if you really want to know who I am, I will whisper it into your ear." He then bent down and I heard one word: "Gestapo!"

"What's that? I have never heard of it before."

He seemed surprised, "Really? It means "Geheime Staatspolizei!— Secret State Police."

"Oh, I see, something like the G.P.U. in Russia, isn't it?"

He did not like the comparison. He then began to tell me about himself. Trained as a lawyer, he is a storm trooper with a high rank—SS Haupt-Sturm-Führer—equal to lieutenant colonel in the Army. He is a fanatic believer in the doctrines of the Nazi Party. He told me about the final aims and goals of the Party, "We intend to destroy all Jews in Europe, as well as the Slavic 'Untermenschen' ('subhumans'). Furthermore, the party considers the Christian Church their greatest enemy. The Catholic as well as the Protestant Church will be eliminated."

In the few months that I've been in Germany, I can't help becoming aware of these Nazi goals. Political propaganda is the life-style here, just as it was in Soviet Latvia. Newspapers, radio broadcasts, speeches by Nazi party leaders expound Hitler's theories daily.

There are no more Jews in Germany. I have not met a single one. The only German Jews I ever encountered were the poor refugees in Riga, marching in a communist parade. I heard the term "Kristallnacht" ("Crystal Night") being mentioned here in Germany. Upon inquiring, I was told that during that night, on November 10, 1933, synagogues were burned all over Germany, and Jewish stores and warehouses ransacked and destroyed. I decided to ask my peculiar fellow traveler a question in reference to this: "Does the Party plan to destroy the churches as the synagogues were destroyed?"

"Oh no," my new acquaintance answered, "we plan to use the churches as meeting halls where, instead of the belief in God, we will teach belief in 'Blood and Race.'" Instead of the Bible, we will read out of our Führer's book, *Mein Kampf,* and instead of the Cross, we will have two crossed swords as symbols of battle and heroism."

I gasped in shock, but he continued, "It is the noblest duty of every German to believe in his German race and in our final victory. All who think otherwise must be destroyed." I thought it wiser not to utter any objections to this and so I continued to listen to his strange tale. "It won't be long now," he went on, "before we occupy the British Isles. The Party has already taken care that suitable men will be prepared for the job of governing England. I am one of them. I am polishing up my English and am being trained in special courses so I will be able to carry out responsible duties in England. We Gestapo men are allowed to listen to broadcasts from England, which are forbidden for everybody else. Last week, I even saw a British war movie. I can't tell you how silly its story was. We all got a big laugh out of it."

This fellow's frankness mystified me: "Listen, why do you tell me all this? After all, I am just a stranger to you and besides that, I am stateless!"

He seemed surprised but he replied, "Well, you certainly belong to the Nordic race, and this is more important than any passport. By the way, how old are you and how many children have you got?" I told him that I was not married and he answered, "Marriage has nothing to do with having children. It is your duty towards your Nordic blood to preserve it in the children you give birth to. You should have offspring as soon as possible." I protested that there certainly were no laws which could force a single girl to bring children into the world. He smiled, "There aren't yet, but there will be soon! Wait until we win the war, an immense change of moral standards will then take place in Germany."

By that time, we had reached Frankfurt and this very strange conversation came to an end. Whatever this man is, one thing is certain—he is deadly serious and convinced about the righteousness of his cause.

It would have never occurred to me that my looks could spell danger for me—danger of being bred by force to produce Nazi-style "superhumans." I never dreamed of such horrible possibilities when leaving Latvia. I left because I was afraid of Siberian slave labor camps.

Was there a way out then in Latvia? Is there a way out now in Germany? There is no answer. All I can do is trust my luck. I'd better not tell Mother about this encounter. My experience might frighten her—or she might accuse me of somehow having provoked the Gestapo man to look upon me with "sinful thoughts."

*June 1, 1941, Whitsuntide* A funny thing happened to me today. I received a most peculiar proposal of marriage. Dr. Merkel, a young chemist who works in the same department with me, invited me to go hiking with him in the Taunus Mountains. We visited the Saalburg—an old Roman fortress erected during the Roman conquest of Germany. The Saalburg was part of the border wall, the "Limes," which the Romans built from the Rhine to the Danube.

The Saalburg is located near Bad Homburg, where Kaiser Wilhelm II used to spend his vacations. Between 1897 and 1907 following Imperial orders, the ancient Saalburg fortress was restored and is now a museum. Pieces of Roman armor, spears, swords, helmets and shields, as well as household goods, earthenware, cups and trinkets are on display. The collection includes leather sandals, which were found well preserved in one of the many wells located on the fortress grounds. The ancient heating system—called hypocaust—strikes me as very ingenious. It is a type of hot air heating. The Romans constructed ducts under the tile floors of the fortress buildings by leaving an open space underneath with low brick pillars supporting the floors. Hot air would circulate through these ducts rising from a hearth in which a wood fire was burning. In this way, the floors and the walls of the fortress were kept comfortably warm.

After the visit to the museum, we started on our hike through the surrounding woods. Dr. Merkel, who for a while seemed deep in thought, suddenly said, "I'm glad we have met." I looked at him in surprise. "You see, I earn about 750 Reichsmark per month, and I guess you get about 500 Reichsmark. That would make a total of 1250 Reichsmark. Besides that, bearing in mind that neither of us would have to pay the 'bachelor's' or 'spinster's' taxes any longer, we certainly would be better off financially." The meaning of these calculations escaped me for a second, then I understood and burst out laughing. That spelled the end of Dr. Merkel's financial dream of matrimonial bliss.

*May 31, 1941* Early this morning Mother took the train to Berlin from where she will continue on to Posen. She wants to visit some of her Baltic friends there.

*June 10, 1941* I have taken a room in a private home. Here, I have met Dr. Ella Brecht, who also is a lodger. She is about my age, tall and blond like me, and the only other female chemist at the plant. She knows all of our young bachelor chemist fellow workers. At night, the house is quite often crowded with young men. They are having a lot of fun, singing, laughing and talking. Once they invited me too, but I somehow don't seem to fit into their company.

*June 15, 1941* Mother writes from Posen/Warthegau that she does not like the conditions. It being a former Polish town, many Poles still live there. They are treated like sub humans, like second-class people. They get much smaller rations than the Germans and they are only allowed to ride in streetcars bearing the sign: "For Poles Only." In the public gardens, there are special benches with the same sign.

Worst of all is the occupation of Polish homes by Germans. Mother writes: "In 1939, the Baltic Germans were settled mostly in Posen and Lodsch, now called Litzmannstadt. Many Polish families in those towns were given orders to move out of their homes in half an hour's time, without being allowed to take any of their property with them. This happened mostly in the evening or at night and so these poor people walked out into the darkness, without adequate clothing or food. The next morning, the new German tenants moved in and found themselves the owners of a complete household with furniture, fully equipped bedrooms, table linens, silver and china, carpets, paintings, and well-stocked pantries. Besides that, there were closets full of clothes.

"Our friends from Riga, Frau Olson and children, for instance, walked into the apartment of a Polish writer. The table was set and a piece of bread partly eaten still lay on a plate. I said to Frau Olson: 'Don't you feel uneasy to think about the horrible shock which the owner of this apartment experienced when she was so suddenly driven out of her home?' But Frau Olson answered: 'Why should I? They are just Poles!' I can't understand this attitude. Don't these people have a conscience anymore?

"Yesterday, I met your friend Karen. She told me a similar story. When she and her husband moved into their new apartment, the beds were still warm from their former occupants. Some time later the same morning, the doorbell rang and a very frightened timid old Polish lady appeared and with tears in her eyes asked Karen if she would allow her to take just one medicine bottle, which she, in all the hurry, had left behind. She did not ask for anything else. Karen is very depressed and is suffering under these bizarre conditions here."

*June 22, 1941* At six o'clock this morning Propaganda Minister Goebbels read a statement from the "Führer" over the radio announcing the attack of Germany on the Soviet Union. German Army divisions have crossed the borders and are invading Russian territory.

Suddenly the "friendship" between Germany and the Soviet Union has turned into war. My German neighbors appear to be shocked and surprised. Goebbels will have a lot of propaganda work to do in order to come up with explanations, why Russia—until now an esteemed political and business partner—starting with today, quite unexpectedly, has turned into the arch-enemy.

*June 23, 1941* Finland too, has again started military action against the Soviet Union. The Finns want Karelia back.

*June 26, 1941* Mother writes from Posen that the war declaration was a great shock to everyone there: "The Germans appear frightened and the Poles seem to have gathered new hope. They are no longer so extremely downcast but somewhat more lively and a kind of renewed spirit gleams in their eyes mixed with an intense expression of hatred for the Germans. On June 22, I heard the speech of a high Nazi official. The essence of it was stated in this sentence: 'We will occupy London but our way to London goes over Moscow!' A thunderous applause answered him."

*June 27, 1941* The people in Germany do not know what the reaction of the western powers towards the new war situation might be. It is forbidden to listen to "enemy broadcasts" under punishment of death.

*June 28, 1941* I have a bad case of the flu and feel awful. I am feverish and my room is terribly hot. My old landlady and Ella Brecht take care of me. The news from the Russian front lifted my spirits somewhat. The German armies are quickly approaching the Baltic States and soon the Soviets will be driven out of my home country. Maybe the German occupation will be the lesser of two evils.

*July 4, 1941* I am still in bed but this morning there was a loud knock on my door. I heard Ella's voice shouting outside: "Riga has fallen into German hands!" I am so excited that the hateful Soviets have finally been thrown out of my home town and that the Red Terror has come to an end there.

*July 10, 1941* Today Mother returned. I met her at the station, The first thing she told me was that Wolfgang, my best beau in high school, was killed at the Russian Front on June 24, just two days after the onset of war with Russia. His parents are now settled in Posen and that's how

Mother heard the news. I am very sad and wonder which of our boys from Riga will be next.

*July 11, 1941* Since Latvia is now occupied by German troops it is possible to send mail to Riga. Today I wrote to Aunt Erika, to Ingmar and to Alfred Pakalns. I have no idea how and if these people—all so dear to me—survived the last days of the Red Terror and the entry of the German Army into Riga. It probably is going to take several weeks before I get an answer and I will have to be patient and hope that they all are well.

*July 12, 1941* My sugar ration card has disappeared. I suspect that the cleaning woman took it. This means that I will have to live without sugar for three months. Ration cards are not replaced if the owner loses them. Well, I'm glad that it wasn't the bread or the margarine card.

*July 14, 1941, Mannheim* I have been sent to Mannheim with my Bavarian office-mate Dr. Kehrer. We are to attend a one-week course on "New Plastic Materials" at the I.G. Farben Plant in Ludwigshafen, located directly across the Rhine River from Mannheim, called Badische Soda & Anilin Fabrik—BSAF, for short.

*July 16, 1941, Mannheim* Tonight, a young mechanical engineer, one of the lecturers conducting the course, took me for a walk through Mannheim. It is a beautiful old town and well-known for its theater. Here Schiller's famous play "Die Räuber" ("The Robbers") was performed for the first time in 1782.

Everyone here is in great fear of air raids and this is understandable when one sees the ruins of burned-out or bomb-destroyed houses which are visible all over town, much more so than in Frankfurt.

*July 30, 1941, Höchst* Now and then we have alerts, but no air raids. I never go into the air-raid shelter anyway.

During lunch today I overheard two male colleagues at the next table referring to me as the "I.G. Häschen" ("I.G. bunny-rabbit"). That's interesting. Is it because of my noticeably younger age or my lack of sophistication? I am not sure, whether I'm mad or flattered. After all, fluffy bunnies are such lovable animals!

*August 1, 1941* I have not yet received any communication from Riga and I am very worried. To make matters worse, the radio broadcasts bring terrible news about atrocities committed in the three Baltic States by withdrawing Soviet troops and by the Communist rabble that fled with them. The advancing German Army has found mass graves in the yard of the Central City Prison. If only a letter would come soon!

*August 3, 1941* Heavy fighting is going on between German and Soviet Forces south of Latvia in the region of Witebsk. Father used to talk about Witebsk. He was there in World War I.

*August 5, 1941* My wish regarding news from Latvia has come true. Today I found a letter from Aunt Erika in our mailbox. She is alive and well and so is her little baby—a girl christened Eva—who was born on June 21, one day before the outbreak of the German-Russian War. Uncle Adi died on March 17. Erika writes: "I am still in my little apartment and have miraculously escaped any direct encounter with the Red Terror, although many of my Latvian friends were arrested and deported. I am scared of the new German military forces that have come into town, but I hope and pray that my baby and I will not be harmed."

*August 7, 1941* German Forces have reached the rivers Desna and Dnieper. German tanks are rolling in the direction of Kiev.

*August 8, 1941, Cologne* I have been ordered to visit the Central Rubber Research Laboratories at Bayer Werke, Leverkusen, near Cologne. Bayer, which is also a member of the I.G. Farben conglomerate, became famous and wealthy for its discovery of aspirin. Last night I arrived in Cologne. The train sped along the beautiful Rhine River. Now I have finally seen this famous stream mentioned in so many German songs. Stepping out of the bomb-damaged station, I came directly upon the famous Cathedral of Cologne. It is located right in front of the station, a monumental Gothic building with two huge towers. I am staying at the "Dom-Hotel" in the old part of town, near the Cathedral. My first glance out of my hotel room window fell upon a heavily damaged house. Cologne has had quite a number of air raids but not as many as Mannheim.

*August 11, 1941, Cologne* The Bayer Plant in Leverkusen employs fifteen thousand people. On top of the main office building, its world-famous trademark the "Bayer Cross," is visible for miles. The Central Rubber Research Laboratory is a very modern building made of steel, concrete and glass. The work halls and laboratories are immense. Only research work is done here, and new synthetic rubber materials called Buna and

Perbunan are tested with specially designed instruments and machines. The Laboratory is headed by Herr Erler, a very short man.

*August 12, 1941, Cologne* Last night, we had an air raid and I went down into the hotel basement shelter. The shooting of the "FLAK" [short for "Flugzeug-Abwehr-Kanone" ("anti-aircraft guns")] became heavier and heavier and we all got frightened and went down one more staircase into the beer cellar underneath the regular cellar, where empty beer barrels are lining the walls. There I sat, listening to the rumbling of the guns, feeling quite safe. After all, a cellar beneath another cellar seemed to me like double protection. This, however, was disputed by my fellow hotel guests. "There is no guaranteed protection in basement shelters against a direct hit," they said.

*August 17, 1941, Cologne* Today is Sunday and the weather is beautiful. I decided to spend the day taking a trip into the surroundings of Cologne. First, I went to Bonn, the famous University town and Beethoven's birthplace. I stood before the great composer's house for a long time and looked at the old door with its knocker, the many small windows with their green shutters and the red flowers on the window sills. Unfortunately, due to the frequent air raids, the house, which is now a museum, is closed to the public.

In the afternoon, I went by ferry across the Rhine to Königswinter, a village at the foot of the "Siebengebirge" ("the Seven Hills"). The most famous of the hills is the "Drachenfels" ("Dragon's Rock")—where, according to the Nibelungen Saga, Siegfried, the shining hero, slew a dragon and bathed in his blood, thus becoming invulnerable.

That evening, I took the Rhine River boat back to Cologne. As we slowly approached Cologne, the silhouette of the ancient town with its numerous church steeples rose darkly into the moonlit sky. The river glistened like molten silver. This beautiful sight created an illusion of perfect peace, but it was only an illusion.

*August 22, 1941, Höchst* I am back here and life goes on as always: work in the laboratory, lunch at the plant restaurant, consisting mostly of boiled potatoes with cabbage or red beets. In the evening I do some reading or mending. All the old clothes have to make do, one can't buy anything new! Sometimes I go to the movies.

*August 23, 1941* At last a letter from Ingmar! He is all right. He stayed with his parents and younger brother in their country home during the changeover from Soviet to German power. There was no fighting in

Sigulda. The Soviets simply packed up and left before German troops arrived. The Soviets apparently had planned large-style arrests in Sigulda: a blacklist with names of people to be deported was found after the hasty departure of the Red Army. Ingmar's parents were on the list, but the arrival of the German troops saved them from a horrible fate.

Other Latvians were not as fortunate, Ingmar writes: "On the night of June 14 nearly 15,000 people were arrested all over Latvia and deported. Of these about 3,000 were children. For the long trek to Siberia the prisoners were jammed together in freight cars without food or water and without sanitary facilities. Under these inhuman conditions many died, especially young children and old people. Whenever such a deportation train entered a station, Russian Secret Police kept away all persons who tried to approach it. No food or water was allowed to be brought to the suffering people in the cars. Some prisoners managed to throw short messages from the moving trains, some written on scraps of paper, some scratched on metal cups, one scribbled in the inside cover of a prayer book.

We, the survivors, have slowly pieced together this information from radio broadcasts, from newspaper accounts and from stories heard through the grapevine.

The situation became truly desperate after the start of the German-Russian war. The Soviets realized that under the pressure of the approaching German army, they would have to leave Latvia in a hurry. Enraged they began to murder right and left and to destroy and burn property all over the country. You would no longer recognize the old part of Riga. The Soviets have destroyed many ancient historic monuments. They set fire to St. Peter's, demolished the Guild of the Black Heads and burned the Town Hall with its valuable library."

I am in a state of shock: my church, seven centuries old, burned to the ground, my home town heavily damaged, thousands of my fellow Latvians—a large part of our tiny nation—murdered or deported!

There is only one comforting thought in this incredibly sad news—Ingmar is alive!

*August 24, 1941* A heavy battle is raging in the region of Kiev.

*August 25, 1941* This afternoon, I was at my office desk, busily calculating test results on my slide rule, plotting a graph, when the door opened and in walked SS-Hauptsturmführer Herbert Ehrland, my Gestapo acquaintance from the train. I stared at him in wide-eyed surprise. He walked right up to my desk and said: "Come on, Irene, let's go for a walk."

"Good Heavens," the thought shot through my mind, "has he come to arrest me? What have I done? Did I perhaps make some careless statements?"

I hedged: "I can't, I've got to work until 5:00."

"Nonsense, Irene, I just spoke to your director. I ordered him to give you the afternoon off."

Reluctantly I rose, grabbed my handbag and walked out with my escort, who, fortunately, was again in civilian clothing. He suggested a hike in the Taunus Mountains (German men seem to like mountain hikes!) and we took off on the next local train to Hofheim. During our walk in the woods the SS-Hauptsturmführer did not say much, just watched me silently. He never touched me, never even smiled.

We ordered supper at a small tavern in the woods, drank apple wine—the famous local beverage—then started back towards the station. It was getting dark. The road crossed over some railroad tracks. Ehrland suddenly grabbed my hand and pulled me onto the tracks explaining: "This is the fastest way back to the train."

I did not dare to protest. Suddenly a railroad guard appeared out of falling shadows and sternly ordered us off the tracks. I was truly relieved but my relief was short-lived: Herr SS-Hauptsturmführer pulled out his credentials, presented them to the startled guard and continued haughtily on the tracks with me in tow.

A glorious August moon rose above the mountains in the East, glowing like an orange Japanese lantern in the dark blue sky. Crickets chirped merrily in the hedges on both sides of the tracks. Suddenly Ehrland stopped and turned towards me: "Irene, I have thought a lot about you these past months. I wanted to see you again. You are lovely!"

Icy fear gripped me. Vague schemes of escape possibilities raced through my brain. What was I going to do? Then, to my utter surprise, I heard him say: "Irene, you can never become a German mother. I have looked you over today. Your bosom is too small. You couldn't nurse a child."

We made it back to Höchst. Neither of us spoke, until Ehrland took his leave. He gave me a military salute—and was gone. I hope I never in my life lay eyes on him again.

*September 2, 1941* More tragic news! Today a letter came from Riga. The sender was Anna, Dr. Alfred Pakaln's sister. This boded nothing good. Cold fear ran down my spine, as I opened the envelope.

"Dear Miss Zarina," she writes, "I received your letter of July 11, 1941 addressed to my brother and wish to inform you that Alfred was arrested on June 26 on the street on his way to the hospital and taken to the Central City Prison. On June 28 he together with hundreds of other victims of the Red Terror was ordered to dig his own grave and then was shot. We found and identified his dead body in the Prison yard, where the victims had been laid out for inspection after the entry of the German troops.

"The horror of this experience will live with me forever, but we must be strong—you too, Miss Zarina—who were Alfred's friend—and bear our fate with courage."

Alfred, three years ago I crocheted a three-colored fraternity ribbon for you in green, gold and blue. May you rest in peace in Latvian soil, amid the velvety green of our meadows and our golden rye-fields swaying in the wind, under the blue of our Northern sky. Alfred, maybe you shouldn't have disturbed young Johnny's sleep in his soldier's grave under the birch tree in the woods near your summer home!

*September 14, 1941, Trier* I decided to spend a weekend in Trier. Mother preferred to stay at home.

I arrived yesterday in this the oldest town of Germany, about which I have read so much. Trier was founded by the Romans. There are still many monuments of Roman times here, the best known being the Porta Nigra and the Imperial Thermal Baths.

The train to Trier took me along the rivers Rhine and Moselle through a beautiful landscape with vineyards and. old castles looking down into the valleys. The name of my hotel is "Porta Nigra" in honor of the old Roman gates by that name just across from the hotel.

Trier, once the seat of the Roman Emperors in Germany, and in the Middle Ages the residence of the Count-Electors, is a town of great historical interest. The Cathedral of Trier is a Catholic shrine. It claims a most famous relic—a piece of the holy robe of Christ.

The market place, with its ancient houses and taverns, looks like a medieval stage setting. I had dinner in a very old tavern, deep down in a former wine cellar. Food was served on bare wooden tables. The guests were seated on long hand-hewn benches. The walls are of rough stone without plaster, paint or tapestry, and old-fashioned lanterns shed a dim light. The ceiling is supported by tall stone columns. In the corners of the tavern are huge wine barrels (empty, I presume!). All this created the illusion of being right back in the Middle Ages. To me, it was an escape from our present-day tensions, worries and uncertainties, a retreat into a romantic, mysterious past, even if it only lasted for a few short hours.

*September 15, 1941, Höchst* Coming home from Trier last night, I noticed something amusing on the train. The usual signs which hang in all compartments, reading "Be cautious in conversations! Enemy listens in!"

had been changed by some joker to read: "Be cautious in love conversations! Mother-in-law listens in!" I saw amused smiles on the passengers' faces as they read this altered version of a sinister warning. There are so few smiles in Germany now!

*September 18, 1941* Today, Dr. Kilian, one of our fellow chemists, warned me to be very careful when talking with or in the presence of Bernauer, our laboratory technician. He is an SA Party man and a fanatical Nazi. There is a well-founded suspicion that besides his laboratory job, he is also engaged in spying for the Gestapo.

Dr. Kilian, short, dark and jovial, told me that several months ago he got into great trouble. He had been careless enough to criticize the Nazi regime in the presence of several people, one of them, Bernauer, and two days later, Dr. Kilian was called to the Gestapo and questioned for hours on end about the meaning of his words. But, Dr. Kilian was smart enough to give the right answers and was finally sent home with a strict warning never to criticize the government again.

*September 19, 1941* Today, I had a chance to observe Bernauer more closely, remembering what Dr. Kilian had told me. He is a short, bow-legged fellow in his forties, with unpleasant glistening eyes and a constant wide grin on his face. He talks in a broad, drawling way using the local Frankfurter dialect.

*October 1, 1941* The German Army is besieging Leningrad and has moved close to Moscow. In the south of Russia German forces have reached the Donez valley and the Crimea. Our German neighbors in Höchst are jubilant.

*October 14, 1941* Today, Mother again accused me: "You have uprooted me, you have taken me away from my cozy apartment in Riga, you have made me miserable!"

"Don't you understand, Mother," I said to her, "that I'm not all-wise, that I can't foresee the future, that I was only trying to make the best decision possible for you and me. Alfred's sister's letter from Latvia confirmed that my fears of the Soviets were justified!"

*October 30, 1941* A great cold wave has swept over the Russian plains, freezing the German Army's forward move. Almost all activity has come to a standstill.

*November 16, 1941* It is quite cold here in Germany and the new room that we rented, our fifth this year, is very dark and damp. We have a little coal stove but its heating capacity declines rapidly at a distance of a few feet. I feel warm only when huddling close to it.

*November 30, 1941* Last night, a special announcement was broadcast from the "Führer's" headquarters. The ace pilot, Werner Mölders, bearer of the highest order of the German Army, "Ritterkreuz mit Schwertern und Brillianten" (the Knight's Cross with swords and diamonds) who shot down one hundred and fifteen British airplanes, died in an airplane crash "undefeated by the enemy." No explanation was given. Nobody knows why or where it happened. Not long ago, another famous pilot, Ernst Udet, also met his death in an air crash.

These deaths, "undefeated by the enemy," seem so strange!

*December 1, 1941* Life is monotonous. We have alerts now and then. I go to work six days a week. It is very cold, and we are living on a near starvation diet.

*December 5, 1941* The Soviets have started a counter-offensive. They are attacking German positions in the north of Russia.

*December 11, 1941* Early this afternoon, while still working at the plant, we were all asked to listen to a broadcast from the "Führer's" headquarters. We guessed what the message would be, and it was no surprise to us when Hitler declared war on America in the wake of the Japanese attack on Pearl Harbor this past Sunday morning. Most of our workmen seemed pleased.

Later on, when a few of us were together in Dr. Kilian's office, he hit his forehead with the flat of his hand to show his indignation and exclaimed: "This idiot Hitler! Does he want to fight the whole world? I am telling you, this is the beginning of Germany's greatest disaster!"

I am quite overwhelmed by this new development. I simply cannot comprehend how one single European nation can possibly fight a World Power occupying the larger part of a continent 3000 miles away.

*December 12, 1941* The Führer has ordered a fur and ski collection among the German populace for the benefit of the soldiers at the Russian Front, who are freezing half to death, not having been property outfitted for Russian winters. This news has unofficially leaked through in letters written from the Russian front.

Little "Hitler boys" go from house to house, from apartment to apartment and pick up items laid out by German housewives for the collection.

*December 13, 1941* An impertinent brat of about eight attacked Mother on the street today and tried to pull her little fur cape from her shoulders. He shouted in a naughty manner: "Off with your fur for the collection! You don't need any fur cape, silly old dame!" I chased him away.

*December 16, 1941* Hitler has dismissed Field Marshall von Brauchitsch, Supreme Commander of the German Army, and has taken over the Highest Command himself.

The Führer, apparently, considers himself fit to be in top control of the German Military Forces. The highest rank this Austrian paper hanger ever achieved during his military "career" in World War I was corporal!

*December 24, 1941* Christmas Eve! For the first time, we are away from home on this Holy Night. We both feel homesick. Just now, during a radio broadcast, I heard the bells of churches from all over Germany, the bells of the cathedrals from Cologne, Frankfurt, Munich, Hamburg, Berlin, Hannover, Bremen, Lübeck and Danzig. Quite unexpectedly, the commentator announced the ringing of the bells of the seven hundred year old St. Mary's Dome Cathedral in Riga. It was a greeting from my beloved country and a wonderful Christmas surprise.

# CHAPTER SIX

## Buna, Bombs and Propaganda

*January 1, 1942, Höchst* This is the first time in my life that a new year begins for me in a foreign country. This morning Propaganda Minister Goebbels read a statement issued by the "Führer" asking the Germans to stand faithfully behind their leader in all storms and troubles which he warned the New Year would surely bring.

*January 3, 1942* We had fish for lunch—nowadays a great rarity. After lunch I read the Latvian newspaper "Tevija—Fatherland" printed in Riga. Latvia is now governed by the German military forces. Life seems to run a fairly orderly course at home. Food supplies are adequate, certainly much better than here! Schools are open, there are concerts, theater and opera performances. The historic feelings of national hatred between Germans and Latvians seem to have vanished. Ingmar's letters corroborate this. "The Latvians would rather be free," he recently wrote, "but after the horrors of the Soviet Terror, the arrival of the German troops appeared to us as salvation from inhuman cruelty, torture and death. The German soldiers were received by the surviving Latvians with open arms, tears of gratitude and flowers. In Riga such welcoming scenes took place on Liberty Street where a crowd had gathered in front of our Statue of Liberty."

According to the paper, Latvian volunteers wearing German uniforms are fighting at the Russian front against the Soviet Army—the arch-enemy of all Baltic people. What will the future of the Latvian nation be? We have been uprooted, our families torn apart, many thousands killed, many thousands deported, with a large part of our people now living on foreign soil. There were only two million Latvians to begin with. How many of us will survive this war and be able to return to our homeland?

*January 4, 1942* Sunday—the only day when I can sleep long enough to really feel rested. On workdays I get up at 6:00 AM.

In the afternoon I took the train to Frankfurt and went for a walk through the old part of town. I passed ancient houses with dark wooden framework on white stone walls, their tiny windows blinking in the fading light. The narrow crooked dark streets all seem to lead to the cathedral in the center of town.

Not far from there stands the "Liebfrauen-Kirche—the Church of Our Lady." Its interior is styled in beautifully curved baroque lines: altar, lectern and pulpit are decked out in gold with many pictures of saints. Tall wax candles were burning, illuminating a Christmas crèche. A large congregation was listening to the sermon of a Franciscan Father in a brown monk's cowl. His subject was the spirit of his religious order. He stated that, contrary to popular opinion, persons who have suffered failure in ordinary life are *not* accepted into the order. "God's realm and God's work require healthy, able, inspired persons. In our times no one is any longer forced to either join or stay in an order. The brothers and sisters in our orders are having a hard time withstanding the new winds blowing in our homeland!"

This monk had courage to state his opinion from the pulpit. No doubt, Nazi spies were sitting in the congregation.

(This 17th century church no longer exists. It was destroyed by bombs. In its place now rises an ultra-modern church building. The old name has been kept.)

*January 5, 1942* I didn't go to work. I have a sore throat. In winter the climate here is damp and foggy—a source of frequent colds. Clear days with blue skies are rare. The Main River valley is usually veiled in a gray haze.

*January 7, 1942* Our furniture container has finally arrived from Danzig where it had been stored for ten months in the open. The contents have been heavily damaged by rain water. My upright piano is ruined. It fell apart while being hauled out of the container. However, I was told that it can be repaired. It is quite old, built in 1880 of heavily veined Brazil nut wood, and I love it. I hope, someday I will be able to play it again.

*January 8, 1942* I saw a movie with an unusual but now very much discussed subject: Euthanasia. Does a physician have the right to end the sufferings of a hopelessly ill person by bringing about a gentle and painless death? The answer which the film gave was "yes." However, it suggested that one person alone should not take the responsibility for such a decision. It should come from a board of physicians.

I assume that films like this are shown in order to prepare public opinion for the day when a government-ordered "Program of Euthanasia" will actually be put into effect.

*January 9, 1942* Quite unexpectedly I received a letter from Joachim, a former fellow student in Riga, who emigrated to Germany in 1939. I had not heard from him in years.

Joachim reminisced about my appearance of long ago: "a white lace kerchief around the neck, a timid smile, blond hair twisted into a knot at the nape of the neck . . ." He still seems to remember me the way I used to be during my freshman year in Chemical Engineering—then apparently a most unlikely candidate for such a severe profession.

Well, I made it. I am no longer a shy little girl; I am now a young professional woman able to stand my ground when dealing with business matters in a male world, further complicated by working in a foreign country which is at war.

I have two choices: either appear mannish or remain ladylike. The first choice is unacceptable to me. I am convinced that feminine charm and elegance can be combined with competence in one's job. Good grooming and nice clothes are important to me, and although we all have fallen on hard times in that respect—nothing new can be bought, we have to make do with our old things—I'm always trying to look my best.

At meetings I usually am the only girl around. It no longer bothers me much. I have learned to deal with my male colleagues, by proving to them that I can do as good a job as they can—or even better.

I fully agree with Schiller: "In deiner Brust sind deines Schicksals Sterne." ("In your breast are the stars of your fate.")

*January 14, 1942* I wrote a report about Chloropren and Propiopren—two synthetic rubber materials tested by my laboratory—to Herr Erler, head of the Central Rubber Research Laboratory in Bayerwerke Leverkusen. Shortly thereafter a young colleague, Dr. Brenner, appeared in my office and we had a long talk about the senselessness of this war. "Civilized nations attack each other," Brenner exclaimed. "The white race seems intent upon destroying itself and it forces colored people, particularly the American Negroes and the Japanese to take part in this mutual destruction. This causes all colored races to lose respect for the 'White Gods,'—here Brenner's voice waxed sarcastic—"if they ever deserved to be respected."

"If all these immense efforts now being made for the war would be made for peace, every person in the countries now at war could live in comfort and safety!"

"You are right, Irene, but instead of this, irreplaceable historic monuments are destroyed daily and countless young lives are lost in the prime of manhood. This is a negative selection, unlike the one taking place in nature where the healthy and strong survive and the sickly and weak succumb; war is the exact opposite."

*January 16, 1942* More philosophical discussions!

I talked about religious matters with our laboratory technician and Nazi spy Bernauer. He insists that the Christian Church is a Jewish institution with the purpose of enabling the Jews to influence Christian opinion. I denied such a possibility. Bernauer went on to say that he hates both the Reds (Communists) and the Blacks (Priests). He denies any belief in resurrection and life eternal. Eternal life, he says, is nothing else but the ability to create offspring and thus live on in one's children.

*January 17, 1942* Being stateless persons we are closely supervised by the Frankfurt Police department and frequent check-ups are routine. Every so often we get a summons to appear in their offices. Today in the waiting room I noticed a young couple, a soldier and a girl. She wore an engagement ring and they seemed to be very much in love. Why were they at the Police Department? My curiosity was aroused. I decided to ask the inspector. With obvious relish he told us:

"They came in for a marriage license, but the girl is half-Jewish, and therefore their application has been refused." And then the none-too-bright looking middle-aged officer went into details about the so-called "Laws of Nuremberg" dealing with marriages between Jews and "Aryans"—"A 'half-Jew' is not allowed to marry an 'Aryan' but may be married to another 'half-Jew.' In case they have children, these too will be 'half-Jews.' A 'quarter-Jew' (one grandparent Jewish) may marry an 'Aryan.' 'Quarter-' and 'half-Jews' don't have to wear the yellow Star of David. This also applies to 'full-Jews' if they are already married to an 'Aryan' partner."

Mother and I listened in silence. Another incredible facet of existence in Nazi Germany! The thought occurred to me that human lives are coldly dealt with, like problems of algebra. Human values—love, devotion, charity, friendship—are thrust aside by the power of some arbitrary and ridiculous "Laws of Nuremberg."

Obviously enjoying his chance to further expound the case of the unhappy lovers, the inspector continued: "The girl tried to convince me that she was not the daughter of her Jewish father—that her mother had cheated on her husband and that she was the offspring resulting from this illicit love affair!"

"Well, it could be possible, couldn't it?" I said.

"Oh, no," the man smiled broadly, "didn't you see her Jewish nose? She can't hide the fact of her racial origin."

*January 19, 1942* Last night I was invited to Dr. Kilian's for a musical evening. As part of my contribution I played Beethoven's Moonlight Sonata. I overheard my office-mate Dr. Kehrer whispering to Kilian: "I had no idea that she plays so well and with so much feeling. She has well managed to conceal this feminine trait of her personality, but now I have recognized her for what she really is."

I was taken aback by these words. I am not aware of making an effort to hide my own true self. I don't know what he means. Dr. Kehrer is a rough and tough Bavarian with very unattractive facial features, married, according to gossip, to a very beautiful but very stupid wife, who at present is still in Munich. He seems pleasant enough in spite of his many witticisms such as: "Dumm liebt gut!" ("Stupid girls love well!")" I wonder if this is a reference to Frau Kehrer?

*January 23, 1942* I had a letter from Riga from my two Latvian friends and sorority sisters Herta and Elsa. "In the spring of '41 during the final days of the Soviet occupation our sorority sisters Mariya, Emiliya and Maiya were deported to Siberia. We, too, expected to be arrested any day. In the final days before the Germans came we hid in the woods." And they continued: "Life is better now, but we are dreaming of the time when our country will be free again of foreign military forces."

*January 24, 1942* Today the newly established "Haus der Technik—House of Technology" was formally inaugurated in Frankfurt. About fifteen hundred chemists, engineers and technicians have come here from all parts of Germany.

I decided to appear in black, wearing my silk dress of Latvian times with Mother's black seal fur cape, all topped by a felt hat. My only ornament was a gold pin. I eyed myself in one of the huge mirrors in the Saalbau, where the gathering took place, and was pleased.

The main speaker gave a talk about Buna—the German synthetic rubber. Germany is totally cut off from any natural rubber imports and must depend entirely on synthetic products. He pointed out that America and England also have started production of man-made rubbers. Then he showed slides from the big Buna manufacturing plants in Germany, their huge distillation apparatus and polymerization columns—a veritable symphony of work. There is no doubt that Buna and Perbunan are of utmost importance in the German War Industry—and I am caught up in the middle of it. When signing the contract with I.G.Farben I was only informed that my work would be in Applied Research. Now I have no longer any freedom of decision. No one in Germany can quit working or change jobs without government authorization. The situation is exactly the same as it was in Soviet Latvia: We are prisoners of the State.

*January 25, 1942* Sunday morning. Snow keeps falling in huge flakes. It has been snowing for more than twenty-four hours, and the snowdrifts in the streets remind me of Riga in winter. As a little girl I loved to stand at the window and to watch the dancing snowflakes, day-dreaming of snow princesses and horse-drawn sleighs with jingle bells.

From these childhood memories I have to return to reality, which in this case means repairing my old gray Persian lamb fur coat. On Wednesday I'm scheduled to go to Berlin to a chemists' meeting with Dr. Haller, and I have to be presentable. I have no other winter coat. I have never been to Berlin before. What will it be like to stay in the capital of a country at war?

*January 28, 1942* Tonight I'm leaving for Berlin by train, where I will be staying for a whole week. During this time I will also have a chance to visit my Baltic German friends in Posen.

*January 29, 1942, Berlin* The meeting of the German Chemical Society today was the biggest meeting I have ever been to in Germany. I was the only woman chemist in a crowd of about 70 men and everybody was staring at me. In spite of my growing confidence this made me nervous and I had to exert quite a bit of self-control to keep calm.

In the evening my boss Dr. Haller took me to a performance of the Lehar operetta "Count of Luxemburg" at the Metropol Theater. It was a splendid spectacle with beautiful music, beautiful scenery and costumes.

I noticed with utmost surprise that in a number of scenes dancing girls appeared naked down to the waist. Such an exposure would have been utterly impossible in Riga.

My dinner at the hotel consisted of a meatless vegetable mix washed down with peppermint tea—a strange and rather unsatisfying combination!

*January 30, 1942* This evening in my hotel lobby I heard a broadcast of Hitler's annual message on the occasion of the anniversary of his coming to power. He declared that he does not know whether the war will end this year, "but one thing is certain, there again will be great and decisive German victories."

Earlier today I considered going out into the street to catch a glimpse of the "Führer" on his way to the Sportpalast here in Berlin, the usual site of his orations. I have been told that crowds always line up along his route. It would be interesting to see this fellow in real life who holds such fascination for millions of Germans. What finally kept me from going was the bitter cold outside.

*February 1, 1942* In the subway this morning I saw a gray-haired old lady wearing the yellow "Star of David" on her overcoat. She seemed withdrawn from her surroundings, sitting there totally alone, her glance unfocused, staring into space. No one dared to speak to her. This is the first time I have encountered a Jewish person in Germany. Since I arrived here less than a year ago I have seen no Jewish people in Frankfurt. I have asked about this many times, but have always received the same answer: "The Jews have left, they have all gone abroad." However, Dr. Kilian told me the truth: Almost all Jewish families have been by force deported to slave labor camps, and their possessions have been taken by the Nazi government. According to Kilian only comparatively few Jewish German citizens were able to escape abroad.

Now I also understand the horrible meaning of the "children's train" which we met on our second day in Germany. These must have been poor little Jewish children heading east—a whole trainload of them—who had been taken away from their families and were carried to some unnamed dreadful destination. No one ever dares to mention the word "murder," not even Dr. Kilian. "What happens to these people in labor camps? Will they stay there till the end of the War?" I wanted an explanation. "I do not know," Dr. Kilian answered . . . .

And now this old lady, wearing the "Star of David" like a medal! Where does she come from, where is she going? Why is she the only one left behind? I will never know the answers.

*February 2, 1942, Posen* Today I took my trip to Posen, which is not very far from Berlin, in occupied Polish territory.

Almost all my Baltic German friends live here. I visited Wolfgang's parents, who are still in mourning over his death. Karen was away visiting her parents in Litzmannstadt, formerly Lodz, another Polish city. Next I called on Frau von Warnecke, Gisela's mother. A grandchild played at her feet—Gisela's offspring. Gisela herself is already expecting her third baby. All my other schoolmates from secondary school, all married by now, also seem to be in various stages of first or second or third pregnancies. I am the only unmarried girl in this group.

Sometimes I am envious—but on the other hand, what suffering it would be to have a husband at the front, having to live with the ever present thought that he may never come back to me, that I may be left alone with a baby! It is happening to thousands of young women daily. Young mothers in "widow's weeds" pushing baby carriages are a common sight these days.

I really believe that under the circumstances I have been given the better deal. Of all my schoolmates I am the only girl with a college degree and with a profession and a career. I am independent and much suffering has been spared me by not having to worry about a husband and children. I'm convinced—my time as "materfamilias" will come eventually.

*February 3, 1942, Berlin* I'm back in the big city. Except for blackout regulations, there are no outward signs of war here, no bomb damage, no destroyed buildings, no people killed in air-raids, still lying buried under rubble.

In the morning I visited the huge department store AWAG (formerly Wertheim—it has been taken away from its Jewish owners). In spite of Germany's third year at war the store was filled with an incredible amount and variety of merchandise: beautiful dresses, hats, fur coats, china and crystal ware, books, oil paintings, carpets, furniture, fabrics and laces. I could hardly believe that all these wonderful things can still be bought in Berlin—if you have the proper ration cards and the money.

Just now I'm on the sleeper back to Frankfurt. I'm dead tired and glad to be able to stretch out in my berth.

*February 4, 1942, Frankfurt* This morning I arrived in Frankfurt. The upper berth in my compartment was occupied by a young, pretty, very elegantly dressed girl. I noticed expensive jewelry on her, many rings and a wristwatch covered with diamonds. We started a conversation. "I'm from Zurich, Switzerland," she said. "I work for a large import and export firm there. I have done much traveling all over Europe."

"How exciting, I wish I could travel like that. All I have ever seen is Latvia, Estonia and some parts of Germany."

"Ah, well," she said, "Europe isn't all that interesting. I find travel in the United States much more fascinating."

"You mean to say you have been to America?"

"Oh yes, I worked there for three years!"

"How lucky you are. America to us Latvians has always seemed like a faraway star—a dreamland—very hard to reach for an ordinary mortal."

"All it takes is a steamship ticket," she laughed.

"I bet, you must be a very hard working girl to have achieved such a fine position in your company."

"I work only for one or two hours daily," she stated flatly.

I looked at her in surprise: "How is this possible?"

"Ah, simple enough—I am the Company President's mistress!"

*February 7, 1942* More and more young men are drafted into the army. Quite suddenly our lab technician Hans has received his notice. Young Dr. Brenner, with whom I chatted the other day, also has been ordered to the front.

*February 9, 1942* We had not heard anything at all from our relatives in Estonia. Today a letter finally reached us from Mother's youngest brother Arno in Tartu. "Our sister Meralda and her husband Karl," he writes, "were deported by the Soviets to Siberia on June 14, 1941. Our niece Elra was left unharmed." And then Arno describes the destruction of Mother's home town.

"The Soviets on one hand and the Germans on the other hand shelled the city of Tartu in the summer of '41 for fourteen days, destroying most of it. Seven hundred houses went up in flames. The historic center with its ancient stone bridge built by Catherine the Great in the 18th century is now rubble." Mother wept all evening. I, too, was extremely depressed, remembering our glorious family get-together for Elra's wedding just three years ago.

*February 12, 1942* Tonight at the movies the newsreel showed Hitler delivering his speech on January 30 and, what was much more interesting, German submarines in front of New York. The submarines emerged from the ocean and at the horizon the silhouette of New York was visible.

*February 14, 1942* On Saturday mornings we have to work until noon. After work I immediately took the streetcar to Frankfurt, where I tried to buy a pair of rubber galoshes, without success. In contrast to Berlin the display of wares here in Frankfurt is very meager. The main street, called "Die Zeil," was crowded with people, although hardly anything can be bought. Snow was melting from rooftops and on the sidewalks were dirty puddles, which made walking hard, particularly without galoshes.

In the middle of all this confusion the sirens began to howl an alert, but no one paid much attention—and no enemy planes made an appearance.

*February 15, 1942* A very dull Sunday. I mended my clothes and my stockings. The stockings, particularly, are getting so worn out that it almost seems impossible to salvage them. Then I had an idea. I put some patches cut from old stockings over the biggest holes. It looks awful—but "c'est la guerre!"

*February 18, 1942* My restored piano was returned and taken to our new apartment, into which we will move shortly out of our one furnished room. It cost 400 Reichsmark to have it fixed, almost a month's salary—but the expense is worth it to me. The piano again sounds wonderful. The tuners have done a great job.

In the early evening, as dusk was falling, I went for a walk. In the west a red glow was fading. The moon hung as a narrow golden crescent horizontally in the sky. Mother says that this means cold weather. And it is indeed getting rather cold again.

*February 21, 1942* This morning Dr. Kehrer, who shares an office with me, came in with a yellow tinge on his face and announced: "I have developed a case of jaundice and must go home to Munich to my wife." I couldn't help but be secretly pleased: for one thing, he would no longer disturb me with his incessant talking; for another, I would no longer have to breathe in fumes from his constant cigarette smoking.

*February 22, 1942* Last night at 11:00 PM we had another alert. We heard heavy shooting, but by now this has become commonplace. Since no bombs were falling I refused to go down to the ice-cold basement air-raid shelter. I lay fully dressed on my bed and soon fell asleep, in spite of all the noise going on outside. The human spirit seems capable of adapting itself to increasing degrees of danger. At 3:30 AM I awoke—all was quiet. I undressed and crept under the covers.

*February 23, 1942* Tonight at the movies the newsreel showed the funeral of Dr. Todt, Minister of War, who was killed in an accident. It is strange indeed that recently so many important men in Germany have been struck down by sudden death: Udet, Mölders and now Todt. Many in the population find this suspect. At the funeral, Hitler was seen kissing Todt's little daughters and patting their cheeks.

*February 28, 1942* We are finally settled into our new apartment. I have done a lot of cleaning, washing, scrubbing, waxing and polishing of windows. Since we have hardly any furniture I am trying to get official permission to buy the bare necessities, like beds and a table and some chairs. I also was able to secure some black plastic window shades—which completely shut out any light from the apartment at night. Every night in all of Germany total blackout is the strict order. Offenders are heavily punished by long prison terms. When night falls, utter darkness reigns in city and country.

This last sentence seems so full of symbolism!

*March 2, 1942, Cologne* My boss is again sending me to the Central Rubber Research Laboratory of Bayer in Leverkusen.

I arrived this afternoon in Cologne. To my horror, the first thing I saw here was a house destroyed by English bombs just yesterday. Eight people in it were killed. I was quite shaken up and could hardly finish my skimpy but expensive supper at the Dome-Hotel where I am staying next door to the Cathedral of Cologne.

*March 4, Cologne* After a whole day spent at the Research Laboratory in Leverkusen, I got back to Cologne late last evening. I had never seen the Cathedral in moonlight before—a dark colossus ascending with two towers high into the sky. To me it seemed like an ancient symbol of strength and power, reaching across seven centuries into our time. Martin Luther's battle song came to my mind: "A mighty fortress is our God!"

In strange contrast to the massiveness of the main structure, the stone carved upper frontispiece looked like a lacy edge against the silver-blue light of the moon. Because of the blackout there were no electric lights in the city, nothing to interfere with nature's own illumination.

For a few moments standing alone before the Cathedral of Cologne, I had a sense of security, of protection. Somehow 1 will manage to live through this war!

*March 5, 1942* On the train back to Höchst.

This morning I had long talks with Herr Erler, head of the Central Rubber Research Laboratory in Leverkusen concerning the performance of Buna under stress, specifically in automobile tires during test driving. Under stress, energy losses are transformed into heat. In comparison with natural rubber, Buna shows poor performance when plotting a graph with energy losses on the vertical axis versus a temperature scale from—50° Centigrade to +200° Centigrade on the horizontal. This means that under extreme temperature conditions—extreme cold like in Russia, or extreme heat as in Africa—German Buna tires cannot be expected to perform too well. In modern wars such technicalities can spell the difference between victory or defeat. These are my own private thoughts. Such matters cannot be discussed in the open. It would be called "undermining the home front," and the punishment for that is: "Off with your head!" I have not forgotten the red posters with print in large black letters: "Today were sentenced by the sword..."

Cheerless thoughts on a cheerless gray day. It's raining hard as the train speeds through the Rhine valley into the oncoming darkness of night.

*Höchst, March 6, 1942* During lunch at the plant restaurant, I became acquainted with a young zoologist, a Dr. Dehren from Berlin. He is a shy, skinny, pale young man with horn-rimmed glasses and poor posture—the typical scientist of the cartoons. He told me that he had a miserable childhood and youth, his parents being very poor. He grew up in the kitchen of a wealthy Jewish home where his mother worked as a cook. During his studies at the University of Berlin, he had to work hard in order to support himself and his mother. He seems to have suffered a lot. He is so depressed and nervous.

*March 7, 1942* I stood in a queue for a full hour in front of a dairy store, with rain pouring down on me. All this trouble for one quart of bluish-looking skimmed milk!

*March 9, 1942* I mentioned to Dr. Kilian that one year ago yesterday, I came to Germany. He looked at me for a while with a strange expression on his face and then he quoted in a grave voice: "Abandon all hope, ye, who enter here!" from Dante's Divine Comedy—the inscription above the entrance to Hell.

*March 10, 1942* Another big fight with Mother.

"Aren't you ashamed to mistreat your poor mother in such cruel ways?" she began. "You have made me into your unpaid servant."

"Don't you realize that I am sharing my earnings with you?" I asked. We have a joint bank account. I pay for all your expenses, including your medical bills."

"It is you who has made me sick," Mother interrupted. "Ever since your father died, I've had nothing but trouble with you. You continuously irritate me with your wild ideas, your stubbornness and your willful ways."

"I am no longer a child; I have the right to my own ideas and beliefs."

"I am still your parental authority, whom you must obey according to the Fourth Commandment. And even if I were seventy and you fifty years old, I still would have the right to give you orders!"

"I most strenuously object to such irrational demands for obedience. Furthermore, it says in the Fourth Commandment to 'honor thy parents' not to 'obey' them." I was close to tears but continued, "I do honor you in any way I can. I do all the house-cleaning and food-shopping so that you may rest. I am always bringing you presents—a book, a handbag, some crystal beads, a leather belt—anything that still can be bought in the stores without ration cards."

"I do not care for your silly presents. They are no compensation for all that I have lost through your rash act of leaving our home country." Anger was welling up in me, listening to these deliberately spiteful words. It is a hopeless case. Mother will never admit that I tried to protect her from harm.

*March 11, 1942* Yesterday's fight with Mother is still in my mind. I'm beginning to wonder if the cruel experiences of her childhood and early youth did not leave a lasting impact upon her sensitive soul. Scenes from stories Mother used to tell me of her early life in Estonia, then a province of Czarist Russia, come back to me:

Mother, then a five year old girl named Ella, having to take care of her little brother Adi, who had the measles . . . Sitting at his cradle Ella heard children playing in the back yard. She threw a blanket over his head so as to protect his eyes from light damage—as she had been told— and carried him outside, in order to join in the games . . . trying to play "catch me if you can" while dragging her heavily bundled-up baby brother around. Her father suddenly appearing on the scene, loosening his belt and giving his little five-year-old daughter a whipping . . . .

My grandfather must have been a brutal man. The children feared him greatly, even the cat started to meow and hid behind the stove when he raised his voice. Whipping apparently was his favorite method of discipline, thereby trying to cure bed-wetting, poor marks in school and even hunger pangs.

Another scene: Ella, seven years old, standing in her father's workshop, talking to Jaan, one of her father's young apprentices . . . Jaan being Ella's favorite, always telling her stories in his free time or playing with her . . . . Suddenly Jaan keeling over, falling to the ground, with blood spurting out of his mouth over Ella's long dress and white apron, gasping: "I am dying" and collapsing on the floor . . . . Ella starting to scream in terror. No one had known he was suffering from TB.

Or this: Ella, seventeen years old . . . in a raging fever—desperately ill with typhoid . . . most of the time unconscious, only once in a while regaining consciousness for a fleeting moment, feeling her mother wrapping fresh cold wet sheets around her burning body . . . . After six weeks the fever was finally broken. Apathetic and exhausted Ella lay in her bed. In walked her father, lifted her up and carried her to a mirror. Ella stared in horror at the tiny yellow face of a bald, old, sunken-eyed Chinese—during her illness all her hair had fallen out.

At that exact moment the bell of the nearby cemetery chapel began to toll. "I wish it were tolling for me!" was Ella's deeply felt reaction . . . . This death wish never seems to have left Mother. She sees no joy in living.

Remembering all this, I know that I'm caught in a web woven of pity, devotion, suffering, revolt against unjust accusations and longing for inner peace. I cannot break out of it. I cannot abandon my mother.

*March 13, 1942* Last night I stood at the window and looked out into the dark blue universe with its sparkling glory of a billion stars. The endlessness of space frightens me, just as the thought of eternity is frightening to me and hard to accept. Even the stars are not eternal, why should our souls be? Some of the stars whose light is reaching us now were themselves destroyed thousands of years ago in immense collisions. They no longer exist, but their light shines on—for a while, but not forever.

*March 14, 1942* An army captain, who recently received the "Ritterkreuz— the Knight's Cross" for bravery at the Eastern Front, visited our plant. He talked about the "Russian soul." He characterized the Russians as rather good natured and frequently quite sentimental, but nevertheless the "Asiatic beast slumbers within their souls, ready to rise upon provocation and commit dreadful deeds of 'atrocity and cruelty.'"

It sounds overly dramatic but—I have to agree. The Red Terror in Latvia proved it. There is one catch, though! Human cruelty is not confined to one particular nationality. Isn't it equally cruel to bomb living quarters in English or German towns; isn't it equally cruel to order Jews and Poles out of their homes and cart them off to labor camps?

*March 15, 1942* This afternoon, I visited our friend, Frau Knoth, who gave a party in honor of her son home on furlough from the Russian front. He is very young and shy, and a great sadness clouds his eyes. He told me that he saw and experienced terrible things fighting in the battlefields of France and now in the "Green Hell of Karelia" high up in the north of Finland. I noticed that he had fine slender hands and I thought what a pity it is that with those hands he has to operate machine guns.

*March 19, 1942* Springtime seems to have come at last! The air is soft, and now and then the sun shines brightly and the snow has almost vanished. The first crocus and snowdrop flowers are beginning to bloom . . . and I sit behind the large windows of my laboratory and see nothing but train engines in clouds of steam, smoking chimneys and coal carts moving in endless rows over a bridge high up in the air right in front of our building. I would love to listen to the gentle murmuring of a spring hidden in blossoming woods. I would love to lie there next to the water watching sunbeams paint golden patterns on the moss—covered ground. Alas, these are but dreams!

*March 20, 1942* To my surprise I found a picture of my former Latvian technician Andris at "Varonis" in the latest Latvian newspaper "Tevija." He was clad in German uniform and is a volunteer fighting against the Soviets. I hope he comes to no harm.

The German newspapers announced that the food rations will be reduced once more. The meat ration from now on will be 300 grams (10 ounces) per person per week. The statement said that no improvement is to be expected before the summer of 1943, because only then will Germany profit by the harvest in the Ukraine. My goodness, when I think of the abundant food in Latvia!

*March 21, 1942* Today, according to the calendar, is the first day of Spring, but the sky is heavy with dark clouds. Not a single ray of sunlight has managed to penetrate. Furthermore, we are having a flood. The Main River has risen tremendously and here in Höchst water is covering the adjoining fields on the left bank and reaches high up to the ancient castle fortification walls on the right bank. In Frankfurt the river water is lapping at the foot of the Römerberg and people living in the flooded area had to be rescued by boats. Fortunately, we have had no enemy alerts.

*March 24, 1942* Every night now for about a week I have been mending stockings. By now my eyes are smarting because I'm trying to repair the runs with a hooked needle by looping the fallen stitches one at a time back up to where the run started. It is a tedious job and very hard on the eyes. How I wish for a pair of nice brand new silk stockings!

I was told in the plant that on March 31, I and two colleagues will be sent to Essen in the Ruhr Valley to a meeting at the "House of Technology" there. The prospect frightens me, because Essen is a large industrial center and is frequently a target of enemy bombing.

*March 25, 1942* This morning, a fellow chemist, Dr. Spiess, told us about his life in America, twenty years ago. He went there because he could not find a job in Germany. He worked as a chemist in New York and in Philadelphia and earned $150-$275 per month. Life is so different there! Most of all, the Negro problem interested us. "The colored people usually work in low professions," Spiess told us, "but there are already quite a few with very good educations. The Negroes are extremely intelligent because the brains of the colored people have rested for several thousand years, but we whites are already relatively tired." I thought this a strange statement. "The educated Negroes," Spiess continued, "usually lead a model family life and are very religious. They have wonderful songs called spirituals. The melodies descend from their African heritage, but the African languages are forgotten. The American poet, Longfellow, wrote words for a few of the old melodies and these have become very popular songs. Some of the Negroes insist that they are descendants of the American Indians."

*March 27, 1942* A fellow chemist announced that he would be soon sent to the German-occupied south of Russia to take over a chemical plant there. I told him jokingly, in case he needed an interpreter, I could offer my services.

*March 28, 1942* Soldiers of a FLAK Company gave a performance in the local People's Institute. The soldiers sang and played in an orchestra and imitated famous film stars. They also produced a magician and several clowns and told jokes:

(Two soldiers talking about their forthcoming furlough) A: "You know, during my furlough, I'm going to visit all the countries and towns which have been occupied by our Army. I will go to Poland, Norway, Denmark, Holland, Belgium, Moscow, Petersburg, London, New York . . . ."

B (interrupting): "Stop, Stop! These cities have not been occupied by our Army yet!"

A: "Well, my furlough is not due until August." Roaring laughter!

B (not wishing to be surpassed and anxious to say something clever): "And on my furlough, I plan to travel by bicycle all over the British Empire!"

A: "And what will you do in the afternoon?" Roaring laughter....

*March 31, 1942, Essen* We are staying in the Krupp Hotel which is a very fashionable place. But Essen is truly a dangerous town to live in. Today, we had four alerts, at 2:00 PM, 5:00 PM, 7:00 PM, and 10:00 PM, so that we spent a great part of the day in different air-raid shelters, rather than at the "House of Technology." I don't think anyone got much out of the meetings there! Tomorrow early we are going back to Höchst.

*April 1, 1942, Höchst* Last night we had an air raid. The German anti-aircraft guns shot violently in defense. Some enemy bombs dropped into the fields and we spent the night partly in the basement shelter, partly on the stairs to it.

*April 5, 1942, Easter Sunday* I went for a walk in Frankfurt, along the Main river, and unexpectedly came to a fairgrounds with merry-go-rounds, a Russian wheel, swings, a laughing cabinet, "trip to Mars," and a monkey and dog show. Munching gingerbread cookies I mingled with the crowds and watched the goings-on. I felt sorry for the poor little animals: the white poodles had to balance on their front legs while dancing to music. Three trained little monkeys perched on a rod and looked at the world with big wistful eyes, except when ordered to perform. Then they had to juggle, dance on a rope, ride a bicycle and balance on a little chair. A monkey mother clutched her three days old baby to her chest; the baby was about four inches long.

*April 6, 1942* I had another discussion with Dr. Spiess about an interesting theme: this time it was about "The Church Fight." The German Christians intend to create a uniform German Christian Church by joining Catholics and Protestants in one big denomination. The Confessional Christians on the other hand, cling to their respective confessions and refuse to be united. This fight has underlying political motives but during the war, the government has ordered cessation of sectarian strife for the Christian churches in Germany.

*April 10, 1942* Being political refugees, we have been ordered to appear before a Commission in Wiesbaden for a "medical and racial" checkup. So, this morning we took the train to Wiesbaden, where a special sanitary convoy on wheels stood on one of the tracks in the railroad station. It consisted of an almost endless row of railroad cars. There we met a large number of people, all from the Baltic States, who were waiting to be checked out.

The checkup was a tedious and complicated procedure. Men and women were separated. Then the screening started. After giving our personal data we were questioned about our ancestors, our family origins, with particular emphasis placed on "Aryan" race, whether "interracial" marriages with Jews had ever occurred in our families.

Then followed an interrogation about professional training, special skills, state of finances and property (nil in most cases!) and church affiliation. After that our pictures were taken. Finally came the medical exam, and blood tests. Then all women were ordered to strip naked, and we were told to file in, one by one, through a narrow door into the adjoining cabin.

As I entered I almost stumbled over a pair of long male legs clad in shiny black lacquered high boots. Their owner, an utterly arrogant SS doctor in uniform sitting in a comfortable arm-chair, had stretched his legs out right in front of the entrance—on purpose, I am sure. I stood trembling in my nakedness. Ice-cold gray eyes looked me over mercilessly and then I heard him snarl: "You are very tall and very skinny. Why are you just bones and skin? Why is your bosom so small?" (Another Herbert Ehrland?)

I felt anger rising in me at these insults to my dignity, and staring right down into his mocking eyes I said in a firm voice: "What do you expect? We live on starvation diets!" And I pulled myself up higher and straighter than before—and stood very still.

My defiance must have somehow impressed the arrogant monster. He considered my answer for a few seconds and then stated: "Well, you have very straight legs anyway!'"

I felt like a piece of cattle being evaluated. I hoped he would now let me go, when he suddenly shot out a question: "Are you Jewish?" It startled me by its unexpectancy, but all I said was: "No, I am not Jewish."

"Can you prove it?"

I did not answer. This was simply cruel mockery. How can one prove anything standing naked and defenseless before a creature with a warped sadistic mind?

After a long silence, while the SS man's stares traveled up and down my body, he waved his hand motioning me to go on to the next cabin. As soon as I got there, a nurse in white uniform grabbed my left upper arm from behind and stabbed it three times with a needle. "What are you doing?" I demanded. "Shut up," she said "and don't ask silly questions!"

Then I was pushed out into a sort of lobby and was finally allowed to dress.

Mother had gone through a similar procedure, except that the SS man had ignored her. Quite unnerved from the experience we eventually got home. There I discovered that the nurse had tattooed my blood group into the skin of my underarm—a big dark blue "A." The same has happened to Mother.

*April 11, 1942* At the movies, the newsreel showed the "Day of the German Army" in Berlin, the English landing attempt at St. Nazaire, a naval battle on the Atlantic, and the bombed town of Lübeck.

*April 13, 1942* On the train to Cologne.

I again have been ordered to go to Leverkusen, this time accompanied by my new associate Dr. Fehrig. He has been recently assigned to my laboratory and is a nice quiet man in his forties. Just now the train is speeding along the Rhine river, which glistens in radiant sunshine. The fields are greening, but not yet the vineyards on the banks of the river, although the grapevines are already carefully tied to supporting sticks.

We had lunch in the "Mitropa" dining car and now Cologne is coming into sight.

In the afternoon I went for a walk through town. There has been a noticeable increase of bomb-damaged houses since my last stay here.

*April 14, 1942* After work (at the Central Rubber Research laboratory in Leverkusen), Dr Fehrig and I drove back to Cologne, where we met Dr. Kort—another I.G. Farben chemist. We had dinner at a restaurant with the peculiar name "Ewige Lampe," which means Eternal Lamp.

We had some Moselle wine and Dr. Kort became quite talkative, insisting heatedly, "Within seven weeks a decisive German victory will occur on any of the numerous battle-grounds in which the German forces are at present involved: Malta, Moscow, Leningrad, the Caucasus, the Crimea, Africa."

"This is not at all certain, Dr. Kort," I argued. Kort became greatly agitated: "I will give it to you in writing, Irene," he exclaimed. And he did just that, stating date, time, place and signing his name. Dr. Fehrig acted as witness. It was a bet. Well, let's see who will be right seven weeks from now!

*April 15, 1942* Fehrig told me this morning that after my departure last night, Kort had called me a "beautiful seductress." He is a conceited character and I am not amused!

In the night we had an alert that lasted into the morning hours. I spent this time in the basement air raid shelter of the Dome Hotel.

In Leverkusen one of their young chemists, Dr. Schöller—an Austrian—invited me to have dinner with him at the Leverkusen plant restaurant, which still serves excellent food. Schöller is really cute, blond with twinkling brown eyes, and his Viennese accent is extremely charming. I like him a lot but I already have other plans. Tonight I'm going to see the first German color film, called "Frauen sind doch bessere Diplomaten." "Women are better diplomats.")

*April 16, 1942, Höchst* The film was produced by AGFA-COLOR. Some of the shots taken are very beautiful, but the colors still are lacking natural hues. There are too many disturbing blue shades in the landscapes, and the skin tones of the actors show too much reddish brown. But of course German color film is only at the beginning of its development and seems to have wonderful possibilities.

Upon returning to Höchst this afternoon I found a letter from my former director Dinbergs written from Riga. He is still at the "Varonis" plant there and is urging me to return and again work for him.

*April 17, 1942* I talked to my boss Dr. Haller about Dinbergs' offer. He categorically refused to let me go, claiming that I was "one of his main pillars in the department—most dependable and a hard worker."

Just now a yellow butterfly flew by my window—a harbinger of spring!

In the afternoon, all chemists were ordered to attend a meeting at the Plant restaurant. A Nazi Party man gave a speech about the principles of duty. He told a story about 1500 Germans in British Africa who at the beginning of this war were asked by Great Britain to decide whether they were opting for England (and thus would be able to keep their property) or for Germany (and lose their investments and their right to stay in the country). Out of 1500 Germans, 1470 decided for Germany and were moved into a concentration camp. The remaining 30 were Jewish immigrants. The man went on: "After one year, the British Government had the Germans transported by Italian ships to Germany. In farewell they were told: 'Go back to Germany and gobble up your "Führer's" meager food supplies!'"

*April 20, 1942* The magnolia trees at the river banks are in bloom. I went for a walk there.

Today is Hitler's birthday, and the whole town is decorated with red swastika flags. Yesterday on the eve of this state holiday Goebbels delivered a speech comparing the "Führer" to Frederick the Great—the famous 18th century king who forged the Prussian nation into a leading European power. What honors next for the "mustachioed little paper hanger?" That's what Dr. Kilian is calling him.

*April 21, 1942* Our boss Dr. Haller informed us that he has been transferred to Berlin to act as middleman between I.G. Farben and a government research group in the north of Germany.

I was perturbed. I like working for Dr. Haller. He is always polite and quick with praise for a job well done. I wonder what kind of person his successor will be?

*April 22, 1942* The evenings at home are rather dull. I try to read but am too tired. So I usually sit around in silence. Talking to Mother is useless, because she will immediately pick another fight. The situation at home is depressing. I am glad that I have a job and can be away all day.

*April 23, 1942* There was a reason behind that mad screening procedure in Wiesbaden two weeks ago! Today we received notification from the Frankfurt Police Headquarters that German citizenship has been conferred on Mother and me "in order to eliminate the Classification 'stateless' for political refugees of suitable ethnographic and Aryan origin in the Third Reich." This means that most of the other Baltic refugees whom we met in Wiesbaden also have been made citizens.

By no means am I thrilled. I'd rather get my Latvian citizenship back—but that is not possible. Mother pointed out that *any* citizenship is better than being stateless, without *any* government to protect you. Dr. Kilian, to whom I talked later, corroborated this. Furthermore, he is of the opinion that should Latvia ever be established again as an independent state, I surely would have no trouble acquiring a Latvian passport.

Anyway, a refusal would be most unwise. The concentration camp is always beckoning. Not only Jews are taken there. Recently a German from our neighborhood, an ordinary working man, a carpenter, disappeared. The GESTAPO picked him up. No one knows why.

Later, to calm down, I went for a walk along the Liederbach, a small stream flowing through farmland on the outskirts of Höchst. On its banks, weeping willows gently waved their hanging light green branches in the evening breezes. I passed quiet little farm-houses with flower and vegetable gardens surrounded by potato and rye fields. The open spaces reminded me of Sigulda in Latvia, where I spent some of the happiest times in my life. Now my home country seems to me like paradise lost. Will I ever, ever be able to return there?

*April 29, 1942* For 48 hours now tremendous winds have been howling around the building and rattling the window panes. All rooms in the apartment are drafty and very cold, because central heating was shut off in our apartment house on April 15 in order to economize.

*April 30, 1942* Late last night the wind finally abated. A full moon rose. I went out for a walk along the Main River. The moonlight was reflected in the waves and formed a golden background for the dark silhouettes of the narrow town-houses of Höchst, huddling close together near the river bank. Some of them were built as long ago as the 14th century, the Justinus Church as far back as 800 AD, presumably by Charlemagne.

The cherry trees are in full bloom and they sparkled in the moonlight as if covered with snow. The old German towns are truly beautiful, especially in spring—and even more so by moonlight when all the restlessness of the day seems swept away and any ugly spots visible in daylight are camouflaged by the interplay of light and shadows.

*May 1, 1942* Today is a national holiday: "Tag der Arbeit" ("Labor Day"). The calendar says "May" but the weather is like November. The only warm spot to be found in the apartment is in the kitchen, near the stove.

*May 5, 1942* Last night, we had two air raids. I hate being in the basement shelter and stayed outside. About 3:30 A.M., the FLAK shot down an English four-engine Wellington bomber near Höchst. I saw the red fire of the explosion lighting up the sky. This morning my assistant Fersen gave me the gruesome details: "The whole crew of the plane, consisting of seven British airmen, were killed in the crash. Their partially burned bodies were found scattered around the remnants of the plane." Dr. Fehrig broke in: "I have heard that these young soldiers will be buried in our local cemetery with military honors."

All military honors of the world combined will not bring these young men back to life. "Countless young lives are lost in the prime of manhood," Dr. Brenner had said. "This is a negative selection . . . ."

*May 6, 1942, Leipzig* In Leipzig I have to call on Firma Schopper, manufacturers of precision instruments, who just now are building an abrasion apparatus for our laboratory.

My train trip turned out to be most unusual. Next to me sat a young mother with her two-year-old boy. All of a sudden it occurred to her to put the youngster on a potty right on the upholstered First Class compartment bench in front of the rest of the passengers including the boy's grandmother, two army officers in uniform and me. The young woman's offspring appeared most indignant and began to yell his head off.

Anyway, it broke the ice, and one of the officers, a captain, just coming from Paris, talked a lot about the wonderful life in France, about opulent meals, good wines and liquors and boxes filled with chocolates. He concluded: "We live there like in heaven!" Next he began sharply criticizing the crews of some Italian submarines stationed at the French Riviera. He claimed that the Italians are cowards and no fighters at all; in fact, they had once refused to go into naval battle. Suddenly the captain's talk was interrupted by the other officer, a lieutenant who addressed his superior in rank in rather strict and clipped tones: "Captain, may I ask you to keep quiet!" The captain immediately shut up and it was a very embarrassing moment not only for the captain but for his fellow travelers as well.

After my arrival in Leipzig, I had a very expensive but not very filling meal at my hotel while a Hungarian orchestra played ravishing melodies.

*May 7, 1942, Leipzig* My visit to Firma Schopper was successful. They promised to reduce their delivery time for the abrasion instrument by a whole month.

In the afternoon I visited the famous St. Thomas Church, the church of Johann Sebastian Bach (1685-1750). The world-renowned "Thomaner Choir" consisting of young boys sang a motet by Bach: "Cantate Domino Canticum Novum!" The voices are so beautiful. At the conclusion, the Thomas-Kantor, Professor Gunther Ramin, played the organ. While listening, the shadows of the war seemed to recede and I felt at peace. I imagined how two hundred years ago, organ music played by Bach himself filled the high dome of this ancient Gothic cathedral.

*May 8, 1942, Leipzig* In the morning I took the train to Halle and from there the streetcar to Buna-Werke Schkopau. The name comes from the Wendic (a now-extinct Slavic language) Scopava meaning sheep-village. ("Sheep" and "scop" appear to be derived from the same Indo-European root.)

The plant is laid out on a large scale with gigantic columns, huge precipitation baths and conveyor belts transporting the freshly manufactured Buna to the dryers. After having spent all day in the research laboratories there, I returned rather tired to Leipzig.

*May 9, 1942, Leipzig* In the morning, I visited the "Völkerschlachtsdenkmal" ("the Monument of the Battle of the Nations"). This battle took place near Leipzig on October 16th to 18th in 1813. This monument was built a century later and unveiled in 1913 on the anniversary of this decisive battle in which Napoleon's armies were defeated in Germany. In a monotonous voice, the guide told his story: ". . . . and fifty thousand dead covered the battlegrounds." We entered the crypt and the "Hall of Fame." The latter is remarkable for its acoustics. A single sound vibrates about twenty seconds in the circular cupola. The guide sang a tri-chord and it sounded as powerful as organ music. It was dark and gloomy inside but as we left the building, lovely sunshine and a warm spring day greeted us.

From there, I went to St. John's Church, a baroque building with a light-colored beautiful interior, where Johann Sebastian Bach's remains rest in a sarcophagus in a vault.

Descending to the vault, I stopped in surprise: a strange bust had caught my attention at an intersection of the stairs. It was half a human face, half a skull. "What is the meaning of this?" I asked an elderly gentleman standing nearby. "This statue was made by a sculptor who also was a surgeon, an anatomist," he replied, "and famous for his knowledge of the relation between facial bones and the corresponding muscles."

"Whose skull is it?" I wanted to know.

"Don't be so impatient, just listen," the old gentleman said. "A skull had been found in an old grave near the foundations of St. John's Church. The minister of the church had commissioned the sculptor to create the face fitting the found skull. The artist performed the given task and to his surprise recognized the features of Johann Sebastian Bach, as he is known from his portraits. The skull given to the sculptor 'incognito' was that of the great musician." And now I too recognized the features on the facial side of the bust, a copy of the original reconstruction.

At the nearby very old St. John's Cemetery, Goethe's love in Leipzig, Kätchen Schönkopf, is buried, and also buried there are the mother and sister of Richard Wagner, the composer.

*May 13, 1942, Höchst* A special announcement from the "Führer's" headquarters was broadcast from the Russian front: Attack on Kertch in the Crimea, 40,000 prisoners, numerous tanks and airplanes were taken. The battle has been going on since May 8.

Dr. Kort was jubilant, because his prediction of one month ago has come true.

*May 14, 1942* Another special announcement: German submarines have sunk USA cruisers at Murmansk.

*May 15, 1942* At home I found a package from Herta and Elsa from Latvia. They had sent me a book by our Latvian author Zenta Maurina, *Dzives Vilcienā* (In the Train of Life)—and a piece of yellow homemade soap. (German soap is horrible—it consists of 80%. sand and 20% fatty material, is non-foaming and irritating.)

*May 17, 1942* Sunday! It is Mother's day and a speech of the "Reichsfrauenführerin" ("Leader of German Women") Gertrud Scholz-Klinke was broadcast. She urged all German women to put their trust in the "superior powers of the 'Führer.'"

*May 20, 1942, Cologne* I'm back again at Leverkusen. Dr. Kort, who is in charge of the synthesis of new Buna materials, seemed rather pleased today. The abrasion resistance of his latest creations has increased as compared to earlier samples.

Last night here we had an air raid. Evil tongues at the Leverkusen Bayer Plant insist, that whenever I appear, I attract the English bombers. They were right again. Some kind of attraction!

*May 24, 1942* Whitsuntide! Mother and I went by train to Hofheim at the foot of the Taunus mountains. From there we walked through the woods to Langenhain, a little village on a hilltop. The woods are in their springtime glory. Between light green birches, maple and beech trees stood tall dark pines. Freshly plowed fields stretched to the horizon and above it all shone a radiant blue sky.

In Langenhain, we visited Franz Sorg, one of my laboratory workers, a World War I veteran, with a bullet still stuck in his lungs. It cannot be removed. He lives with his daughter in a cozy little old farmhouse with tiny windows and flowers on the window sills. Everything was sparkling clean and reminded me of the house of the seven dwarves in Grimm's fairy tale about Snow White.

Franz Sorg took us to see the maypole in the middle of the village square. It is a high wooden mast decorated with green garlands, colored paper bows and streamers. Just as though there were no war, village children were dancing around it celebrating May time. We too celebrated

May time by drinking some "Appelwoi" (apple wine in the local dialect) in an ancient dark village tavern. This forgotten little Taunus village seemed like an oasis of peace, untouched by daily strife and nightly air raids.

*May 26, 1942* At the movies, the newsreel showed Hitler playing with his German Shepherd dog "Londi." What's the matter with him? Doesn't he have a girl somewhere? Or is this kept a secret?

*May 28, 1942* Our old caretaker's son Hans Herzelt is home on furlough from Riga. He told me of the conditions there. The Latvians are much better off than they were under the Red Terror, but are not really happy under the German Occupation either. The Jews are treated worst of all. They receive only 200 grams (7 ounces) of bread daily and are forced to do hard labor. He has seen many collapse on the streets from undernourishment and exhaustion.

It may all of a sudden occur to these "supermen" that the Baltic people, based on latest "research," also belong to the group of "sub humans" and therefore must be stamped out. I can well imagine how much fun some SS-men (like the two characters whom I have encountered) would have to stamp *me* out!

*May 30, 1942* In the afternoon, the radio broadcast the speech of a Hindu, an associate of Subhas Chandra Bose, who talked about the struggle for freedom of the Indian Nation. He seems to be in league with the Nazi government.

*May 31, 1942* Sunday I went into the Taunus mountains to a lookout tower, high above the green woods. The weather was very clear and I saw the landscape spread out before me: the mountains of the Odenwald, the Vogelsberg and the Pfalz, the towns of Frankfurt, Königstein, Soden, Höchst. In the distance the River Main glistened like a silver ribbon. I stood high on the tower with a powerful wind blowing around me. It gave me the illusion of feeling completely free, completely disconnected from the depressing and troublesome life going on down there in the cities and villages. But eventually I had to descend and go back.

Dusk began to fall and clouds of mist rose and veiled the mountains in silver-gray haze. Slowly and solemnly the moon ascended above towering dark trees like a great golden sphere. In my mind I heard the sounds of Beethoven's immortal song: "The heavens are telling the Lord's endless glory, through all the earth his praise is found!"

*June 1, 1942* Summer is here! My thoughts go back to university days in Latvia when after having passed my spring exams I immediately went to Grandma Amalia's country estate for three months of "dolce far niente" ("the sweet life of doing nothing"). And now? I'm a cog in an endlessly humming gigantic machine. I'm caught; I can't break out. I have no freedom of decision!

*June 2, 1942* I have started to make myself a dress out of some soft-textured material which I acquired under the pretense of needing window curtains. It is impossible to buy any clothing at all. So, I cut out the dress, but this is a complicated affair for a beginner and it took me a long time. The task was finally completed at midnight.

*June 4, 1942* I get along quite nicely with my sewing. I have attached the sleeves and the skirt to the waist, but the hemming and finishing still remain to be done. Tomorrow I'll have a new dress!

*June 5, 1942* The papers brought the news that the "Führer" paid a personal visit to Marshall Mannerheim, the leader of the Finnish Army, in honor of his 75th birthday. Mannerheim is fighting for the freedom of his country against the Soviets. He has a noble bearing and already long ago, during his first visit to the Imperial Court, when Finland still belonged to Russia, the Czarist noblemen respectfully referred to him as "the Knight." Mannerheim is forced to go with Hitler because no other country is willing to help him guard Finland against the Soviet invasion.

At night I heard the broadcast of a concert from Helsingfors in honor of Mannerheim's birthday celebration.

*June 6, 1942* Dr. Spiess, who today returned from Cologne, told us about the terrible destructions there after a heavy air raid. Thirteen churches and a great many houses have been destroyed; 200,000 people are homeless and 2000 were killed; 200 FLAK soldiers also lost their lives. There were not enough coffins in town for all the dead. The population of Cologne is bearing all this sorrow with "calm resistance" (says Dr. Spiess—who appears to be a Nazi). As he talked, the bright colors of the summer day seemed to fade. We ask ourselves how long it may take before Frankfurt experiences the same fate.

*June 7, 1942* Tonight we were ordered to attend an air-defense meeting, discussing counter-measures in case of air attacks. We were shown how to extinguish English incendiary bombs.

*June 12, 1942* During lunch, I had an interesting talk with my former Latvian physics professor, Dr. Kalns, who now also works at I.G. Farben, about the beginnings of life on earth. Some scientists believe that life on our globe is nothing but a "'mistake of nature" an unintentional accident which took place either because the "primeval cell of life" coming from somewhere in the universe got lost on our globe, or because through a mysterious chemical reaction, life was suddenly created. Maybe, he said, in time, chemists will be able to synthesize living protein cells.

At home I found a letter from Elsa, describing the wedding of Anna, one of our sorority sisters in Latvia, which took place in grand style, just as in the "good old days". Enormous amounts of food were consumed as well as hundreds of liters of homemade beer. Elsa also confessed that she has lost her heart to a blond giant named Hans—a sergeant in the German army.

*June 15, 1942* A special announcement came today from Army Headquarters in Africa: German and Italian troops under the leadership of Rommel have split the British Army in two and, having, reached the coast, have taken Tobruk and encircled the western part of the British Army.

*June 22, 1942* Today I received a notification from the local "Wirtschaftsamt" ("Office of Supplies") that I have been granted permission to purchase a bicycle. I am very glad. Nowadays bicycles are the only possible means of private transportation. All motor cars were immediately requisitioned by the Army at the beginning of the War in 1939. Furthermore, gasoline is not available for private use. All gas stations in town have been closed for years now.

*June 23, 1942* Today Dr. Dehren told me the sad story of his life. During his studies, he suddenly was struck by an attack of schizophrenia and taken to a mental hospital. He stayed there for a year and was then released. In anguish Dehren exclaimed: "Ever since, the fact that I once suffered from a mental illness has haunted me. I am in constant danger of being sterilized. My fiancée is in Berlin. I cannot get permission to marry her. My life and also my girl's life have been completely warped!" Poor fellow! I felt so much pity for him and tried to come up with some kind of advice. I suggested he should try to get out of Germany. To my surprise he answered: "That is all arranged. I know of an escape route to Belgium. I will not let them emasculate me!"

*June 24, 1942* St. John's Day! But here in the south of Germany are no celebrations. I remember "Ligo Night" two years ago in Latvia: a fire was built in the open—Ingmar and I jumped over the flames and then walked hand in hand through woods and fields until the sun rose again. Now the war has separated us.

In the afternoon I visited the old church in Unterliederbach which lies in the middle of an ancient cemetery. This tiny country church is 500 years old and, therefore, under special protection as a historic monument. During the Thirty Years' War, while the battle of Höchst was fought, the peasants of Unterliederbach sought safety in their little church from the cruelties of the looting soldiers. In the cemetery, I found many oddly shaped crosses and gravestones out of the 16th and 17th centuries under blooming jasmine bushes. I thought of the endless stream of people who entered through these church doors in the course of five centuries, who were christened, married, and buried there. I thought of the laughter of young children, the smiles of brides and the tears which were shed over those now forgotten graves. And now, nothing remains but memories! This is the law of life: Eternal change!

# CHAPTER SEVEN

## Past and Present Meet

*June 25, 1942, Cologne* This morning I arrived here once again on my way to Bayer-Werke in Leverkusen. The city is badly bomb-damaged: destroyed buildings, burned-out department stores, and rubble are everywhere. However, the streets are full of people and whatever stores still exist are crowded with customers—all persons who lost their belongings and who, having been reimbursed by the government for their losses due to "acts of war", are trying to replace their destroyed furniture, bedding, house wares, linen, clothing, silverware, etc.

I am amazed that all these goods still can be purchased in Germany. In my opinion it has become too dangerous to stay overnight in Cologne. I have a reservation for a room at the guest-house of the Bayer-Werke in Leverkusen.

*June 27, 1942, Leverkusen* I'm furious at Erler, the diminutive director of the reference laboratory here! This morning I told my nice Austrian colleague Dr. Schöller the whole story. He laughed merrily: "Calm down, Irene, don't you know that little pots are apt to boil over!" Amused by this comparison, I too burst out laughing. But still—the effrontery of that individual!

Erler invited me yesterday after work to his garden at the outskirts of Cologne: "Won't you help me pick strawberries, which otherwise would go to waste?" His wife and five kids have been evacuated to farm country away from the dangers of further bombing raids in the city. I found the prospect of having fresh strawberries for supper rather tempting.

Promising Schöller, who had invited me for dinner, that I would be back after a couple of hours, Erler and I set out by streetcar to his home. It took us about an hour to get there. It was still light outside, and we went at once to his "garden." I was very disappointed. All I saw were a few rows of tiny dusty plants with hardly any red berries on them.

Erler mumbled some excuses, but I told him point blank: "I am taking the next streetcar back to Leverkusen!" He escorted me to the stop, but no streetcar came. We waited and waited—in vain. Finally a man, passing by informed us: "The last streetcar back to town left about an hour ago."

I could have strangled the little fox, who was standing there pretending to be greatly perturbed. "Oh, I'm so sorry, Fräulein Zarina, I had no idea . . . ." His game was up, but on the other hand—what was I to do? We were practically in open country. All there was were a few rows of homes with no hotel in sight. To stay out all night in the open was dangerous—in case of an air-raid and the shooting of the FLAK.

I had no choice but to return to Erler's home, where he showed me the guest room. I noticed that the door had a lock but the key was missing. "Where is the key?" I demanded.

"I don't know, it must have gotten lost."

I knew he was lying. I closed the door, pushed a small chest of drawers in front of it and lay down in my clothes on the bed. I was very hungry and very upset. My biggest worry was the possibility of an air raid. During the big enemy attack in early June, a 100-pound bomb had come down into the adjoining fields, shattering all windows and doors in the neighborhood. This Erler had told me earlier. Thoughts raced through my mind: "There is no public air-raid shelter here, nowhere to hide. I am not afraid of 'Tom Thumb,' this skinny little man. I know I can handle him easily! But what if it starts 'raining bombs'?" I lay in the darkness and waited and listened to the clock in the hall strike the hours with deep ringing bangs and every quarter hour with a silvery staccato tone. I must have dozed off after midnight.

Suddenly the door creaked open. I sat up in bed, my muscles tensing. It was pitch dark. For a few moments nothing happened. Then I heard Erler's thin trembling voice coming from the door: "May I cuddle up next to you for a little while?"

"Not unless you wish to be squashed by my shoe like an insect!" my voice rang out. And, indeed, I was ready—shoe in hand. A hoarse groan, then silence—but he was still in the room. "Get out and shut the door!" I commanded. He obeyed and troubled me no more.

Early in the morning I took the first streetcar back to Leverkusen.

*June 29, 1942, Höchst* Lunch today was extremely skimpy and I am plagued by hunger pangs. Dr. Fehrig gave me some candy drops to chew.

I changed my old black wool dress into a jacket by cutting some of the bottom off and opening up the front. From the cut-off part, I made a tie belt. "Krieg macht erfinderisch" is a modern proverb, coined by the Germans—war develops your inventive talents.

*June 30, 1942* I received confirmation of my reservations for a double room in an old inn near Kaiserslautern in the Palatinate, a province adjoining the French border. Mother and I will spend my vacation there starting on July 12. The inn called "Klug's Mill" is seven hundred years old.

*July 1, 1942* I'm in bed early tonight. The windows in my room are open, a gentle breeze is moving the curtains. Little fluffy clouds are slowly traveling across the evening sky like a herd of spring lambs. The linden tree before my window forms lacy patterns against the fading light. Good night, beautiful world! At this moment the War does not exist for me!

*July 2, 1942* Tonight I went to communion at the little old Unterliederbach Church. 1 had not been to communion for a long time, and I do need divine guidance. I am very alone.

*July 3, 1942* I could have been dead, smashed by a heavy truck! But the good Lord protected me. It is like a miracle. Riding my bicycle on my way to work, I passed through a narrow alley between two buildings on factory grounds. Suddenly a huge truck came around the corner bearing left, instead of right. In a split second its front loomed before me like the gigantic gray snout of a monster. My last thought was: "This is the end!" The next moment I was flying through the air and then hurled to the ground. I closed my eyes thinking: "The heavy truck will roll over you and you'll be dead." Strangely enough, in that moment there was no outburst of a ferocious will clinging to life—instead, only calm acceptance of what the next moment might bring.

But nothing happened. I opened my eyes. The truck had managed to brake just in time. The truck driver and some workers lifted me up—there was general commotion, I must have fainted. Slowly I came to, tried to stand up, carefully felt my bones, if some might be broken—but except for some bruises and skin lacerations on my legs I seemed to be all right. The bicycle looked like a pretzel, though!

I limped to my department and here I am—at my desk, shaken up but alive. In my heart I'm sending prayers of thanks to God for protecting me from almost certain death or horrible maiming. I am repeating the verses of the 91st Psalm which I learned in Sunday School long ago: "He shall give his angels charge over thee to keep thee in all thy ways."

*July 4, 1942* My bruised right knee and hip hurt very badly all night, but I've not told Mother about my accident, because she would get upset. At work I put cold compresses on my knee, using Dr. Fehrig's big yellow handkerchief.

Quite unexpectedly six Russian slave labor girls arrived this morning at our department. I talked Russian to them; their eyes lit up and they crowded around me for protection like frightened lambs. They have come straight from the Crimea and have traveled for ten days. Two of them have been assigned to my laboratory for cleaning and dishwashing services. Their names are Lydia and Natasha. Lydia, who is sixteen, has more spirit than the rest of the group. Her bright gray eyes are very observant and seem to take in the unaccustomed sights and scenes here in Germany with much curiosity. Her questions addressed to me are intelligent: "Where did you learn to speak Russian?" and "Will I be wearing a white coat like you?"

Fifteen year old Natasha, on the other hand, is like a little larva in a cocoon. In spite of the July heat she was wrapped up in a heavy quilted, dirty jacket, with a thick gray wool shawl wound around her head. All I could see of her at first was a tiny pointed yellow nose sticking out of her wrappings and a pair of black, beady, frightened eyes. She refused to shed her "armor" and complained: "Mnye cholodno, ya boyus!" ("I am cold, I am afraid!") So I let her be.

My fellow workers, having heard of my accident, are very nice to me. I found a basket-full of beautiful red cherries from an unknown benefactor on my desk.

*July 5, 1942* Tonight at the movies, the newsreel showed the capture of Tobruk and the storming of Sevastopol. For the first time, the newest German artillery weapon, a huge gun which moves on tracks, was shown. It was as high as a two-story house and its barrel was approximately 20 meters long and had a diameter of about one meter. Sounds of surprise were heard in the theater: "Look at that beautiful monster! Look, what power, what might!" The audience seemed overawed when the cannon began to shoot and clouds of smoke and fire rose on the screen.

*July 7, 1942* Two special announcements came through. In Russia, the railroad center Voronesh was captured and, at Murmansk, 28 American transports out of a group of 38 have been destroyed by German submarines. The people here are in a jubilant mood.

*July 12, 1942* Mother and I got up early, ready for our trip to "Klug's Mill." Before leaving, Mother sprinkled moth powder into all our rooms, quite unnecessarily I thought. "We have no rugs or valuable furs or woolen blankets, Mother, so why bother!"

"You will never be a good housewife, you have no feminine traits. Stick with your male profession!" was Mother's sharp reply.

The train took us over Worms on the Rhine River to Kaiserslautern. From there we took the local train to Karlstadt, a small town. Then we had to walk about two miles, carrying our cardboard suitcases, through a beautiful green valley, the "Karlstal." We reached the Mill on the bank of a fast moving brook in late afternoon. An ancient huge mill-wheel driven by the water's force went slowly round and round. Enormous maple trees cast green shadows on mill and stream. On the other side of the sandy road sunlight was cascading down upon some white-washed stone buildings: a barn and a guest house. Above the mill, high on a mountain top, rose the ruins of the castle Willenstein, supposedly built by the Emperor Barbarossa in the 13th century.

This is indeed a beautiful valley, and here we will stay for a whole month.

*July 13, 1942* Our room in the guest-house next to the barn is small but cozy. At night we hear the mooing of the cows and the clanking of their chains. We also can smell them.

I went down for breakfast into the dining hall located in the mill itself. As I entered I heard a high-pitched voice from one of the tables exclaiming: "You must be Fräulein Zarina. My husband is quite wild about you. He adores you! I am Frau Erler." I stared in amazement—so did the other guests. At one of the tables, surrounded by five young children, sat a tiny blond woman. She rose, came over and shook hands with me.

It turns out that Klug's Mill is very popular with people from various I. G. Farben plants. That's how I heard about it.

*July 14, 1942* It is so beautiful here. I spend most of my time walking in the woods or along the mill-stream. Today I met a fragile old peasant woman who joined me on my way home. She took me to the ruins of the

Castle Willenstein and told me a story about the young and lovely daughter of one of the lords of Willenstein, who fell in love with a shepherd. "Her father was outraged when he discovered her love for the low-born boy," related the woman. "In despair, the young lady threw herself into the stream down there in the valley. The shepherd also drowned himself, and they were buried in one grave in the nearby village."

"When did all this happen?"

"Oh, it happened a long, long time ago, centuries ago, when the old castle was still standing—long before that great war that lasted for thirty years!"

I sensed from the woman's tale that the people here have a strong feeling of being part of their ancient soil, from whence they came. The local history and legends are interwoven with their own roots, their own lives. It almost sounded as if the old soul had lived through the Thirty Years' War herself, just as I am now living through a great war.

*July 15, 1942* The sky has clouded over and a cold wind is blowing. Nevertheless I again went walking. Frau Erler joined me with her five noisy kids. I decided to mention her husband's ridiculous behavior. She laughed merrily: "Oh, Fräulein Zarina, I know all about it. He confessed to me how he tried to make a pass at you and how furious you were. Don't give it another thought!"

And then she proceeded to tell me about her romance with Erler, who at the time was studying—of all things—for the priesthood in the Catholic Church. "We wanted to get married and could think of one solution only. We tried—unsuccessfully for quite a while—to get me pregnant, so as to enable Fritz to break away from his Seminary. Our ruse eventually worked. Fritz was jubilant when I informed him about being with child. Then finally we got permission from the church to get married," Frau Erler exclaimed happily.

Listening to these outpourings, I silently admired Frau Erler for her determination in wanting to get married to a such a man—and to produce so many children with him. It must be true love!

*July 18, 1942* It has been raining for three days now. The guests, including me, spend their time in the dining hall, playing cards or talking. I busy myself with embroidering a table cloth. We have some nice people here: the wife of an Army captain from Hannover with her two children (he is away at the front), a Frau Zehner from Mainz with her two year old little boy Franzl, also some older couples. The food is good and plentiful.

At night Frau Zehner laid the cards for me and predicted a long trip and a "handsome boyfriend with lots of money." Idle dreams! All eligible men are at the front!

*July 22, 1942* It is still raining—worse than ever. A whole week of nothing but rain! Our spirits have sunk quite low. We are trapped in the inn and bored to death. The children, eight in all, are beginning to get on our nerves with their wild games, their fights, their screaming and yelling. To make matters worse, we are cut off from any news. The newspapers have stopped coming and the only radio in the house has broken down.

*July 23, 1942* It rained a bit less and I ventured out for a walk. I quite unexpectedly discovered an old cave. In its interior I found a stone cross and a memorial tablet into which in (now barely visible) middle-high German script, a prayer was carved.

I had come across the hermit's hide-out, which is tied in with the Willenstein legend: The unhappy girl went to the cave to see the old monk and asked for his help. He refused to marry the ill-fated lovers without Lord Willenstein's blessings, and so it all ended in tragedy. Not far below the cave I could hear the waters of the brook, rushing by: centuries ago it must have been much deeper. Nobody could drown in its shallow waves today.

The old script, which I was partially able to decipher, has almost convinced me that this German medieval "Romeo and Juliet" tragedy may be based on truth: the inscription asks the reader to pray for the souls of the unhappy lovers.

Following an impulse I knelt before the cross and said a prayer, when suddenly I heard heavy rumbling. A thunderstorm had surprised me. It turned dark in the cave, rain was pouring down and lightning flashed. I was trapped there and spent a ghostly hour alone before the medieval cross. Once, as a stroke of lightning outside filled the cave for a split second with an eerie green glow, I seemed to sense the presence of a figure in a monk's cowl looming in the background.

My imagination was playing tricks on me, but still—I was scared and glad to get out as soon as the downpour stopped.

*July 24, 1942* In the morning it was still raining, and half in jest, half in earnest I decided to spite the old rain-god by applying some "anti-rain magic." I put on my brightest summer dress—white with little red blossoms and a red satin sash (my own creation, recently made from curtain material). While dressing I *willed* that the rain should stop by chanting over and over: "Today the weather will change!" During breakfast I informed the astonished guests: "Cheer up! The sun will soon be shining!" No one believed me, since we just had another downpour.

But, lo and behold—in about an hour the clouds suddenly parted, disappeared in an inkling, and for the first time in almost two weeks, we saw the sun again.

The sunshine has brought the newspapers back. I read quotations from a speech which Secretary Backe delivered on July 19 in the region of Oberdonau (Upper Danube Valley): "Today we have reached a turning point. Thanks to the efforts of our 'Wehrmacht,' the problem of 'Lebensraum' ('living space') in our Fatherland is already solved. Now great tasks are set before the German farmers: to populate the new regions and to win them for the German nation . . . . The Eastern expanses are now ready to be Germanized and the German farmers will have to pour their blood into these new lands."

This shows clearly enough the intent of the Nazi government not only to subdue but even to eliminate the people of the conquered Eastern countries, including the Baltic States. In accordance with this, the report also quoted SS "Reichsführer" Himmler: "It is our task to Germanize the East, not in the meaning of former times, i.e. to force upon the local inhabitants German language and German laws, but to take care that in the East only people should live who have German blood!" This is worse than I suspected. Once again the Baltic States are caught in a power struggle between East and West—true to the historic pattern of seven hundred years of strife—and once again we are the losers.

*July 25, 1942* It is not just my country that is caught in a power struggle; I too am torn. On one hand I feel an immense grudge against the political governments of Soviet Russia and Nazi Germany for having caused death, destruction and untold misery to millions of lives—on the other hand I am fervently clinging to my belief in the "Brotherhood of Man."

My entire existence has been drastically altered due to the war. I have met cruel and nasty people, but I also have had the experience of a refugee being treated with much kindness and sympathy.

I like the miller and the guests in the Mill here: they all mean well; they all take a genuine interest in each others' problems; they all have their crosses to bear caused by the war, by the bombings and by the separation from their fathers, brothers, husbands, sons, who are at the front.

They are Germans, I am a Latvian—our backgrounds differ, but fate has made us live together for a while. How and where does the "Brotherhood of Man" begin? Certainly not by hating each other! These

German women and children are not automatically guilty of the Nazi atrocities, just as I am not automatically guilty of the Soviet atrocities, having come from Soviet Latvia.

Maybe the answer is that I should think of myself as a human being among human beings—and make the best of it.

*July 26, 1942* Ever since my "anti-rain magic" ritual the weather has been perfect, with sunshine every day. The guests have jokingly nicknamed me "La Sylphide" ("the Wood-Elf") and are claiming that I have peculiar powers. Mother hearing this remarked dryly: "Don't let them turn your head. You are conceited enough as is."

*July 27, 1942* One year ago the only son of the mill owner was killed at the Russian front. He was only nineteen years old. For seven hundred years the mill has been in the Klug family, there always was a son to take over, when the old miller died. This chain from one generation to the next is now broken. The Klugs have only one daughter left, no other direct male heir. Frau Klug cried bitterly telling me this.

Later she mentioned that her daughter is going to marry her first cousin who bears the same family name, and thus hopefully the long line of descendants will not be interrupted. It has been quite difficult to obtain this marriage permission: the new laws in Germany forbid marriages between first cousins.

*July 28, 1942* While we here in the Mill are living in comparative peace and safety, terrible battles are going on in Russia: Rostow has been captured and the Don River crossed by German troops.

*July 29, 1942* This afternoon, I went for a walk in the woods with Frau Erler. We came to a clearing and Frau Erler told me a fascinating tale which is not found in any history book.

In the year 1862, King Ludwig I of Bavaria visited the Palatinate and was received with much splendor by the Baron von Gienanth, to whom all the land in Karlstadt belonged. In honor of the seventieth birthday of the King, this clearing in the woods was prepared for a grand celebration: Tables and benches, arcades, a bowling alley, a rifle range, a dance floor were set up and a maze was laid out, consisting of numerous intertwining paths between tall bushes. The king celebrated his birthday in the midst of the woods in great splendor. The most fascinating attraction of the party was the famous dancer, Lola Montez, the king's mistress, who gave a moonlight performance on a specially built stage.

But the royal splendor has vanished long ago, the nobles have gone to their graves, moss covers the dance floor. The bowling alley, the rifle range, and the maze are now an overgrown thicket. Only the wind has not changed. It is still singing its song in the trees.

In the evening, we, too, celebrated a birthday; not that of King Ludwig, but of Frau Almsburg, the army captain's wife. At three o'clock in the morning, I proposed a moonlight walk. The dark pines along the road stood in two rows like sentries on parade; the brook murmured in the valley; high above us stars were sparkling. We walked down the road arm-in-arm and sang. We ended up by dancing a country jig. Even the elderly captain, who is 20 years older than his wife, having just arrived on furlough from the front, jumped around and joined the chorus:

> "A nightcap with a tassel
> Goes around and round with us.
> Dideldum, dideldum, dum, dum!"

And all this spontaneous joy of life after having consumed nothing stronger than "Ersatz"—coffee! For a few hours the war, its horrors and its dangers had sunk into oblivion.

*July 30, 1942* Today some of our ladies went for a walk to the German fortifications at the French border, the "West-Wall." They told me about bunkers, built-in tank traps, burned out tanks and deserted villages. They even had been on French soil. It sounds frightening but also fascinating. These are impressions from the war of the battle fields, a totally different aspect as compared to war at the home front—the nightly air-raids.

*July 31, 1942* I sat on my favorite spot on top of a hill at the edge of the woods. Far in the distance, I heard a muffled rumbling and assumed that it was a thunderstorm brewing. But, later on, I learned that it was gunfire and bombing. English bombers have raided Saarbrücken and also Kaiserslautern. There is a general rumor that the British Army plans to establish the "Second Front" this summer. That means the invasion of the continent!

*August 3, 1942* Frau Almsburg showed me an English leaflet which her children had found in the fields and which must have been dropped by an English airplane. It was printed in German, of course, and described the heavy losses of German submarines. The leaflet called the submarines "floating coffins." It is strictly forbidden to read any "enemy leaflets" or to pass them on to other persons. Now, Frau Almsburg and I are guilty of the crime of spreading "enemy propaganda,' which means execution by the sword, if caught.

*August 4, 1942* Life here is monotonous, but restful. In the afternoon I took the children with me for a walk in the woods. I told them stories I had heard from my mother about Sutta the tomcat, about the two frogs, the silver-fox, the little pony and the glass mountain. The kids, of course, were enraptured. My favorite is Andreas, a blue-eyed little boy with flaxen hair. The radiance of his innocent eyes seems to reflect a shimmer from a paradise long lost to us adults. Andreas and the other little ones do not yet know what forces of evil are raging on this our planet Earth.

*August 7, 1942* I have made friends with my old peasant woman, who so loves to tell stories. I visit her frequently. She reminds me of Grandma Amalia with her frail build, her blue eyes and her silvery white hair. I promised to send her a scarf from Frankfurt.

*August 8, 1942* Tomorrow we are leaving, and so we went for a last walk through the Karlstal. The hills and valleys, ripening cornfields and orchards lay before us in bright sunshine, and white clouds sailed slowly through a blue sky. I certainly hate to leave and go back to the city life where there is noise, restlessness, dust, sooty smoke, and the perpetual danger of air raids.

*August 9, 1942, Heidelberg* Mother and I are stopping over in Heidelberg for a few days on our way back to Höchst. We are staying in the "Holländer Hof." Tonight we went for a walk along the river Neckar. Before us was the panorama of old Heidelberg, its castle perched high above the town houses.

*August 10, 1942, Heidelberg* This morning we visited the castle. The guide there told us some of its fascinating history: "The oldest part was built in the 13th century. The castle was the residence of the Counts-Palatine. In the courtyard, tournaments were held with the ladies watching from the window of their "Kemnate" ("Ladies' quarters"). We saw the old kitchen and its huge fireplace where whole oxen could be roasted on long spits. We walked through the large banquet ball to which wine was pumped from one immense barrel in the cellar.
    In the chapel are statues of the Counts-Palatine who resided in this castle. The guide continued: "The castle was destroyed by the French,

who, after the French Revolution broke into Germany in 1793 and swept through the southwestern part of the country, looting, burning, and murdering." One hundred fifty years have since elapsed, but human nature has not changed one iota.

In the restored part of the castle, there now are splendid halls decked out with wall and ceiling paintings, beautiful silk tapestries, old tile stoves and antique furniture.

Finally, we descended into the cellar to see the world-famous wine barrel which can hold 222,000 liters (approximately 55,000 gallons). There we heard the story of the dwarf Perkeus, court jester and also wine butler to the counts, who supposedly drank 15 bottles of wine daily.

These excursions into the past give me a greater sense of my own time in history. I am but a speck in a never-ending chain of generations and events. Thinking in those terms, the daily troubles besieging me seem to lose some of their importance.

*August 11, 1942, Höchst* On the train back to Frankfurt, 1 overheard a conversation between two soldiers who were just returning from the Russian front. "I was present at the capture of Sevastopol. and took part in the battle before the 'Maxim Gorki' fortress. I'm telling you, brother, the Russians fought like desperate savages, but we finally took the fortress."

"I am coming from the Peninsula Chersonnes," related the other, "where the rest of the beaten Soviet Army had withdrawn. You never saw such killing before, man! We piled the dead up—friend and foe alike—and used them as barricades, from behind which we could take aim and shoot."

Both fell silent. After a while, the second continued: "In the hot weather the bodies decomposed fast and the stench was unbearable. In the waters of the Black Sea, puffed-up corpses were floating like huge fish."

I was amazed that in spite of all these terrible experiences, both soldiers seemed very optimistic and quite certain that Germany would win the war,

*August 12, 1942* On our first night at home, about 2:00 A.M., the sirens began to howl and soon after we felt powerful detonations. Frightened, we hurried into the basement shelter. This morning, we heard that English bombers have heavily raided Mainz which is about 30 kilometers from Frankfurt. Everyone is very upset.

*August 13, 1942* Last night, again at 2:00 A.M., we had another alert and felt heavy explosions in the distance. The English once more have bombed

Mainz and completed their destructive task started the night before, in a most thorough way. The whole town is in ruins! The famous cathedral and seven churches are destroyed, and the old part of town is erased. The damage is said to be even greater than in Cologne.

*August 15, 1942* I bought gas masks for Mother and me. We have been advised that in case of a "direct hit" (i.e. a bomb falling straight into our apartment house) the ensuing destruction is liable to cause so much dust in the air-raid shelter underneath that we might suffocate.

*August 16, 1942* Yesterday I was fortunate to be able to purchase fifty pounds of potatoes. I dragged the heavy bag home on my bicycle, which again is in good shape. It was fixed during my vacation in the I.G. Farben machine shop. The supervisor there took pity on me.

*August 17, 1942* At lunch, I met Dr. Dehren, who is depressed and miserable as usual. He has broken the engagement to his girl because the German doctors refuse to let him get married.

My former boss Dr. Haller is now in Berlin holding a job as middleman between I.G. Farben and a research group on the Baltic coast. He visited our department today. Upon my question in what type of research he is now involved, Dr. Haller made it a point to avoid the issue. I have a feeling that this project is not to be discussed.

I met our new boss Dr. Gellinger. He was very polite, but I sensed that he was appraising me while discussing professional matters. I wonder how I'll get along with him.

It always amazes me anew to observe how we all here in the department are play-acting: the boss pretending to be infallible and all-knowing, the chemists subservient and simultaneously politely critical, the technicians obedient, the workmen passive and disinterested. In actuality all persons working here have rather strong opinions, which they dare to expound only among trusted friends. The Nazi regime has put its unmistakable stamp on all public relationships. No true freedom of expression is possible in the Third Reich. We all are forced to wear masks. My mask is slipping ever so often.

I'm afraid I'm an unruly spirit!

*August 18, 1942* Sure enough, today I had ample opportunity to prove that I am indeed an unruly spirit and not given to knuckling under.

Our Technical Director, Dr. Lehr, asked me to come to his office. I had no idea what he wanted and so I was very curious. Dr. Lehr received me politely and then, without preliminaries, told me about complaints from several older chemists: "You, Fräulein Zarina, a woman, so young and not even a native of Germany, are holding a very good position as group leader of a laboratory. There is much envy because you have been sent frequently to technical meetings and to visits in associated laboratories which, as you know, is considered a favor."

"Dr. Lehr, I have not traveled for the fun of it but because I had been ordered to go. Why was my job as head of a laboratory not given to any of these complaining gray-haired or bald-headed gentlemen long before I even appeared on the scene?"

Dr. Lehr's evasive and surprising reply was: "Don't forget, it is the first time in 80 years of our Company's history that a woman chemist, and so young at that, holds such a job. In Germany, the male has always been in a preferred position in all aspects of life and we can't break this rule either. We have given you an associate, Dr. Fehrig. Normally you should be his senior in rank, if not in years, but we can't do this to a man who holds a degree similar to yours. To have a female supervisor would be an insult to his male dignity. You should know that at I.G. Farben you will never achieve a higher position than the one you have now!"

Dr. Lehr gave it to me point blank. I was shocked but kept my control. I told him coldly: "I will return as soon as possible to my home country, where such traditional discrimination against women was never the way of life." After a brief silence I added: "Furthermore, I want you to realize that you have just killed my initiative and my interest in doing a good job?" A look of perplexity crossed Lehr's face. I turned and walked out of the office.

*August 19, 1942* At 9:30 this evening, a special announcement came through: English, American, Canadian and deGaullist troops, in the strength of one division, this morning attempted to land in Dieppe on the French Coast, but were driven back and had many losses. The Germans captured 1500 prisoners, including 16 Canadian officers. I assume that this invasion attempt is the result of the meeting on the Crimea between Churchill and Stalin.

*August 20, 1942* Lydia, our little Russian cleaning girl, told me that last night several Russian laborers got hold of wood alcohol and drank it. One of them died, the rest are very sick. "We Russians here are all homesick and terribly depressed. We hate to live in barracks. Life is unbearably dull and monotonous. Oh, if only I could get back to the Crimea!" And Lydia broke out in tears. I promised to invite Lydia and

Natasha to my home, as soon as I could get permission for them to leave camp for a day.

*August 22, 1942* Saturday afternoon. I decided to visit Frankfurt and the birthplace of Goethe, Germany's greatest classical author, particularly now since the possibility of damage or destruction of this shrine is greater than ever.

The house shows the wealth of the Goethe family. I particularly liked the kitchen of Goethe's mother. On the stone hearth under a huge hood I saw an assortment of old kettles, pans and pots. A manually operated water pump in the kitchen, 200 years ago, was a sensational innovation. The illumination was poor: only two tiny oil lamps gave some light. On one of the walls copper baking moulds for cookies in the shape of animals, stars, flowers, and lobsters were gleaming in the semi-darkness. The staircase in the big entrance hall has a cast-iron railing decorated with the family initials.

On the second floor, the "bel étage," are the sitting rooms. The walls are covered with linen tapestry and decorated with oil paintings showing Chinese motifs. The furniture consists of tables and high-backed chairs with silk upholstery. Across the hall in the music room is a red clavichord on which the young boy Wolfgang and his sister Cornelia used to practice.

On the third floor is the room where Goethe was born on August 28, 1749. In it now stands a bust of the young poet. On the pedestal lies a wreath sent as a birthday greeting in 1939 from Shakespeare's birthplace in Stratford-on-Avon, just two days before the war started. No more wreaths have since been sent from England. This, again, impressed upon me the senselessness of this war between two nations who both possess such a profound cultural heritage.

I also saw the rooms of Goethe's sister, Cornelia, and the reception room of his mother, who, as wife of a State Councilor, on Thursdays and Saturdays entertained the ladies of Frankfurt.

In Goethe's own room, the walls are decorated with silhouettes of his parents and of his girlfriends, Kätchen Schönkopf and Charlotte Buff. The latter is the heroine of the novel which made Goethe famous: *The Sorrows of Young Werther.* He placed Charlotte's silhouette on the wall opposite his bed so that in the mornings his first glance and in the evenings his last fell upon her image.

In Goethe's father's library, long shelves full of old books bound in pigskin embossed with gold cover two walls from floor to ceiling. The father was a well-educated man, very serious and very strict, 19 years older than Goethe's mother. How determined and strict he was is indicated by his insisting on having a window put into the fire-wall of his house, against the city's building ordinance. He wanted to check up on young Wolfgang's late homecomings. However, the youthful sinner outwitted his father by sneaking into the house through the kitchen entrance.

The boy entered the house from a small back yard, where nowadays ancient linden trees are casting heavy shadows over a white stone bench and some white statues seem to be playing hide-and-seek in the bushes. In Goethe's time the view was unobstructed all the way to the Main River, and the Taunus mountains were visible in the distance. Now the yard is enclosed by a high stone wall.

Goethe's writings are part of my life, and I felt at home in his house, although transferred 200 years back to another time. I greeted the black silhouettes in Goethe's room and particularly Kätchen and Charlotte like old acquaintances: "How lucky you girls are! Your young friend Wolfgang made you immortal. You will be known as long as his writings are known!" Hours like these let me forget as if by magic the depressing present and give me new strength to carry on.

(In 1944 the Goethe House was destroyed in an air raid. Only one fragment of the stone staircase was found. Fortunately, the furnishings had been stored in a safe place and after the war were reinstalled in a reconstructed building.)

*August 23, 1942* Last night was filled with terror. At midnight, the sirens began to howl and heavy gunfire started. We hurried into the basement. Soon we heard bombs exploding close by. We put our gas masks on. The whole house shook and waves upon waves of a tremendous air pressure deafened us for a while. It was a terrible experience to sit completely helpless in our tiny air-raid shelter, not knowing what the next moment might bring. Suddenly we heard a rustling noise and then a great crash next door.

Shortly thereafter, the people in the neighboring basement broke a hole in the brick wall partition between our two cellars and one by one crept into our shelter. Their house was on fire and they could no longer escape in any other way. Most of the houses in the neighborhood had been hit by incendiary bombs and were in flames. Any moment our house, too, could catch on fire and then we all would be trapped.

Suddenly the air-raid warden in charge of our city block appeared in our shelter and shouted: "Leave instantaneously! A delayed-action bomb has been found in your back yard which may explode any moment and kill you all!"

We all rushed out of the cellar, but I, on impulse, dashed up into our apartment and, in a few seconds, gathered some clothes and bed covers into a sheet. Countless fires all around us in the neighboring houses were burning making a loud rustling noise, and their huge flames illuminated our apartment with an eerie orange glow. On our stone balcony an incendiary bomb was spinning round and round, in the process splashing burning phosphorus in all directions. Any moment expecting an explosion, I ran downstairs with my bundle and joined the others who by now were standing on the opposite side of the street watching a row of houses go up in flames.

Suddenly a woman fell into my arms screaming hysterically: "Curse you, Adolf Hitler, killer, murderer, Satan's accomplice! Go to Hell, where you belong!" I knew I had to stop her lest these words put her in danger. I clamped my hand over her mouth and pressed her head against my shoulder, thereby managing to shut her up. Between sobs, she whimpered: "My husband, oh my God . . . my poor man! He is terribly burned . . . an incendiary bomb fell through the ceiling of our apartment . . . splattering burning phosphorus all over his face. He is badly hurt . . . they have taken him to the hospital. He will go blind . . . he will die! Oh God in Heaven, deliver us from evil!" I held her for a long time. She finally quieted down. We both stared silently into the flames on the opposite side of the street.

(After many months, this woman's husband was released from the hospital, his face badly scarred but fortunately not totally blind.)

The morning has come and the fires have been extinguished by our local fire brigade, but the whole town is covered with smoke. Our street is closed to traffic. All kinds of stuff that the owners managed to save are piled up in front of the burned-out houses: furniture, linen, household goods, bags and bundles Out of the blackened ruins, heavy clouds of smoke still rise. In the midst of all this, like a miracle our house is completely intact. We heard that eight magnesium incendiary bombs and half a dozen phosphorus bombs had fallen into our back yard and burned out there without causing any damage. A number of explosive bombs landed in the adjoining fields, tearing huge funnel-shaped holes in the ground. They had caused the changes in the air pressure that broke the windows and displaced furniture (including my heavy piano, which had sailed right across the room). One incendiary bomb fell through the roof and through the attic into the top floor where our 72 year old janitor Herzelt lives. He managed to extinguish it. The big "delayed-action bomb" which had so alarmed us last night turned out to be an ordinary large phosphorus bomb. It had buried itself deep into the ground and thus was mistaken for an explosive bomb. We will be allowed to move back into our house later in the day.

We are lucky; many neighbors have lost all their belongings. But fortunately no one was killed. One man said: "Now all that is left are my wife and my eight children!"

I have decided from now on to keep our clothes in bags in the basement. It is terribly inconvenient, but it is far safer in case of fire or bomb damage.

*August 26, 1942* This noon I had a long talk with Dr. Gellinger. Our new boss is of the opinion that I have been receiving preferential treatment due to my "feminine charms," as he expressed it, while his pale red-rimmed eyes in a long, haggard face watched me speculatively. "I shall be very strict and very just," he announced, "but I have the impression that you are a most stubborn young woman!"

"Exactly, and furthermore, I have the courage of my convictions, namely, that women can be just as successful professionally as men," I countered.

Gellinger's upper lip rose in a sarcastic smile, showing long, ugly protruding teeth. What an unpleasant character! At best there can only be an uneasy truce between us.

*August 27, 1942* I had another letter from Joachim von Velden, who seems to be in love with me. I wish I were in love, too! However, there is no one to be in love with. I would be so happy to again feel the flaming enthuasiasm, the yearning, that makes the whole world appear in a more beautiful light. Even Ingmar seems so far away, so unreal. Love even seems to transform one's own looks. Two years ago in Latvia, when I was so much in love with Ingmar, and so very happy, our laboratory cleaning woman at "Varonis" told me one morning: "Miss Zarina, your eyes grow daily more beautiful and more radiant. What may be the cause of it?"

I bet she guessed what the reason was!

*August 28, 1942* We have had a few quiet nights without alerts and I feel more rested. Today I went by bicycle into the Taunus villages to try and buy fresh fruit there. It is strictly forbidden to buy fruit directly from the farmers, but so far, I have not seen any berries, plums, apples or pears in the stores. In spite of all restrictions, people just go out into the country and buy fruit on the sly. If they are caught they are fined or even imprisoned, on grounds that they are "disturbing the German war economy." However, the "German war economy" does not seem to function very well regarding fruit and vegetables. This produce has completely vanished from the open market.

I was lucky to be able to buy a big basket full of yellow plums, which I carried home in triumph on my bicycle.

*August 31, 1942* Mother was rather nervous tonight. "Why are you always so quiet and so sullen?" she started to complain. "You remind me more and more of your Grandma Amalia. You look like her and you inherited her personality. She was an unattractive woman, pale and skinny and had no feminine charms! You are the same way."

"But Mother, if my grandma was all that plain and dull, how come she made such an excellent second marriage to a high official in Czarist Russia?"

"Oh, he was some years her junior and he didn't know any better. She seduced him, she was totally immoral!"

"What was so immoral about her?"

"Just that, that she married a younger man. A decent woman would be ashamed to marry a younger man!" Mother ranted on.

I could take it no longer. I rushed out of the room, took my bicycle and rode to Sulzbach, a small village nearby. There I sat on a bench and watched the evening colors fade in a glass-clear sky and the outline of the Taunus Mountains get more pronounced as dark blue shadow slowly began to spread over them. In the distance the red tiled roofs of the houses in Bad Soden glowed in the setting sun. The church steeple of Sulzbach pointed like an index finger into the sky. A precious feeling of peace and evening quietness was in the air. Slowly my inner turmoil abated and I felt new hope rising from some mysterious inner source.

Someday all will be well! Someday I will live in peace!

# CHAPTER EIGHT

## Shadows of Death

*September 2, 1942* Today in the movies, the newsreel showed the invasion attempt at Dieppe on the French Coast which ended in destruction of the American, Canadian and English forces. The seashore was covered with dead soldiers and with heavily damaged tanks, motor boats and ships—a terrible sight! The survivors—American, British, and Canadian soldiers—marched in long rows into captivity, some barefoot, many clad only in shirts. The Americans and Canadians were for the most part strong, tall, and good-looking men in spite of their disheveled appearance—certainly a lot better looking than our local "home front" heroes.

*September 8, 1942* Last night, we had another air raid. Incendiary bombs were dropped on Höchst, but fortunately, this time the bombs fell mostly into the vegetable gardens at the outskirts of town. One factory and the prison caught fire: both burned to the ground. From the windows on the top floor of our house, I saw heavy fires in Sulzbach, my peaceful tiny village. Its church steeple now rose above a sea of flames.

The tension in the air-raid shelter was unbearable. I trembled with fear, could take it no longer and rushed to the top floor. I'd rather face the danger head-on than try to hide from it. I'm beginning to understand why soldiers on furlough have repeatedly stated that they prefer the trenches at the front to the air-raid shelter at home. In the trenches they at least have a chance to defend themselves.

*September 11, 1942* Today, I attended a church wedding. The groom, our old custodian's son, soldier Hans Herzelt, who is stationed in Riga and who told me about conditions there, got a one-week marriage furlough and came back to wed in his home town. His bride Barbara wore black. In surprise I asked her why. "Because of the hard times," she answered. Her only decoration was a bouquet of white carnations. She was, thus, an unusual bride, but beautiful nevertheless—a tall girl with dark hair, olive-colored skin, pale lips and luminous black eyes. I experienced a strange foreboding, though, gazing at this "bride in black," a feeling of dark clouds approaching—of disaster.

*September 12, 1942* I had a chat with the wife of my old cobbler. She told me about her youth. She had been a cook in a large Jewish household in Berlin. At the same time, her future husband had served in Berlin as a soldier of the Imperial Guard. They met, fell in love, and got married. "The good Lord gave us six children, but then it pleased Him to take three youngsters back," the old woman stated quietly. "Now we have been married for 40 years. My husband spends all his days and part of the nights working hard repairing shoes, most of which are terribly worn indeed. I take care of the household and our small vegetable garden. During the day I also watch my grandchildren. My sons are all at the front and my daughters-in-law go out to work!"

"Are you happy with your life, Frau Schultze?" I was curious to know.

"Well, Fräulein, I am content. I trust in the Lord—and my old Johann and I are truly happy together. He is over seventy, but you know"—and there she lowered her voice to a conspiratorial whisper: "You know, he still has his fun in bed every night!"

I looked at her in surprise. A resigned quiet smile had spread over her withered face. Her pale blue eyes twinkled under wisps of gray hair. She had folded her hands under her bosom, whose sagging outline showed through a faded cotton dress.

"Her world is still in order," I thought. "She does not doubt God's wisdom or justice. She accepts her fate unquestioningly. But can that be called happiness?'

*September 13, 1942* The English have bombed Düsseldorf. This city seems to be next on their list after Cologne and Mainz. In Stalingrad, heavy fighting continues between Soviets and Germans.

*September 14, 1942* I saw a Japanese film: "The Wild Eagles of Nippon." It is a propaganda piece about the life and principles of the fighter pilots in the Japanese Air Force. Life in an academy for pilots is shown based on rather strict military discipline; there are also scenes from air fights.

To die for their country is considered heavenly bliss. The Japanese believe that the spirits of their war dead still continue to fight with their comrades if they take the ashes of the dead in urns with them into battle.

One thing indeed baffles me! I can't understand why the Nazi Government so intensely emphasizes the superiority of the "Aryan" race and yet shows so much admiration and friendship for the Japanese, an Asiatic people with their unique culture and traditions who, very likely, don't feel any sympathy at all for Europeans, including the Germans.

*September 15, 1942* Last night I committed a "blackout crime!" I forgot to pull the black shades down in my bedroom before turning the lights on. Shortly thereafter, I heard noises of an angry group right under my windows but I had no idea that all the excitement was caused by me. Then, there was a loud ring at the door. It scared me right out of my bed. Slipping a housecoat on I rushed to the door. Sure enough, there stood an officer. "You are under arrest!" he thundered.

"Good Heavens, what have I done?" I asked, thoroughly frightened.

"You are sending light signals to enemy bombers in the sky!" he roared.

Then I remembered that the black shades in my bedroom were still up and that my bed lamp was on. I dashed back to my bedroom and switched the light off. The policeman was right on my heels. "Don't try any tricks, young woman—you can't escape me!" and he grabbed me by the arm.

"Why should I want to escape you? I have done nothing. I just forgot to pull the shades down!" I countered, gaining some of my courage back.

"Anybody could say that, but now I have recognized you for what you are. You have an accent, you are not German: you must be an enemy agent—a spy." I had a fleeting vision of myself in iron and chains, a Mata Hari being made ready for shooting at the stake. The officer pulled himself up to his full height, all blazing righteousness and grandeur— "defender of the home front." The polished buttons on his uniform and the buckle on his belt gleamed menacingly in the shaded green light coming from our hall fixture.

Then I remembered my German passport. Little had I known that this unwanted document would come in handy. "Your accusations are sheer nonsense," I declared in a firm voice. "I am a chemist working at the I. G. Farben Plant here in Höchst. Furthermore, I am a German citizen!"

The officer demanded to see my passport. After having examined it most thoroughly—probably making sure that it was not forged—he announced grandly: "Ich werde Gnade vor Recht ergehen lassen. (I will put mercy before right.) But you have to pay a 100 mark fine." And with this he stalked out. He is coming back tomorrow to collect the money.

*September 16, 1942* I again have been ordered to go to Bayer-Werke in Leverkusen, but this time I will go part of the way by boat on the Rhine River.

*September 17, 1942, Cologne* The boat trip started in Mainz. Mainz is nothing but ruins. A man there told me that about a thousand people are missing under the rubble.

I had lunch on the boat, during which Rhine wine and fresh grapes were served. This is most unusual nowadays. After about an hour, we reached Bingen with its famous "Mice Tower" and then we continued through the lovely Rhine Valley. Here the river really is the "Green Rhine," as it is called in so many songs, because the green hills and vineyards are reflected in the water. Slowly we passed the castles and villages of Rheinfels, Rheinstein, Bacharach, Rüdesheim, Oberwessel, Boppard—all names reading like a wine list—then we came to the famous rock where, according to legend, fair Lorelei used to sit and comb her golden hair while singing irresistible songs, causing the shipwreck and death of many a sailor.

At Oberwessel, a group of Spanish girls, who were touring Germany—strangely enough, right in the middle of a war—embarked and soon began to sing Spanish songs, accompanying themselves with castanets. I have never seen Spaniards before and their coal-black hair, dark skin, black eyes and heavy makeup seem very exotic to me.

*September 18, 1942, Cologne* Everywhere I looked I saw ruins and rubble, heavy destruction caused by British bombers. Twenty thousand apartment houses have been destroyed and thousands of people killed. Someone told me that the British have dropped leaflets which read: "We will erase Cologne! Only the Cathedral will be left standing to indicate where Cologne once rose!" And, indeed, the Cathedral has not yet been damaged.

*September 19, 1942, Leverkusen* After work, I went for a walk through the park there, laid out by Carl Duisburg, the founder of the Bayer plant in Leverkusen, for the benefit of the factory workers. There is even a swimming pool supplied with warm water produced by the factory's turbines. One part of the park is called the Japanese Garden. It is decorated with Japanese statues, bridges and small temples, all of which Carl Duisburg received as presents from Japan.

He expressed the wish to be buried in the park and his grave lies among beautiful flower beds in a small circular marble temple. The goddess Flora carved in marble hovers over his grave and the white temple front bears this epitaph in gold letters: "Edel sei der Mensch, hilfreich und gut!" ("Noble be the human, helpful and good!")—a quote from one of Goethe's poems.

My escort, Dr. Sterker, who is a devout Christian, murmured: "The tomb of a pagan!" Above park and plant rises the world-famous Bayer cross on top of the administration building.

*September 20, 1942, Leverkusen* I spent the day with Dr. Sterker's family. After lunch, we went for a walk into the "Bergisches Land—Hilly Country" and the village Neuenkirchen. All houses and barns there are painted white with black half-timbering ("Fachwerk") and green shutters. Brightly polished brass door-knockers shine on black doors. The houses were built after the Thirty Years' War.

*September 24, 1942, Höchst* I saw a beautiful film about Rembrandt. All scenes are photographed in the style of his paintings: "between light and shadow." Rembrandt's fate is dramatic: He loves Saskia, his beautiful wife, with all his heart. She dies and he is very lonesome. Later on, he finds the second companion of his life, his servant Hendrikje, but she too dies and Rembrandt passes his old age in bitterness, loneliness and great poverty.

He paints his final picture, a self-portrait showing a miserable old man with a strange, almost insane smile. Before dying Rembrandt has a chance to once more see his painting of the "Marksmen's Guild" in Amsterdam, the painting which his contemporaries rejected. He realizes that he has not lived in vain and that his paintings will never be forgotten. Neither light nor shadow can hurt him any more! He is finally at peace.

This film has moved me deeply. Suffering seems to be a necessary part on the way to inner growth, to strength, to fulfillment, to peace! I derive comfort from that thought.

*September 25, 1942* Autumn is in the air. We have a lot of rain. In the mornings, the world appears gray and sad. I can't get rid of the feeling that my present living conditions are only of a temporary nature, that the present situation cannot last much longer, that a change must soon occur.

*September 26, 1942* This afternoon I had a strange encounter. I attended an organ concert at St. Catherine's Church in Frankfurt. Music by Bach, Schütz and Händel was played. On my way out I started a conversation with an older very refined lady. She mentioned that the present minister at St. Catherine's is a direct descendant of Pastor Fresenius, the priest who baptized Goethe in 1749. Suddenly she looked at me and said: "You are a chemist, aren't you?"

"Yes, how do you know?" I answered.

"I see it in your eyes!" was her surprising reply. I would have never thought that my profession can be read from my eyes. This lady must have peculiar intuitive powers.

*September 28, 1942* Bad news from Estonia and Latvia: Mother's brother Arno in Tartu has contracted tuberculosis; X-rays show big lesions in his lungs.

Aunt Erica, Uncle Adi's widow in Riga, has no income and does not know how to support herself and little Eva. No money can be transferred from here to the occupied Baltic countries, and there is no way to help our relatives. Mother and I are very depressed.

*September 30, 1942* Today at the beginning of the fourth "Winter Relief Action," the "Führer" delivered a speech. He started by ridiculing the "unsuccessful efforts" of Germany's enemies to cover up their "failures." Then he talked about the heavy battles at the Russian front, and the sufferings and sacrifices of the German soldiers there. He insisted that the German Army "certainly will take Stalingrad" and then he growled: "What we possess, we will never give back!" He also mentioned the bombings of German towns and promised "revenge."

*October 1, 1942* For the first time in two years I have visited a hairdresser. I am pretty good at creating my own hairdos, but since my supply of shampoo has finally run out, I had no choice. Shampoo can no longer be bought. I have to look well groomed, because tomorrow I'm scheduled to go to Berlin for another round of scientific meetings.

*October 2, 1942, Berlin* During my free time I went to visit my friend Nina from the refugee camp in Schwarzbach. She now lives with her parents in Berlin. Shortly after my arrival, Nina's sister appeared together with a part-Japanese, part-German girl, Fräulein Jokoy, a tiny, very Asiatic-looking person. I was quite surprised to see her suddenly start a Bible lesson in which we all had to take part. Jokoy told me that she is very happy in her

Christian faith. In her early youth, she suffered from the dichotomy of belonging to two races, but now she feels safe in God's hands and as a child of His kingdom. I can understand that this thought must be a great comfort to her.

*October 3, 1942, Berlin* In the afternoon, I met Dr. Haller, my former boss, and we strolled down the famous Kurfürstendamm. It was a sunny day and the street was filled with people, for the most part quite well-dressed, enjoying a walk or sitting in the sidewalk cafes sipping "Ersatz" coffee. Berlin has never been bombed.

Later we had supper at the hotel "Fürstenhof" in a very elegant dining room with a crowd of waiters and two "piccolos—little bus-boys" serving us. The table was lavishly set with at least five china plates and three crystal glasses as well as a generous assortment of sterling silverware for each place setting. After all these preliminaries, I expected an opulent meal, but was bitterly disappointed. The food consisted of a watery soup, a tiny bit of meat with two tablespoons of rice, very salty "Ersatz" gravy and some brightly colored jello made of cellulose, not gelatin. This dessert has no food value. It only serves as a stomach filler. With that, we drank "Ersatz" coffee and some wine. The waiters all assumed a busy attitude, rushing to and fro and changing empty plates for other empty plates. When this "luxurious" meal finally came to an end, the bill, accordingly, was "luxurious." But the whole situation struck us as so funny that Dr. Haller paid laughingly.

*October 4, 1942* Walter, who saved me and Mother when he was still at the German Embassy in Riga by helping us escape from Soviet-occupied Latvia, has now been transferred to Berlin. He phoned and we arranged to visit Potsdam.

First, we saw the old part of town which was built during the reign of Frederick the Great. The castle, St. Nicolaus Church, the Garnison Church and other old buildings are all constructed in the neoclassic style of the 18th Century. The architects of the "Third Reich" are trying to imitate this old style in their modern buildings. This is obvious after seeing buildings such as the "Neue Reichskanzlei," the New State Chancellory.

Frederick the Great is laid to rest in a vault of the Garnison Church together with his father, the "Soldier King" Frederick William I. Frederick the Great's sarcophagus is decorated with laurel wreaths. Old standards of the King's Grenadiers and of the Garde du Corps regiment are placed against the walls of the vault. The colors of the banners are faded and show holes torn by bullets during battles. Reverently, Walter and I stood before the coffins; then Walter whispered: "Here rests the King—contrary to his wishes—in a heavy coffin amongst memories of vanished glory. He wanted to be buried on the terrace of his beloved palace 'Sans Souci,' together with his greyhounds which he considered his best friends."

The guide's voice droned on: "In the year 1805, on November 4, this vault was visited at midnight by Czar Alexander II of Russia, King Frederick William II of Prussia and his wife, Queen Luisa, in order to ratify the Russian-Prussian Treaty at the coffin of the Great King.

"About one year later on October 25, 1806, Napoleon stood before the coffin of Frederick, whom he greatly admired, and spoke the words 'Sic transit gloria mundi!' More than 125 years later, Adolf Hitler, the "Führer," in this same church opened the first Reichstag of the Third Reich. In front of him sat Marshall von Hindenburg who, after the session, put wreaths with black and white ribbons on the coffins of the two kings in the vault."

The wreaths are still there. We saw them. They bear the inscription, "March 21, 1933." Walter made another comment: "Hindenburg was in his nineties, probably already touched by senility. Being at heart a monarchist, he must have taken delight in placing the wreaths decorated with the Prussian colors on the coffins of the royal forebears of his former lord and master Emperor William II."

"I wonder, Walter, what fuzzy notions may have prompted the old warrior to endorse Hitler's bid for power."

"No one will ever know, Irene, but Hindenburg's endorsement was the beginning of one of the greatest tragedies the world has ever seen." (In the final stages of World War II the royal coffins were removed to some salt mines, where they were discovered after the end of the war. They now have found a resting place in the Hohenzollern Castle in Hechingen, where the Prussian royal family originated.)

From the Garnison Church we went directly to "Sans Souci," Frederick the Great's charming palace, which lies in a beautiful park with flower terraces, fountains, white marble statues, shady alleys, green lawns and idyllic vistas.

I waxed romantic: "Can you imagine, Walter, how two hundred years ago, the lonely king supporting himself on a cane, took a walk on this terrace accompanied only by his little dog Biche."

"Frederick was an embittered unhappy old man in spite of all the glory and splendor surrounding him in Sans Souci. His was a miserable life, Irene."

After a rather skimpy but expensive supper—again in the "Fürstenhof"—Walter took me to the train back to Frankfurt. In a gentle voice tinged with a slight Russian accent (Walter had a Russian mother.) he joked as we were reaching the train:

"Do you remember, Irene, how ladies used to travel in Riga in the 'good old days'—with at least ten coffers, two hat boxes, containers and baskets filled with food? A train trip was a very exciting and very memorable event. But look at you now: one small bag and a reservation for the Wagon-lit. Very sophisticated indeed!" We stood on the platform before the first class sleeping compartment. The conductor called out: "Bitte einsteigen!" I jumped onto the doorstep and hanging on to the handrail, waved a last goodbye. Walter grabbed my hand and held on to it as long as he could.

The train picked up speed and I had to climb inside. Thus we parted. It was a nice time, but I must face reality.

*October 7, 1942* "Reality" nowadays mostly means to try to supplement our meager food supplies. This evening I again bicycled to Neuenhain in the mountains to see my farmer friends there in the hope of organizing some produce. I was lucky. They sold me pears and tomatoes. On the way home it got pitch dark. Suddenly an alert sounded. Searchlights began to play at the horizon, searching for enemy planes. It was an eerie feeling to be totally alone on a deserted road in the darkness of night with no place to hide in case of a bombing attack. I heard the humming of approaching enemy planes, but they flew on—further eastward.

I got home safely.

*October 8, 1942* At the home of Frau Knoth, our former landlady, I met an admirer of her daughter Ulrike. Karl used to be her classmate and is now a soldier on furlough from the Russian front. Short and good-humored, he spoke of the terrible conditions there, the heavy battles, and the almost unbearable stresses the soldiers have to endure. On his uniform he wore a red ribbon, a mark of distinction given to all participants in the Winter Campaign of 1941. The soldiers mockingly call this ribbon "Gefrierfleisch-Orden—the Order of the Frozen Flesh."

*October 13, 1942* A letter from Ingmar! His architectural studies are going well. The content is always the same: "I love you!" I have not seen him in one and a half years now. How will it all end?

*October 14, 1942* There is no heat in the apartment, and it is getting very cold. No improvement is to be expected. Central heating will no longer be provided. Mother is in a bad mood, and I am bearing the brunt of it: "If it weren't for you, I would now be in my warm bedroom in Riga. You should have left me behind when you went to Germany. I hate it here, I hate this country."

"Have you forgotten what happened to your sister in Estonia?"

"Ah, but she and her husband were 'capitalists.' I am a poor old widow and no one would have hurt me!"

"You aren't all that old: you are still in your fifties!"

Another hopeless and senseless argument! I cut it short by going out for a walk. This fight had again stirred up frightening memories. Uncle Karl was executed by the Soviets as soon as they crossed the border out of Estonia as a "capitalistic enemy" of the people. Mother's sister Meralda has since succumbed in Siberia to exhaustion and exposure to extreme cold. All this Arno had written us.

*October 15, 1942* Ulrike's friend Anna Schulz has died under tragic circumstances. I once met Anna at the Knoths.' She was a pleasant young girl, a student at the University of Frankfurt. "Last week Anna's landlady found her unconscious in the kitchen before the open gas stove," Ulrike told me. "Besides sticking her head into the stove, she also had swallowed concentrate of vinegar in a double effort to commit suicide."

"For goodness sake, Ulrike, what was the reason?"

"She was pregnant! Don't you remember Alf, the young engineer, with whom Anna was in love?"

"Oh yes, the fellow who for some unknown reason was never drafted!"

"The same! He refused to marry Anna. Furthermore, she found out that he had cheated a girl once before and had left her with an illegitimate child."

Ulrike continued her sad tale: "Anna was taken to the hospital in serious condition. A young minister, who lives in the same apartment building as she, visited her daily. She couldn't talk because her tongue was badly swollen. She just looked at him with sad questioning eyes. Shortly before her death, she was able to talk again and whispered: 'Don't you condemn me for what I have done?' The minister assured her that no one criticized her and that all hoped she would recover. Anna, gathering her last strength, tried to overcome death by sheer will power but it was too late." Tears were rolling down Ulrike's cheeks. I felt like crying, too.

*November 4, 1942* The battle in Stalingrad continues. The fights in the northern part of the town are terrible. The German troops have suffered great losses.

In Africa, the joint campaign of the American and British troops against the German Army has begun.

*November 5, 1942* The German troops in Africa were forced to retreat from their positions due to the overwhelming strength of the Americans and the British. The people here are all very depressed.

As usual I left work at 6:00 PM and went home by bicycle. The night was pitch black and to make matters worse it was pouring. The "blackout" cover on my bicycle lantern lets through only a few rays of light and I could see nothing. My ride home was very troublesome. First, I fell into a big hole on the factory grounds. I scrambled out and started off again, and promptly had a collision with the gatekeeper's booth at the exit. In the streets I went through several deep puddles and got my feet wet before finally reaching home. I assume these conditions were not unlike the conditions the people in the Middle Ages had to endure if they ventured out after dark. And here we are, at it again, in our technically far advanced progressive Twentieth Century.

*November 8, 1942* On account of the anniversary of the Armistice after World War I, the "Führer" delivered another speech in which, as usual, he dealt with the war situation and the air raids on German towns. He growled:

"We will repay the English with interest and compounded interest. The German inventor spirit does not rest, and we will direct such blows at the English that their sight and hearing will fail them!"

After this speech, our German neighbors have recovered some of their optimism.

*November 11, 1942, Leverkusen* I am again working for a few days in the Rubber Research Center of Bayer-Werke. This morning I discovered a Russian girl in one of the laboratories here, who seems very intelligent. I began to question her in Russian. Her name is Yevgenia Pavlovna Riabova and she is 23 years old, a slim, very tall, very pretty girl with blond hair and blue eyes.

Yevgenia was delighted to be able to communicate in her native tongue. The information she gave me was fascinating: "I am a chemical engineer, a graduate of the Academy of Sciences in Leningrad. It was very difficult to get into the Academy. We had 22 candidates for one place. We were called 'distinguished students' and therefore, besides our studies, were also offered many recreational possibilities: visits to the opera, the theatres, museums and concerts."

"Yevgenia Pavlovna," I interrupted her: "I, too, am a chemical engineer. I wonder, did you have many girl students in the Engineering department at the Academy?"

"Oh yes, about half of all students were girls!"

"In Latvia I was one out of three girls in a group of 150 males."

And then we compared our courses of study and found to our surprise and delight that we had both run through a practically identical program in order to get our degrees. "1 know what the reason is, Yevgenia Pavlovna: our Latvian University in 1919 simply took over the chemistry course program from the Czarist Polytechnical Institute in Riga and carried on in the old Russian tradition, although in Latvian."

Yevgenia asked me for my first name and father's name. "Irina Konstantinovna," she exclaimed, "It must have been fate that we have met! Horrible memories are haunting me. I can find no peace, no rest. I cannot sleep nights! Cruel nightmares torture me!" An expression of deep suffering crossed her beautiful face. "I must tell someone! Will you listen, Irina Konstantinovna?"

"Of course I will, Yevgenia!"

"It all began last year with the siege of Leningrad by the German Army. The German headquarters had sent a demand to our military leaders to have Leningrad declared an open city and to hand it over without resistance. Otherwise, Leningrad would be completely destroyed by the Germans. But we refused, and so the siege started. The German enclosure of the town was almost complete; transportation of food and fuel was cut off. It soon grew cold and, as all windows were shattered from gunfire and bombings, it was as cold in the interior of the houses as out in the streets:—40°C. The daily food ration per person consisted of 125 gr. (4 ounces) of bread and twice a day a soup made of flour and water. Twenty-two thousand people daily died of starvation. Of 7000 Academy students, 4000 died; one of them was my fiancé. I, too, was near death. My body was nothing but skin and bones, my limbs terribly swollen and my hair had fallen out. I was almost insane from hunger and once I ate glue and glycerin which I had found in the laboratory. Under such conditions, I still tried to study for my final exams."

"I took my exams in an ice-cold laboratory. All windows were broken. The professor tried to warm the room by lighting some gas burners. The body of a student who had died the day before still lay in a corner. Under such inhuman circumstances I received my Chemical Engineering degree. The memory of these horrible days will haunt me as long as I live."

I listened in shocked silence. Yevgenia continued: "The following spring I managed to get out of Leningrad—the city of the dead—I went to my parents in Rostov where I stayed for one month in a hospital. Slowly I recovered from my ordeal. My body began to fill out, my hair started to grow back."

"The German troops captured Rostov and I fell into their hands. I was transported to Germany for work—and here I am."

Deeply shaken, I put my arm around the girl's shoulder: "You have gone through hell, Yevgenia Pavlovna! You must be very strong to have been able to survive such incredible sufferings."

Tears wet her cheeks: "I had hoped that I might be able to use my chemical training here, but instead I have to do manual labor, scrubbing laboratory floors and cleaning glassware. I have to live in primitive barracks crowded together with uneducated and noisy girls. You can't imagine, Irina Konstantinovna, how desperately I am longing to have my own little place again where I can enjoy being alone in peace and quietness!"

"Dorogaya"—I said to her, "dear girl—hang on a while longer. The war can't last forever and then you will go home, back to your family and friends, back to your native soil! I, too, want to go home!—Ya tozhe hochu vernutsa domoi!"

We embraced and exchanged the Russian farewell: three kisses on the cheeks. I gave Yevgenia all I had with me—a big red apple and some cash. I wished I had had something more to give!

*November 12, 1942* On the train back to Frankfurt.

I had a couple of hours in Cologne before the train left and I went shopping. I couldn't believe my eyes when suddenly in a perfumery store I saw a lilac-colored intricately shaped powder box with the name "Vera Violetta" written on it in gold letters. Mother had had such a box when I was a little girl. She kept postage stamps in it. I used to admire the box for its lovely color and its graceful shape, which reminded me of a flower petal. The gold letters on it were so pretty. I asked Mother what they meant. "Vera Violetta," she said, and then she told me how before World War I, she used to send for this face powder to St. Petersburg. This cosmetic was manufactured in France and apparently very popular in Russia. A first inkling stirred in me, an inkling of the expanse of our world, of countries different from mine. I knew I lived in Latvia, I seemed to remember someone having mentioned Russia, but I had never heard of France!

The little lilac powder box held so many fascinating mysteries for me. And now I have found this magic box again. I'll give it to Mother for Christmas!

*November 13, 1942* Singing lesson with Fräulein Brettlein! She insists that my voice has a nice timbre. I have been taking lessons with her for half a year now, practicing up-and-down scales: do-re-mi-fa-sol-la-si-do and back: do-si-la-sol-fa-mi-re-do. I have done exercises and sight reading. Right now I am studying Schubert's serenade "Leise flehen meine Lieder." I love to sing, but I'm afraid I'm not talented enough.

*November 14, 1942* Today English troops captured the fortress of Tobruk. The Germans have retreated "according to plan." If this goes on, the Germans will soon be driven out of Africa, but right now, German submarines are inflicting heavy damages to the American and the British Forces. The Allies have to transport provisions to their troops in Africa, and a certain massing of their transporters and cruisers before the North African Coast is unavoidable. That is where the German submarines attack them. Today, again, a special announcement was broadcast: Two hundred thousand tons of Allied shipping has been destroyed in front of the African coast.

*November 15, 1942* Sunday. I have made good my promise and taken Lydia and Natasha for a visit to my home. These girls, apparently, have never seen a Western European apartment. Everything surprised them. "What is this?"

"This is an upright piano!"

"Does it belong to the Government?"

"No, it is mine!"

"How can it be yours? Big pieces like this always are nationalized."

Then, pointing to the wrought-iron chandelier—one of our few Latvian possessions—"But this surely is government property?"

"No, Lydia, I brought it with me from Latvia." Lydia eyed me dubiously.

The bathroom fixtures provided an unending source of excitement and delight. "Do you heat the water in pots on the stove and then pour it into the tub?" Natasha demanded.

"No, we have an automatic gas heater." I showed the girls how it worked.

"May we take a bath!" both girls shouted in unison. Soon they were sitting happily in the tub splashing warm water over each other and over the bathroom floor.

I could not feed them; there is not enough food in the house. The quality of our food is just about as poor as that of the Russians in the barracks: mainly potatoes, cabbage and beets.

I walked Natasha and Lydia back for supper to their camp.

*November 17, 1942* Besides singing lessons I'm also learning to type, using the "ten-finger-blind" system. This course is sponsored by the I.G. Farben administrative offices and I have signed up for it. To be able to type should be very useful.

*November 19, 1942* In the morning, I had an interesting talk with Dr. Scholl, another chemist who has been assigned to my laboratory. In contrast to my associate Fehrig, Scholl is a grumpy impolite fellow. Furthermore, he is quite deaf and has a speech impediment. His main purpose in life seems to be to expound Nazi theories.

He talked about heredity and inbreeding in connection with the Nazi German racial ideas. He told me that at the Egyptian Court, several thousand years ago, the laws of heredity and inbreeding had been investigated and used in the royal family.

With great enthusiasm Scholl spouted forth: "These ancient studies have now been repeated in Germany, experimenting with mice. Mice from one litter were paired and, in the next generation, the same was done with their offspring, etc. The first generations showed many degenerative traits of inbreeding but the sick mice were always eliminated and only the sound ones were allowed to pair. This was continued up to the 10th generation, after which no more signs of inbreeding appeared, because by this method of selective pairing, all degenerative genes had been eliminated.

Starting with the 11th generation, only the 'pure and healthy blood' was inherited. The same was done in the royal house of Egypt. Cleopatra, for instance, was the daughter of a brother and a sister who were also children of a brother and a sister. Cleopatra's great-grandfather had first married his sister and after she died, had taken his own daughter for his wife. So, Cleopatra had only two grandparents and only two great-grandparents."

"By our standards, this is incest and a most terrible thing, but in those Egyptian Pharaoh days, it was looked upon as necessary in order to secure the purity of the royal blood." Thus Dr. Scholl.

I'm not sure what he wants of me. Does he want to make a Nazi convert out of me? Or does he want me to take part in breeding experiments à la Egyptian Court? Alas, I have no brother! What insanity!

*November 20, 1942* Sure enough, I was right. Today Scholl informed me that I was the "prototype" of the Nordic Race and therefore "superb breeding material." He tried to interest me in taking part in a special program to that effect.

"Not far away from Munich," Scholl said, "is a 'Breeding Institute for Humans' named 'Adlerhorst—the Eagles Nest'—where young, healthy and specially selected SS Men are assigned to turn young girls into 'single mothers'. In this way, the government plans to further a numerous, healthy, new rising generation."

I almost did not believe my ears but Scholl assured me that this is the truth. After all, if an SS Man, bearer of the Golden Party Badge, insists that things like these happen in Germany, I might as well believe him.

*November 21, 1942* At my dentist's I met a fellow chemist, a Dr. Schumann who has recently returned from America to Germany. It was not clear to me how he managed to reach Europe from California, where he had worked for 14 years. He seems to be in his late thirties, has an unlined face, but graying hair. Timidly, he asked me for a date. We plan a visit to the theater in Frankfurt. I made the mistake of telling Mother. She, of course, disapproves and we had another fight.

*November 22, 1942* Day of Remembrance! We went to our little old Unterliederbach Church. Mother asked me to go with her. She apparently is no longer mad at me. The memory of our family members and good friends who all had died within a short period had softened her heart: my father, her brother Adi, her sister Meralda, Uncle Karl, my friends Wolfgang and Alfred. Mother and I both cried during the service.

I must learn how to control myself better. Mother seems to be near a nervous breakdown. She has lost a tremendous amount of weight and is skin and bones, which, of course, aggravates her condition! I, too, am starving, but being young I am better able to withstand the deprivations and stresses of our daily life.

*November 24, 1942* Today, one of my laboratory workers, young Kätchen, told me about her fiance, 21 years old, whom she had visited last week in a hospital in Berlin: "Seppl was badly hurt at the Russian front, he has lost one hand and his sight. After he regained consciousness in his hospital bed and found out that he was blind and a cripple, he wanted to die. He refused all food for eight days. Finally, in order to save him, the doctors told him a lie that there was hope he might partially regain his eyesight. This helped Seppl to overcome his first utter despair." In answer to my question whether she still intended to marry him, Kätchen replied with a firm "yes." Her big brown eyes had filled with tears and I saw deep suffering in her pale young face.

*November 27, 1942* Today brought a shocking announcement from Army headquarters. The French fleet sank itself this morning at the port of Toulon because German and Italian troops had occupied Toulon the night before. This heroic action on the part of the French Navy has had a greatly upsetting effect on the German people. The news from the Russian front is likewise disturbing: Soviet forces have broken through German lines in the vicinity of the Don River and at Rshev; they have reached Toropez which is only about 200 km away from Latvia.

*November 28, 1942* Today I had my date with Dr. Schumann. We went to a Gerhard Hauptmann play in Frankfurt: *Und Pippa Tanzt* (*And Pippa Dances*)—an allegory, a fairy tale from the Silesian Mountains. I found the play rather strange. Afterwards, we had some "Ersatz" coffee at Café Rumpelmayer—one of Frankfurt's landmarks. I wore my red silk dress, which I had given a new look by appliquéing a big black velvet flower onto the skirt. Schumann told me about his life in the USA. He held a job as production manager in Los Angeles:

"I earned a good salary, had my own car, and was very active in sports, particularly tennis and golf. In the USA this is considered a fashionable way of life. When the war started, I decided to leave because I could not pretend to be hostile toward Germany, which I was expected to do. I traveled over Asia and Russia back to Europe. In Moscow, I lived in the Intourist Hotel and saw only those parts of Moscow which my Intourist guide was permitted to show a foreigner. I came to Frankfurt in early 1941 and got a job with I. G. Farben, but I must confess I miss the good life in America."

I found Schumann's account interesting, but I find him a bit dull.

*November 29, 1942* Today is the first Sunday of Advent. We went to morning prayer in our little old church which was nicely decorated with pine branches and an Advent wreath with four candles. Just as in St. Peter's Church in Riga, one more candle will be lit each following Sunday.

Christmas is in the air. I had a feeling of expectancy although we have nothing good to expect.

*December 1, 1942* This morning started with much excitement in our department. The boss, Dr. Gellinger, called a meeting in the course of which he severely criticized one of our fellow chemists, Dr. Nehr. Dr. Nehr got mad and, turning white, suddenly banged his fist on the table right in front of Gellinger and told him in plain language what he thought of him. I could not help feeling pleased that finally a man stood up in this country where utmost servility is the law.

I applauded inwardly while our boss, also turning white, withdrew to the door and saved his dignity by walking out. The meeting was over and we all filed out. Behind the door, Gellinger tried to cover up his defeat by grinning sarcastically. But this grin transformed his face into the sad mask of a clown: white face, red-rimmed eyes, lopsided downward-curving mouth, wisps of hair sticking out at the sides and on top above his high forehead.

*December 2, 1942* At lunch, I met a very interesting man, a certain Herr von Lorch, a Baltic German. He told me that he is the newly-hired interpreter for the Russian workers' camp. He gave some details of his fascinating life. "During World War I, I was a fighter pilot in the Russian Army. My chief was Prince Alexander Michailovich, a cousin of the Czar. The prince was a very pleasant man, but his wife, Princess Xenia, the sister of the Czar, although beautiful, was very proud and arrogant."

After the Revolution, Herr von Lorch lost his estates and was forced to find some kind of occupation. "I became a ballet master. My wife was the ex-prima ballerina of the Opera in Kiev. Together we gave Russian Ballet performances and in this way made a living. We traveled all over Europe: Greece, the Balkan States, Italy and France. I was present at the funeral of Prince Alexander in Nice. Princess Xenia died two years ago in Denmark. As you may know, her mother, the old Czarina, had been a Danish princess."

In the course of our conversation, we found out that Lorch is the uncle of my fellow high school student in Riga, Ina von Lorch. We marveled at how small the world is!

*December 3, 1942* This morning I went to City Hall to try to get some ration cards for clothing. I had to wait in line for about two hours and, during that time, I saw and heard of much misery.

Wounded and crippled war veterans quite often live in extreme poverty. They get very little financial support, only 28 marks per week, and with the exception of their worn uniforms have no other clothes, nor underwear, nor warm winter coats. I was very amazed, indeed, to hear about this. I expected that the very least the Nazi government could do for their war veterans who have lost their health and frequently also their limbs in this Nazi war, would be to take proper care of them. But the veterans were told: "This is the fourth war year, and textiles are no longer available."

*December 4, 1942* Heavy fighting has died down on the battlegrounds in Russia and in Africa. Local skirmishes are still going on there but, lately, no more important or unusual news has been broadcast.

*December 5, 1942, Saturday.* I took Lydia with me to our old pastor's home in Unterliederbach. He lives with his two unmarried elderly sisters in a parsonage next to the ancient church. The old ladies received us with coffee and homemade fruit cake. (The surrounding farmers occasionally help them out with food supplies.) Lydia was delighted. Furthermore, the ladies had made a collection and presented Lydia with an assortment of wool sweaters, pullovers, wool stockings and a skirt. Later Lydia had an opportunity to duly admire the parish menagerie, consisting of one old dog and two skinny cats. After that I escorted Lydia back to her barracks.

The local Germans do feel sorry for the Russian slave laborers. I have frequently observed our plant workers who are fortunate enough to have little farms on the side, hand sandwiches and fruit to the Russian boys and girls. This is strictly forbidden by the Nazi Government and is punishable. But the spirit of charity is strong.

*December 6, 1942* We went to Giessen to visit some Baltic friends there. On the train we met a soldier, on furlough for the first time in two years. He was quite excited because the train was approaching his home town. Asked about his experiences in Russia, he told us: "Turkestanian regiments are now fighting on the German side against the Soviet Army at the River Terek in Russia. They seem to be proud to wear German uniforms and they are fighting like devils for the German cause. Soviet prisoners are used as engineers and scouting patrols in the German Technical Corps." The soldier concluded: "Generally speaking, we can depend on them. They are fighting with much bravado." This puzzles me. Maybe the explanation lies in the fact that many of the Soviet soldiers or their families were victims of the Red Terror and therefore, like the Latvians, feel no loyalty for their Soviet masters.

*December 13, 1942* Early this morning there was a ring at the front door. Mother opened and came back with tears in her eyes. Our dear old pastor is dead! He succumbed to a heart attack last night.

He was alive and well two days ago when I visited the parsonage after work. I had talked about the power of prayer, and how it can protect us from evil. It had gotten very dark and the old gentleman insisted on escorting me home. In parting I thanked him and my final remark was: "Nun müssen Sie den dunklen Weg alleine gehen." ("Now you must walk the dark road alone.")

The ominous double meaning of these last words only now is becoming apparent to me and makes me shiver.

*December 15, 1942* I finished reading a book by Gustave le Bon: *Psychology of the Masses*. Dr. Kilian had given it to me, pointing out that the contents of the book most elegantly describe the conditions existing in Germany today: "A ram is leading a herd of sheep to their destruction!"

*December 16, 1942* Our parson's funeral. Adjoining the cemetery chapel is a hall with small chambers. These are used as lying-in-state rooms for the deceased. Each has a door with a glass window, through which the corpse can be viewed. I hardly recognized our pastor!

He looked much younger in death. He lay peacefully in his coffin clad in his minister's black robe and white collar, a black velvet beret on his head. After the funeral service in the chapel, the coffin was carried to the grave. An immense crowd had gathered.

It was very cold and windy. My feet were frozen because I have no rubbers or boots, and I could take it no longer. I left before the ceremonies were ended, hurried home, soaked my feet in hot water and drank steaming tea. Sometimes the profound and the profane seem to be found in rather close proximity.

*December 21, 1942* I caught a bad cold at the funeral in spite of my efforts to avoid it. I had to stay in bed for several days. Today back at work Dr. Fehrig repeated to me a sarcastic remark which our boss Dr. Gellinger had made during my sick leave: "Never fear, Fräulein Irene will be back as soon as she has finished her Christmas shopping!" I wish he were right, but, alas, there is no chance of buying any presents at all. The stores are empty.

*December 23, 1942* I'm deeply shaken up—one more tragic death! Another of Ulrike's girl friends, Inge Mart, also has committed suicide. Her reason, though, was not betrayed love; it was exaggerated ambition! She failed to pass her finals at the University of Frankfurt. That day, she did not come home. Her mother searched frantically for her all through the night and the following morning. In the afternoon Inge was finally found.

She lay dead in the kitchen of her grandmother's apartment. Her grandmother had recently died and Inge had gone there to kill herself. She had first taken an overdose of sleeping pills and then sat down in front of the open gas stove, just like Anna Schulz. "Inge's limbs were twisted as if in agony," Ullrike told me. "One hand was clutching her heart; her rigid eyes were open, still expressing a nameless terror."

"I fail to see why anyone would want to kill oneself for such an insignificant reason!" I interrupted Ulrike.

"Inge's mother was very ambitious and was always prodding her to do more and better work in her studies. Just before the finals Inge told me: 'If I don't make it, Ulrike, I'll kill myself!' I thought she was joking!" Tears were streaming down Ulrike's face. Not long ago she had shed tears for her friend Anna.

"I can sympathize with Anna," I said to Ulrike, "being pregnant and abandoned by the man she loved, she could see no other way out. It did not occur to her that her death was actually rather neatly solving her unscrupulous lover's problems: how to rid himself of an unwanted girl and an unwanted child. That thought alone would have kept *me* going!"

In spite of her sorrow, Ulrike had to laugh: "I bet you, you would, but Inge was not like you. She was too frail to withstand the tremendous emotional strain caused by the war conditions, which we all have to bear day-in, day-out."

"You mean her reason was 'Lebensangst' ('fear of life')! I consider this cowardice. Life is there to be lived, and if the going is rough, one has no choice: one must fight or lose out. Inge lost out."

"I do not understand," mused Ulrike, "how this gentle girl could do such a cruel thing to her parents. Her only brother is at the Russian front, fighting at Lake Ilmen, trapped in a kettle, cut off from the German lines; and it is very doubtful if he will ever come out of there alive. Inge was aware of this!"

"What a horrible double tragedy! What a nightmare life has become—especially for the younger generation. We have just come of age, and we have nothing to look forward to but desolation, destruction and death!"

"Maybe that's why Inge killed herself, Irene," Ulrike replied softly . . . .

"Maybe so, but yet every fiber within me revolts against the thought of saying 'NO' to life."

Inge was strikingly beautiful, with a lovely face and body, her eyes a radiant blue, her silken hair shining like spun gold, her complexion the proverbial "peaches and cream." It seems unfathomable that such a person blessed with so much beauty and charm would have the will and the desire to destroy a perfect work of art—her own body—given to her as a priceless wondrous gift by our Creator.

The death notice in the papers read: "Our joyful sunny child has quietly slipped away from us."

*December 24, 1942* Holy Night. Mother and I lit six small wax candles on our tiny Christmas tree and gave each other our presents. I got some writing paper and a songbook with Christmas carols. Mother was pleased with her lilac "Vera Violetta" powder box. I also gave her a nightgown with lace ruffles, which I had been lucky enough to buy from an old lady.

*December 29, 1942* I saw a very interesting film, which recently has been released. Its subject is the discord between Kaiser William II and his "Iron Chancellor" Bismarck. Its title is: *The Dismissal.*

The film begins in 1888 with the death of the ancient Kaiser William I. His funeral cortege is winding its way through Berlin, past the Brandenburger Gate, with a banner reading: "Vale Senex Imperator!" Behind the casket walks solemn and alone Prince William, the old Emperor's grandson. The prince's father, the new Emperor Frederick III, stands hopelessly ill at a window of the royal palace supported by his wife Victoria—oldest daughter of Queen Victoria of England—and salutes his dead father for the last time.

Ninety days later Frederick III dies of cancer of the throat and his young son ascends the German throne as William II. Soon disagreements arise between him and Bismarck. Impressive scenes are shown of Bismarck giving the young and authoritarian monarch his clear-cut opinion without much ado. After years of tensions and arguments the Chancellor finally asks for his dismissal. William II is jubilant; he believes that he now has gained more power. What William II does not realize is that he has lost one of the greatest political leaders of his time.

The film was a masterpiece and not marred by Nazi propaganda, for which I was grateful. On the other hand it surprised me! I fully expected that the "Führer" would somehow get tied in with the image of Bismarck. Who knows, propaganda minister Goebbels may do that yet in one of his forthcoming speeches!

*December 31, 1942* "Sylvester"—as the Germans call it—last day of the year. I went to evening prayer during which the names of all persons who died this year in the parish of Unterliederbach were read off while organ music played softly: sixty-five names in all, of which 15 were soldiers killed at the front. This is a large number for such a small village. By now most women in Germany are wearing black—they are in mourning. There is hardly a family that has not lost a son, brother, husband or father in the war. The congregation sang the medieval chorale:

> "Mitten wir im Leben sind
> Von dem Tot umfangen"
> ("In the midst of life
> We are surrounded by death.")

Latvian Crest, developed in honor of Latvian Independence Day, November 18, 1918.

Irene at age 19 in Riga.

Riga in 1572 (engraving).

Riga. Monument of Peter the Great of Russia, replaced after Latvian independence by the Liberty Monument.

Riga. Monument to Liberty, erected in 1935.

Riga 1942. The Riga City Hall Square with medieval statue of Roland, bodyguard and nephew of Charlemagne. In the background is the destroyed church tower of St. Peter's.

Tallin (capital of Estonia) before the war.

Tartu, Estonia. The "Steinbrücke" (stone bridge) erected by Catherine the Great of Russia. Destroyed in 1941 by the Soviets.

1873. Irene's paternal grandparents, Karl and Amalia (née Dessain) Zarin.

1900. Grandma Amalia, second husband Ernest and daughter Cecilia.

1895. Irene's father, August Konstantin Zarin, at age 21.

1919. Irene age 3 with her parents, August Konstantin Zarin, and Elfriede (née Lahne) Zarina.

Aunt Cecilia de Dobroliuboff.

Cecilia's husband, Vladimir Mihailovitch de Dobroliuboff.

1939. Cousin Elra's wedding in Tallin, Estonia.

1940. Irene in her sorority colors, as vice-president of the sorority.

September 1938. University of Latvia, Irene's alma mater. Irene standing honor guard as the Latvian president, Dr. Karlis Ulmanis, and the university president, Dr. M. Primanis, walk by.

The ruins of Sigulda Castle, built in the 13th century, where Irene danced in the moonlight with Ingmar in 1939.

1939. Ingmar in Riga.

June 15, 1940. Graduation Day at the University of Latvia. Irene is in the second row, third from the right. (The other women are Pharmacy graduates.) Villis Zwaigznite (his name means "Little Star"), the first on the right in the second row, was deported to Siberia only a few months later.

1940. Irene's first job as chemical engineer at Varonis Rubber Plant, Riga.

The I.G. Farben Industry AG complex in Hoechst, Germany, before the war. Irene worked here during the war from 1941 to 1945.

The "blonde tiger." Irene at her desk at I.G.Farben, Hoechst, Germany.

Frankfurt am Main. The original Goethe-Haus. The great German writer Goethe was born here 8/28/1749. It was totally destroyed by bombs and rebuilt after World War II.

1943. Irene in Germany in her green "peau-de-soie" dress.

Irene's best friend, Karen (on left) and her sister Helga.

1945. American Occupation Forces Officers' party. The hostesses, including Irene, were all invited.

1944. Irene's husband Merit P. White at the Institute of Advanced Studies, Princeton, New Jersey.

The wedding party. Merit, Irene and her mother.

1960. Front row : Irene, daughters Elizabeth, Irene and husband Merit.
In back, oldest daughter, Mary.

# CHAPTER NINE

## Love and Laughter versus Total War

*January 1, 1943* It is utterly discouraging to wait and wait . . . and wait . . . for this war to end—but it doesn't end! It goes on from year to year. We have horrible weather: it has been raining for two days now. In spite of the chilly wetness I took the streetcar to Frankfurt and visited my friends Ilona and Hilda Alt. Ilona is wildly in love with an older married man, with whom she has had an affair for five years now. He keeps promising to divorce his wife and marry her. He is an executive, exempt from the draft, Ilona is his secretary. She travels a lot with him. I do not wish to shatter Ilona's illusions, but I am convinced that her boss is just taking advantage of her loneliness and naiveté.

Later in the evening we drank some "Ersatz" coffee and I told the girls and their very charming and refined mother their fortunes by laying out cards. All three listened in rapt attention and seemed very happy about my forecasts.

*January 3, 1943* Sunday, Mother and I visited my pilot-plant worker Franz Sorg in Langenhain in the Taunus mountains. Trudging up and down on steep mountain roads on our way to the village, we saw snow-covered hills and valleys stretching in gentle rows all the way to the horizon, ever so often interspersed by dark pine woods. One last slippery ascent—and before us in the valley lay Langenhain, the village church in its center, before it the snow-covered commons with their ancient linden tree. Around this focal part of the village crouched old half-timber buildings, their tiny windows blinking sleepily in the sunlight, as though peering out from under fluffy white nightcaps that had settled on their red tile roofs. It looked like a setting out of Grimms' fairy tales. Franz Sorg and his young daughter had prepared a veritable feast for us: pork chops and vegetables and for dessert coffee and home-baked plum pie.

On the way home we met a seventy-year-old man who told us his life's story. In 1916 during World War I at age 43 he was drafted into the army and badly wounded. He lost one leg and the use of one arm. He had been a leather tanner but could no longer carry out his profession. He is still supporting himself by working as a night watchman in a leather factory. He has four daughters, one of whom is married in Argentina. The old man was very pleased that I took such an interest in his tales. He insisted on giving me two large bags filled with apples. I, in turn, was very touched by his kindness.

The simple German people strike me as being helpful, charitable, hard-working, brave, long-enduring and most devoted. This I have witnessed over and over again, when mingling with country folks. Why are the Germans as a nation hated world-wide? I don't quite understand, unless it be that the educated middle classes, the nobility, the political leaders with their conceit, their alleged superiority, their arrogance, have permanently destroyed the reputation of all Germans.

*January 7, 1943, Leipzig* Just now I am sitting in bed—the only warm place—in my room at the Hotel "Stadt Rom" in Leipzig. "City of Rome!" What a silly name for an inn in the middle of German Saxonia, where the population speaks "Sächsisch," a most horrible Saxonian dialect, very far removed in sound from melodious Italian. I find it hard to believe that the creator of modern German—Martin Luther—actually spoke this kind of dialect. But he stated it himself: "Ich rede nach der sächsischen Kanzlei—I speak according to the Saxonian Chancellor's office."

But back to my trip from Frankfurt to Leipzig. My fellow travelers on the train were quite interesting: A lieutenant who had lost his arm in the war and who was reading "The Heroic Passions" by Kolbenmeyer, two middle-aged couples and a tall, handsome major who was deeply engrossed in "The Death of Wallenstein" by Schiller. Since I was reading "The Sorrows of Werther" by Goethe, I noticed with amusement that we seemed to have quite a literature-minded group in our compartment. We finally started a conversation, in which the major introduced himself as a professor from a German university. All others including me preferred to remain incognito. It snowed as we arrived in Leipzig. Darkness fell and I could hardly find my way to the hotel.

*January 9, 1943, Berlin* This morning in the hotel lobby I quite unexpectedly met an acquaintance, Herr Grissel, from Riga, who is here on business. We had lunch together at "Kempinsky," the famous Berlin restaurant. There we were joined by a Herr Hohlmann, a friend of Herr Grissel, who also works for I.G. Farben. Herr Hohlmann amused me greatly. He was short, fat, blond, red-cheeked with watery blue eyes, and seemed to be somewhat dull of comprehension. He began to laugh about a joke only after the rest of us had already forgotten it. But, at the same time, he told quite interesting tales about his stay in South America where he worked as a representative of I.G. Farben in Lima, Peru. He spoke about the hot climate there which, nevertheless, did not prevent him from taking part in all kinds of amusements and parties, mostly at the "German Club." Herr Hohlmann also met beautiful dark-haired girls in Lima, but, he said, with an expression of distress and regret at the same time: "It's quite hazardous to date one of these girls. If you are seen once or twice with one of them and after that don't propose marriage, it may happen that her father or one of her brothers will push a knife between your ribs!" I could not help but laugh at this description, imagining poor, red-cheeked, blue-eyed, pale blond, stodgy Herr Hohlmann in so dangerous a society of glowing, dark-haired, passionate beauties. But Herr Hohlmann was deadly serious about it and could not understand why I thought his words so funny. He continued his tale.

"At the beginning of the war I was interned, together with other Germans, and for half a year transported from one camp to another, partly by railroad, partly by boat. The treatment and the food were very good. Then, due to exchange of interned persons between Germany and America, I finally came back to Germany; but before I was sent home, I had to take an oath not to fight in this war." Herr Hohlmann showed me the statement. It was written in English and had been attested by an American notary public. It read: "I swear not to bear arms in this war . . . ." The German government honors this oath and Herr Hohlmann will not be drafted.

*January 10, 1943, Berlin* I had lunch with Dr. Haller, my former boss from I.G. Farben, in a restaurant near the river Havel in Grunewald, a suburb of Berlin. The weather was wonderful and we went for a walk through the snow-covered woods, where thousands of Berliners enjoyed this winter Sunday. All hills were crowded with families on skis and sleds, children fought snowball fights, shouting for joy, little scotch terriers, pugs and dachshunds rolled and sneezed in the snow and everyone was happy.

*January 11, 1943, Berlin* This morning I went by subway to the Technical University in Berlin-Charlottenburg. It is a very large imposing building. At the main office I inquired about the necessary formalities and examinations in order to start work for a Ph.D. degree.

*January 14, 1943, Höchst* Today, our new boss, Dr. Gellinger, called me to his office and scolded me for having stayed at home because of a cold. I asked him whether he expected me to come to work while ill. "Yes, I, myself, went on a business trip with a temperature of 104° F," said Gellinger.

"If you go on trips while sick, it's your private business. My 'Zeal of Servitude' comes to an end when my temperature rises above normal."

"So you won't admit you were wrong?"

"Why should I? I haven't done anything wrong because I had a cold. What actually do you want of me?"

"Military discipline!"

"I am no soldier and besides that, I grew up in a free democracy." He stared at me furiously, but I smiled and left the room.

*January 17, 1943* Sunday. Two old ladies came to visit. They are sisters and both in their sixties. Frau Hertzelt is the wife of our custodian and the mother of soldier Hans Hertzelt, whose marriage to the "bride in black" I attended last year. The older sister, Frau Huber, told me about her experiences during World War I. She stayed alone with seven young children, while her husband was at the battlefront. The family lived through extreme miseries: poverty, hunger, cold, sickness. They even boiled the cadaver of the family cat, which had died of old age, and ate it. Life for so many of the older people here seems to have meant much suffering, and has indeed been "a vale of tears." Now these same people are going through similar harrowing experiences—or even worse—for the second time.

*January 19, 1943* One of our fellow chemists has recently been transferred to Prague. Today, we got a letter from him. He writes that life in Prague is better than in Germany: on the black market (which does not exist here because of the utmost control exerted by the Nazi regime) it is still possible to buy quite a good many things, but, of course, for very high prices. For instance:

    1 Kg coffee—200 RM (half of a young chemist's monthly salary)
    1 Kg pork—20-30 RM
    1 pack of cigarettes—15 RM

*January 25, 1943* The news from the Russian front and from Africa is depressing for Germany. In Stalingrad the German troops are enclosed by Soviet forces. German divisions had to retreat from Velikie Luki and from Voronesh. In the Caucasian Mountains, the Germans likewise had to withdraw to new positions. In Africa, Rommel was forced to clear out of two villages near Tripoli.

*January 30, 1943* In connection with the anniversary of Hitler's coming to power, Goebbels delivered a speech and read a proclamation of the "Führer." The content is always the same: belief in the final German victory, but Goebbels had to admit that the situation in Stalingrad is hopeless. A whole German Army is enclosed and prey to destruction by Soviet forces.

The other day a German mother showed me the farewell letter of her son who is in Stalingrad. He wrote that he knows he will never again see his home. "But don't be afraid, Mother," he writes, "that I will ever fall into Russian hands. My last bullet is for me!"

*January 31, 1943* Sunday. We went to Mainz to visit friends of ours. Mainz shows terrible sights of destruction—whole blocks and streets have been erased by the English air raids of last summer. Everywhere there is nothing but ruins. Now and then, in the heaps of rubble, I saw some remains of furniture and household goods. In Mainz, which had a population of 150,000 people, 60,000 have lost their homes. The exact number of victims is not known, because many persons are still buried under the ruins of their houses. I saw funeral wreaths that had been placed on the rubble, in memory of the dead underneath. A woman told us about one of the many tragedies which have occurred in Mainz:

"During the night of terror, last summer, a young woman gave birth to her first child in the air-raid shelter of her house. Her mother-in-law assisted her, but the newborn child had only a short time to live. A bomb destroyed their house and killed grandmother, mother and child, who were all buried under the rubble. The young father was summoned home from the Russian front. Finding his house in ruins, he immediately started to search for the dead. First he dug out his mother, then his wife and the newborn baby. He threw himself over the dead bodies, kissing them, sobbing loudly, screaming curses at Hitler. He was taken to the insane asylum."

On our way home, we had to cross the bridge over the Rhine. It was dark, but the stars shone and their light was reflected in the waters of the stream. These sparkling stars were like a symbol of peace, and remembering the vast destruction I had seen, and the sad stories I had heard, a prayer arose in my heart that this cruelest of all wars would soon come to an end.

*February 3, 1943* Army Headquarters today announced the defeat of the German forces in Stalingrad and gave a description of the tragic event. "Our soldiers gathered for the last battle and hoisted the swastika banner above the highest ruins of the town. Then they fought shoulder to shoulder, generals, officers, soldiers, down to the last man. At the repeated summons of the enemy to surrender, they proudly refused."

*February 8, 1943* After the loss of Stalingrad, Germany was in mourning for four days. All cinemas, theaters and opera houses were closed and the radio brought only mournful music, instead of the usual bouncing military marches and soldiers' songs.

*February 12, 1943* We had some trouble at the plant, because some of the Russian girl laborers have stolen denatured alcohol and distributed it in the Russian barracks. Many Russians were poisoned by drinking the stuff.
   This morning there was more trouble. Last night, Lydia, my Russian laboratory worker, attempted suicide by taking two pellets containing a mercury compound, which she had stolen from the lab. With foam on her lips and bloodshot eyes, she was taken to the dispensary where her stomach was pumped out, and thus she was saved. This morning she was all right again, although very pale. On my strict questioning, she explained that she wanted to die. Bernauer, our big Nazi agent, had beaten her because she had resisted his amorous attentions. I know he is a heel, but there is no proof, and we can't do a thing about it, because the Gestapo covers all his actions.

*February 19, 1943* Last night, Goebbels delivered a long and blaring speech, in the course of which he announced "Total War." That means that the civilian population—every man, every woman, every child—is now at war with Germany's enemies. It also means that Germany's towns will be more heavily bombed than ever before.

*February 24, 1943* At today's departmental meeting Dr. Gellinger announced that all males up to age 39 will be drafted. Three of my technicians have to go next week.

*February 25, 1943* My fellow worker, Dr. Scholl, is getting more and more unpleasant. I guess Germany's failures on the battlegrounds are making him nervous. The other chemists don't like him much either and tease him whenever there is an opportunity. This morning, Dr. Kilian put the picture of a beautiful, dark-haired senorita from Las Palmas, which he had cut out from some magazine, into Dr. Scholl's bookcase, with the following inscription: "The ideal of the Nordic man! His complete surrender is to be expected." Upon discovering this, Dr. Scholl was greatly annoyed and questioned me over and over again as to who had done it. But of course, I did not give Dr. Kilian away.

*March 3, 1943* News from the Russian Front continues to be bad. Soviet troops are advancing and pushing the Germans out of the Ukraine. In India Mahatma Gandhi is supposedly on his death-bed. In England Churchill is claimed to be seriously ill.

*March 4, 1943, Berlin* I'm again in Berlin. After the meeting at the Chemical Society today, which I had been sent to attend, I walked down the street "Unter den Linden." I saw several bomb-damaged houses, before which large crowds had gathered, gazing uneasily at the ruins. I was not as impressed because I had seen so much more destruction in Mainz and Cologne.

The Berlin War Memorial is located on the same street. It is a circular hall with a cross in the center and two high posts on both sides of the cross, on each of which burns an Eternal Flame in memory of the dead of both World Wars. The relatives of the war dead honor the memory of their fathers, brothers, husbands and sons who are buried in foreign soil, placing wreaths bearing inscriptions at the foot of the cross in the hall. I saw countless wreaths piled almost to the ceiling, and I thought: "Each wreath means a dead soldier!" On the inscriptions I read words of heartbreak, grief, great love and deep mourning.

The people in Berlin are all terribly upset about the latest air raids, because this city never before has been seriously bombed and the population felt quite safe—especially because Hermann Göring, the much bemedalled, overfed, mountainous Marshall of the German Air Force had declared: "If ever an enemy airplane reaches Berlin, my name shall be 'Mayer.'" Now the Berliners have nicknamed him "Mayer." But in spite of this failure, "our Hermann," as the Germans call him, still seems to be quite popular. They tell jokes about him and make songs about him. Some time ago, the hit of a cabaret program was the chant of a nightclub performer with the following refrain:

> "The Hermanés, the Hermanés
> On the right-lametta,
> On the left-lametta,

And the belly gets still fatter!"

(Lametta" is angel hair, decoration on Christmas trees, in reference to Göring's zeal for collecting medals.) The storyteller did not report whether the singer, a girl, got into trouble with the Gestapo or not. Göring strikes me as vain, lazy, an insignificant clown, in spite of his vast bulk.

*March 5, 1943, Berlin* During my free time I visited the Imperial Palace of Berlin and the Dome Cathedral which lies opposite the palace. The palace was built by Andreas Schlüter, a great 18th century German architect, at the time of King Frederick I of Prussia. The rooms for state receptions are splendidly decorated with wall and ceiling paintings, statues, gilded panels and purple and brocade drapes. Very beautiful is the "White Room" where the great court receptions took place and where the Prussian kings and later, the Emperors, delivered their speeches from the throne. In this room, also, the royal weddings were celebrated with the traditional "Fackeltanz—Torch Dance," a stately dance in which the male courtiers hold torches. [Author's note: In 1950 the Soviet Occupation forces ordered the palace to be blown up, in order to make room for a replica of the "Red Square" to be laid out in Berlin.]

Kaiser William II had the Dome Cathedral built at the end of the 19th century. It is a vast building under a circular cupola and did not impress me favorably. A burial vault for the imperial family is located under the church.

*March 6, 1943, Berlin* I once more went to the Technical University in Charlottenburg. During last week's air raid, one wing of the huge building was burned out and the air in the corridors and offices was still filled with. smoke. While there, I also visited the palace and the Mausoleum of Charlottenburg. The royal palace, which lies in a beautiful park, is much smaller than the one in the center of Berlin. Unfortunately, the palace was closed to the public.

After Queen Louise's death, Frederick William III remarried and continued to live in this same house with his second wife, who was not of royal blood. In the Mausoleum, Queen Louise, her husband, King Frederick William III and also their son, Emperor William I, victor over the French in 1872, and his wife, Augusta, are laid to rest in a vault underneath the Memorial Hall. At the entrance to the Hall stands a marble Angel of Death. Mysterious blue light shines through colored windows, high from the ceiling, onto four memorials dedicated to the dead royalties. On these memorial stones the figures of the dead carved in marble rest in all their glory, as though asleep. Most beautiful of all is the figure of Queen Louise. Her face bears the expression of angelic beauty and calm. She was a good and heroic queen, dearly loved by her subjects and respected even by Napoleon. The last years of her life were filled with great suffering. In 1807 she humiliated herself in vain at Tilsit before Napoleon, begging for more tolerable peace terms for Prussia. Three years later she died at age 34. Her second oldest son became Emperor William I of Germany in 1872.

After this excursion into the past, I returned to the busy center of Berlin, and went to a play, "Anna of Austria and Charles III." It sounds very historical, but is actually a modern play about marriage problems. All evening long only two persons performed on stage, an actor and an actress. I find it amazing that in spite of increased bombing attacks theater and opera performances are continuing.

*March 7, 1943* The last day in Berlin . . . I had dinner with Walter in a. Russian restaurant "*Medvedj*—The Bear," but the only Russian things there were the names on the menu card. We ordered:

>   Cotelet a la Posharsky
>   Borscht
>   Kasha a la Gurieff.

The cotelet turned out to be a spoonful of ground meat, the borsch was watery vegetable soup, and the kasha a peculiar version of cream of wheat.

When it came time to pay the bill Walter discovered to his great consternation that he had forgotten his wallet. In nervous haste he groped through all his pockets, but in vain. Trying to save him from embarrassment I handed him my purse under the table. With a sigh of relief he grabbed it, fumbled through the ten and twenty-mark bills and paid the waiter. I watched Walter and suddenly noticed how very much he has changed since we last met. He has aged, his hair and eyebrows have grayed noticeably, and he seems to be very absent-minded and high-strung. Maybe he too, like so many of the people around me, is losing his moral strength, his capacity to withstand hardships.

On the train back to Frankfurt, I was not able to get a berth in a sleeper and was lucky to find a seat in a crowded compartment. Up to Halle, the trip was not too uncomfortable, but then an enormously fat man appeared. (How he had managed to stay fat after three and a half war years is a mystery!) Unfortunately, he decided to squeeze himself between me and my neighbor. I was so annoyed, that in my mind, I nicknamed him "Jumbo." "Jumbo" got drowsy and leaned his great hulk more and more heavily on to my shoulder. I felt as though I were suffocating. I could stand it no longer and suddenly hissed at him like a cat. He jerked back and bothered me no more.

*March 10, 1943, Höchst* I finished the typewriting and shorthand course which I had started several months ago. At present I have no need for it, but I have a feeling that some day this newly acquired skill may be of use to me.

*March 13, 1943* Herr Grissel from Riga, whom I recently met in Berlin, is now in Frankfurt (I suspect him of being a wheeler-dealer). He asked me to have dinner at the Frankfurter Hof, the most fashionable hotel in town. There we were joined by Dr. Tann, representative of I.G. Farben in Japan, who traveling over Asia and Russia two years ago came to a meeting in Germany and was prevented from returning to his post due to the outbreak of war with the Soviet Union.

The dining rooms of the hotel are beautiful, and I am surprised at what good food still is served there, though of course, for a very high price. For the fourth war year in Germany, it was indeed a remarkable menu:

> Appetizer: Sardines and tuna fish served with Italian southern wine
> Chicken Consommé
> Wild duck with vegetables served with Moselle wine
> Pudding
> Champagne.

The table linen was snowy white; the crystal glasses and the sterling silverware sparkled in the soft lights flooding the rooms. The walls were decorated with pink and brocade tapestries. One could almost forget that there is a terrible war raging.

*March 15, 1943* I saw the second German color film, "The Golden Town," a story which takes place mainly in Prague—therefore the name. The colors still do not appear to be natural, but are already so much better than in the very first color film, one year ago.

*March 20, 1943* Spring has come. The bushes are greening and young juicy grass is merrily growing along factory fences.

*March 21, 1943* Memorial Day for the War Dead! The "Führer" gave a short speech from Berlin. He said that now the danger from the East is completely banished, and he also mentioned the number of Germans killed in this war: 542,000. I can't believe it; the losses must be much, much higher.

*March 20, 1943* I received a letter from Ingmar. His studies of architecture at the University of Riga are going well. He is still dreaming of romance, reminiscing about moonlight walks in our beautiful Gauja river valley.

*March 29, 1943* Dr. Tann, who is a member of the German-Japanese Society, invited me to a lecture by a Japanese Professor Dr. Muratta, who had come to Frankfurt from the Japanese Institute in Vienna. His subject was: "The position of the Japanese woman in the family and state." Prof. Muratta, a tall, very skinny man, talked in a high voice and seemed to have trouble pronouncing "r" and the German "sch" properly. The "r" he usually pronounced like "l."

At the end of his lecture Prof. Muratta stated: "European people often have the impression that the Japanese woman has no freedom and, therefore, cannot be happy. But this is a European point of view. The Japanese woman does not know and does not want anything else, but faithfully and dutifully to serve her family, and thereby the state and her ancestors." That's what Muratta says. I wonder how a young Japanese woman really feels about her status in society.

After the lecture, I talked with a Dr. Hajo, another Japanese, who is professor of the Japanese language at the University of Frankfurt. His German was somewhat halting, but he knew Russian very well and we used this language to communicate. He is a linguist and told me that he is very interested in the Latvian language. He was small and bespectacled like most Japanese.

But I can't warm up to him or Dr. Muratta—Their manners are so entirely different from what I am used to among Europeans and I always have the suspicion that behind their politeness shadows lurk. And indeed, at the end of his lecture, Professor Muratta said, proudly raising his voice: "Japan is a World Power!"

*March 30, 1943* I saw a most unusual film about the Schäfer Expedition: "Secrets of Tibet." In 1938, a small group of German scientists started an expedition from India through the Brahmaputra Valley up to the Highland of Tibet. The Germans even succeeded in reaching the "Town of the Golden Roofs," Lhasa, the seat of the Dalai Lama. Never before had a European been allowed to enter this town.

The film showed the difficult ascent on narrow paths, through wild mountain valleys, crossing torrential waters, higher and higher up to the region of eternal snow. There in the mountains live nomad tribes with rather strange customs. When greeting a stranger, they show their tongues as far as possible. They live in great poverty and terrible dirt. Their children are quite cute, but indescribably dirty and covered with vermin.

The Highland of Tibet is a desert. Only steppes, grass and salty swamps cover the vast surfaces of this huge plateau. Beautiful are only the wild horses, which in large herds, following their leader, are roaming through the steppes. After enduring many hardships, the expedition finally reached Lhasa. There, the houses are built in a very strange style with curved roofs and bizarre towers.

During a reception in a temple, the fat lamas sat on thrones and smiled benevolently. The greeting ceremonies were very solemn with countless bows and mutual compliments. The guests received gifts of foodstuffs consisting of butter, flour, peas and dried pork. The religion is Lamaism—all religious services and the hopes of the faithful are directed towards the life hereafter; asceticism is the ideal. In Tibet there exists a monastery town, which is inhabited by 50,000 monks, whose only occupation consists of turning their prayer-mills all day long and murmuring prayers with the help of a type of rosary.

Their religion is characterized by fear of countless gods and evil spirits, who are continuously endangering the human soul during its lifetime and also after death. By constantly praying, the monks are hoping to banish the danger. But worst of all are the burial customs in Tibet. The naked bodies of the deceased are laid out on a mountain slope. There, the priests grind the bodies to pieces with stone hammers and then throw them to the vultures. I never saw anything so revolting before!

*April 1, 1943* The French pianist, Frederick Ogouse, gave a Chopin concert performance. His playing was beautiful, elegant, and he showed a brilliant technique, but I missed the pathos, the deep feeling which, in my opinion, Chopin's music inspires. The applause was tremendous and the artist had to give three encores. I noticed an expression of sadness and exhaustion on his face. He looked extremely frail and tired, but his audience cruelly demanded more music—and he complied.

*April 4, 1943* I attended the opera "Troubador," by Verdi, at the Opera House in Frankfurt. The performance was very good, except for a comical incident caused by the tenor. He sang the famous aria, "Di quella pira" with much bravado and at the end of the song, elegantly reached a flawless high C. The public applauded vehemently and asked for a repeat. The tenor returned radiantly smiling and with much enthusiasm started the aria all over again. Now came the high C. The audience listened expectantly, but instead of a beautiful sound there came an ugly squeak. This time the tenor did not make it. He disappeared like a flash of lightning behind the curtain, but the people were tactful enough to give him, nevertheless, a thunderous applause.

*April 7, 1943* Last night at the movies I met Ulrike's mother and walked home with her. A tremendous windstorm had arisen. We could hardly move forward. The wind was howling through the streets and in the heavens, playing with the clouds, tearing them apart and again bunching them up into huge black forms, then racing them across the sky. But the sky itself was starlit, high and wide and glowing in dark blue luminescence.

As we came to the bridge across the Liederbach I heard the waters of the usually very peaceful brook roaring and thrashing against its stone embankment. I saw the still naked branches of the nearby trees bending to the ground under the impact of the elements. It was scary, but at the same time I felt elated. I too wanted to shout, to sing, to howl with the storm, to jump and bend and swing with the branches, to race with the wind. This unleashing of nature's forces must have awakened some primeval instincts in my soul, must have stirred some deeply buried memories spanning millions of years back to the animal beginnings of homo sapiens.

*April 10, 1943* During the night we had an air raid on Frankfurt. Bombs fell and we could feel the detonations in the distance. We stayed most of the night in the air raid shelter.

*April 18, 1943* Sunday. A marvelous sunny spring day. Mother and I took the local train called "Bähnche" to Königstein in the Taunus mountains and hiked from there to Falkenstein—a medieval castle now in ruins—and on to Kronberg, which once was the seat of Victoria, Empress Friedrich, daughter of Queen Victoria of England, and mother of William II, the last German Kaiser. Her Emperor husband Friedrich III died after a rule of only 90 day.

By the time we got home the moon had already risen. I stood at our living room window. Three linden trees are growing right in front of our house. Their budding leaves and branches cast intricately woven lacy shadows onto the moonlit asphalt. Ever so often the tiny slit opening of a "blacked-out" bicycle lantern would emit a quickly passing reddish glow of light, as the rider sped by on the street. It reminded me of fireflies dancing in the meadows of Sigulda, which Ingmar and I had so often watched, when we still were together in Latvia.

*April 21, 1943* Dr. Tann visited us. He brought me sheets of piano music by Schuman and Chopin, which he had managed to find in a store in Frankfurt. Dr. Tann is thirty years my senior, older than Mother, much older than Walter, but I have the feeling that he is falling in love with me.

The War has destroyed the natural balance of things. We are all lonely, I for my friends in Latvia, he for his wife in Japan. There is no way for him to return to Tokyo, ever since the Russian Offensive started in 1941.

*April 23, 1943* Good Friday! The weather is beautiful. I went by bicycle into the country and lay down in the grass under an old linden tree and looked out into the green valley with its blossoming orchards. Here and there I saw people taking a walk. It was like a picture by Moritz Schwindt, the German painter of the Romanticism period. Suddenly a deep growling voice stirred me out of my reverie: "Dieser Sauköter, verflixter!—This lousy pooch, darn it all!"

I turned in surprise and saw an old man with a long white beard standing before me in "Lederhosen" (traditional German leather shorts) and green jacket. "Are you talking to me?" I asked politely.

"Of course! There is no one else to talk to. Have you perhaps seen a brown dachshund? My daughter and I went walking in the woods and he ran away. Now we can't find him. We have been looking for him for hours!" The old man sat down on a bench under the linden tree and together we commenced waiting for his daughter. And so it happened that I heard yet another life story. The man was 83 years old, had been married twice and had five children. He had worked in the Inorganic Products Department of I. G. Farben, where concentrated sulfuric acid is manufactured.

Eventually the daughter appeared, happily leading her lost-and-again-found dachshund puppy on his leash. The doggie was an adorable, charming, lovely and happy creature with silky golden brown fur, which frolicked and rolled and jumped for joy. Father, daughter and dachshund took off to the railroad station and I hopped on my bicycle and rode to Sulzbach, the little village on the way home.

In the church there, on wood paneled walls, I found tablets with the names of soldiers killed in the wars of 1870-71, 1914-1918 and the present war. In this war, Sulzbach has already lost 25 men, a great number for such a tiny village.

*May 1, 1943* International Labor Day (a state holiday here)! Dr. Tann visited us. He appeared with an enormous bouquet of flowers. He also brought along some pictures of his wife, his home in Tokyo and his summer place in the Japanese countryside. As executive director of the I.G. Farben branch in Japan he seems to have led a very elegant life there. Half jokingly he asked me if I would be interested after the end of the War to take a job in his laboratories in Japan. "Why not?" I said. "I'd love to see the world." Mother gave me dark looks but made no comment.

*May 4, 1943* Yesterday I received a post-card from Ingmar, and today another two cards from him. We have now been separated for over two years, but we still care for each other. I hope to see him again this summer.

*May 8, 1943* I saw Macbeth played in the Schauspielhaus in Frankfurt. The actors were good and the stage trappings very simple in a truly Shakespearean style. In his time, the settings usually consisted of signs only, which read, "wood," "churchyard," "battleground," or "castle," etc. The technique here was a little better. Instead of mere signs, light projections were used, which made very quick changes of scenery possible and, in addition, were very impressive. The witches' song in the fourth act struck me as strangely symbolic, expressing the horrors and upheavals of our own earth-shattering times:

> "For a charm of powerful trouble,
> Like a hell-broth boil and bubble.
> Double, double toil and trouble;
> Fire burn and cauldron bubble."

*May 11, 1943* I'm still wild with joy. This morning we received a letter from Berlin, that we have been granted permission to visit Latvia for a period of four weeks. Upon reading this message I performed what I imagine to be an American Indian Victory Dance with much stomping and shouting and waving of arms. Then I immediately started planning for the trip and how best to utilize the allotted time. But I have problems: I have no travel clothes and no fabric to sew anything either. I badly need two new summer dresses. My blue wool suit is rather out of style, but I will try to alter it, thus making it look more fashionable. Anyway, what does it matter! All I can think of is that I am going to Riga, to Riga! Mother too, seems happy. "Now I will be able to visit the graves of my dear ones," she said.

*May 15, 1943* Dr. Tann sent me an invitation to a ceremony in connection with the visit in Frankfurt of General Oshima, the Japanese Imperial Ambassador to Germany. The streets leading to the "Saalbau," where the visit was celebrated, were blocked and only people with invitations were permitted to pass. Hitler Youth lined each side of the way to the entrance. The hall was terribly crowded and it was very hot. At 5 o'clock precisely Ambassador Oshima and his escort appeared and were received by "Gauleiter" (Provincial Leader) Sprenger, who then gave a brief address. After that, General Oshima, a short, stout, tough-looking man talked; and then his attaché, a Japanese major named Endo, delivered a speech about the fighting spirit of the Japanese.

It was the same old story, a glorification of Japan, which everyone in Germany by now has heard over and over again, and I almost fell asleep. The ceremony finally came to an end by saluting the "Tenno" and the "Führer," that is by shouting three times, arms outstretched, "Sieg Heil!" for the Tenno and three times "Sieg Heil!" for the Führer. The whole thing was terribly boring and I was glad to get out into the fresh air again.

*May 18, 1943* English bombers have destroyed the dams across the Eder Valley and across the Möhne Valley. The immense water masses—in the Eder Valley alone there were 250 million cubic meters—cascaded into the valleys and submerged many villages. Thousands of people were drowned. How terrible it must have been for these people when suddenly, in the middle of the night, a huge wall of roaring water plowed through their villages bringing destruction and death. Some of them may have thought before they died that this was a Second Deluge, or the Day of the Last Judgment. It was—for them!

*May 19, 1943* I attended a concert of the well-known pianist, Elly Ney. She plays solely Beethoven's music. Her appearance is very impressive. She is tall, with curly grey hair and beautiful hands. She wore a long white dress with wide sleeves. But it is too bad that she mixes art with political propaganda.

She started her program by first reading several letters from German soldiers in Russia whose content was a praise of the Nazi Government. After the concert, I went for a walk along the Main River. All was so quiet. The beautiful silhouette of the old town rose majestically into the moonlit sky, but I kept asking myself how long Frankfurt would remain undamaged.

*May 20, 1943* At the movies, the newsreel showed the destruction of an American airplane carrier by the Japanese.

*May 24, 1943* Last night I attended in Frankfurt what surely must be one of longest operas in existence: "Die Meistersänger" by Richard Wagner. Mother and I sat through five and three-quarter hours of orchestral music and arias. However, I didn't mind it at all; it was beautiful.

Only one thought disturbed me: the possibility of an air raid. We all live with this fear day-in, day-out, and night-in, night-out. Any moment the sirens may start to howl announcing approaching enemy planes. The opera performance would immediately be stopped, the curtain would come down and the audience and artists alike would rush to the nearest air-raid shelter. Fortunately no disturbance occurred, and one could almost forget that we are truly living on borrowed time.

*May 27, 1943* I have finished the alterations on my blue wool suit—the only suit I possess. Removing the cuffs, narrowing the lapels and taking it in at the waist has simplified its lines and improved its fit. Its blue color matches my eyes; it really looks nice on me now.

Our severe food rationing is good for something—after all. It gives you an elegant appearance. I am so skinny, that I could easily compete with any of the slim plaster-cast mannequins displayed in department store windows, the only difference being that they don't feel any hunger pangs, but I do—constantly.

*May 28, 1943* Today I had an appointment with our technical director, Dr. Lehr. In order to bolster my confidence I wore my "new" blue suit. He had called me to his office to talk about my position at the plant. Gellinger apparently has complained about my being rather independent. "Do not be surprised that everything you do or say is reported to me," Lehr told me. "You, being one young woman among 300 male chemists, seem to be a most interesting person to your fellow workers and are, therefore, right in the limelight and closely watched." (The other girl chemist, my former housemate Ella Brecht, recently got married and has left.)

"And let me tell you," Lehr concluded his speech, "even if nothing else is functioning here in I.G. Farben Höchst, the 'Central Intelligence

Agency' is certainly functioning, and at that exceedingly well!" This last statement struck me as very funny and I burst out laughing. But nothing happened to me. I guess I have been warned.

*June 1, 1943* In the afternoon, I stood for one hour in a long queue before a vegetable stand in order to get some cherries. They were selling a quarter of a pound per ration card, so I got half a pound for two persons. It was the first time that I had been able to buy some fruit on the open market.

*June 5, 1943, Saturday* Dr. Tann came to visit with another big bouquet of flowers and more sheets of music. This time he brought compositions by Beethoven for piano and voice. I know the "Adelaide" aria from my singing lessons. Dr. Tann accompanied me on the piano and we staged a little concert, singing and playing all my favorites, mostly Schubert "Lieder."

Mother sat on the sofa listening and watching. I am scared; I wonder what thoughts she is mulling over in her mind. She has started to be very abrupt with Dr. Tann. On parting Dr, Tann said, "What a pity that I have to go. Life is so beautiful here!" He must be blind not to see the tension between Mother and me. After Dr. Tann's departure Mother remained seated on the sofa, not talking, just smiling menacingly at me.

*June 8, 1943* Yesterday my singing teacher (Fräulein Brettlein from the fourth floor) brought us a package of frozen grapes, which she had been able to buy in a store. There must have been something wrong with them: Mother ate some and today she is sick in bed with stomach cramps and a temperature.

*June 12, 1943* The last days have been very hard on me. Mother is still ill and I have to nurse her, prepare her breakfast and clean her bedroom before leaving for work. During my lunch hour I come rushing home to fix some food for her, then bicycle back to my laboratory. After working hours I do the daily shopping for food (standing in queues mostly) and then more cooking and more house cleaning. I never get to bed before 1:00 AM. I am exhausted.

*June 13, 1943* I saw a very good film about Mozart's life called, "Whom the Gods Love." The performance of the actors was excellent and the accompanying music, all by Mozart, was most beautiful. The film brought scenes out of Mozart's famous operas, "The Escape from the Seraglio,"

"Don Giovanni," and "The Magic Flute," and also parts of his "Requiem." The scene of Beethoven's visit with Mozart shortly before the latter's death was marvelous: Beethoven, serious, strong-minded, and determined, Mozart already tired and without his usual gaiety, although still so young.

*June 14, 1943* Whitsuntide here as in Latvia is a religious and a state holiday. I took advantage of my free time and visited the medieval "Römer", the town hall in Frankfurt, where in former centuries many of the emperors of the "Holy Roman Empire of the German Nation" were crowned, and which is still Frankfurt's main administrative building. The large Gothic hall is decorated with paintings of all the emperors. Some of these were painted in modern times after busts and tombstones, others are genuine portraits.

One or the other of these majesties I greeted as old acquaintances from Miss Aronett's history classes in high school, way back in Riga. On the square before the "Römer" stands an old fountain decorated with the statue of the goddess of Justice, who is blindfolded, holding a scale in her uplifted hand. In the Middle Ages, the inhabitants of Frankfurt celebrated the coronations of their emperors on this square and around this fountain, with feasting and drinking. Whole oxen were roasted on spits and from the fountain flowed red and white wine. In this century, although now interrupted by the war, open-air performances of Goethe's famous play, "Götz von Berlichingen" (about a leader of the medieval peasant uprisings, also known as "The Knight with the Iron Hand") were staged in front of the "Römer."

In the old part of the town, I found another relic of the past—the Carmelite Cloister, which was build about 1500 AD. The cloister garden is enclosed by a covered walk with columns. Flowers, herbs and green ivy grow in abundance. This quiet walled-in spot reminded me of our 13th century Dome Cathedral in Riga which also has such a beautiful inner garden. Before the war Goethe's "Urfaust" was performed summers in these settings—the tragic play of Dr. Faustus' love and betrayal of Gretchen.

*June 16, 1943* My assistant technician, Faller, came back from Aachen, where he had visited his relatives. He told me about terrible scenes which had taken place during the British air raids on Aachen, Cologne, Barmen, Dortmund and Düsseldorf. The British dropped burning phosphorus on the towns. Phosphorus is very difficult to extinguish. Furthermore, turning to liquid, while burning, it runs like a hissing stream of fire into basements and air raid shelters trapping the people therein. The towns soon were in a sea of flames and thousands of persons burned to death.

In Barmen, many people with hair and clothes afire jumped into the River Wupper, in order to extinguish the flames, and were drowned. The loss of life was very high. After an air raid in Aachen, Faller saw a dead woman whose body had been smashed against a wall by a bomb explosion and who, while dying, had given birth to a child. The baby, still connected by his navel cord, hung from the mother's body. This story made me tremble in fear. What will be the end of this insane orgy of murder? Is there indeed no way out of this inferno?

*June 18, 1943* Dr. Tann invited me to a play by the famous Spanish writer, Lope de Vega, in the "Schauspielhaus" in Frankfurt. It was a lighthearted and charming comedy called "El Perro del Hortelano—The Gardener's Dog."

Lope de Vega, father of Spanish drama and a contemporary of Shakespeare (whose works were unknown to Lope) is a phenomenon as a writer and poet. In his lifetime of 73 years, he wrote 1600 secular plays, 20 big volumes of novels, about 3000 sonnets and 400 religious dramas. Besides that, he still had time for numerous amorous adventures, in spite of the fact that he was a priest. Although Lope de Vega lived during the darkest time of the Spanish Inquisition, he cleverly managed to avoid serious conflicts with the Church, which frowned upon his adventurous life and on the frequently daring contents of his plays.

*June 19, 1943* I've been thinking about Dr. Tann. He is a fine man, very intelligent, full of energy, with lots of personality, but also quite an idealist, fascinated by the arts, music, poetry. Amazingly enough I no longer seem to notice that Dr. Tann is so very much older than I. I like him immensely, but my friendship for him is mingled with a great deal of respect. In his presence I feel at peace and protected from my everyday miseries and from my mother's nagging.

I love to hear Dr. Tann's wonderful stories about exotic places, exciting adventures—all stories out of his own life. Never before have I quite so strongly realized that it is the spirit that moves us that counts. There is hardly any doubt in my mind: he and I are tuned in on the same wavelength. Am I falling in love with him? No, I don't think so.

*June 20, 1943* Sunday. The weather was wonderful and Mother and I packed our meager lunch, consisting of cold, boiled potatoes, in a paper bag and took off to Bad Homburg, the famous former summer resort of

Kaiser William II. The large park there was filled with sunshine, the birds sang and all was peaceful.

In the afternoon we hiked to Kirdorf, another village in the Taunus mountains. On a country road with the peculiar name "Höllsteinstrasse"—Hellstone Street—we passed a most beautiful monument in memory of the dead of the war of 1914. It depicts a soldier, one hand still clutching the gun, the other resting on his breast. His helmet is lying by his side. His coat is draped over his feet. On his face is the calmness of death. The monument is surrounded by tall dark oak trees. Piled high in the background are heavy gray granite blocks. The inscription at the base stirred me deeply:

> "Horch, es rauscht in den Eichen,
> Die Totenklage der Heimat . . .
> Hark, the roar in the oak trees
> sounds the country's death lament . . ."

*June 21, 1943* The morning was full of sunshine but in the afternoon, a heavy thunderstorm raged with lightning and hail. In spite of these weather conditions, we had an alert. English airplanes were approaching. The air raids in the west are steadily increasing. The Ruhr district and the Wupper Valley are by now thoroughly devastated. So far, we still have been lucky here in Frankfurt and suburbs.

*June 22, 1943* I wrote a number of letters to my friends and relatives in Latvia and Estonia announcing our arrival there in early July, which I then sent to the "Ostland—East Land" as the Baltic States are now called.

Later I went to the "Wirtschaftsamt—Office of Economics" to pick up our monthly food ration cards. Quite unexpectedly, as a bonus all persons over twenty-one years of age received a smoker's card entitling one to buy some cigarettes. The clerk refused to give me such a card with the remark that I was obviously under age. I found his opinion very flattering, but since cigarettes are an important bartering item, I insisted on my rights by producing my German passport—as proof that I am over twenty-one.

*June 26, 1943* In connection with my travel plans to the "Ostland," I had to get permits from the "Arbeitsamt—Office of Labor" and from the Police Department in Frankfurt. I also had to go to the "Devisen-Amt—Office of Foreign Exchange" in order to get some "Reichskreditscheine—

State credit certificates". I requested 800 Marks worth, with which to finance our stay in the "Ostland." It took me all morning to secure these needed papers.

At noon I met Dr. Tann at the Frankfurt railroad station to see him off. He is going to Bad Kissingen—the famous spa—for a month's vacation. We waited for the train from Cologne, which finally arrived three hours late. Enemy planes over the Rhine valley had caused the delay. The train, as usual, was incredibly crowded. With much difficulty Dr. Tann squeezed his big-boned frame through the door into the narrow corridor, where he remained stuck in a tight cluster of tense and sweating human beings. One last wave, the doors were slammed shut, the train rolled on and sped out of the station. I looked up at the station's huge glass-covered dome, blackened by decades of smoke and soot, and had a vision of one single bomb smashing it into myriads of splinters in an instant.

*June 27, 1943* Air attacks on German towns seem to be increasing in intensity. The population is daily suffering heavy losses. This is the all-out "Total War" that Goebbels announced so proudly earlier this year.

*June 28, 1943* There is a fight raging between me on one hand and Doctors Gellinger and Heyden on the other, over rights to a patent for "Olefin oil 100." The dated entries in my laboratory notebook prove conclusively that I was the first one to come up with the idea of using this oil as a softener in "Buna S" formulations. Dr. Heyden claims "rights to prior art" based on verbal statements made before my first dated entry. Dr. Gellinger is supporting him, not me: two men against one young woman.

Never, upon my life, was I aware of such statements by Heyden. I am plainly furious and defending myself with teeth and claws. I won't give in. Not in vain have my colleagues nicknamed me "the blond tigress." The old pet name: "I.G. Farben bunny" is long forgotten. I have long since learned to fend for my rights here.

*June 30, 1943* The British have bombarded the Dome Cathedral of Cologne and caused heavy damages to this venerable and ancient building. I don't blame the Germans for being furious. I am extremely upset myself over this senseless destruction. I realize, of course, that the German Air Force has probably damaged and destroyed churches and cathedrals in England, but does one barbaric deed set to right the wrongs of another barbaric deed? What has become of our ancient cultural heritage, our proud traditions, our teachings of Christianity, shared by British and Germans alike, in fact by the whole Western World? What is emerging now is uncontrolled bestiality clothed in human form.

*July 1, 1943* I have won the patent fight and feel much calmer now.

*July 2, 1943* Tonight we are starting on our trip to Riga. Many preparations in a great hurry—final arrangements at my laboratory, trips to the bank and the Ration Card Office, packing of bags, farewell visits—but on Sunday, I shall be in Riga!

*August 5, 1943, Höchst* My last entry was made more than one month ago. I did not dare to take my diary with me into the occupied Baltic Territory, for fear that the military police on the trains might confiscate it. We arrived in Riga after a trip of 40 hours, which it took to cover the distance of 700 miles from Frankfurt. The first thing we saw when entering Riga by train was the old part of town in ruins, out of which rose the spire less socket of St. Peter's pointing heavenward like a symbol of sinister accusation. This sight shocked me deeply, although I had been prepared for it. I knew that Riga had been heavily and willfully damaged by the Soviets in July of 1941 before they fled town.

At the station we were greeted by Aunt Erika and by my friends Herta and Elsa, who presented me with a huge bouquet of roses. Laughing and crying we fell into each other's arms. Erika took us to her apartment in the suburbs where I saw my little cousin Eva for the first time. She now is two years old, and, of course, has no idea that her daddy died before she was born. She is the sweetest, cutest, light-blond, blue-eyed creature imaginable and extremely lively. She right away made friends with me, and soon she was showing me all her little playful tricks, like rolling on the bed, hiding under the table, jumping at me, peeking from behind doors. The family resemblance between her and me is remarkable: she could be my own child.

The next day we went down town. Life in Riga has completely changed. The people are poorly dressed, the stores are empty, except for bookstores. Only German political pamphlets and Nazi propaganda material are available. The only store which is filled with valuable goods of Latvian origin is the former Army Economical Store, now renamed "German Department Store," where only Germans are entitled to buy. The Latvians have no possibility whatsoever to buy any clothes, underwear or stockings. This merchandise simply is not available to them. They have no ration cards for clothing.

Food is strictly rationed, but the rations are much larger than in Germany. Furthermore, the Germans here get double rations. Fortunately, the Latvians don't starve either. The black market is flourishing and it is possible, although for high prices, to buy any wanted amount of butter, milk, eggs, bacon and meat. Besides that, almost all Latvians living in the capital have relatives somewhere in the country and can always get surplus food from them.

Aunt Erika's cooking is excellent and we tremendously enjoyed the sumptuous meals she served us. Unfortunately, our digestive systems were no longer used to large amounts of proteins and fats, and Mother and I both promptly got sick. Our stomachs and intestines revolted in the most violent way. Erika called her doctor, who explained what the trouble was. We had to go back to our old starvation diet, only gradually starting to add foods of high nutritious value.

One of the first places I visited was my Alma Mater, the Chemical Department of the University. Many of my old friends were still there, professors, assistants and students. Their unanimous opinion seemed to be that I had undergone a remarkable change. Young Professor Balins summed it up: "Life abroad has made you much more outgoing, Irene, you have become a very interesting person." I was amazed. I had not thought of myself in those terms.

After having spent a week in Riga, Mother, Aunt Erika, little Eva and I went to visit Uncle Arno and his family in Tartu, Estonia. It is extremely difficult to get permits for travel within the "Ostland," but I was fortunate. In the German Office for Transportation I quite unexpectedly met my former high school fellow student Sigrid Stein, who is chief secretary there. Sigrid still looks the same: plump, blond hair hanging into her face, merrily squinting eyes and a kind smile on her wide mouth. I had no trouble whatsoever to get permits for our entire family. However, there was yet another hurdle to overcome. We had to get certificates from a doctor especially appointed by the German Occupation Government certifying that we were free of body lice. This paper is required from every traveler in the Baltic States.

The trip to Tartu, in Estonia, was very tiresome and boring. It took us 20 hours to cover the short distance of 160 miles, because our train had to wait whenever military hospital trains came from the Russian Front and had to let them pass by. Thus, I sometimes could catch glimpses of the wounded soldiers lying in their berths—row upon row of them—an endless procession of misery and suffering. My heart went out to them, but what could I do? We civilians are powerless to do anything at all. It comforted me to think that these wounded soldiers actually were the lucky ones. Hundreds of thousands of their comrades have died on the battlefields of Russia.

In Tartu Arno and his entire family awaited us at the railroad station. My thirteen-year-old cousin Sven and his six-year-old sister Hiye took me by the hands and gaily chatting pulled me along on our way to their house through deserted city streets, leading past endless rows of destroyed buildings. The whole town is a field of ruins. Only a narrow ring of houses at the outskirts of town is still left. Aunt Meta told me that in 1941 the Soviets, during their fight with the approaching German forces, directed their gunfire for 14 days into the town, with the sole purpose of destroying it. Arno had already written us about this to Germany, but I had the same reaction as in Riga when first seeing the destruction myself. I was deeply shocked.

I felt bad about the fact that the Soviets have blown up the beautiful old stone bridge over the river Embach, which the Russian Empress, Catherine the Great, had ordered built in the 18th century. It was a famous historical landmark and bore these proud words in Latin and German:

> "Stream, tame here your course,
> Catherine the Second commands it.
> Her generosity brought about this construction
> And adorned Livonia with its first stone bridge."

And now I stood at the bank of the river looking down upon the massive fragments of the bridge that had sunk into the waters. The stream is still running its course, but the bridge is gone, in spite of Catherine's imperial orders.

The return trip to Latvia was equally as boring and uncomfortable as our train ride to Estonia three days earlier. Little Eva became extremely restless, climbing, jumping and running about the corridor and could hardly be controlled. In Cesis on Latvian territory my great-aunt Kristina came to the train. I had written her that I would pass through her town. She must be nearly ninety and has become very frail. She brought me a present, a package containing bacon, eggs and a cake. I was deeply touched: Kristina is so old, poor and sick, with painful sores on her legs, and still thinking of me. We cried when we said our farewells. We both knew that we'd never meet again in this life.

Grandma Amalia used to tell me how proud and beautiful Kristina had been as a young woman—tall and golden-haired, a perfect example of our Swedish ancestry dating from the 18th century, and how many suitors she had had. Though married twice, Aunt Kristina never had any children. The proud bearing is still there; I heard no complaints from her. Kristina carries her lonely old age and her many tribulations with dignity.

We arrived in Riga at two o'clock in the morning. No streetcars were running and Erika's apartment is three miles away from the station. We made a quick decision, hired a porter to transport our suitcases, I carried little Eva, Erika carried our handbags, and we started out on foot, trudging through the early morning dawn.

On the next day I went to Sigulda, where I saw Ingmar again. Ingmar, my love! He had come to the train station to meet me. He stood there, handsome, in the prime of youth, looking at me with his radiant, green eyes, wearing the ruby ring I had given him as a pledge the night before I left Latvia two years ago. My memory went back to the days in early 1941, when I made the decision to leave my country. Ingmar had asked me to stay, to become his wife, so that we might face the approaching peril together. But, I knew I had to go; the warning in my heart was stronger than our romantic dream.

And now, over two years later, we met again. I was a guest at his parents' home in Sigulda. Ingmar's mother was extremely concerned over my skinny looks. She insisted that I drink six glasses of fresh milk daily, and fed me plenty of eggs, butter and cheese. After each meal I was sent out to the orchard to eat raspberries and blackberries straight from the bushes, or else feast on plums, cherries and apples.

I felt as though I had been transported to the Garden of Eden. I would lie in the tall grass under the fruit trees, enjoying the cool shade on hot summer afternoons, trying to forget howling sirens, exploding bombs, cities burning, death swinging its sickle at the battle fronts and in the cities of Europe. With each passing day the disturbing memories became fainter and fainter.

My days were not just filled with shade and rest but also with sunshine and activity. Ingmar and I would roam the countryside, visiting the lovely lookouts on the high banks of the river Gauja, imposing castle ruins, romantic taverns and ancient chapels, all of which held such dear memories for us. It seemed like ages ago that we had walked through these same daisy-covered meadows and surveyed the woods and the valley from the high tower of the castle Krimulda, built by the Teutonic Knights in the 13th century.

We stood in a forgotten graveyard trying to decipher the inscription on an ancient memorial. Suddenly, I felt an overpowering surge of gratitude welling up in me. I was overcome by the sheer happiness of being alive, of feeling my heart beat and my blood rushing through my veins, of being young and strong and of still having a future. Almost without words, I communicated these thoughts to Ingmar. Our time had not yet run out, our abode was not yet a cold and silent grave! We were in the midst of life, glowing, wonderful, radiant life!

Nature all of a sudden seemed transformed; the sky was bluer, the sun more radiant, the red roses redder and the birds sang more jubilant songs! Hand in hand, we walked out of the graveyard, away from death, back into life. And our hearts were filled with many hopes in spite of Total War!

While enjoying every moment of my stay in Latvia, I nevertheless had a foreboding that it was going to be a long, long time before I would see my country again—if at all. This made me more aware than ever how beautiful my homeland is.

One afternoon, Ingmar and I went for a bicycle ride to the country estate where Grandma Amalia had grown up and married, and where in the 1880's my father, then five years old, had played with the young Count, son of the German lord of the manor (who according to Grandma Amalia, was in fact her half-brother). The young Count got mad at little Yussy (short for August, my father's name), and tore the lace off Yussy's pretty blue velvet suit. Grandma Amalia used to claim that the true reason for this nasty behavior was jealousy on the young count's part: Yussy, according to her, was much handsomer and much more nicely dressed. Ever since hearing this story I have imagined my father looking like Little Lord Fauntleroy as a boy.

Ingmar and I had a lovely ride through the countryside. The rye was cut and had been stacked together in upright bundles. The now empty fields stretched to the green woods at the horizon. The sky had the intensely clear blue color characteristic for northern landscapes with big, white fluffy clouds slowly sailing across its wide expanse. Suddenly Ingmar burst out: "Look at the sky, Irene, look at the fields, look with all your heart, and keep this memory forever! This is our country—your country, the place where you belong!" And I looked, and I will never forget!

The day of parting came much too soon. Again we had to say goodbye to each other. The train whisked me away and I saw his figure slowly getting smaller and smaller until he vanished in the distance. "Ingmar, will I ever see you again, or are you just a dream without fulfillment?"

Latvia is such a small country that it does not take long to cross the 250 miles from the western to the eastern border, or from the south to the north. I went north to the Baltic Sea. I wanted to see the shore again where I had spent so many happy vacations as a child. Together with my friends Herta and Elsa, I swam in the clear, cold blue waters of the Baltic and sunbathed on the soft white sand of the beaches. We listened to the gentle lapping of the waves and the murmur of the wind in the pine trees on the dunes, and it was so good to be there—to be home again.

One afternoon, we all three went to a concert in one of the summer resort places on the Baltic Sea. Our well-known Latvian tenor, Arthur Priednieks-Cavarra, sang arias and tunes from operas and operettas. The concert hall was decorated with flowers; the people in the audience were sun-tanned; all seemed content and glowing with health. The ladies wore brightly-colored summer dresses. A pleasant breeze came through the open windows and with it the faint rustle of the waves from the sea. The tenor received a huge bouquet of dark red roses which he placed on the piano-grande, where they formed a colorful background while he was singing. It was like a beautiful summer symphony, created of music, sunshine, flowers and a joyful audience. Once again the memory of a cruel war raging all around our little island of peace seemed to have vanished like a shadow.

In the evening we walked home along the beach. And there we saw another symphony—a symphony of colors, the red and the orange, the golden bronze and purple of a glorious sunset, and watched the glowing ball of the sun in the Western sky slowly sinking into the sea. At midnight, I once more went to the beach. The water shone like an enchanted mirror in the twilight of the northern summer night, while tall dark pines kept their vigil on the dunes above the sea.

It was hard to leave all this beauty, but our permit was running out and we had to return to Germany. Furthermore, the Soviet Front was moving closer daily towards the Baltic States. Sometimes we could already hear the rumbling of cannons in the distance. Early in August we started on our trip back to Frankfurt, back to reality, back to war and air raids, back to hunger and fear. The short respite was over! What better proof of this than the crowds of refugees from Hamburg who entered the train at Berlin? The night before Hamburg had suffered a devastating bombing attack and all Hamburg was in flames. The population had had terrible losses. The people boarding the train had been lucky enough to escape death, but all were extremely upset and badly frightened. Many had soot-smudged faces and torn clothes.

"Abandon all hope, ye who enter here!"—the inscription over the entrance gate to Dante's Inferno—flashed through my mind. While we were in Latvia, a very important political event had taken place. On July 25, 1943, Mussolini was forced to resign and the old King Victor

Emmanuel and Marshal Badoglio took over the reins in Italy. That, of course, means the end of Fascism and there is a general rumor all over Europe that Italy will soon stop fighting.

*August 6, 1943, Höchst* Yesterday we arrived in Höchst. Climbing out of the train I was most surprised seeing Dr. Gellinger standing on the platform. He, of course, had not come to meet me. It was a chance encounter. "Welcome back, Fräulein Zarina," said he. I noticed how extremely pale and tired he looked.

"I thought you were away on vacation, Dr. Gellinger?"

"I had to postpone my trip: we had too many delays in the department due to time losses caused by increased frequency of air alerts. Enemy bombers by now are daily flying east over Frankfurt and the entire Main River valley."

I am scared: it is almost certain that our area will soon come under heavy attack. Up to this point we have been spared by the Americans and the British for reasons unknown to us. As a matter of fact, the population has nicknamed Höchst "The Air-Raid Shelter of the Reich," because in four war years no major damage has yet occurred in our little town.

*August 7, 1943* We are lucky still to have an apartment. When leaving in July I was secretly afraid that we might come back to ruins. I'm grateful for every day on which we still have a roof over our heads.

*August 13, 1943* This morning Dr. Gellinger called our office to take his leave. He is finally going to Garmisch-Partenkirchen in the Bavarian Alps for the vacation which he had to postpone. I took the telephone message and spontaneously responded, "You mean to say, we won't see you again?"

"Don't be silly, Fräulein Zarina, of course, you'll see me again. I'll be back in three weeks," and Gellinger put the receiver down. I'm embarrassed to have blurted out these words without thinking.

*August 15, 1943* Work in the department is much nicer without Gellinger around. There was so much hostility between him and me; he makes me feel tense. And yet, in a way I'm sorry for him. Misery is written on his face. Once he remarked to me, "It is as though I'm carrying a sign around my neck: 'Watch out! Ferocious dog!'"

I have since heard through the grapevine that he is married to a much older woman, the former widow of a butcher. He supposedly chose her for her riches. She brought a daughter into her new marriage who by now is nineteen years old. Nasty tongues in Höchst are chuckling:

"Why didn't Gellinger wait a few years, he could have married the daughter instead!"

*August 17, 1943* Saw Dr. Tann again. He told me about his stay in Bad Kissingen. According to him this spa at the foothills of the Fichtel Mountains is another "oasis of peace in the middle of a raging war," just like Latvia. No bombs have ever dropped on Bad Kissingen and the food served in the hotels there is of much better quality than in Frankfurt.

*August 23, 1943* This morning Herr Kroll, our office manager, called a meeting and in an emotion-filled but subdued voice announced: "Our boss Dr. Gellinger died last night in Partenkirchen." We were stunned by the news. Gellinger was only 36 years old. We later heard that several weeks prior to his death he had been suffering from intestinal hemorrhages but had paid no attention to these danger signals. An ensuing blood infection ended his life.

Gellinger seemed to be an unhappy, bitter man. Despite his avoiding military service through his "Efforts on the Home Front," for which he recently received the Wartime Service Cross, he has now joined in death the thousands of his age group being killed daily at the military front. And one more puzzling and even frightening aspect: my last words on the phone to Gellinger had an ominous double meaning. It has happened to me once before—last year when our old parson died.

*September 1, 1943* We live in daily fear of air raids, but in spite of very frequent alerts in the Main River valley no attacks on Frankfurt and vicinity have lately occurred.

*September 8, 1943* Very late last night came the news that Marshal Badoglio has surrendered and that Italy has stopped fighting. The German radio informed its listeners that the armistice between Badoglio and General Eisenhower was already signed on the 3rd of September, but until the 8th this was kept a secret. In those days after the surrender, but before the 8th of September, the Americans had still bombed Naples. The Germans retaliated by occupying Rome and parts of Northern Italy and by disarming parts of the Italian troops who were within their reach. Right now, heavy fighting is going on between German and American forces at Salerno.

*September 15, 1943* More sensational news from Italy—German airborne troops, led by a mechanical engineer from Vienna, Otto Scorzenny, liberated Mussolini who had been kept a prisoner of Marshal Badoglio in a practically inaccessible place high in the Abruzzi Mountains. On September 12, Scorzenny landed there in a small plane, rescued Mussolini and took off for Germany. Right now, the "Duce" is with the "Führer". After his liberation, Mussolini gathered together some of his faithful servants and party members, changed the Fascist party's name to "Republican Fascist Party" and released the Italian troops from their oath to the "treacherous king" Victor Emmanuel. Scorzenny, meanwhile, is being celebrated in Germany as one of the greatest heroes of all time.

*September 18, 1943* I had dinner with Dr. Tann, during which he lost some of his usual reserve: "If I were twenty years younger, Irene, I would have a hard time to control my feelings for you, and I wouldn't be accountable for my actions, I'm afraid."

"You sound positively dangerous and I'm glad you aren't twenty years younger," I joked, trying to ease the tension. "Don't forget that you are a married man!"'

"Irene, I don't want to vegetate; I want to live! You are so natural, so uncomplicated, so full of enthusiasm for all things beautiful. You have made my lonely life here brighter, have put a sparkle into it."

"I'm glad that you think so, Dr. Tann."

"Stop calling me Dr. Tann, call me Bruno. I know that I'm much older, and that I have no right to interfere with your life, but I don't want to lose you. Promise to come to Japan with me after this miserable war is over! I'll make you head of my research laboratories there. You will see another part of the world and will have a wonderful time!"

Tann looked at me pleadingly. The sudden passionate outburst of this much older very dignified man scared me—I was at a loss for words. "Irene, don't be frightened. Northern Germans have the reputation of being cold, composed and controlled. I am a Northerner, but if you only knew what a storm is raging in my heart!"

"I like you very much, Bruno, but I was born too late for you, much too late! Let's not forget that fact," and I rose to go.

*September 21, 1943* Mother seems to sense that Tann is in love with me, and is full of suspicions: "Aren't you ashamed to be taking up with a man who could be your father?"

"I have not taken up anything with anyone! Dr. Tann has been most kind to me and also to you, Mother, inviting us to concerts, the opera, the theater, asking us out to dine, to enjoy excellent meals in beautiful surroundings at a time when food is severely rationed. He simply is lonely and likes our company." But it is no use arguing with Mother. If she could only understand that human relationships are much more complex than the restricted rules and regulations that govern her world. I wish I could tell her the truth about Tann's feelings for me and ask her advice.

*October 5, 1943* It finally happened late last night. Our fears and premonitions of long standing came true. About 9:00 PM the American Air Force started a massive bombing attack on Frankfurt. We in Höchst sat in our basement air raid shelter, hearing the detonations in the distance, not knowing that all of Frankfurt was already in flames. At midnight the sirens gave the "End of Alert" signal—a long drawn-out howl. Coming out of the shelter we saw an intense red light blazing in the sky above the city of Frankfurt which is eight miles away.

This morning I heard some details about the horrible damages wrought. The "Römer" has burned to the ground—only the stone facade still stands, the old part of town surrounding it is very badly damaged. Many suburbs are either completely destroyed or in bad shape. In Sachsenhausen a bomb fell on a children's hospital burying 730 children and their nurses under tons of rubble: 90 children, 14 nurses and one woman doctor were killed.

*October 15, 1943* The bodies of about 500 Frankfurt citizens who lost their lives in the great air raid of October 5 have been identified and their names and ages today were published in the newspapers. These unfortunates, mostly old people or young women and their children, many of them infants, have been buried in a new cemetery especially dedicated to "War Victims of the Home Front".

Next to the loss of life the loss of immense material values does not seem to count for much—large parts of Frankfurt are in ruins—but I would not want to be one of these poor people who are finding themselves homeless on a devastated street in a devastated city. This is your Total War—Herr Propaganda-Minister Goebbels! The sinister presence of death and destruction is all around us. It can happen to any of us: any day may be our last day!

*October 28, 1943* My birthday! Dr. Tann sent a bouquet of beautiful yellow chrysanthemums. Mother frowned and made nasty remarks. There was no celebration. The mood for parties is gone.

*October 29, 1943* Work at the plant is depressing. My colleagues are distraught, the laboratory workers restless. We spend much time daily in the plant air-raid shelter waiting for enemy planes to either attack Höchst or else pass us by. So far, Höchst, incredibly enough, has been spared. But this not knowing what the next moment might bring, this utter helplessness in the face of ever present danger is nerve-racking indeed.

*November 9, 1943* As usual on this date commemorating the end of first World War, the "Führer" delivered a speech. It was a mixture of boasting, threatening and fanatical belief in the final German victory. I will quote some of his statements: "As always in world history, the final battle alone will bring the decision. But this time the German people will not lose their power of resistance, even under the greatest tribulations. It is an impudence of our enemies that they now behave as if they alone were able to solve the problems of the world, they who could not even solve their own problems. We will never again repeat our mistake of 1918, that is, we will not put our weapons down at a quarter to twelve. The one who will put her weapons down last of all will be Germany, and that at five minutes past twelve! [Thunderous applause] . . . ."

"And then finally one more thing: I read every week at least three or four times, that I either suffered a nervous breakdown, or that I dismissed my friend Göring, and that Göring has gone to Sweden. Then again, Göring has dismissed me—then again, the German Army has dismissed the Party, or vice versa, the Party has dismissed the Army—and then again, the generals have started a revolution against me—and then again, I have arrested and imprisoned the generals, etc. You may be convinced: Everything is possible but that I ever lose my nerves is completely impossible! [Thunderous applause]"

Regarding the bombing terror, Hitler said, "And you may be sure: our towns we shall rebuild again, more beautiful than ever before, and this in the shortest of time! [Thunderous applause] The Americans and the British, at this time, are planning the reconstruction of the world, but I, at this time, am planning the reconstruction of Germany! [A storm of applause] And there will be only one difference: while the reconstruction of the world by the Americans and the British will never take place, the reconstruction of Germany by the National Socialist Party will be carried out with precision and according to plan! [Thunderous applause]"

*November 10, 1943* Today was the funeral of one of the important men in our I.G. Farben Plant, Director Kron, who died several days ago of sudden uncontrolled diabetes. He was a convinced Nazi Party member and held a top rank in the party. He was also the representative of the Ministry of

War for our district. His funeral was the funeral of a pagan. There was no religious ceremony, but some high Nazi Party officials gave speeches and representatives of the plant said a last farewell. At intervals, organ music, rendering heroic motifs from Wagner's operas was played. Finally, before the casket slowly disappeared from the catafalque behind a curtain, one of the Nazi officials stepped forward in front of the coffin, opened Hitler's book "Mein Kampf", announced, "We will now listen to a word by the Führer . . ." and then read a paragraph from that book. This struck me as sheer blasphemy and I remembered the words of the Gestapo man on the train two years ago: "Instead of the Bible, we will have the Führer's 'Mein Kampf' . . . ."

*November 24, 1943* The war goes on and on and there seems to be no hope that it will ever end. Our daily troubles have become routine by now: an unheated apartment, poor food, long queues before the food stores, disturbing alerts, frequent air raids on the Main River valley. Work at the plant is monotonous. The late Dr. Gellinger has been replaced by a Dr. Wernicke, a short, frail, high-strung little man. He seems to be equally as disagreeable as his predecessor. It does not help my depressed mood to have to share an office with Dr. Scholl, who still spouts Nazi slogans daily.

*December 10, 1943* Today a Dr. Wolkov, from the I. G. Farben Plant in Bitterfeld, visited our laboratory. He is the inventor of PNCL2—phosphorous nitrogen chloride, which is the subject of my dissertation. I was surprised to learn that his father was a Russian and his mother a German. His father was director of a bank in Siberia, and after the Russian Revolution emigrated in 1917 with his family to Paris. There Dr. Wolkov studied chemistry at the Sorbonne. Two years ago, being part German, he came to Germany to stay. He speaks German poorly, but of course, Russian and French very well. I wonder why he left Paris. In my opinion this move was a big mistake and Wolkov may some day regret it.

*December 25, 1943* Christmas Day! We are still away from home and there does not seem to be much hope that we will ever see Latvia again. The Russian Front slowly but steadily continues to move westward. We had a little Christmas party at our home. Dr. Tann gave me a big textbook on organic chemistry by Paul Karrer. I promised to study a chapter a week.

    I had a nice present for Mother: a shopping bag made of red plastic material, now being manufactured at our plant. I had fashioned it myself by punching holes around side and bottom edges and then looping heavy white plastic strands through them. I used the same technique to attach the handles. Mother seemed very pleased. "No one else will have such a bag," she announced in a happy voice.

*December 28, 1943* During lunch, we chemists in our department made a resolution: we should indeed enjoy every day on which we are still alive and still have a home. Therefore, we decided unanimously to celebrate the approaching New Year's Eve in grand style.

I will be wearing my new green "peau de soie" dress, which I was able to buy in Latvia this past summer. There was hardly any selection in the "German Department Store" in Riga, where I found the dress. It was a monstrosity, an immense size 52, probably a relic from the "good old days" when people still were fat. I could have used the dress as a tent. I have since altered it to fit me, and out of the excess material I have fashioned a long-sleeved bolero.

*January 1, 1944* The big party took place last night at Dr. Kilian's home. Almost all of the chemists in our department and their wives attended. Mother, too, was invited. She as usual wore her black silk dress, and sat quietly in a corner of the sofa most of the evening talking to the older ladies present.

I received many compliments on my new green dress. Fortunately, we were not disturbed by any air raids and had a joyous time with talking, joking, singing, playing the piano and even dancing. In the midst of all this gaiety, I suddenly remembered the old teacher's words in Latvia about life on a volcano. We truly now seemed to dance on a volcano which could at any moment erupt and destroy us. But I managed. to suppress my pessimistic thoughts.

After Dr. Kilian brought in the punch, which Dr. Heyden—my recent adversary in the patent fight—had concocted from wine, champagne, and preserved fruit, we all began to feel quite merry. At the stroke of midnight, Dr. Kilian got up and declared that the time had come for a speech. He pulled his hair low onto his forehead. and indicated a moustache under his nose. We, of course, immediately recognized whom he was going to portray—the "Führer" himself. Kilian began in a growling voice:

"Party comrades, fellow countrymen, twenty years ago, we stood before next to nothing! Now, we again are standing next to nothing and our enemies are hoping to find in our midst people who are against us. But I am telling you, we are not afraid to destroy these 'elements of decomposition' wherever we may catch them! It does not bother me in the least to sign a death sentence or two and to have a dozen rascals, criminals and traitors executed!" And at that, Dr. Kilian rolled his eyes wildly and banged his fist on the table. We almost died of laughter; the imitation was so perfect and so extremely funny. But even in our laughter there was peril. One treacherous word and we all were doomed!

After Kilian's remarkable speech we proceeded to cast our fortunes. Heating a bit of lead in an old soup spoon over a gas burner in the kitchen, each person took turns to pour the molten metal into a bucket of water. The solidified shapes then were carefully scrutinized either directly under the lights or by casting their shadow against the wall with the help of a candle flame. A variety of shapes emerged from the bucket: a boot, a lion, a tree, a steeple, a heart, a star. Numerous predictions were made.

I cast a shape that looked like an ocean liner with two smoke-stacks. "There is a big voyage in Irene's future!" someone shouted.

"Sure, down the Rhine to Leverkusen," said I.

Mother cast a wreath. "Another funeral!" she sighed.

Our hostess was the last to cast her fortune. When she held her solidified metal piece up for inspection we all exclaimed in unison: "Frau Kilian, a cradle!—You will have a baby!"

"What nonsense! Me—a baby? I wouldn't dream of it! I'm over forty and I'm quite content with my two teenage boys!"

"But, Frau Kilian, it is such a perfect cradle! Just look at it!" we teased her.

"It is a cradle all right, but it has nothing to do with my future!" Frau Kilian exclaimed.

We celebrated until 4:00 AM and then went home, arm in arm, in a long row down the street. Even Mother joined in the parade, linking arms with me and with Dr. Heyden. It has been an exhilarating night—one that I will never forget—an intensely vibrant hour of life in spite of terror and death looming in the background. To me it was a manifestation of the human spirit at its best, an expression of courage, the will to live and the will to enjoy life against all odds!

# CHAPTER TEN

## Terror

*January 2, 1944* Another war year has started. The fate of us all is invariably connected with the fate of Europe and the outlook is devastating: war and more war, more bombings, more destruction and more death!

*January 8, 1944* We have alerts quite often, but since last October no more heavy bombings have taken place in Frankfurt. We all hope that Höchst, for some mysterious reason, will be spared.

*January 11, 1944* Today Dr. Kilian got a letter from Berlin, describing a frightful incident which took place there recently. A young officer whose face had been terribly disfigured in battle at the Russian Front and who after many months in a hospital now is stationed in Berlin, one evening entered a restaurant. He was wearing his captain's uniform. At another table opposite him sat a man who felt disturbed by the captain's maimed face. Calling the waiter he ordered him to deliver a message to the officer: "Will you please leave, I cannot bear to look at you!" The waiter—he must have been a half-wit—carried out the outrageous order, bowing deeply. The officer, remaining outwardly calm, asked politely to have the guest pointed out to him, which the waiter did. The officer then drew his pistol, took aim, shot and killed the man.

    This story reminds me of the young lieutenant whom I saw standing on a street corner during my last stay in Berlin. When I first caught sight of him his dreadfully maimed face gave me an awful shock. Practically all that was left of it were his large dark eyes. He had no more nose, only two holes and an upper lip. The chin was gone. He wore an olive grey kerchief over the lower part of his face, matching the color of his uniform. A sudden breeze had lifted the mask and revealed for an instant the horror that it was supposed to hide. It was the sight of a living skull and I could not help shuddering.

Then compassion was welling up in me for this young human being, probably even younger than myself. Having to live with the symbol of death—a skull—for a face could mean nothing but indescribable agony and utter despair. I wanted to go over and touch him and give him some loving words. I dared not! I would have been totally misunderstood! In spite of war and disaster there are inviolate taboos against young ladies approaching total strangers on street corners in a big city.

*January 17, 1944* In these days a new song is making the rounds in the "Anti-Nazi" group of our department. I don't know where this song originated, but we all enjoy singing it, making sure of course, that no Nazi spies are about. It is a satire about a group of ten persons complaining about the Nazi terror. From this song I learned a German slang word for "complaining", namely "meckern," meaning bleating of a goat. I had not heard this expression before. A person who likes to criticize is thus called a "Meckerlein."

This is the song (Author's translation into English):

> Ten Little Meckerlein
> Ten little Meckerlein
> Last year together had some wine.
> One of them told a cutting joke,
> And there were left but nine.
>
> Nine little Meckerlein
> Once thought about their country's fate.
> One of them dared to think aloud,
> And there were left but eight.
>
> Eight little Meckerlein
> Wished Adolf's death as a gift from heaven.
> One mentioned this to a good friend,
> And there were left but seven.
>
> Seven little Meckerlein
> Talked about Goebbels and his tricks.
> One of them said: "He is a heel,"
> And there were left but six.

Six little Meckerlein
Complained about their gruesome life.
One of them said it was like hell,
And there were left but five.

Five little Meckerlein
Rented a piano from a store.
One of them played "God Save the King,'
And there were left but four.

Four little Meckerlein
Once listened to the BBC.
One told his neighbor what he heard,
And there were left but three.

Three little Meckerlein
Declared the War is not yet won.
This heard a Nazi and arrested two,
So there was left but one.

One little Meckerlein
Got mad and called the Nazis swine.
To Dachau he was taken soon,
And there he met the other nine.

*January 21, 1944* Dr. Scholl, as so often, again annoyed me with his nasty behavior, so I decided to teach him a lesson. I wrote a quotation on a piece of paper and handed it to Scholl: "Whenever a man rises above average, he will be attacked at once, but if ever a woman dares to get into competition with men, the 'Lords of Creation' become downright rude." Bismarck

Scholl read it, glared furiously at me but didn't dare to protest. He considered it wiser to keep quiet than to oppose Bismarck's statements. Bismarck is revered as one of the Nazi Party "Saints," being highly honored and respected by the Hitlerites. The film "The Dismissal" which I saw two years ago bears this sentiment out very strongly. Furthermore, Bismarck is forever quoted in Nazi speeches. Bismarck was a great statesman and I suspect that were he alive he would most strenuously object to having his words misused by a ruthless gang come to power.

*January 22, 1944* It is downright dangerous to think or speak in such critical terms, not to mention making such statements in writing as I did yesterday. However, it is almost a compulsion for me to write, thereby getting these daily frustrations out of my system. I have found a very effective hiding place for my diaries—at least, I do hope that it is effective. I keep them in a locked drawer to which only I have the key. To be truthful, I was actually more compelled to hide my writings by Mother's snooping, rather than by fear of political persecution.

Most of the Nazis I know seem to adore me because I apparently represent their party-line defined ideal of the "Nordic Woman". They can't imagine that such a "Nordic Woman" could have some ideas of her own, objecting to their crazed theories of "Blood and Race" founded on outer physical characteristics rather than basing one's evaluation on simple, plain, old-fashioned goodness of heart.

Mother's insistence on wanting to read my diary I find at present much more worrisome. She is not after my political convictions; she is after my feelings for Dr. Tann. She is convinced that I am having "sinful relations" with him. Mother started anew: "I have the right to know what you are doing at all times, to read your diary and the letters you receive. It is my duty to guide you!"

"You can't, Mother! I know much more about daily battles than you do. You have always lived a sheltered life. First your father protected you and then my father. At barely twenty you became his wife."

"I hated to be married to him. I loved my Russian sweetheart Andrei Kudrashov!" And Mother rushed to her finely chiseled polished mahogany treasure chest, pulled out Andrei's picture and gazed at it lovingly: "Look at his large, dark eyes, look at his black curls! Oh, how happy I was with him!"

"But Mother, for goodness' sake, why then didn't the two of you get married?"

"I have told you this before, Irene. We weren't allowed to: he was Russian Orthodox, belonging to an ancient sect, the "Starovertci—the Old Believers". I was a Protestant, a Lutheran. Neither set of parents gave their permission for this match."

Mother was almost in tears. "How old were you then?"

"Seventeen."

"And you have never forgotten your first love?"

"Never!" Mother was crying now.

I don't know enough about the workings of the subconscious, but could this unhappy love story be part of the reason for Mother's strange brooding moods and concepts—plus her harsh early childhood experiences?

*January 29, 1944* Saturday. The sirens began to wail in the early afternoon. I was still working in my laboratory. We all rushed into the air-raid shelter assigned to our department. Soon afterwards we could hear heavy detonations, though far in the distance. Frankfurt today has been severely bombed. Several bombs fell on the Main Railroad Station that was crowded with trains and people. The loss of life was very high. Exact figures are not known, but it must go into the hundreds, not counting the injured.

Dr. Kalns, my Latvian compatriot, a professor of physical chemistry, whose course I took at the University of Latvia during my graduate studies, and who now is my next door neighbor in our apartment house, arrived pale and shaken from Frankfurt in the late afternoon. The terror was still lurking in his usually mild-looking light blue eyes: "It all happened very suddenly. The sirens hadn't stopped yet when the bombers were already upon us. I managed to run out of the railroad station and into the nearest underground air-raid shelter. A large crowd of frightened people was trying to rush down the steps leading from the open square in front of the station to the shelter underneath. The first bombs began to fall. A soldier appeared at the top of the stairs and jumped in panic right down into the milling mass of terrified humanity on the steps. He landed on a frail woman holding a baby. Both were knocked unconscious by the impact of the 'noble warrior's' heavy Army boots."

"My God, Dr. Kalns, what happened to the mother and child?"

"I don't know, Irene, the crowd surged forward in terror and I was pushed along with them. I'm afraid mother and child may have been trampled to death!" I felt sick to my stomach, reeling, steadying myself with one hand against the cold corridor wall connecting our apartments. But worse was yet to come.

"I don't know how I survived the terror of the stay down there in the air-raid shelter," Dr. Kalns continued, "with one heavy detonation after another shaking the ground, with the lights going out, and nothing else to do but wait for death. Between explosions I could hear the people moaning, whispering prayers, children crying helplessly. Every minute stretched like an hour in that pitch-blackness around us."

"How long did the air raid last?"

"I cannot tell—one loses all sense of time. It must have been more than an hour before the sirens finally gave the signal for 'end of alert'."

"What happened then?"

"I emerged to find a scene of devastation. The railroad station is heavily damaged, its restaurant, filled with passengers when the alert started, was completely destroyed. Many apartment buildings in the vicinity have been erased by bombs. The famous concert hall The 'Saalbau', was struck by a bomb, while the artist Elly Ney and her audience sat in an air-raid shelter underneath the building. The artist and some of the people were hurt."

"I'm so glad that these people weren't killed and that you are safe also, Dr. Kalns!"

"Irene, I'll never forget the last horrible scene I saw before boarding the train back to Höchst! I'm not sure how I can live with this memory!"

"Tell me!"

"I don't want to talk about it."

"Tell me!" I had to know. Not knowing was worse than knowing. Nameless fears were harder to conquer than facts. "Tell me, Dr. Kalns!"

He gazed at me for a long time. Then he spoke: "Approaching the railroad station on my return home I saw seventy coffins lined up on the square before the building. Each contained a corpse. These were the bodies of the bombing victims killed in the station restaurant. The coffins had been nailed together of rough white pine boards. The lid of one coffin did not quite close. Out of it hung a woman's long blond hair!"

Silence. We stared at each other. Words no longer could convey the tragedy, the horror, the insanity of this war.

*February 3, 1944* Maybe I should not have insisted on Dr. Kalns telling me all. For three nights now I have had a nightmare about a woman in a coffin with her blond hair hanging out of it. The woman is always me. I can talk to no one about it, certainly not to Mother. Upon mentioning death she has one response only: "Why didn't I die when I was seventeen and had typhoid! I didn't want to live! Life is a vale of tears!"

*February 6, 1944* I had supper at the "Frankfurter Hof" (which is still standing!) with Dr. Tann. After a while a short, thin, dark-skinned man joined us. He turned out to be a Hindu from India, a friend of Subhas Chandra Bose, whose broadcast I had heard some time ago. The Indian has left his country for political reasons and has now found asylum in Germany. He told us that he is a Brahmin, a member of the highest Indian caste. I thought it an excellent opportunity to talk about the Latvian language and Sanskrit.

Latvian and its sister language Lithuanian are the most archaic Indo-European languages in Europe, still bearing significant resemblances to Sanskrit. I began to ask a great many questions and to my delight and satisfaction I found that indeed many Latvian words are closely related to Sanskrit words expressing the same concepts, particularly such primeval terms like: "earth", "water", "sun", "stars", "heaven", "father", "mother", "child." We started talking about names, and I told him that my last name means "little branch". He responded that in Hindi Zarina means "flower"! How strange, how delightful—my name reaches back several thousand years, keeping its original meaning (or so close to it) through waves of migration northward and westward from India

*February 10, 1944* Dr. Wernicke ordered me this morning to go to Leverkusen to a meeting in the Bayer-Werke Rubber Research Laboratories there. I refused. Train travel and visits to cities in the Rhineland have become extremely dangerous. Trains and cities are attacked by bombers daily. Air raids can be expected anywhere, anytime. The British attack by day and the Americans by night. Dr. Wernicke shot poisonous glances at me, mumbling something about "lack of discipline noticeable in the foreign elements in this country," but let it go at that. I chose not to challenge him on this. The situation in the department is rather tense these days. I have a feeling that our "favorite" Nazi spy Bernauer is watching me closely.

*February 11, 1944* Sure enough! This morning I was called to the boss's office: "Fräulein Zarina, you better start using the German greeting 'Heil Hitler!' immediately, rather than clinging to the old-fashioned reactionary 'Guten Morgen'. There has been a complaint from a venerable trustworthy Party member that some of our fellow chemists and especially 'the ladies' don't use the proper all-German greeting form."

Dr. Wernicke glared up at me from his short height trying to look imposing and threatening. Towering above him by a head's measure I stated sweetly: "'Vivat Caesar!' from which the all-German greeting seems to have been copied had some justification indeed. Caesar was a great man!" I saw puzzlement in Wernicke's face, the wheels in his brains were turning: "Now, what am I to make of this? Is she serious or is she making fun of me?"

He decided to act out the role of Imperator Rex. Pulling himself up to his most erect stance he announced grandly: "I wish to point out to you that you are at present enjoying the protection of the German Reich and therefore owe loyalty and devotion to our Führer and our government. If there are any more complaints we will take measures, my dear young lady!" I was dismissed with a Napoleonic wave of a small pudgy white hand.

*February 12, 1944* No use fighting windmills! I might as well be more cautious. The war can't go on much longer. Germany is being attacked on all fronts. Her cities are in ruins, her population is desperate. Any day gained is a day nearer to the end of this cruelest of all nightmares.

*February 14, 1944* This morning I met our Nazi spy in the hall in front of my laboratory: "Heil Hitler, my dear Herr Bernauer!" I shouted, "and how are you today?" He seemed surprised about such sudden ironclad enthusiasm on my part, but then caught himself and clicking his heels together, right arm outstretched, responded with military formality:
"Heil Hitler, Fräulein Diplom-Ingenieur."

*February 20, 1944* During my visit at Frau Knoth's tonight I heard some very sad news from Ulrike: "Irene, do you remember my friend Karl, the little soldier who was on furlough from the Russian front over a year ago?"

"I do, Ulrike, the one who was decorated during the winter campaign with the 'Order of the Frozen Flesh,' as he called it?"

"Yes, that was Karl, the fellow who had loved me all his life!"

"Ulrike, is he dead? Did he get killed at the Russian front?"

"Yes, he is dead!" Ulrike broke out in tears. "I feel incredibly guilty, I was always so nasty to him, I did not care for his love, I didn't want him!" Ulrike wailed. "I realize now that Karl was a good and loving person—he couldn't help it that he was so short. I should have been grateful for all the love and devotion he gave me. I laughed at him instead!"

I tried to calm Ulrike down: "It is human to make mistakes like that, that will haunt us later. It has happened to me, too!"

"Irene, if I only could ask for Karl's forgiveness, for all the hurts that I have inflicted upon him!"

"Knowing Karl's gentle ways, Ulrike, I am quite certain that he would forgive you with all his heart!" Ulrike kept on crying, but I am convinced that Karl had never held a grudge against her, because he loved her truly. Within a year Ulrike has lost her three best friends: Anna, Inge and now Karl. And what about my friends? The words of a sinister poem are echoing through my mind:

> Ich bin der grosse Völkertod,
> Ich bin das grosse Sterben.
> Mir ist kein junges Blut zu jung,
> Kein Leib ist mir gesund genug,
> Mir ist kein Herz zu fromme.

(I am the force that kills whole nations
I am big death itself.
No young blood is too young for me,
No body too healthy for my reach,
No heart too pious for my touch.)
(Hermann Lingg, *Der schwarze Tod (The Black Death)* Author's translation)

Of my male friends only Ingmar is still left. Wolfgang and Alfred are gone.

*February 25, 1944* I have felt despondent for a couple of days. Karl's death has shaken me up. But today my "joy of life" broke through again. Fortunately for me there is a power or a spiritual force—call it what you will—residing in me, that eventually always comes to my rescue. This morning the sun was shining brightly as I walked the two miles to work. (My bicycle tires seem to have gone on a prolonged strike. Repairs no longer help. They have become so brittle, that I have another flat tire practically every day.)

I held a monologue with myself: "Why worry? Why be full of sorrows? Fate is immovable; it will not bend to our wishes, our desires, our dreams, our hopes! The only way to survive is to be strong, never to give in to weaknesses. I will find my way, as I always have. Maybe I am living in an illusion, but so far this illusion has unfailingly protected me from grave danger.

"As a child I used to think: 'No harm can possibly befall me, because I am the one and only Irene Angelika Zarina in this world. How can anything ever happen to ME?' It was a childish thought, of course, but my Guardian Angel seems to have listened. I believe he is still listening." On this happy note I started my working day.

*February 28, 1944* There seems to be an abundance of political jokes about the high Nazi officials. Almost every day a new story is popping up. Dr. Kilian theorizes that this telling of jokes is like a safety valve for the German people, who are getting more and more depressed daily about the whole situation: the bombings at home and the failures at the Eastern Front. Since there is no freedom of speech or press, the people may be experiencing a certain relief in the telling and retelling of jokes, satirizing the Nazi gods. These stories, of course, are told in strictest confidence only.

The latest runs like this: The "Führer" recently told his barber to give him a new hairdo. "I am tired of the lock falling onto my forehead," he said. "I want a crew-cut instead with the hair standing up like a bristle."

"At your service, my Führer," said the barber and went to work, but try as he might, he couldn't make the leader's hair look like a bristle. Completely exhausted, he finally mumbled: "If you only knew, my Führer, what your own people are thinking of you—your hair would stand on end by itself!"

*March 1, 1944* The atmosphere in Europe is filled with tension. "Invasion here!" "Revenge there!" are the battle cries of the Allies on one hand, of the Germans on the other. The invasion from the West seems only to be a matter of time, the invasion from the East has already begun. Slowly but steadily the Eastern Front is moving westward. The Baltic States are once more gravely endangered by approaching Soviet Forces. Latvians, Estonians and Lithuanians have been drafted by force into the German Army—many also having joined voluntarily—and are fighting together with the German soldiers against the Red Army.

There is no doubt in my mind, that every Latvian, or Lithuanian or Estonian, who loves his country and who is able to bear arms, will try to protect his homeland from the terror of another Soviet occupation, even if he had to join forces with the devil himself. The Baltic people simply have no choice. They are totally alone in their plight, in their losing fight for national freedom.

The same sentiment was expressed in Ingmar's latest letter, which I received today. He expects to be drafted any day and sent into training in an East Prussian Army Camp. He sounds sad and depressed.

*March 2, 1944* Mother is in a very melancholy state. Today I talked to Fräulein Möhler in Unterliederbach. She is our late parson's youngest sister and has some connections to the Hohe Mark, a sanatorium located in the Taunus mountains. She might be able to secure a place for Mother.

*March 4, 1944* The "Frankfurter Hof" seems to be a haven for all kinds of Orientals. Oshima, the Japanese Minister of War, was there last year. Recently I met there the learned Brahmin refugee from India. Today I saw the Great Mufti (supreme Muslim authority) of Jerusalem walking through the lobby with several attendants. He is a tall man who wore a high white lamb's fur cap and a long black caftan. He has recently escaped from Palestine and is on his way to see the "Führer" in Berlin, stopping over briefly in Frankfurt. Dr. Tann still seems to be in good spirits, in spite of the dismal all-around situation. So am I.

*March 13, 1944* Another Nazi joke! Question: Who are the three greatest inventors of the Twentieth Century?
Answer: Hitler, Göring and Goebbels! Hitler invented "Voluntary Compulsion," Göring discovered "Modest Pomp" and Goebbels the "Dressed-up Truth."

*March 19, 1944* Last night American bombers again attacked Frankfurt and did heavy damage. Fortunately, nothing happened here in Höchst, but the tension-filled hour in the air-raid shelter was hard to bear.

*March 23, 1944* Another air raid, this time one that involved us in Höchst directly. I am still quite shaky from last night's terror attack on Frankfurt and Höchst. This was the worst yet, although it seemed to start harmlessly enough! The sirens began to howl at 9:00 PM. The radio announced just one enemy airplane visible on the radar screen covering our territory. I sat in the living room studying my French lesson for Dr. Torgau's class which I have recently joined, reading page 61 in Volume II of my textbook "Französisch für Deutschsprechende—French for German Speakers," by Karl Müller:
"Plusieurs maisons ont été complètement détruites et un grand nombre de magasins endommagés—Many houses have been completely destroyed and a large number of stores damaged." I had barely scanned that sentence, when dark foreboding struck me that the words I had just read might in some mysterious way indicate what was to occur tonight. I dropped the book and fled in panic, rushing down to the air-raid shelter, in time to hear one split second later a terrible detonation. The whole house seemed to rock, the lights went out and left us in total darkness. Then came blow after blow, each shaking the house to its foundations. In between, loud rumbling noises could be heard and the shattering of glass.
I was scared out of my wits, for the first time truly feeling the imminent presence of death—a horrifying experience possibly comparable only to the anguish of the condemned, who is left in ignorance whether his execution has been stayed or not. Pulling my gas mask over my face,—in order to protect myself from choking to death by dust in case of a direct hit on the house—I crouched in a corner on the ground, instinctively rolling myself into a ball with my head on my knees. My whole body trembled, my throat was completely dried out, I could no longer swallow.

I crouched and trembled and whispered prayers. No one spoke, no one moaned or cried or groaned. No noise whatsoever was coming through the pitch-black darkness from the group of people cowering there like me suspended between life and death.

Every second could be our last and every second lasted an eternity. We survived through seventy such eternities, listening to the whistling of the bombs as they came down from heaven. Each bomb's flight downward started with a high whine, grew louder and deeper as it approached the ground and ended with an ear-splitting crash. There seems to be a theory that as long as you can hear a bomb, it is too far away to hurt you. Legend or truth, I don't know and I don't care! I never want to hear another bomb come screaming from the sky!

When finally all became quiet, the FLAK gun-fire ceased and the sirens gave the "End of Alert" signal, we ventured out, shaky but alive and unhurt. I went with a flashlight through our apartment. In the living room I discovered the largest part of the ceiling on the floor and on the sofa, where I had sat studying my lesson. I would undoubtedly have been killed by the heavy chunks of plaster had I not fled just in time. My heavy piano and the large bookcase filled with weighty volumes had been pushed away from the walls by the immense air pressure of the detonations. To my amazement no windows—though all were closed—had been broken in our second-floor apartment. Plenty of windows had been smashed on the upper stories.

The morning dawned upon total destruction in Frankfurt. All that has made Frankfurt a famous and beautiful city is gone. We heard it on the radio: The "Römer" and adjoining buildings have suffered additional damage and the "Römerberg" is now nothing but rubble. The "Hauptwache—the old Police Station", another landmark, is completely destroyed. The churches of St. Catharine and St. Paul, where in 1848 the first German National Assembly took place and the Dome Cathedral, built in 1330, are in ruins, as is the old part of town with its medieval houses and ancient streets. The Opera and the theater—the "Schauspielhaus"—no longer stand, neither does the "Frankfurter Hof," Dr. Tann's hotel. I do fervently hope that Tann managed to escape with his life. All telephone connections are broken between Frankfurt and Höchst. Thousands of people have been killed.

I am particularly upset about the destruction of the "Goethehaus"—the poet's birthplace I visited so recently. An explosive bomb tore this early Eighteenth-Century building apart, stone by stone and scattered it through the rubble that is left of Frankfurt. I am incredibly upset about this killing of people and this senseless destruction of irreplaceable historic monuments and beautiful old landmarks. What savage barbarians are the ruling classes of our Twentieth Century, here in Germany and in the rest of the so-called civilized Western World, not to mention the Soviets?

In Höchst several heavy bombs fell on the Railroad Station and on apartment houses opposite from it. Many people were killed; among them our pretty little blue-eyed "mailgirl", who delivered our letters. Her dead body was discovered hanging head down in the steel frame of a destroyed building. The cashier in the ticket office of the station, a girl, was killed while at work. Her body was found naked, her clothes stripped off by the air pressure from the detonations. The first heavy explosion that so frightened me last night was caused by a super-bomb which fell 300 meters from our building on a schoolhouse, destroying it and two adjoining apartment houses. Many people there were killed.

Dr. Scholl last night after the air raid helped to dig up bodies from under the rubble of the destroyed houses in our neighborhood. He told me that he found a dead mother still holding her completely unhurt and very much alive baby. The mother had been hit on the head by a collapsing beam, and by fully receiving the blow had saved her child from death. After hearing this I said to Scholl: "This is your Total War now, how do you feel about it?" A look of uneasiness and fear came into his face but he replied, "The sacrifices are terrible but we must go on and win the war. Otherwise there would be no sense in our resistance and in our fight!" Sorrow and fury seemed to choke me. I could not reply.

*March 24, 1944* Early this afternoon Frankfurt was bombed again and one of the main business streets, the "Kaiserstrasse", was laid in ruins. By now about all of Frankfurt is gone and I hope the Allies realize that it does not especially pay to throw bombs into ruins. At best, they would only kill more innocent people. There is still no news from Dr. Tann.

*March 25, 1944* "I can't take this bombing any longer," Mother said to me last night. "When the sirens start howling I feel like screaming, like banging my head against the wall, just to shut out the horrible sound and the horrible fear."

"Mother, maybe I could secure you a quiet place in a sanatorium in the mountains, far away from the city, so that you could rest."

"Where would that be?" asked Mother, suspicion rising in her voice.

"In the Hohe Mark near Oberursel."

"I've heard that name before. It is a place for mentally disturbed people, isn't it? The Germans have nicknamed it 'Klapsmühle'—meaning 'Mental Mill.' No ten horses are going to drag me there!" Mother was furious.

"You are exaggerating, Mother, our friend Fräulein Möhler has gone there several times for a rest, and as you very well know, she is a normal person and no raving maniac."

"I will not hear another word about it," was Mother's reply. I dropped the matter.

*March 26, 1944* I've heard the most incredible story of an event taking place during the night of the heavy air raid on Frankfurt four days ago. An American bomber was hit by gun fire. Most of the crew were either killed or wounded, but one flier managed to jump out. He parachuted into the city, landed on the roof of an apartment building and found his way down into the basement air-raid shelter. This was the only sensible thing to do, because it was too dangerous to remain outside with all the bombing and FLAK firing still going on at full blast.

The inhabitants of the house most certainly must have experienced a tremendous shock when the door of their air-raid shelter suddenly opened and an American flier appeared in full battle dress. He calmly asked for a cigarette, but none of the Germans had any because this article is no longer available. The American sat down and waited with the rest of the people until the air raid was over. Then he was taken to the nearest police station and thus became a prisoner of war.

*March 31, 1944* Why doesn't Germany quit fighting? Resistance is completely senseless. The terrible German sacrifices at both fronts and at home are sheer madness! If the Nazis suspected that I was thinking such treacherous thoughts "undermining the faithful, long-enduring and steadfast Civilian Home-Front," I would be instantaneously hauled off to prison and in short order to the executioner's chopping block. But I am not the only secret rebel. There are thousands thinking like me.

*April 3, 1944* We have finally received a letter from Dr. Tann. He has lost all his belongings that were in his hotel room. The "Frankfurter Hof" went up in flames on the night of the great attack on March 22. He sat in a basement air-raid shelter nearby. The house above was hit by a bomb and collapsed. Fortunately the strong beams of the shelter were able to support the weight of tons and tons of debris above, so that the people huddling in the shelter were not hurt. They managed to escape by breaking through the wall leading into an adjoining shelter.

In that manner they forced their way through a total of five basement shelters until they finally reached open air. Dr. Tann is now with friends in Darmstadt and I understand that he will soon be leaving Germany altogether. He will be transferred to one of the Balkan countries, which are all occupied by the German Army.

*April 4, 1944* For some unknown reason I thought of Wolfgang today and of my first formal ball. It was one of the most wonderful days of my life: I danced with Wolfgang in a beautiful long blue silk gown; he was my first love. I still remember the radiance in his dark brown eyes, his charming smile, his proud face, high cheekbones, his aquiline nose. Now he is dead, is no more, his light extinguished! My youthful dreams were beautiful, and although they never materialized, they were still full of bliss and I am grateful for such lovely memories.

*April 9, 1944* Easter Sunday! It is raining and life appears unbearably sad! One sits around waiting for a change that would take all this misery and terror away and would let us live in peace again. I am constantly tired and hungry; there is neither enough sleep because of nightly alerts nor enough food.

Lately, the Soviets also have started bombing attacks. On March 9 they bombed Talinn, the capital of Estonia, and inflicted heavy damage. Talinn is over seven hundred years old and up to the present had preserved its medieval character. I can't bear to think that its Gothic churches, its high narrow townhouses, its ancient city walls interspersed with watchtowers, and its medieval castle high on the hill overlooking the city might all be in ruins, destroyed, dead, like Frankfurt on Main! Hungary, likewise, is now being heavily bombed by the Soviet Air Force.

*April 10, 1944* Fräulein Möhler came to call. I, of course, had instigated the visit. Our guest chatted amiably with Mother and pretty soon I heard Mother complaining: "The events of the last weeks have completely unnerved me. I can no longer take the stresses of our daily existence. I am feeling faint and our starvation diet doesn't help either."

"I could secure you a place in the Hohe Mark, Frau Zarina. Life is very peaceful there, the food is still excellent, and you would get plenty of rest, which you need badly. I can see that, Frau Zarina." I held my breath. Would Mother agree?

"Are you sure that I will not be looked upon as a madwoman, Fräulein Möhler? I refuse to undergo electro-shock treatment and be submitted to restraining jackets and ice-water baths!"

"Come on now, Frau Zarina. The Hohe Mark is no insane asylum; it is a sanatorium for nervous disorders and mainly a place for rest and recuperation."

"All right, Fräulein Möhler, if you say so. I will go there for rest and recuperation." I heaved a sigh of relief. It will be good for Mother to get away from air raids and hunger—and for me from Mother.

*April 14, 1944* This afternoon I took Mother to Hohe Mark. It was a one hour ride by streetcar from Frankfurt. The sanatorium is located in beautiful surroundings, at the foot of the Taunus hills. Mother's room looks out into green and peaceful woods.

*April 16, 1944, Sunday* I went to visit Mother. Interestingly, part of the Sanatorium has been reserved for American and British prisoners of war. The officers are housed in one of the clinic's main buildings on top of the hill, the enlisted men in barracks at the foot of the hill. Mother says she meets the captured officers during her daily walks in the surrounding park.

"One of them, a tall British major, bows deeply every time he encounters me during my stroll and greets me most politely."

"What does he say, Mother?"

"He says: 'Gutt mahnink, Madame!'" and Mother, her eyes shining, tried to imitate the Britisher's Oxford pronunciation.

"And what do you say, Mother?"

"I don't say anything, I just bow my head in acknowledgement. The patients are forbidden to speak to the prisoners of war."

"Mother, knowing you, I don't think that would keep you from talking to them."

"You are right, but I don't speak any English!"

"But maybe the British major knows some German."

"Maybe he does, who knows, Irene, maybe he does?" And Mother smiled.

I doubt that I have started an international romance, but these daily encounters will at least divert Mother's thoughts from the complaints and frustrations so deeply engrained in her psyche.

*April 17, 1944* The I.G. Farben Personnel Department has distributed leaflets with instructions in the event of damage or destruction of the workers' homes. Rule #1 reads: "All members of the I.G. Farben staff, professionals and workmen alike, have to report to their working places at their usual working hours in spite of damage or destruction of their homes."

Rule #2 reads: "In case of destruction of our I.G. Farben plant a general meeting place for all workers will be made known, with orders to report there for further instructions." At a departmental meeting presided over by Wernicke we were told as an encouraging example the story of a man who in one night lost his family and his home. The next morning, he—big hero of the Home Front—appeared as usual at his work bench. Our workmen did not seem to react with much enthusiasm to this gem of loyalty. "The poor devil must have been out of his wits, in a state of shock, not knowing what he was doing!" I heard one older man mumble to his neighbor.

"He was just plain stupid," answered the other.

*April 20, 1944* The program on the radio is always the same, either political propaganda or martial music. The only song I really like is "Lili Marleen" which is being broadcast from all German radio stations many times a day:

> Unter der Kaserne
> Vor dem grossen Tor
> Stand 'ne Laterne
> Und steht sie noch davor . . .

The tune is eminently catching, rhythmical and lilting—sung by a woman with a scratchy alto voice. Her name is Lale Anderson and she has made the song famous. The other day, a radio commentator gave a short history of the song. The words were originally written in 1917 and were already sung by German soldiers in World War I, although to an entirely different tune. The song was forgotten until Norbert Schultze, a German composer, wrote a new tune for it in the 1930's. In 1941 a radio station in Belgrad, Yugoslavia, operated by German soldiers, started broadcasting the song nightly as the closing number in their repertoire, because the song is accompanied by a bugle playing taps. That's how "Lili Marleen" began to gain fame.

Last night, I tuned my radio in to the BBC station and in spite of German disruptive noises interfering with the British broadcast, to my great surprise I heard a familiar melody. It was "Lili Marleen," although with English words:

> Underneath the lantern
> By the barrack gate,
> Darling, I remember . . .

I wonder how the British ever got hold of "Lili Marleen?"

*April 23, 1944* I visit Mother every Sunday. She likes it at the Hohe Mark. She gets no medications, no therapy. The only treatment is rest and decent food. Her absence is a great relief for me too. It is wonderful to be alone in the apartment, not to have to check every word, before uttering it, not to be afraid of temper outbursts and unjustified accusations.

*April 29, 1944* Sometimes little capsules of beauty and enchantment still burst open in our desolate existence. Tonight I attended the premiere showing of the latest German color movie: "Münchhausen" in Frankfurt. It is the story of an 18th century German baron who could tell the most wonderful and colorful lies about his travels and his adventures. These colorful lies have been made into a charming colorful film, a fairy tale for children and grown-ups alike. This is the third German color film, and it is greatly improved as compared to its predecessors. The color tones are very natural and have depth and brilliance. It amazes me that such remarkable progress still has been possible in the German film industry in spite of ever worsening research and working conditions.

Münchhausen's story has a special interest for me. He, being a historic figure, at one time did military service under Peter the Great in Livonia, as Latvia was then called, where he was married to a noblewoman, supposedly a forebear of Grandma Amalia's aristocrat father. Some of the highlights of the film: Münchhausen goes to Russia, meets the famous magician Count Cagliostro there, has a love affair with Catharine the Great, and finally travels from Russia by means of a cannon ball to Turkey. From there, fate leads him to Venice. There he meets Casanova, the great lover. Later he is forced to fight a duel and must flee the city.

Münchhausen's last adventure is his travel to the moon, floating up, higher and higher, with a big balloon. Eventually he again lands on our globe and settles down in his ancestral castle, where he goes on living "happily ever after." The daredevil baron was played by daredevil Hans Albers, tall, blond and keen-eyed, one of Germany's most dashing actors, well known from the film "The Blue Angel", where he appeared in the role of Marlene Dietrich's young lover.

*May 3, 1944* Spring has come again and is casting a golden veil over the forsythia bushes in our backyard, but the colors seem muted to me as though seen through a "glass darkly". War and Death are ever present. There is constant talk about the "Second Front" which is expected to be established any day now. This means Invasion! Scholl said today: "Let the Allies come, they will bash their skulls in running against our Atlantic Wall!"

*May 12, 1944* Dr. Kilian told us a story which caused much laughter in our "Anti-Nazi circle." In the year 1960 a stranger arrives in Berlin and takes lodgings at the hotel "Adlon," the famous hangout of the Nazi bigwigs. The white-haired venerable bellboy shows the guest to his rooms on the second floor—the "bel étage." Handing the servant a tip the stranger asks with a heavy British accent in his German: "What became of the man who used to stay in this room twenty-five years ago?"

"Which gentleman do you mean, Sir?"

"Oh, the one with the forelock and the moustache and the bellowing voice!"

"I think I know to whom you're referring, Sir. He went back to Austria and is again painting houses, Sir."

"I see! Well, what became of that big fat fellow with the wobbly tummy covered with decorations, who also frequently used to stay at this hotel?"

"Oh him, Sir! He went to Sweden and is now building airplanes in his own plant there, Sir."

"Well, well, that's interesting. But tell me, do you remember the pint-sized fellow with the clubfoot who was a buddy of the other two?"

"I sure do, Sir! He went to Switzerland and opened up a bookstore there, Sir."

"Hm, hm, is that so!"

Silence.

After a couple of seconds the bellboy has an afterthought: "Excuse me, Sir, may I ask you a question, Sir?"

"What is it?"

"How come, Sir, that you're so well informed about our guests who used to stay here way back in the thirties?"

The stranger in broken German: "Ich sein Lord Hess from London!- I be Lord Hess from London !"

*May 17, 1944* This afternoon while still at the plant we had an alert. Large formations of American airplanes flew over our territory, looking like silver birds high up in the sky. One of our men counted five hundred planes. They went east and after having completed their mission (wherever that may have been) returned flying back above our town. The deep humming of their motors could be heard for about an hour.

*May 18, 1944* Today the American 8th Army occupied the town of Cassino in Italy. After heavy and long fighting the Germans finally were forced to surrender this remote mountain spot. The town and its famous cloister are completely destroyed. Nothing is left but rubble.

*May 24, 1944* Scholl outdid himself this morning in sheer cruelty. A little sparrow flew through the open window into our office by mistake and, frightened, started bumping into walls, trying to escape. Scholl, jumping up from his chair, caught the poor bird, squeezed it in his huge hairy fist and threw it through the window taking aim to smash it against the outside brick wall.

I screamed in anguish and running up to Scholl, grabbed him by his shirt front and shook him: "Be damned, you cruel monster! I hate you! You miserable killer! God shall crush you as you crushed the little bird!" And I broke out in tears, but Scholl just grinned, showing his big yellow ugly teeth.

*May 29, 1944* The sanatorium "Hohe Mark," where Mother is staying, has been bombed. Two super-bombs fell about 100 meters from the building housing the allied prisoners of war. Fortunately, no one was hurt. It would have been strange if the Americans had killed their own officers, now there in captivity. The bombs fell into soft ground in the park, tearing up two huge holes, 40 feet in diameter and 20 feet deep. Today I visited Mother and the holes in the ground were the sensation of the day. All visitors were taken there to inspect them.

Mother's nodding acquaintance with the British major never developed any further, because the prisoners lately have been kept behind barbed wire. No more walks in the park! Mother has heard from one of the nurses that the POWs and their German guards, surprisingly enough, are on rather friendly terms. The Allied officers frequently get food packages from the USA through the intervention of the International Red Cross. They regularly share their supplies—canned meat, chocolate, biscuits, cigarettes—with their guards. So, every time a new package arrives, captives and captors alike are delighted.

On the way home I passed a group of American soldiers escorted by German military police who were returning to their prison camp. One of them looked at me and grinned. He was a handsome dark-haired fellow, and I noticed with dismay that he had lost his left arm. A huge dark brown spot of blood showed on his empty khaki uniform sleeve, where his arm should have been.

*May 31, 1944* To cheer us up Dr. Kilian again told us a joke: The Reich's Propaganda Minister Joseph Goebbels is delivering a speech about the enemy terror attacks on German towns and the promised German revenge: ". . . and if the English fly to Germany with 500 bombers we shall fly to England with 1000 bombers! And if the English fly to Germany with 2000 bombers we shall fly to England with 4000 bombers! And if the English fly to Germany with 10,000 bombers then—we shall go into our air-raid shelters!"

Kilian delivered this remarkable oratory with a most solemn expression on his face in dramatic tones sounding indeed very much like "little Jupp" himself. We thought his performance excruciatingly funny.

*June 2, 1944* The staff in my laboratory has increased. Frau Lehr, the technical director's wife, is now working with us as an assistant technician, due to the new regulations of the "Führer": Every housewife without small children at home has been ordered to work in a plant. Frau Lehr does not seem to be a very pleasant person, and my fellow chemists have already nicknamed her "the goat," because of her rigid posture and her bleating voice. Teasing me they frequently ask me how I get along with "Frau Direktor Doktor." These are the titles which this woman bestows upon herself as a reflection of her husband's glory.

*June 3, 1944* Today Rome fell into the hands of the Americans. The Germans have declared it an open city and have moved out. The Americans have moved in. I'm so happy that the Germans had enough sense not to start the destruction of that glorious place, which is looking back upon a history of three thousand years.

*June 4, 1944, Sunday, Bad Kissingen* I'm spending the weekend in this resort town, having accepted Dr. Tann's invitation, who is vacationing here. I arrived last night. Bad Kissingen, located on Bavarian territory, is one of the most famous watering places in Germany. Its salt deposits were used even in prehistoric times. The Bavarian kings, especially the art-loving Ludwig I, best known for his affair with Lola Montez, had a great share in the development of the town. One of Bad Kissingen's steadiest and most celebrated guests was Bismarck.

I couldn't believe my eyes when I first stepped out of the train into a completely intact beautiful city with not a single house damaged, with no ruins anywhere, with life going on harmoniously as though no war existed. The shady streets are lined with flowerbeds filled with red geraniums, blue morning glories and pastel-colored roses. Happy, well-dressed crowds of people can be seen in the Kurgarten at the famous Rakoczy mineral spa, taking the waters there or moving along on the Promenade.

Last night Dr. Tann and I had dinner in an elegant restaurant. The food was surprisingly good and the servings much more generous than what can be had for ration cards in Frankfurt. After dinner we attended an enchanting performance of "Il Trovatore" at the opera house, which is decked out in gold and red velvet—the usual 19th century style. It was lovely to be surrounded by elegantly dressed and relaxed people—mostly ladies and older men, like Dr. Tann, since all young men are at the front—and to listen to Verdi's stirring music, without having to fear an interruption by approaching bombers.

This morning Dr. Tann picked me up at my hotel and we went for a walk in a spacious and well-kept park. Coming to an old linden tree I noticed a heart and two initials carved into its thick brown bark. "Another fellow in love," remarked Dr. Tann. I kept quiet. "You must have noticed, Irene, that I adore you," continued Dr. Tann.

I looked at him in silence. Bruno Tann is a very good-looking, stately man, accomplished, polite, charming, with a wide field of interests. His company is so much fun. We can talk for hours about music, history, poetry, paintings, travels, anything at all—and chemistry as well. I wish he weren't so ancient. Furthermore, he has a wife.

Bruno motioned me to take a seat on the bench which had been placed strategically under the old linden tree. The view was beautiful, opening into a vista across the green lawns of the park and out to a sun-filled valley with gently sloping hills at the horizon. "I know that I am old enough to be your father," said Bruno, taking my hand, "but I can't help it, Irene. I love my wife dearly and miss her terribly, but my feelings for you do not interfere with my feelings for her." He sounded very sincere and very honest.

"I believe you, Dr. Tann. I like you too—very much so—and I thank you for your frankness . . . . but that is where we have to stop."

"You are so right, Irene, it would be crazy to get involved. If I were younger and free, I'd marry you on the spot." I had to smile about so much enthusiasm, and jumping up I extended my hand to Bruno.

"Come along, let's make the best of it. Let's enjoy each other's company without getting dramatic or sentimental about it. We can't change the fact that I was born one generation too late for you!" Bruno rose and suddenly embraced me. I gently extricated myself and gave him a peck on the cheek. "Cheer up now, Bruno, we have a lot to be thankful for. We are still alive, that is the main thing. The war has not really done irreparable damage to us. Eventually you will be reunited with your wife and all your problems will be forgotten."

I know, I sounded horribly cold and unemotional, but I have to keep my wits about me. All these peculiar problematic relationships would simply not arise if there were young men of my age around, with whom I could be friends. Before my mind rose the warning example of my acquaintance Ilona Alt, who is wasting her time and her emotions on her married, much older lover, involving herself more and more deeply in an insoluble torturous situation. I for one am for clarity in human relationships. If Mother only knew how determined I can be, if I have to. Tonight I'm going back to Höchst.

*June 6, 1944* The Allied Invasion has begun! Heavy military action started early this morning and it seems that the Allies have been able to establish a bridgehead on the coast of Normandy, between Cherbourg and Caen. I heard the news at the plant. Scholl, of course, is greatly agitated, but our "Anti-Nazi circle" feels relieved that "things have finally started rolling." Now there is at least some hope that in due time the war will come to an end. The tension of the last months and weeks has indeed been hard to bear.

*June 10, 1944* German divisions are involved in fierce battles with Allied troops fighting under the American General Eisenhower.

*June 15, 1944* The Invasion forces are approaching Cherbourg. Rundstedt, the Commander-in-chief of the German Armies, is trying in vain to hold the Allies back. The peninsula Cotentin was taken yesterday by Allied Forces.

*June 22, 1944* Today three years ago the Germans started their war with the Russians. In honor of this anniversary, it seems, the Soviets this morning began their summer offensive against the German Eastern front. Scholl, although looking rather nervous and distraught, has not given up hope yet for Germany's final victory: "der deutsche Endsieg" is his dream of glory.

*June 30, 1944* The fall of Cherbourg to the Allies was announced today.

*July 1, 1944* These days, a mechanical engineer from the Physics Department has started to argue with me about ethical versus Nazi-Party principles, whenever we meet in the plant's air-raid shelter, which usually is several times a day. Herr Evers is a convinced Nazi and his ideas are strictly along the lines of Scholl's and that Gestapo officer's I met on the train three years ago. Evers tries to cover up the hopelessness of the German situation with dry sarcasm. Today he remarked, as we were finding a seat on a bench along an outer wall of the air-raid shelter: "Let's try to secure a window seat in the mass grave!" I felt goose pimples prickle out all over me!

*July 2, 1944* This morning Frau Lehr made a speech: "The Allied Forces are moving nearer daily! How will this all end? I try and try to find an answer, but I simply can't imagine what the outcome will be!" And at that she gave me a nervous grin displaying her big square protruding teeth.

"The answer is very simple and quite obvious, Frau Lehr," said I. But she just stared at me with a blank expression on her face.

*July 4, 1944, Sunday* This afternoon I brought Mother home from the Hohe Mark. She seems much more relaxed and quite pleased to be back in the city. I hope we have no air raid tonight, so she won't get frightened on her first night home.

*July 8, 1944* Last night I tried to listen to a broadcast from the Allies, as I do sometimes. It is very difficult to hear anything, because the Germans are quite successfully disturbing "enemy" broadcasts with drilling and whistling noises. Besides that, of course, I have to tune in with a very low sound, so as not to let the neighbors know what I am up to. Right under us live determined Nazi fanatics, the Buchners, who would most gleefully consider it their patriotic duty to turn me in for listening to enemy propaganda. I got the BBC and also the "Voice of America." Both stations gave news about the rapid advances of the Allied and Soviet forces at the Western and the Eastern Fronts. Since the Allies this time around obviously are the gainers, there is no need for them to exaggerate and I am convinced that they are telling the truth.

*July 9, 1944* Caen has fallen.

*July 14, 1944* Early this afternoon, there was great excitement at our plant. We had an alert, as is usual for this time of day, and soon a group of British airplanes appeared and flew over Höchst. The FLAK began to fire and happened to hit one of the aircraft which caught on fire and, leaving a trail of smoke behind, started to move in towards the west. One of the crewmen managed to jump out and hanging from his parachute came slowly floating down, landing right in the middle of our factory territory.

Scholl and I had not felt like going to the air-raid shelter—one eventually gets used to danger, even bomb scares, unless it is a massive air raid—when suddenly the door opened and in burst our young laboratory technician Fritz: "The factory guards have just arrested a British soldier, who came parachuting down from an airplane!"

Scholl jumped up from his seat. "Where is he?" he shouted, purple in the face with big veins standing out on his forehead.

"He is very young, almost a boy and badly hurt, Dr.Scholl," Fritz said pleadingly. "His face and hands are burned and he can hardly walk. The guards had to support him!"

"These details don't interest me!" yelled Scholl, "I want to know where he is!"

"The guards are protecting him from a crowd of furious workmen who are trying to lynch him!" Fritz whispered, now thoroughly frightened by Scholl's menacing behavior.

"And right they are!" Scholl screeched in a rage—his voice climbing to a falsetto squeal—"Wait 'til I get there! I'll make mincemeat of him!" and out he raced, slamming the door behind him.

"Fräulein Zarina, do you think he will really kill the poor boy?"

"He no doubt would, if he could, Fritz," I answered, as a vision of a frightened little sparrow in a hairy fist flashed through my mind. "But don't worry, the guards won't let that maniac commit murder. They are armed—Scholl isn't." Later I heard that the guards had whisked the British soldier to the Police Station and to safety, before Scholl could reach him.

*July 17, 1944* Today came the news that field marshal Rommel's car was attacked in Northern France by British fighter bombers. The car was forced off the road and overturned. Rommel received serious head injuries and is in poor condition. The Germans are very upset. They adore their "Volksmarschall—the people's Marshall" as they have lovingly nicknamed him.

*July 20, 1944* About 7:00 PM tonight Mother and I were returning to Höchst after a long, hot and dusty day in Frankfurt spent at a number of government offices in quest for a vacation travel permit. We had barely reached our house on Königsteinerstrasse when Frau Buchner, our downstairs neighbor and most staunchly devoted Nazi follower, came rushing out of her apartment gesticulating wildly: "Have you heard the news? An assassination attempt has been made on our 'Führer'!"

I couldn't believe my ears: "It isn't possible, Frau Buchner! What happened?"

"He is all right! Destiny has protected him," Frau Buchner declared with much pathos, "but several of the 'Führer's' staff have been killed!"

Silently Mother and I ascended the stairs to our apartment. Once we were alone we looked at each other and suddenly both burst forth simultaneously: "What a pity that he wasn't killed!" And then we started contemplating what a blessing Hitler's death would have been for Germany and the entire world. It would have spelled the end of the war.

"Because he still lives thousands more will have to die, and that could include you and me, Mother!"

"He must have a pact with the devil himself," was Mother's reply.

*July 21, 1944* Late last night the "Führer" in person broadcast a short statement over the radio, probably in order to prove to the people that he is indeed still alive. "Destiny has spared me for great future tasks," he shouted. "It is but a small clique of traitors that desired to eliminate me. The rest of the nation stands by me more faithfully than ever." I wonder what percentage of that "faithful" nation is right now extremely sorry that their beloved "Führer" has not yet gone to Hell.

*July 22, 1944* The assassination attempt is the only theme of discussions. Everyone is talking about nothing else and the opinions are divided. The Nazis rejoice that their leader was spared and the Anti-Nazis regret it. Today all plant workers and staff were ordered to listen to a speech by Robert Ley, one of our top Nazi officials. The topic, of course, was the assassination attempt. We assembled in a large work-shop and soon Robert Ley's rough uncultured voice came through the loud-speakers. The speech indeed did honor to his reputation of being a ruffian, a drunkard and an uneducated bore. It was a conglomeration of threatening, swearing and name-calling. Even our workmen, who are not too easily shocked, were thoroughly disgusted.

Robert Ley's wrath was mainly directed against the German nobility, whom he called "blaublütige Schweinehunde—blue-blooded swine-dogs." Rumor has it that the "small clique of traitors" seems to be a large organization spread all over Germany, led by quite a few members of the German aristocracy.

*July 25, 1944* The Allied Forces have begun a massive breakthrough from Normandy into Britanny. France is sustaining heavy losses in this fight for her freedom, because the Allies are forced to bomb many strategically important French cities and villages in order to drive the Germans out. All European nations are suffering alike, the conquerors and the conquered, the victors and the losers, and Death is playing the fiddle in this merry-go-round of terror.

# CHAPTER ELEVEN

## "To be or not to be"

*July 26, 1944* I just read a poem by Ricarda Huch that has touched me deeply and also has given me a strong uplift. It is called "Einsamkeit—Loneliness"—and the last verse is incredibly beautiful:

> Sei deine Welt, dein Stern, beglückt wenn deine Glut
> Am goldnen Leben schafft.
> Und fordre nichts, dir wird kein andres Gut
> Als deine Kraft.

> Be thy own world, thy star, and blessed if thy glow
> Adds to life's golden flame.
> Ask nothing more, there is no other prize but
> Strength that's thine alone.
> (Author's translation)

*July 27, 1944* We have a "tempest in a teapot" situation at our department. Frau Lehr, who has been in my laboratory for about two months now, announced this morning with her usual grin, "In a few days I'm going on a six—week vacation to my estate in Prussia!" Our workers were stunned: "But how can you get away for six weeks? The normal vacation period for anybody at I.G. Farben is 21 days!"

Franz Sorg spoke up: "In order to get 21 days off you should have worked at least three years. You have been here two months!"

Fritz chimed in, "You can at best get two days off, one for each month!"

The "nanny goat" continued to grin: "Oh don't worry, my husband will take care of that!" My workers are furious, particularly since last week my technician Liesel Schneider wanted two days off to visit her ailing aunt, her mother's older sister, who is reportedly near death. Her request was not granted. A group of our workers beseeched me this afternoon to see that justice was done and that Frau Lehr was prevented from enjoying special privileges.

"I'm just as disturbed about this as you are, but let's face it: Frau Lehr's work in our laboratory is nothing but a farce, just to satisfy government regulations. Her contribution doesn't amount to much, and I don't think we are losing much."

"You are right, Fräulein Zarina, but we too would like a six weeks' vacation!"

"So would I, but all I'll be getting is three weeks!"

"Do something about it!"

"It seems to me, you yourselves are much better equipped to protest this injustice. I am a foreigner; you are natives, living under a National-Socialist government that is claiming equality for all Germans. Go and insist upon your share of this equality! Speak to Dr. Scholl, your local Party ideologist!" Franz Sorg, Liesel, Frau Schmidt, Anna Berg, Fritz and the rest thought this over, while I stood there in my white laboratory coat waiting for their reply. The reply never came; they turned and silently filed out of my office.

*July 27, 1944* This morning word came from the Technical Director's office that Frau Director Dr. Lehr has been assigned to do six weeks of work as a farmer's helper on an estate in Prussia during harvest time. This evoked much laughter: her husband has indeed risen to the occasion and figured out some "reasonable" excuse to satisfy the workers and the Party, whose badge he is so proudly displaying on his lapel, not to mention the shining example the director's wife is setting: toiling away under the hot August sun on her own country estate and when the going gets too rough, seeking refuge in her own mansion. Rumor has it that Frau Lehr is the sole owner of this Prussian estate and not her husband, and that he married her strictly for her riches.

*July 28, 1944* Nowadays it is very difficult to take a vacation trip to a distant place, because only very limited transportation possibilities exist for civilians. Most of the available engines and trains are now used only for troops and war supplies with the slogan: "Räder müssen rollen für den Sieg!—Wheels must roll for victory!" This statement can be read everywhere, not only in stations and on railroad cars but also painted in large black letters on the ruins of houses and even on street pavements.

So Mother and I, following latest strict government regulations, having secured special travel permits in Frankfurt last week (on the day of the assassination attempt on the Führer), this morning changed our food ration cards into travel food coupons at the local Wirtschaftsamt and picked up enough money from my bank savings account to last us through the vacation trip. Now all we have to do is to pack our bags and then we will be ready to start off tomorrow morning for Gaschurn, a little village in the far-away Austrian Alps, where we are planning to spend my precious twenty-one vacation days.

*July 30, 1944, Gaschurn* After an adventurous trip of about thirty hours we have finally arrived here in this remote little place in the mountains. The journey started with a bang—an air alert, as we were sitting in the streetcar on our way to the Frankfurt Railway Station eight miles away. We had no choice but to simply ignore the alert since the streetcar kept moving along. Fortunately, no bombs fell.

As the trip continued things got increasingly hectic. The next shock was my discovery of having forgotten my big handbag in the streetcar. My friends jokingly call it the "port-starboard bag" because one side of it is made of red plastic material, the other of green (compliments of the Synthetic Resin group at I.G. Farben). The bag contained my passport, our travel permits, our food coupons and eight hundred marks in cash. There wasn't the slightest doubt in my mind that in case of loss we might as well forget about our vacation trip. Money and passport could be replaced, but not the travel permits and the food coupons.

With a sinking feeling in the pit of my tummy I dashed to the Hauptwache—police station in former centuries and now streetcar office in the center of town—bomb-damaged but still functioning—and told the man in charge there about my loss. He immediately phoned to both end stations of streetcar line #12 inquiring about my bag. No one had seen it.

I, meanwhile, tense and nervous, paced the pavement in front of the Hauptwache back and forth—back and forth—for two of the worst hours in my entire life, it seemed. What was I to do? Someone had very likely taken my bag. No one would ever return food coupons and the much-coveted travel permits. It seems silly now, but thoughts of suicide crossed my mind. Why not jump into the Main River rather than face Mother's fury and my own horrible disappointment?"

My "Guardian Angel" came to my rescue. It seemed as though a voice began to whisper, "Don't be ridiculous: what are twenty-one vacation days compared to a lifetime thrown away for nothing? You will survive your mother's wrath, as you have before. What, after all, can she do to you? Millions of people have lost everything they ever had, but consider themselves lucky to be alive. What is the loss of food ration coupons compared to that?"

I heaved a sigh of relief, ready to accept the inevitable: no trip and three hungry weeks ahead! At that moment I caught sight of a flash of red and green. I almost didn't want to believe my eyes, but a streetcar was approaching the Hauptwache and my "port-starboard bag" was clearly visible on the window seat in front of the driver. I got the bag back, its contents untouched: the documents were there and the 800 marks were there also.

In my mind I blessed the honest people in the streetcar, including the Italian foreign workers who had found the bag and alerted the conductor. In a split second my feelings bounced from resignation to joyous happiness and I ran all the way back to the Railroad Station to tell Mother about the fortunate ending of my ordeal.

The train to Constance that we had been scheduled to take had since left and we had to wait for the 7:17 PM train. This meant night travel and I felt great apprehension. Night after night now enemy airplane formations were flying over Germany, bombing cities and attacking trains. We very likely were in for a bad night. Dusk was falling as the train sped through open country—fields, meadows, woods—ever so often passing peaceful villages and stopping in cities on the way south. Coming into the vicinity of Stuttgart the humming noise of approaching enemy airplanes was suddenly heard and large formations of bombers flew over our train.

The train stopped somewhere in an open field. Orders were given to extinguish the dim blue lights in the cars, so that not even a tiny ray could sneak by the dark covers of the blacked-out windows. There we sat in total darkness, and helplessness, listening to the roaring of the engines above us. No one spoke. Eventually the engine noises faded and soon we heard heavy detonations in the distance. The earth shook and with it our car. The more brave, including me, ventured out to take a look. We saw searchlights wandering over the black sky and a red blaze growing at the horizon. Stuttgart already had been bombed the two previous nights, I heard from some passengers, and now the Americans continued their attack on the town.

After an hour in the open field our train again began to move and finally we reached the small town of Villingen. There we were ordered into an underground air-raid shelter, which was nothing more than a deep ditch covered over by a makeshift roof of beams and branches, supporting a three-foot layer of soil above. We crawled into the shelter and found ourselves in the midst of a larger number of bombed-out refugees from Stuttgart, mostly women and children. The eerie blaze of reddish flickering lanterns cast light and shadows over these poor people and I could see the horror still written in their haggard, exhausted and soot-smudged faces. I heard frightful tales of destruction, explosions, houses collapsing, a sea of fire, fields of ruins, and thousands of people killed or trapped under rubble, suffocating to death. It was the same hellish story, heard so often before in these last years, a story to which no feeling human being can ever get adjusted—another version of Dante's Inferno.

I wanted to protest, to scream, to cry out against this horrible torture, this endless murder, this insanity, shake my fists, rave . . . . It was no use, we were utterly helpless, without power, all victims of evil, dark, merciless forces. Is that what history is made of? It seems to be—it has been through the ages.

Exhausted, I slept for a while, perched on a narrow wooden bench between Mother and a sad-faced young woman holding a baby. At dawn we were told that our train would continue its trip south and in the morning we finally arrived in Constance, the ancient town at the shore of the Bodensee—Lake Constant. The lake is almost like an inland sea. It is huge, bordering in the south on Switzerland and in the east on Austria; the west and north shores are German. We took the next boat across the lake to Bregenz on the Austrian border.

Our small white steamship chugged merrily through the waves. From the Swiss side high mountains, partly hidden in clouds, greeted us. I was quite overawed—being a native of the lowlands at the Baltic Sea, I had never seen mountains before in my life. The sun suddenly broke through the morning mist and to my surprise and delight the waves changed from dark gray to a bright blue-green. In spite of my excitement my chemically trained mind demanded an explanation for this unusual water color. All I could think of was that the waters of the lake probably contained some iron salt complexes with traces of copper mixed in, thereby forming beautiful blues with sulfates and bicarbonates.

We passed the famous towns of Petersburg, Bad Chechen, Landau and Friedrichshafen, all on the German side. Friedrichshafen was in ruins, totally destroyed by American bombers. I would not have enjoyed this boat ride so much had I known what I heard upon arrival in Austria, that the day before Allied bombers had attempted to sink this same white little steamboat. Fortunately the bombs fell into the water and the boat and passengers escaped without damage.

Upon entering Bregenz we were already in Austria and from there we went by train higher and higher towards the mountains. On the boat I had had a first glimpse of the Alps, but now I could observe them in more detail: Immense gray steep granite walls covered with fir trees, between them ever so often the silver rivulet of a brook trying to wind its way among enormous rocks down into the valley. The clouds hung low, even lower than the mountain tops. To me the sight seemed oppressive, overwhelming, awe-inspiring. I was not sure if I would be able to breathe freely in the mountains.

In Bludenz we changed to a small-track mountain railroad. The undersized engine puffed its way slowly into the Montafone Valley, working hard to pull train and passengers along. The end station was Schruns, a village nestling deep in the valley. From there it took us another three hours by horse and buggy to finally reach our destination: Gaschurn, 2700 feet above sea level.

Mother was very quiet all through the trip and not complaining. She even took the night in the underground shelter in good spirits. Maybe the rest at the Hohe Mark has helped her. We were kindly received in our inn called "Gasthaus zur Krone"—The Crown Tavern—and taken to our room. The inn, just like every other house in the village, is built in the Swiss Alpine style with a low flat over-hanging roof, low ceilings, wood-paneled rooms and a second floor balcony with a carved railing, encircling the entire building.

The most prominent piece of furniture in our room is the double bed sporting two immense goose down-filled red and white-checkered featherbeds which were puffed up almost to the low-hanging ceiling. The first thing Mother and I did was to remove those monstrosities from our bed. I, for one, was certain that I would have nightmares sleeping under them. Then we opened up the windows leading to the balcony to let the stuffy air out. Looking at the sky I noticed that the clouds had sunk even lower, and were now almost touching the village roofs and swirling in lacy patterns. The world seemed gray in gray, encapsulated in walls of mist, and I felt trapped, a depression coming on.

*July 31, 1944* I awoke in the night and heard the rain drumming on our roof-top. Hoping for sunshine in the morning, I fell asleep again.

But the sun isn't shining, it is still raining. We've had breakfast, consisting of "ersatz" coffee and one white roll with one pat of margarine and two teaspoonfuls of jam.

That was all, I'm still hungry.

For lunch we had some noodles with "Ersatz" gravy, another cup of Ersatz coffee and for dessert a pudding that quite suspiciously looked to me to be made of cellulose, with no nutritional value whatsoever, the same kind that I was once served in the restaurant in Berlin.

It is still raining and I'm still hungry.

Dinner wasn't much better: "spätzle"—a kind, of wheat-flour product made of cut-up, boiled, small pieces of dough and more Ersatz gravy with it: no meat was in evidence. Dessert consisted of a starchy-tasting red jello with a make-believe vanilla sauce, also rather starchy in consistency. With that we were served chamomile tea with an artificial sweetener.

I'm hungrier than ever and it is still raining.

By now I'm almost convinced that I've made a colossal mistake in choosing this desolate spot for a vacation. It is hard to stand Mother's wailing: "Why didn't you leave me in Höchst, there at least we had our regular food rations, here we're starving to death!" (Mother's old spirit is coming back: She is again starting to complain. This time she is right for once, and I am miserable.

It is still raining.

*August 3, 1944* We had to endure two more dismal days of steady rain, but suddenly last night the weather cleared. The clouds disappeared and a full moon rose in shining glory above the mountains, first peeping down into our valley and then traveling higher into the dark blue midnight sky.

This morning the sun shone brightly and the village came alive: people were hustling and bustling in their tiny front yards, traveling up and down the one and only narrow village street, children were playing, dogs were barking, chasing goats that were being taken out of their barns to graze on the nearby lower mountain pastures. Even the geraniums in the flower boxes under windows and on balconies seemed to have put on a much brighter red color to honor the reappearance of the sun. I heard swallows chirping happily under the eaves where they are nesting.

My depression fled with the rising sun, my constant companions—the hunger pangs—were forgotten. The first thing for me to do, obviously, was to climb a mountain. The landscape appeared magically changed: green alpine meadows were glowing like patches of emerald on granite mountain sides, which, reflecting the morning light, seemed enveloped in a rosy-golden haze. Above the meadows, blue pine forests rose into the transparent, crystal-clear cool air. It seemed such a joy to be alive!

Right behind the village a mountain path wound its way steeply up leading me higher and higher, until after a couple of hours I reached the summit. I now was 6000 feet high—for the first time in my life on a mountain top. It was exhilarating standing up there in wind and sun, deep below me the tiny village. My first oppressive fear of the mountains came to my mind. How foolish I had been! Only on mountain tops can one truly breathe freely, where there is nothing at all between you and space.

I saw rows upon rows of purplish gray mountain chains stretching to the horizon under a brilliantly lit sky. I would have loved to sail from peak to peak and peer into all the valleys below that now lay hidden from my gaze. I could only guess their presence. A tremendous sense of freedom from worldly fears and everyday worries came over me. At my feet a multitude of bell-shaped gentian violets were blossoming, painting big patches of blue on the green of the meadow, as though reflecting the color of the sky.

Pink and red alpine roses clustered in low bushes around me, spreading their sweet fragrance. I stretched out on the soft grass in the midst of all this glory of summer, sun and flowers, above me nothing but the sky. As I was observing the sailing clouds my thoughts and longings seemed to be floating away with them to a land of tranquility and peace. Goethe's verses describing the moment of perfect bliss came to my mind:

> Werd ich zum Augenblicke sagen,
> "Verweile doch, du bist so schön! . . ."
>
> When thus I hail the moment flying:
> "Ah, still delay—thou art so fair . . ."
> (Translation by Baynard Taylor)

*August 5, 1944* I have found some companions, who like me love to explore the mountains rising above our Gaschurn valley. These are two middle-aged ladies from Berlin, who also are spending their vacation here. I have repeatedly invited Mother to come along, but she refuses. With a look of utter disdain she told me yesterday: "What, me, climb mountains?! Have you forgotten that I have been suffering from a heart condition for the last ten years now?"

"Mother, this is all your own imagination. Dr. Weiss in Frankfurt recently examined you most thoroughly and couldn't find a thing wrong with your heart!"

"How dare you say such a thing? I know better than any doctor, whether my heart is afflicted or not! And anyway, Dr. Weiss is a perfect fool!"

"I wouldn't say that, Mother! He is a well-known heart specialist and I trust his judgment."

"Have you forgotten that Dr. Rikste fifteen years ago in Latvia declared me to be suffering from a heart ailment?" Indeed, I had not forgotten. I was a child then, but I vividly remember how Mother—at that time in her forties—came home one afternoon from the doctor's office, all excited:

"Dr. Rikste told me that I have a heart condition!" She smiled happily and repeated this—to me rather frightening-sounding message—in a gleeful voice, almost singing it out in a high vibrant tone: "I have a heart condition!"

Yesterday we three decided to climb up to a dairy hut on a pasture high in the Alps. On our way we passed the Garnera waterfall, stopping and admiring the glistening water cascading down over the rocks. It is such a pity that photographic film for years now has no longer been available in Germany. Cameras are lying empty and unused in dark drawers; beautiful sights and scenes can no longer be captured on film, only in our memory.

The mountain pasture plus dairy hut, alas, was somewhat of a disappointment to me, so unlike all descriptions I have ever read about life in an alpine dairy high in the mountains. There everything is supposed to be utterly romantic with pretty maidens and handsome lads, with cowbells tinkling, with heavenly fragrance of flowers and freshly mown hay in the air, and cows decked out with flowers between their horns cavorting on sunny pastures.

The maidens were there all right, quite pretty too, buxom and well-fed. There also was one young handsome cowherd. I wouldn't be surprised if he had a happy time with this half a dozen lovely girls for company. But the rest was extremely disappointing.

The dairy itself is situated in the center of a half circle formed by tiny sheds—one for each cow. These sheds are so constructed that the rear part of the animal when standing in it is sticking out—evidently for practical purposes. The result is a smelly combination of heap and puddle—and this multiplied by twenty gives a stench that defies the imagination. The cows are never let out, they have to stay in their sheds day and night, all summer long, just like being in prison.

Only with great difficulty could we thread our way to the dairy, trying not to step into the odorous puddles. It was a pleasant contrast to find the interior of the dairy hut sparkling clean: the wooden benches and the table were well scrubbed, the huge kettle, in which cheese is made, shone in polished blackness, a number of assorted milk cans sparkled like silver in the sunlight coming through a tiny window in the rear.

I saw no bedsteads and so I asked one of the girls where they slept. "Oh, we sleep up in the attic in the hay," and she pointed to a ladder leading up.

"And where does the cowherd stay during the night? Does he stay outside with the cows?"

"No, he sleeps with us in the hay!" My spinster ladies from Berlin seemed shocked but said nothing.

The three of us had hoped to be able to buy some of the good food in evidence in the dairy: whole milk, cheese, cream, butter. But our longing eyes beheld them only from afar. Upon our timid questions we were told by the pink-checked voluptuous girls in unmistakable terms, "Our entire produce is strictly rationed and we are not allowed to sell anything. But if you wish, we could let you drink some buttermilk!" We were happy to get at least that much and drained our big brown earthenware mugs containing cool refreshing buttermilk with much relish.

*August 6, 1944* It is Sunday and I attended services at the Catholic Church in Gaschurn. It is the only church in the village. The entire population is devoutly Catholic. I noticed with much appreciation that on Sunday apparently all women without exception are wearing their national costume: a. long, heavy, wide black skirt and a tight black long-sleeved spencer with a large dark-colored silk apron tied around the waist. With this a stiff black straw hat is worn with a wide flat circular brim, on top of which perches a huge bow made of black silk ribbon. The women look extremely solemn and serious in this dark-colored Sunday best, holding their prayer books and a tiny nosegay of little flowers, walking slowly down the road to church.

The men are less strikingly dressed, mostly wearing long pants and short jackets made of dark loden cloth. With that go alpine hats and silver buttons on the jackets.

The cemetery is located opposite the church. It seems rather tiny for the size of the village, and so I asked an old man if this was their only cemetery. He replied in the affirmative and. told me that they bury their dead three rows deep, one above the other. I noticed that the inscriptions on the gravestones called all unmarried women "virgins" (Jungfrau) and all unmarried men "lads" (Bursche) regardless of whether they had died at eighteen or eighty.

The population seems to be poor and this is understandable, because the people here are farmers with hardly any land. Each farmer has some little fields on very steep mountain slopes. Working the land is difficult and can be done by manual labor only. Besides that the fields are covered with heavy granite stones. Only a few can afford to keep cows and send them up into the mountain pastures during the summer. Most of the farmers have only goats. A few people keep bees and sell the honey. Their main income, no doubt, is tourism!

*August 8, 1944* Last night an Alpine Army troop moved in on horses in order to carry out some maneuvers in the mountains. This morning the main dining room in our inn was filled with soldiers. I talked to them and soon found out that all of them were recruited Austrians, and that they all loathed the Nazi regime. "The Nazis have taken 'Gemütlichkeit—coziness' out of our dear old Austria!" a corporal complained.

"We hate to have those Prussians in our country!" exclaimed a young fair-haired soldier, "they have brought us nothing but misery!"

I was lucky enough to be able to persuade one of the soldiers to sell me some surplus dark Army bread. Maybe this bread will somewhat appease the continuous hunger that is gnawing at my insides. The food situation has not improved, it is as bad as on the day of our arrival.

*August 10, 1944* In the afternoon I met a dark-haired, rosy-cheeked, extremely attractive young girl. She was tending flowers in a garden as I walked by and singing a Russian folk song. Of course, I immediately stopped and spoke to her in Russian. The girl's name is Yevdokiya—Dushenka for short—and she was brought to Austria as a slave laborer from Russia to work on a farm here. With a twinkle in her soft brown doe-shaped eyes Dushenka told me that the son of her employer, Franz Hubermeyer, is violently in love with her. She has taken him on to be her Austrian sweetheart. Franzl is just now stationed in Italy with the German army and is sending her presents frequently, imploring her not to forget him. Upon my question whether she planned to marry him after the war was over, she said:

"No, oh no, Franzl is a good boy, but my longing to go back to Russia is stronger than my attachment to him!" Dushenka sold me some honey that her farmer boss had in storage. I doubt that this was a legitimate transaction on the girl's part, but I wasn't going to object.

*August 11, 1944* We have been leading a peaceful existence in this remote mountain valley—there are no alerts, no air raids, no bombers—although we've paid for it by a chronic state of hunger. Today, however, this illusion of peace was shattered by the headlines in the papers. At one end of the valley a tiny white chapel dedicated to "Maria im Schnee—to St. Mary in the Snow" is located on top of a hill, surrounded by the Alps in the background with the village street ending at the foot of the hill. I love to sit there quietly, in the grass, my back against the chapel wall, surveying the landscape or reading.

Upon unfolding the morning daily from Innsbruck, glaring headlines leaped at me: "Traitors of July 20th Sentenced to Death by Hanging!" The lengthy article gave a detailed description of the final session of the "People's Court of Justice," which had conducted the trial of the "traitors." The main leaders of the resistance movement that have been tried are von Witzleben, Hoeppner and Hase.

I wonder whom that "People's Court" actually represents. No Germans I know have ever been asked about their opinions or have had a chance to speak up. As a matter of fact, no one would ever dare. There is not the slightest doubt in my or anybody else's mind that the selected judges in the "Peoples Court" are nothing but puppets of the Terror Regime. But the Nazi officials keep screaming all over the country that the "whole German nation has unanimously condemned the criminals of July 20th to death by hanging."

The lies and the pretense are exactly the same tactics I saw in Soviet Russia, the same maneuvers are being used to fabricate the "will of the people" and Goebbels' "dressed-up truth" is being forced upon the population daily in newspapers and broadcasts. Herr Propagandaminister's tirades of burning hatred and bloody revenge are vibrating triumphantly all over Germany and Austria. My soul is sick and I long for refuge somehow, somewhere, out of this hell!

*August 12, 1944* The food situation has become unbearable: the last of the loaf of dark Army bread has been eaten and Dushenka's honey pot is empty. We can no longer stand the hunger here bordering on starvation, so tonight we are leaving, trekking back to the Bodensee, to Lake Constant, the way we came, and then on to Karlstal and "Klug's Mill" in the Palatinate for the last week of my vacation.

*August 13, 1944, Karlstal* We made it to "Klug's Mill", but the trip was even more trying than the ride from Frankfurt to Constance two weeks ago. The first part of the journey back to Bregenz on the shore of Lake Constant was uneventful and the boat ride across the lake to Constance was quite pleasant, in spite of our fears of a possible alert. All remained calm, though.

The troubles started in Constance. It was very hot and the train to Ludwigshafen was so incredibly crowded that there was no way to enter the train through the doors. People were climbing in and out through windows. First I propped Mother up, she grabbed the window frame and by me pushing and passengers inside pulling, we managed to get her in. Then I followed, more or less in the same fashion. Somehow we had also managed to squeeze our bags in. The compartments and the corridor running alongside were tightly packed with people, the majority standing, the luckier ones sitting. Toilet facilities could not be used because it was impossible to move at all, and also because four passengers had jammed themselves into the tiny rest-room, plus their bags.

As darkness fell we again were surprised by American airplanes, saw searchlights, felt detonations, heard the steady roar of hundreds of enemy engines and the firing of the FLAK. Again the train halted in an open field, this time near Heidelberg. We were very scared because more and more frequently now moving trains are being bombed by Allied fliers.

The danger passed, the train moved on and about midnight we arrived in Ludwigshafen. It was very dark as we pulled in—there was no moon, no stars—and I could hardly discern anything. Most passengers left the train there. Mother and I had to wait until early morning for our connection to the Palatinate. We remained in the car.

In the dawn's first gray light I ventured out of the car expecting to find a railroad station, ticket offices, a restaurant and rest rooms. To my immense shock there was nothing there: no building, no walls even, only a railroad track and rubble as far as the eye could see—a whole city of rubble, not a single building anywhere in sight, miles and miles of wasteland around me where Ludwigshafen once had stood.

For a fleeting moment I had the impression that I was experiencing a nightmare. The scene was incredibly grotesque: not a living being anywhere, nothing but one lonely train on one lonely track, in the middle of nowhere. I remembered how I had arrived in the same spot there in July of 1941 to attend a one-week summer course on Synthetic Materials at the world-renowned Badische Anilin und Soda Fabrik (BASF) in Ludwigshafen. The city and the railroad station then had been a lively place bustling with activity, and now three years later a whole city had disappeared, been swept away, was gone.

Grotesque or not, I had to face reality. It was so! In my mind I seemed to hear a growling voice reverberating: "We shall erase their cities..." The curse has come home.

*August 14, 1944, Karlstal* I have since been told that Mannheim, the town across the Rhine from Ludwigshafen, is likewise totally destroyed. What I find amazing is the fact that some semblance of railroad traffic is still continuing to and from these cities in ashes and ruins. They apparently are still serving as relay centers.

The trip from Ludwigshafen to Karlstal was uneventful. Life here is very quiet, except for Allied bomber formations which, coming from the west several times daily, are flying over our valley. The best part of being here is the food: it is adequate, we are getting enough bread and fresh vegetables to feel hungry no longer, although meat and fat are absent from our diet.

*August 15, 1944, Karlstal* The past week has been disastrous for the Nazi regime. Turkey broke its relations with Germany, Bulgaria is just now seeking peace terms with the Allies, Rumania is considering doing the same. Allied troops have today landed in Southern France. I heard all this on the old radio in our room tuning in on the BBC late at night, when all are asleep.

In Poland and the Baltic States losses are mounting for the Germans. The Soviets have swept over Brest-Litovsk, Bialystok and Lvov and are approaching Warsaw and Riga. South of Warsaw the Soviets are moving towards Silesia on former Czechoslovakian territory.

*August 19, 1944, Karlstal* In France the Allies are steadily gaining. They are now heading straight for Paris, Bordeaux, Toulon and Orleans. It seems that German resistance cannot last much longer and I have great hopes that the war may be ending this year. Just now the French Underground Movement is fighting the Germans in the streets of Paris.

*August 20, 1944, Höchst* Today we returned home. On our walk from the railroad station to our apartment we saw a rather strange figure painted in black on house walls and garden fences. It is the shadow of a man in a hunched-forward position, looking much like a thief or murderer. No one seems to know what this is all about and why the black-painted figure can be encountered everywhere.

*August 25, 1944* Paris has been liberated! The Germans here—with the exception of the Nazis—don't seem to care that their army had to withdraw from Paris. The people now are interested in one thing only: End of War as soon as possible! Their endurance is at the zero point. In Paris General de Gaulle has established the fourth French Republic.

*August 26, 1944* Mother and I are no longer using our basement air-raid shelter at home. After having seen whole cities turned into rubble, it is quite obvious that basements cannot give adequate protection. So we, as soon as the alert sounds, are now rushing to the "Bunker" nearest to our house. The "Bunker" is the strongest type of air-raid shelter devised by the Germans, built of steel girders encased in 9-foot-wide cement walls with an 18-foot-thick cement roof. It has six floors. On each floor are small cabins connected by long narrow corridors. The outside cabins have tiny rectangular ventilation holes built into the thick walls. There are ventilators for the inside cabins. The only furnishings are long narrow wooden benches.

The city fathers expected that Höchst, being an industrial center, would be heavily attacked and therefore had six huge "bunkers" built for our small town. For this reason the people of Frankfurt envy us. Their supply of "bunkers" is most inadequate for their city of half a million population. These bunkers have proved to be truly safe! Explosives and incendiary bombs can't damage them. They have withstood countless heavy bombings all over Germany.

By now the bunker is our sole refuge. More and more people are feeling the same way and the place is always crowded. One meets one's friends and colleagues there—almost like in a social club—and since we all feel relatively safe, we chat and even laughter can be heard, while outside the FLAK may be firing, and airplane engines humming. Whenever there is a detonation, even at a long distance away, the bunker catches the shock waves from the explosion and begins to sway. It is an eerie feeling as though experiencing an earthquake.

Last night I noticed Hella and her mother in our cabin. Hella is our departmental office manager's niece. Herr Kroll is a dark-haired swarthy type, but Hella a natural platinum blonde with fair skin and immense blue eyes. Hers is an angelic beauty and she has a lovely personality to go with it. She is always smiling and a very gentle girl. I wanted to ask her how her studies at the University of Frankfurt were progressing, but Hella seemed very tired. She was resting her head on her arms, hair reclining on a bench. Her silvery hair fell over her pale beautiful face and over the sleeves of her rose-colored blouse.

*August 31, 1944* The mystery has been lifted from the big black painted wall shadow: an official Nazi government newspaper release stated that the figure is to represent the "Shadow of the Enemy Agent", who listens in on conversations in order to discover German secret war strategies. The reaction of the population is derision mixed with indignation:

"Any fool can see through this cheap propaganda! Enemy agents! War strategies! 'Blöder Quatsch!—Idiotic nonsense!' We have nothing more to lose at the fronts!"

"This ridiculous figure surely is meant to be the approaching shadow of General 'Männerklau—kidnapper of men'—to replenish the decimated German Army."

"No, you're wrong, it's 'Kartoffelklau—Potato thief'—and he's the reason why we no longer can buy potatoes!"

"To me he looks like 'Kohlenklau—Coal robber'—he's stolen all our coal for heating and therefore we shall freeze this winter." "Klauen," I learned, is a German slang word for stealing, hence the inclusion of the abbreviated verb in the "Shadow's" mock names.

Dr. Kilian gave the final verdict: "This childish propaganda was started by a desperate regime in order to distract the attention of the population from the general disaster at both fronts and at home."

*September 1, 1944* There is great excitement in our department and all over the plant. Bernauer has been arrested, of all things—by the Gestapo itself—for one of the greatest crimes a Nazi can think of: "Rassenschande!—Race Crime!" This means to have sexual relations with a person of any of the "inferior" races: Jews, Poles or Russians. Bernauer's crime was detected when a pregnant Russian girl named him the father of her child. He was questioned at length and finally broke down admitting his guilt. While on voluntary duty as guard of the Russian girls' barracks he had forced one of the girls by brutal threats to submit to him—a repeat performance of his attack on Lydia.

Bernauer is married and has two teenage children. This incident, of course, is extremely embarrassing not only to Bernauer's family but particularly to the Party and all our local Nazi bigwigs. Scholl prefers to keep quiet about the whole sordid affair, while I'm needling him with remarks about the Nazi ideals in theory and the Nazi attitudes towards their own ideals in practice. I get no answer from Scholl, just furious glares. We in the department are all predicting that Bernauer will either be executed by the sword or simply hanged as a "traitor to the cause."

*September 3, 1944* Another blow for the Nazi warlords! Brussels today was liberated by Allied Forces!

*September 8, 1944* Frau Lehr has returned after six weeks as "farmer's helper," tanned, rested and grinning as ever. She looks as though she has put some poundage on her angular big-boned frame, but one thing is certain: she is full of energy and enthusiasm. Today she made a speech: "Our heroic German Army has covered itself with glory. It is true we have had a few setbacks here and there, but that should inspire us all to work even harder at the home front to reach our goal: the final German victory—'der deutsche Endsieg!'"

Her only supporter was Scholl. Bernauer, alas, was no longer there to click his heels and to deliver the German salute. So Scholl did his best to uphold the Party line, shouting with right arm outstretched: "Sieg Heil! Sieg Heil! Sieg Heil!"

The rest stood silent.

*September 10, 1944* The Americans have devised a new strategy. They now are not only throwing bombs on moving trains but are also shooting at them from small fighter planes with machine guns. Today a local from Höchst to the Taunus hills was attacked by a "strafing plane." Several passengers were killed and many wounded.

These suburb trains are of no military importance whatsoever, and the people traveling on them are poor hungry civilians, going into the country to buy some fruit or vegetables, or else commuters to and from work. This is murder, unjustifiable murder!

*September 11, 1944* At the plant I heard some details about yesterday's shooting attack on the train to Limburg. Hildegarde, one of the technical assistants in our department, was on the train together with her fiancé, young Dr. Hermer. Hermer was only recently released from an Army hospital where he had spent the better part of a year in a cast. He had been seriously injured at the Russian front.

In tears, pale and shaky, Hildegarde told me her story: "Heinz and I were on our way to Limburg to visit his parents when suddenly a single fighter plane descended and began firing on the train. The train stopped, we all rushed out and tried to hide under a nearby railroad underpass. People were clinging to each other and screaming in terror. I hung on to Heinz."

"What a nightmare, Hildegarde!"

"I heard the machine-gun rattle come nearer and nearer. The American plane followed us and started to shoot into the crowd in the underpass."

Hildegarde was sobbing now: "Several people were hit and fell. I heard horrible moaning . . . and the clatter of the gunfire . . . Heinz flung his arms around me . . . . trying to protect me. Suddenly he fell forward . . . with blood gushing out of his back . . . I tried to support him . . . but it was in vain . . . ."

"Hildegarde!" I could say no more.

"His blood was all over me . . . a few moments later he died in my arms!" The girl's face was like a tragic Greek mask, pale like marble and filled with inconsolable grief. Despite her tragedy, company regulations require her to come to work.

*September 12, 1944* I cannot forget Hildegarde's horrible tale. What incredible depth of shock, terror and suffering the human soul can endure and survive! But not all people are equally strong. Anna and Inge could not stand up under stress—they killed themselves; Yevgeniya Ryabova, the Russian girl, survived. Hildegarde, the German girl, also seems to have the necessary resilience to overcome this tragedy.

*September 13, 1944* Last night Frankfurt was again bombed. More people were killed and. more buildings destroyed.

*September 14, 1944* The Allied Forces have broken into the Siegfried Line east of Aachen. Parts of the Baltic States are again occupied by the Red Army. From Berlin comes the news that the Nazi High Command is viewing the losses with "sovereign calm"—true to their motto: "We shall never surrender."

*September 20, 1944* Luxemburg has been taken and Brest, the largest port in Europe, today was captured. by the Americans.

*September 25, 1944* This afternoon, Frankfurt was again bombed. Most of the bombs fell into ruins, but two large public air-raid shelters (not Bunkers) were also hit. Since the attack occurred during working hours, these shelters were crowded with people from nearby stores and offices: many were hurt, many killed. It amazes me to hear that a number of business places in Frankfurt are apparently still functioning, in spite of the immense damage in the center of town.

*September 26, 1944* A new special fighting unit has been established. It is bombastically called "Der Deutsche Volkssturm—The German People's

Storm". All German men between the ages of sixteen and sixty who are able to bear arms, and who are not yet at the front, will be drafted. "It was to be expected, wasn't it?" I heard our custodian Herr Herzelt, 70, from the sixth floor, say to Herr Keller, 50, from the first floor. "First they kill off our young men in their prime, and now they are after our grandfathers and our children. It will be my turn next!"

*September 27, 1944* Herr Kroll is very worried: his niece Hella is missing since yesterday. It was her first day on a new job as secretary at a bank in Frankfurt. She did not come home last night and her widowed mother is in terrible distress begging her brother to search for Hella. Herr Kroll will go to Frankfurt today.

*September 28, 1944* Hella is dead. Herr Kroll helped dig out her body from under the rubble of one of the two public air-raid shelters in Frankfurt. He was visibly shaken when telling us about his ordeal this afternoon. "Our poor Hella must have been instantly killed. Her body was badly mutilated, parts of her limbs torn off, one buttock missing and there was a large hole in her abdomen. I recognized her by her blond hair and by the blue shawl which I had given her as a birthday present . . . ."

Tears were streaming down Herr Kroll's face. "My sister is in a deep state of shock, Hella was her only child!" The thought is unbearable that this beautiful girl, to me one of Nature's most lovely creations, has been destroyed, is no more! She was like a flower, torn out by the roots and broken by dark unfathomable forces. I thought of the Ninetieth Psalm:

> Thou dost sweep men away;
> they are like a dream,
> like grass which is renewed in the morning.
> In the morning it flourishes and is renewed;
> in the evening it fades and withers.

This, but by the grace of God, could have been me.

*September 29, 1944* The Germans recently announced the evacuation of the civilian population in Riga. This means that Riga's fate is now decided. Soon the Soviets will move in again.

*September 30, 1944* Today, upon coming home from work, a great surprise awaited me: Aunt Erika and little Eva were there. They had managed to get out of Riga with the help of the German Army. Together with thousands of other Latvian refugees they had been bundled into trucks and. transported into East Prussia from where they slowly found their way to Frankfurt, mostly by train. Three-year-old Eva was exhausted and slept; Aunt Erika looked haggard and tired: "I have left behind all my possessions, my furniture, my clothes. All that we have is in two bags."

"Don't feel bad, Aunt Erika. It is much more important that you and little Eva have not been hurt and are now here with us!"

Erika gave me a grateful smile: "I guess you're right, Irene."

*October 1, 1944* Erika told me this morning that at the beginning of the Soviet offensive against the German forces in Latvia, the German authorities invited women and children to leave on a voluntary basis. As the military situation worsened, evacuation orders were issued and enforced. In the final stages of the German retreat a regular chase for men took place in the streets of Riga and other cities. Latvian men were caught by special Gestapo units and by force shipped to Germany. They weren't even allowed to notify their families about their departure into East Prussian military training camps. I'm very worried about Ingmar and his brother.

*October 2, 1944* Our predictions regarding Bernauer's punishment have turned out to be completely wrong. He has been sentenced to only two months in jail. His wife has let it be known that after his prison term he will be provided with another job somewhere in some distant town. Upon hearing this Dr. Kilian quoted an old German proverb: "One crow never picks out another crow's eye!" That settles the Bernauer case.

*October 9, 1944* Fall has come with rains, cold and dampness. Leaves have turned yellow and then brown and are being blown away by high winds. People are trudging along to and from their jobs. In the wake of the assassination attempt on Hitler our working hours have been tremendously increased. We now work eleven hours daily, from 6:45 AM to 6:15 PM with half an hour's lunch time.

To justify this, Wernicke in one of his rallies for the workers shouted: "We shall prove to the world that Germany's will of resistance is now greater than ever!" The I.G. Farben crew doesn't seem to think so. Everyone already arrives dead tired in the mornings—after having spent another sleepless night in the air-raid shelter—and by the time 6:15 PM rolls around, we are all completely exhausted, particularly since we have several alerts daily, which are spent in the I.G. Farben "bunker." All this, plus the steady hunger, is utterly nerve-wracking and is depleting us of any energy reserves we might still possess.

*October 10, 1944* The German military situation appears to be hopeless. France is liberated. Rumania, Bulgaria and Finland have quit fighting and almost all of Holland and Belgium has been occupied by the Allies. Practically all of the Baltic States are again under Russian control.

*October 14, 1944* Late today it was announced that Erwin Rommel died of injuries suffered in July, when he was attacked by British planes. All Germany is in mourning. Rommel, the "Desert Fox," was their most brilliant and most popular general.

*October 16, 1944* Liesel Schneider, one of my lab workers, today told me a most amazing story about her black tomcat "Mohr." The animal seems to sense beforehand if there is going to be a dangerous air raid on the town or if the alert only is heralding the appearance of enemy air-planes in transport over Frankfurt to other parts of Germany.
 Whenever the alert sounds, Liesel and her parents watch the cat. If Mohr gets very agitated, starts to meow and rushes downstairs into their basement shelter, hiding in the darkest place he can find, they know that there will be a severe bombing attack. If the cat remains calm and unperturbed when the sirens start howling, the Schneiders are certain that the alert is only perfunctory. Liesel claims that it works every time. Well, it could be. My Grandpapa Ernst used to tell me stories about animals' extrasensory perception.
 Mohr, by the way, is quite some cat. Last year, when we still once in a while were issued ration cards for butter, he one day got hold of the entire family's supply consisting of 100 grams and ate it up. Liesel found him, licking his chops. The much coveted butter was in Mohr's tummy. Since that day the Schneiders are calling him "Buttermohr." This story has a funny twist to it. There is an apothecary's shop in town that for the last century or so has belonged to a family named Mohrbutter. So we now have a Dr. Mohrbutter, the pharmacist and a "Buttermohr," the cat, in our fair megalopolis of Höchst.

*October 25, 1944* After a long silence I have finally received a letter from Ingmar. As I feared, he is one of the Latvian boys who were transported by force into East Prussian camps and are being trained in an SS Division there. All the Latvian boys have been forced into SS uniforms.
 Ingmar writes about the last fights in Riga between the Germans and the Soviets on October l2th-l4th. "The Soviet artillery attacked the town, destroying houses and causing great fires. The Germans, on the other

hand, blew up all strategically important buildings, and some dark elements did the rest by setting fire to the National Opera House and by looting stores and homes. Finally the Germans were forced to retreat and the Soviets moved in."

That is the end of our hopes for freedom!

Ingmar continues: "German pilots flying over Baltic territory reported that they have seen long columns of people moving slowly eastwards into Russia. We know where these columns are headed and of whom they consist. These are our parents, our families, our friends, our fellow countrymen—our Latvian, Lithuanian and Estonian brothers! All being taken to Siberian slave labor camps. Shall we ever see them again?"

I'm terribly worried about my Latvian friends and what fate awaits Ingmar.

*October 26, 1944* Every night for hours and hours on end we hear the roaring of enemy bomber formations above our town. We are in an almost continuous state of "air-raid alert." There must be thousands of airplanes coming in wave after wave. By now they are able to reach every city in the whole Reich, and we are daily hearing reports about new terror attacks on the middle and eastern parts of Germany.

We spend almost every night in the "Bunker," bundling little Eva up and either I or Aunt Erika carrying her the half-mile stretch to the shelter, with Mother trudging behind grumbling about the weight of the bag assigned to her, containing our documents, food ration coupons, personal jewelry and some emergency clothing.

*October 27, 1944* Leverkusen on the Rhine has been heavily bombed and Bayer's Central Rubber Research laboratory is badly damaged. Once more we ask ourselves: "Will Höchst be next?"

*October 28, 1944* It is my birthday! Bruno Tann sent me yellow roses. I wonder where he still was able to find a functioning florist's shop in Frankfurt. He recently was ordered back from Bulgaria, where he had spent several months doing administrative work for I.G. Farben subsidiaries there. I saw Bruno the other day. He is still devoted to me, treating me as though I were a precious, delicate China doll.

Doesn't he see me as I really am? Independent, a fighter of a thousand daily miseries, troubles, hazards brought on by the war; a lonely young woman determined to survive. I get no moral support from Mother whatsoever. She is only adding to my burden, nagging, criticizing, attacking my will to live, trying to undermine my confidence. Her stay at the sanatorium has not changed her.

On one hand adoration, on the other hand rejection . . . no wonder that I am grateful to Bruno. He is making life more bearable for me, but I also have to admit to myself: I wish he had stayed in Bulgaria—there is a tension growing between us.

*November 1, 1944* Another letter from Ingmar from his Prussian camp with news from Latvia: "Some more Latvian refugees have now come to Germany by way of the Baltic sea on the German boat 'Steuben.' There were ten thousand passengers. The boat was attacked by fifty Soviet bombers. Fortunately, they didn't manage to hit the ship directly and the bombs fell into the water, but the people panicked and there was a horrible commotion."

*November 7, 1944* Many of my Latvian friends are now in Germany, all in the east. Herta wrote from Dresden: "We Latvians have been put into a camp here—an incredibly dreadful place, filled with people from all 'known and unknown' European and Asiatic nations. It doesn't pay to waste words about the hygienic and sanitary conditions here. At the gate stands a guard watching us day and night: no one is allowed to leave camp. We are virtually prisoners . . . ."

"My only longing is to go back to Riga, although the town is now in ruins: the Opera House, the University, the Court House, the great hotels, the Ministry of Finance and many other buildings are either severely damaged or destroyed."

*November 15, 1944* Ingmar wrote me the farewell letter whose arrival I had so dreaded, knowing that he would soon be sent into combat at the Russian front: ". . . The time has come to say goodbye to you, my love. Tomorrow at dawn we will leave our Prussian training camp and will be heading east to join the German forces in a losing fight with the Red Army . . . .

"Do you remember Lenski's Aria before the duel with Yevgeniy Onegin in Tchaikovsky's opera which we heard together in Riga?

'Kuda, Kuda, Kuda vy udalilis,
Zlotiye dni moyei vesny?'

('Whither oh whither have you escaped,
You golden days of my life's spring?')

"This is how I feel, Irene ... Mana darga sirds draudzene (My dearest friend) so close to my heart, our attachment was always a happy and lighthearted one. We both were too proud, too reserved to talk about our innermost feelings, but before I go, I want to tell you that you were the most wonderful thing that ever happened to me! I had been drifting along, not really knowing what to do with my life. You gave me hope and strength and a goal! You were my guiding star! ..."

I am numb with heartache and fear.

*November 20, 1944* This morning Dr. Wernicke called me into his office to discuss some test reports. Suddenly looking at me he queried: "Why do you look so depressed, Fräulein Zarina?"

"I find nothing to be cheerful about!"

"It could be a lot worse!"

"This is bad enough."

"I'm sure things will straighten out again. We must go on with our daily duties, and that with much fervor!" Wernicke sounded just like Frau Lehr and it annoyed me.

"For heaven's sake, don't you realize that any fervor has become utterly senseless? Why are you continuously urging us to increase our work output, why are we forced to work for eleven hours daily? Nothing can be achieved with dog-tired and starving people anyway! Isn't it about time for Germany to quit this senseless fighting?"

Wernicke stared at me for a long moment, then muttered: "Nonsense, we all have our duty to do!"

"Not having been raised in this country I will never understand your Prussian "Kadavergehorsam (cadaver-like obedience)!" I rushed out of the room. Only now am I beginning to realize that I have been most careless to speak so frankly. What if Wernicke turns me in?

*November 25, 1944* Wernicke, although greatly annoyed, has not reported me to the Gestapo. Maybe he, after all, is admitting to himself that I am right. But, of course, being the boss, his opinions have to closely follow the official pattern, or else he would not be the boss.... Once a month he conducts a roll-call for the workers of our department. He starts out, quoting "a word by the Führer." Then comes the usual pep talk covering increase of work load, request for more enthusiasm and greater incentive—didn't I hear this before way back in Soviet-occupied Latvia? A word or two are thrown in about duty to the Fatherland and the "Führer". The next phase consists of criticism of the department members regarding their "failures" in work or political attitude—this too sounds familiar to me! Then Wernicke ends the roll call by giving the German salute and by shouting three times the familiar "Sieg Heil!"

The workers have to follow suit, have to raise their arms and have to repeat the shouting in chorus. What a farce! Didn't I witness this before? It was a Russian version, though!

*November 29, 1944* I received a letter from Dr. Paul Starker in Leverkusen., in which he describes the present living conditions in their part of the Rhine Valley: "We are constantly reminded of the nearness of the front by droning enemy airplanes. Our alerts continue with almost no interruption. Alerts, so to speak, have become a 'chronic disease.' The time without an alert is now the exception.

"This morning the first alert started at 5:30 AM and lasted through the noon hour. At 3:00 PM the sirens again began to howl, and not far from our home a bomb fell and exploded—an unwanted salute from a single airplane cruising high in the sky.

"What you write about Latvia is tragic and shocking. We here still don't seem to be able to fully grasp the bitter fate of these poor unhappy people who have been forced on their way into Siberian slave labor camps and into hopeless misery.

"Now, here too, long columns of fugitives from the West are passing by daily—a most pitiful sight! And we don't know yet how much further into German country the fury of the war will throw its flaming torch! Maybe my family and I and our whole community soon will have to leave our town trying to seek refuge from the bombing terror.

"We are grateful for every day which we still are allowed to spend in our own home—by tomorrow it already may be destroyed. All we can do now is hope and pray for peace!"

*December 1, 1944* There is still some fighting going on in Kurland—our quaint little Latvian province where German forces are making a last stand trying to hold the Red Army back. The radio is repeatedly bringing news about some small German gains, but there is no longer any hope that the Soviets could be severely beaten and again driven out of the Baltic States. Thousands of Latvian refugees from all over the country are bunched together in the small space behind the German battle lines, not yet occupied by the Russians. These are the people who didn't get out in time—either across the Baltic Sea or by taking the land route southwest into Germany. There is scarcely a hope for them; they all will fall into Soviet hands.

*December 2, 1944* Erika has been able to rent a room a few blocks away from us. She must have sensed Mother's hostility and I'm glad for her and little Eva that they are now by themselves, even though their place is not very comfortable. The room is dark and poorly heated and Erika has to share kitchen and bathroom with her landlady. Mother is pleased, of course: "Now we again will have some peace and quiet!"

"Yes, with sirens howling and bombs dropping!"

"That's not what I mean, Irene. Erika just irritated me."

"Everything irritates you, Mother! I like Erika very much. She is warm-hearted, gentle, always smiling. Adi loved Erika very much and she made him very happy during the short time of their life together. Have you forgotten, Mother, how Erika nursed Adi with utmost devotion as he lay dying of cancer?"

"I agree, she did nurse him well," Mother suddenly said, much to my surprise. There were tears in her eyes, not for Erika or Eva—I'm sure—but in memory of Adi, her younger brother, whom she had helped to bring up.

*December 5, 1944* We no longer undress at night, just lie down on our beds. As soon as the sirens begin to howl—and they do every night—we jump out of bed, grab our overcoats and our two "emergency" bags and instantly leave for the bunker.

Last night I tried a new way of transportation. I put Mother on the package support above the back wheel of my sturdy "Wanderer" bicycle and hung our two small bags on the handles in front. Then I jumped onto the bicycle and by maintaining a precarious balance, managed to transport myself, Mother, bags and all, to the bunker in the short time of four minutes. Walking takes 15 minutes. Every minute counted, because we already could see the flashes of detonations at the horizon and hear the humming of approaching bombers. To make matters worse, I had to find my way through pitch-black darkness. Neither moon nor stars were out. I felt very much as though Death itself was racing us. Suppose a bomb had dropped on the street in front of us!

*December 7, 1944* I wonder what happened to the "Volkssturm?" None of my acquaintances who would be eligible for it have been drafted.

*December 9, 1944* Herta writes from Langenvolmsdorf in Saxonia. She and other Latvians were able to get out of their refugee camp and Herta is now working as secretary in an office. Her letter is very bitter: "It seems

I got into the poorest part of Germany. The population here appears to be extremely ignorant. Only rarely do I meet a person who has any kind of intelligence.

"I have visited quite a number of villages here and talked to many people. I have come to the conclusion that the farmers in this part of the country have not had a chance yet to benefit from the advances of civilization or culture. They are still threshing their grain with flails and. working their fields with oxen (as they did one thousand years ago) and their living rooms and cow barns are under the same roof!

"Here too, we are treated like prisoners of war and are not allowed to express any opinions. Today I found out that even the local hairdressers have strict orders to refuse service to us Baltic people.

"Of course, it would never occur to a German that such an attitude toward us can only create bitterness. They seem to be surprised that we—the foreigners—don't show them the expected devotion and gratitude!"

I am in agreement with Herta. This has been one of the biggest German mistakes in all the countries which they occupied during the war: to treat the native population with haughty contempt—"super-race" lording it over "sub-humans."

*December 8, 1944* The Allied bombing crews continue to use their very frightening and very efficient signaling method during air raids on German cities. Last night Hanau, about 20 miles east of Frankfurt, was attacked. Since no bombs were falling in our vicinity I stepped out of the bunker to watch. As usual, I saw a display of fireworks high above me in the dark night. Red, green and white lights appeared, singly or in patterns and seemed to be hanging in the sky for a long time.

When first observing these signals earlier this year the population seemed bewildered. "What is the meaning of this?" people wanted to know. We soon found out what these "fireworks" signified. These signals are set by the Americans to indicate the target area scheduled for bombing. The Germans have nicknamed them "Christmas trees." They may look beautiful but they spell terrible danger.

*December 11, 1944* Trying to occupy my mind with something besides worries and fears, I have again taken up French with Dr. Torgau, who is a combination of linguist and I.G. Farben patent chemist. Our group meets twice a week at night. Besides me our group consists of Frau Berger, a doctor's wife, my German friend Veronika Arnheim and several young girls. It is a nice group, and we are having lots of fun with all the mistakes we are making trying to speak French. Frequently, our laughter intermingles with the howling of sirens; then we continue our lesson in the nearby bunker.

*December 16, 1944* Saturday afternoon. Surprise attack on Höchst! All of a sudden a few single planes appeared, seemingly out of thin air—no alert was ever sounded—and started throwing bombs onto the old part of town: the tiny narrow houses huddling close to the medieval castle of Höchst, as though for protection. The castle could not save them from destruction! About a dozen houses have been hit and reduced to rubble.

Several people were buried under the ruins of their houses, trying to get out, frantically giving knocking signals, while a Nazi-organized "emergency crew" was equally frantically trying to dig these poor trapped victims out. I imagine that Scholl was there also. Their efforts have been in vain. Digging through rubble from collapsed houses with spade in hand takes an awfully long time. The knocking noises were heard for four hours; then all was quiet. When the emergency crew finally reached the people, they were dead—suffocated.

In another basement shelter a young girl has been found who was trapped for six hours. She is alive and unhurt, except for shock. Collapsing beams had formed a cage-like structure around her, protecting her, somehow letting in air. Both her parents are dead, buried under tons of rubble.

The greatest shock for me is the news that Frau Berger, our co-student at Torgau's French class, has been killed in this air raid. Her end was a freak accident, as though Death was amusing himself by playing a prank. A piece of shrapnel from either an exploding bomb or FLAK came flying through a window of Frau Berger's apartment and hit her in the right temple. She screamed in anguish. Her sister entering from another room, saw Frau Berger make a few steps, heard her cry out: "Help me, oh help me!" saw her collapse. Rushing to her side she found her lifeless, with blood oozing from under her dark curls, running in rivulets over her face. Frau Berger's husband is at the Russian front. He has no knowledge of his wife's death.

*December 17, 1944* Yesterday General Rundstedt began a great surprise offensive at the Western front in a last attempt to stop the Allied Armies. The German military reports today sound very optimistic, but the German people are no longer in a hopeful mood. No one believes in miracles any more. And especially here in Höchst everyone is still so upset about yesterday's bombing attack that no one pays much attention to what at present is going on at the front.

*December 24, 1944* Instead of church bells ringing in Christmas, the sirens began to howl. The prelude to Christmas Eve was a heavy air raid on the Rhine-Main Airport. This important airport lies on the other side of the River Main directly opposite Höchst at a distance of about twelve miles. We were in the bunker, but the detonations were so heavy, that the whole bunker shook and swayed like a boat on a high sea.

*December 25, 1944* In spite of the hard times I arranged a small Christmas celebration for Aunt Erika and Eva. I had also invited Dr. Tann. Our party was twice interrupted by alerts, but nevertheless, we have been as happy as we could expect to be under the circumstances. In preparation for Christmas I had fashioned a number of presents: a knitted sweater, a little dress and a hand-crafted shoulder bag for three-year-old Eva. Mother, Erika and Dr. Tann received handmade calendars, book covers, glasses cases and purses, all "created" by me from leather scraps, bits of plastic materials and odds and ends. It is completely impossible to buy anything at all that would be suitable for a gift.

During the course of the "festivities" Dr. Tann put on his heavy overcoat and a beard made by me out of cotton and appeared as Santa Claus to the great surprise and joy of little Eva, who firmly believes that she has seen the real Santa: "Ziemas Svetku Veciti—little old Grandpa Christmas".

*December 27, 1944* Herta wrote that she is going back to Latvia. Her profound longing for home seems to have made her lose all caution. I am very upset about her decision. Herta most certainly will fall into Soviet hands there and that will mean the end of her freedom. I'll never hear from her again!

*December 28, 1944* Rundstedt's winter campaign in the Ardennes has ended in failure. This was to be expected, considering the overwhelming strength of the Allied Forces.

*December 30, 1944* Today I received a short note from Ingmar's mother. Contrary to my expectations of doom, the remaining Latvian refugees in Kurland, fortunately enough, have been transported by boat across the Baltic Sea to Germany. Among them are Ingmar's parents. His brother Leonid is also at the Russian Front.

*December 31, 1944* It is the last day of a tragic year. I am glad that it has gone, and I am grateful that Mother and I are still alive and that we still have a roof over our heads! Hamlet's question "to be or not to be?" has truly for us also become the issue of the day.

This year has taught me a primitive kind of humility: nothing matters but the Will to Live, in spite of Danger, Terror, Fear and Death!

# CHAPTER TWELVE

## Apocalypse

*January 1, 1945, New Year's Day* For the past three years now on this day I have fervently hoped for the end of war to occur within the next months. At this point I no longer seem to feel the urge for hope or prayer. All my energies must go towards survival on a day-to-day basis. I do not wish to think of the dismal weeks and months ahead, only how I can get through one day at a time.

    The howl of sirens woke us this cold gray morning and off to the bunker we went on my bicycle. In the afternoon we "celebrated" New Year's with cake made of flour mixed with boiled mashed potatoes and yeast. This concoction was baked without fat, not to mention eggs or milk, which we haven't seen in years. And again we were disturbed by an alert, again we rushed off to the bunker. The fear of bombing attacks has become the bane of our existence, much harder to bear than cold and hunger.

*January 3, 1945* Not having heard from Karen—my best friend since childhood—in many months, I was quite happy to receive a letter from her today. But the news did not sound cheerful: "Life in Posen is filled with tension. The Soviet Forces are too close for comfort. The Polish population here is reacting to the military situation by showing the local Germans their anger and contempt more and more openly. I feel as though I'm living on a powder keg.

    "To make matters worse I'm very pregnant. My third child is due by the end of this month. Erich is at the front and I'm all alone with my two little sons Bernd and Wölfchen. Wölfchen is not quite three years old yet and a fragile child. You can imagine how terribly worried I am about the immediate future.

"No, more than that, I'm scared out of my wits! Not of the forthcoming birth, mind you. I've had no problems in the past with my first two babies. But in my present state I'm pretty helpless, big as a house and awkward. Suppose we have to evacuate Posen, have to run? What will happen to me and my babies, born or yet unborn?

"Of course, our 'Gauleiter' keeps reassuring us that the German population in Posen may put all their trust in the superiority of our Army, that we will be protected from all evil, that no harm will befall us, that Posen will remain a German city 'through the ages.'

"No further comment is needed. I'm sure, you are fully aware of my opinion about all this. Think of me in the hour of my need.

"Your old friend, Karen"

Poor Karen: in our carefree childhood we never imagined what the distant future might bring.

*January 5, 1945* This morning I took my little cousin Eva to work with me. I had told my laboratory people about her and they expressed a wish to see the child. Eva was on her best behavior. She curtsied, held out her dimpled hand and blue eyes sparkling under a mop of platinum blond hair, said politely "Guten Morgen!" with a very nice Baltic German pronunciation. Little Eva can't help it: her only contacts in Germany have been her mother, her "Aunt Ella" (i.e. my mother), and myself— and we three speak Baltic German, which sounds somewhat different from the Reichsdeutsch spoken here.

Eva wore the red and yellow striped dress which I had made for her as a Christmas present from I.G. Farben dye lot samples. She was much admired by my lab crew. After the introductions were over, I lifted Eva onto my swivel chair in front of my desk, gave her paper and crayons and asked her to draw me a nice picture. This kept her occupied until lunchtime, when I took her home seated on the back of my bicycle.

This morning, oh miracle of miracles, we had no air raid warning, almost as though the Americans knew that they mustn't scare a little child on its first outing into the working world of grownups.

*January 6, 1945* The aftermath of my little cousin's visit to my I.G. Farben laboratory is a ridiculous rumor. Frau Berg was in her usual working place at the machine testing the tensile strength of our latest synthetic rubber samples, when she saw me come in. She stopped her work and the following conversation ensued: "Good morning Fräulein Zarina, we very much enjoyed little Eva's visit yesterday! She is a darling child, . . . 'wie Ihnen aus dem Gesicht geschnitten—the spitting image of you'!"

"That is understandable. We are first cousins, Frau Berg!" There was a strange look in Anna Berg's eyes.

"But you are at least twenty years older than Eva, Fräulein Zarina!"

"That is correct. Eva was born after I left Latvia in 1941."

A small group gathered around the tensile tester. Suddenly Mitzi Meyer's high voice shrilled out: "But maybe Eva was born before you left?"

I looked at her in astonishment: "I don't see what difference that would make?"

There was no answer. The people in the group stood there, staring at me and grinning. And then it dawned on me: my workers actually suspected Eva of being my own illegitimate child, whom I had somehow managed to hide all these years in Latvia. A strange mixed feeling rose in me, partly anger, partly amusement, partly fierce tenderness for Eva, this little being—budding twig on my family tree—a copy of the child I once was.

"Mitzi Meyer and all of you, I thank you for entertaining the flattering thought that I could be the mother of such a lovely child! I would be happy if little Eva were mine but she isn't. Her own mother is here in Germany with her."

In answer I heard an embarrassed mumble, the group quickly dispersed and Mitzi's big brown somewhat calf-like eyes, that had stared at me insolently just a minute ago, were suddenly down-cast and averted. Gossip indeed seems to be the spice of life. Even in these dark days fraught with danger and terror, my dear fellow humans find it in their hearts to fabricate the most colorful lies, apparently to liven up the hour. Could this be another safety vent, another way to make life bearable, serving the same purpose as the underground "anti-Nazi" jokes?

*January 7, 1945* Last night Dr. Kilian became the proud father of a little girl. This morning he told us the news. My thoughts went back to our New Year's Eve celebration on Dec. 31, 1943, in Dr. Kilian's home a little over a year ago, when we all had cast our fortunes, and Frau Kilian's molten lead had taken on the unmistakable shape of a cradle.

In view of the regularly occurring alerts, which could be expected any time of the day and night, Dr. Kilian had deemed it best to prepare a lying-in room in their basement air-raid shelter for his wife's confinement. He whitewashed the cellar walls, put a bed and a baby crib into the room, and installed bright lights, an electric space heater and facilities for the proverbial boiling of water, also fitting in a medicine chest with medications and first-aid equipment. The plan was to get Frau Kilian to the hospital if possible, but in case of an air raid the emergency room in the air-raid shelter was to be used.

Last night about midnight Frau Kilian went into labor and, as feared, the sirens almost simultaneously began to signal approaching enemy airplanes. Frau Kilian descended to her basement "hospital room." It was impossible to notify the midwife. I understand that in Germany, just as in Latvia, a physician is called in only if complications arise. During a normal delivery even in hospitals only a midwife is in attendance.

Frau Kilian's hour was approaching; bomb detonations were heard in the distance; the FLAK was firing. Dr. Kilian rolled up his sleeves, scrubbed his hands and forearms, put on a gauze mask and delivered his own child, a 6 pound little girl.

"Weren't you scared, Dr. Kilian?" I asked him.

"No, not really—I grew up on a farm in Saxonia and I had to help my father when our cows were calving."

I couldn't help but laugh loudly: "But Dr Kilian, there is a slight difference between a baby and a calf!"

"No, not really," he again repeated the same phrase as before. "The birth process is similar. In my opinion, delivering a calf is more complicated than helping a human baby into this world."

I stared at him in disbelief. "You aren't serious, are you?"

"Oh yes, I am. Many a time when playing veterinarian in my father's barn did I have to reach inside a cow and turn the calf around if it was in the wrong position. To deliver my baby daughter was comparatively simple. All I had to do was receive her, wait for the placenta, then cut the navel cord and bandage her little tummy. Oh yes, not to forget—the first thing I did, of course, was to hold her upside down and spank her, to start her crying and breathing." I am truly impressed by Dr. Kilian. He is an amazing fellow: frank, honest, down to earth, strong, capable of handling any situation, apparently any situation at all.

*January 10, 1945* We finally had a letter from Mother's brother Arno. He and his family are now living in Rothenstein near the city of Jena in Saxonia. They managed to get out of Estonia last fall, just hours before Soviet forces reached Tartu, where they had lived all their lives. The children are now attending German school; Sven is fifteen and his little sister Hiye is eight years old.

Arno writes: "The kids are in good health. It does not bother them in the least to have lost their home. We, the grownups, are miserable and homesick. Refugee life is a hard life. Meta seems to be better able to stand up to our daily troubles and tribulations. I am in rather poor shape, a mere shadow of my former self. My lungs are affected and I'm suffering from a heavy cough!"

Reading this Mother paled: "My God, he is my youngest brother and the only one left in my immediate family. He has TB, the same sickness that killed my father and my oldest brother." And she broke out in tears: "Nothing but death all around us. All my dear ones are either dead or sick and dying. I can sense another tragedy occurring in the near future."

I said nothing. I too felt a strange foreboding that I could not shake.

*January 16, 1945* It has suddenly grown extremely cold. Icy winds and heavy snowstorms are sweeping over Germany, coming from the East, from Russia. But what is infinitely worse is the news that Soviet forces have broken through the German lines in the east and are swiftly moving westward. The Red Army is already deep in Polish territory and is approaching the so-called "Warthegau." There does not seem to be much German resistance left. What will become of Karen and her babies and of all my other Baltic German friends in Posen?

*January 17, 1945* General Rundstedt's winter campaign in the Ardennes has ended in failure. The American General Patton has crushed this last desperate German attempt to turn the tide in their favor. I heard the American broadcaster refer to this military action as the "Battle of the Bulge." Why? The reason for such a name is entirely unclear to me.

*January 19, 1945* Today I visited Frau Kilian and her little daughter. Liliane looks just like a little China doll, with dainty features and perfectly formed arms and legs and tiny fingers and toes, each endowed with a pink nail the size of a split pea. Her mouth is the size, shape and color of a rosebud and was busily engaged in nursing at her mother's breast.

Frau Kilian told me that Liliane's big brothers aged fifteen and sixteen are beyond themselves with delight over their little sister's arrival and are constantly fighting over the privilege of carrying the baby in her bassinet to the air-raid shelter, whenever the sirens begin to howl. I'm sure there should be no lack of opportunity for them to do so. Dr. Kilian's teasing nickname for Liliane is "Kellerassel," which means "cellar bug," because Liliane started life in a cellar.

*January 20, 1945* From the Eastern Front comes the news that Warsaw, Litzmanstadt, and Posen have been taken by the Soviets. The German population in the Warthegau has been evacuated and transported back to the Reich. This is what the official government reports are saying. No one here in the south of Germany knows what really has happened to the people in the Soviet-occupied parts in the east. To make matters worse, the cold wave continues and if anything, has increased in intensity and the temperatures in Eastern Germany have reportedly dropped to—40°C. This can only mean disaster for the refugees fleeing from the Red Army.

*January 23, 1945* The tension that had been building up over the past months between Frau Lehr and me finally erupted today with a big bang. After her return from her Prussian estate last fall she has managed to become more and more obnoxious, trying hard to take over the running of my testing laboratory, which is really my job. She gives orders, she checks attendance, and she reprimands people for being late to work. I have done my best to ignore this, just to keep the peace within our generally tense, tired and depressed laboratory crew. But this morning the inevitable happened. The collision occurred.

Upon checking yesterday's results for 52 synthetic rubber samples sent over to us from the Organic Research laboratories, I noted a very strange thing: the tensile strength for all 52 samples was equal to zero, which literally means that the rubber samples would fall apart upon touch. For any material with a rubber-like elastic consistency this is an impossibility. I investigated the matter and soon found out that Frau Lehr had done the testing of all 52 samples and had made a colossal mistake when handling the testing instrument. She had thus spoiled our laboratory's and also the Organic Research Lab's previous work, because the tests are interdependent and also because our neighbors, the synthetic chemists, produce only very small individual samples, just enough material needed to run through our test procedures.

I told Frau Lehr just that, politely but firmly in the presence of our lab crew, who were trying to restrain themselves, but were obviously enjoying the spectacle. Frau Lehr was terribly offended. No longer grinning, but giving me a poisonous stare, she huffed in her haughty high-pitched voice, "I will not take this insult from a foreigner. I'm going straight to my husband's office." She turned and rushed out of the laboratory, carrying her nose high up in the air.

There is hardly any possibility that I can win in this duel of power. But frankly, I no longer care what will happen next in my job situation, as long as the Nazis don't throw me into jail! For what? For sabotage maybe or for demoralizing the workers at the home front, just to follow the Soviet pattern!

*January 23, 1945* I have received the verdict. Wernicke called me this morning into his office and glaring at me from behind his desk declared with venom in his voice: "Fräulein Zarina, your arrogance has become unbearable. You have dared to criticize the technical director's wife. Who do you think you are? Director Dr. Lehr told me in no uncertain terms: 'My wife and this . . . this . . . woman chemist'"—Wernicke firmly spat this description of my person out as though it were an insult—"Ahm . . . I repeat: 'My wife and this woman chemist cannot work together under the same roof. One of them has to go!'"

"I do not have the slightest illusions as to whom at this stage in the game you consider more important for maintenance of your position, Dr. Wernicke."

"You will be transferred to another department. You shall report tomorrow morning to Dr. Dietrecht at the Physical Chemistry Department, Fräulein Zarina." That was the end of the interview.

*January 24, 1945* My new working-place is in a veritable shack in a back yard of the plant, a dark and dreary place containing long tables along the walls and in the center of the room a contraption made of glass and steel, supposedly a viscometer. My new project is concerned with this contraption. I am to help Dr. Dietrecht further develop this instrument to measure the viscosity of liquids based on an entirely new, unusual principle. I was somewhat surprised to hear about this research project from my new boss: by no means is there a great need for viscometers. They abound in many makes, sizes and shapes. But here I am and planning to make the best of it. I can't say that I miss my job at the Applied Research testing labs. After the tension and commotion there, being virtually alone all day in the viscometer shack is a not unpleasant change.

There is another advantage to my new work location: the shack is quite close to the newly built "super-modern" I.G. Farben bunker, which displays the best facilities to be had in air-raid shelters, namely individual ventilation systems for each cabin, forced air heat, wide passages, ramps to the different floors and easy access to the bunker from all parts of the plant as well as quick exiting possibilities, so that no crowding is possible. Since we spend at least half of our working hours in the bunker, the latter is becoming more important than any working place.

*January 25, 1945* Today at Ulrike Knoth's home I met a woman, a Frau Bergmann from the Warthegau, who ten days ago managed to escape with her family from Posen just before the onslaught of the Red Army. They were lucky enough to make their way to Höchst, where they have relatives. From Frau Bergmann we heard a firsthand report of the double disaster that befell the German population in Posen due to the Soviet breakthrough and the extreme cold wave:

"The people, particularly the ones who were trusting the 'Gauleiter's' assurances, were totally unprepared for the suddenly developing emergency. It all happened so quickly that there was hardly any time to plan the next steps.

"People grabbed their children and a few belongings and ran, mostly to the railroad station. Soon the few trains available were totally jammed. The German Army provided open trucks: soon these were completely packed also. Some lucky persons had been able to organize horses and wagons; the rest were trying to make it on foot, many pushing baby carriages crammed with children, household goods, clothing, odds and ends.

"Any organized effort to direct the stream of panic-stricken refugees soon broke down. All movements were severely hampered by the extreme cold. Soon bedlam broke lose, and everybody was on his own."

"But Frau Bergmann, why didn't these people simply stay where they were, rather than risk freezing to death?"

"We all were scared of the Poles. The moment they heard of the approaching Soviet Forces, they assumed a threatening attitude. We couldn't stay—the Poles would have attacked us, not to mention the Russians."

"I don't blame you, Frau Bergmann, for being scared. I myself am terribly scared of the Soviets. As for the Poles I can't blame them either. They too have terribly suffered in this war." Frau Bergmann did not respond to my remark, but started to wail, "We have lost everything, all our worldly possessions!"

"But you are still alive and still have your children!"

"That is true. Many of the refugees did not make it. They froze to death in the open trucks, even in the trains. The losses among children and infants were especially high. I saw mothers holding dead babies in their arms while the tears froze on their faces. They eventually were forced by the other refugees in the train compartments to throw the stiff little bodies of their infants and children out of the windows. There was no space for the dead—the living had barely standing room themselves. We were that tightly crammed together!"

"What a nightmare, Frau Bergmann!"

Frau Bergmann nodded, unable to continue her tale. Big tears were rolling over her haggard face.

*January 27, 1945* We have been ordered at the plant to look through all our notebooks, reports and laboratory records, collected over the years, and to mark important matters with red labels. These fiery red patches indicate: "Burn in case of approaching enemy forces!" So, finally, the factory administration is silently admitting that the German military situation is hopeless.

*January 29, 1945* I hadn't heard lately from Bruno Tann. Today I received a letter from him from Berlin, which surprised me. His message is quite unexpected: ". . . I have been ordered to go to Berlin to meet with our I.G. Farben representatives there. It is an urgent matter and I am not allowed to divulge any details.

"I may never see you again, Irene, but I will always remember the radiance in your eyes, your youth, your spontaneity, your beauty. You are the most wonderful thing that has happened to me ever since I found Ruth many years ago. Now I am separated from my wife by thousands of miles, and will be separated from you, probably forever.

"I love Ruth and I love you, but in different ways. You are a symbol of my youth that is gone forever, of my ideals, of my longing for beauty that was only partially fulfilled. In my heart I'll send you roses and loving thoughts every day. You were and still are my saint.

"Farewell, Irene, Yours, Bruno"

I didn't know that Bruno was a poet, at least this letter sounds like poetry to me. This parting is hurting me too, but I have to admit to myself, it is for the best that Bruno has gone away. The role of saint simply does not fit in with my nature, my outlook on life.

*January 30, 1945* Each afternoon when I get home from work I'm hoping for some news from Ingmar and from Karen. There is nothing! Are these my dearest friends still alive? Where are they? What has been their fate? I know nothing. I can only hope and at the same time fear the worst.

*February 1, 1945* My work at the "viscometer shack" is incredibly dull. Neither I, nor my new boss Dr. Dietrecht, nor our technicians display much enthusiasm for the job. It is almost impossible to keep one's mind on the experiments at hand, when another air alert can be expected any minute and we all have to rush to the bunker.

Lately Herr Evers, the engineer who kept me company last summer in the old plant air-raid shelter, has again made it a habit to join me during alerts in the new bunker. Herr Evers is amusing enough when he forgets to talk about his Nazi ideas. But usually they are foremost on his mind, in spite of the rapid decline of Nazi military power. But what is infinitely worse: he too has suddenly discovered the "Ideal Nordic Woman" in me and makes it a point to display rapt adoration, trying to hold my hand, whispering endearments, giving me lovesick stares.

And all this, while outside the FLAK is firing and enemy airplanes are droning above our heads. The man is in his forties, married, with a large family. I have no use for him as a suitor, although as a human being he is much to be preferred to Dr. Scholl, our Nazi #1, whom I despise with all my heart. Evers is not mean, just deluded.

*February 3, 1945* The sirens began to howl at about 11:00 PM and. the approach of heavy bomber formations was announced on the radio. My bicycle is out of order. The inner tubes are so covered with patches that they are no longer holding together. One can't very well put patches upon patches. One also can no longer find new tubes anywhere.

I set out on foot to the bunker. Mother, again mad at me, went to our basement air-raid shelter. Halfway down the street I already heard detonations and saw flashes of explosions coming nearer and nearer. I realized that I no longer could make it to the bunker. The Western Front by now has come so close that it takes enemy airplanes only a few minutes to reach Frankfurt and vicinity. The howling of the sirens frequently coincides with the droning of the first approaching bombers.

Terrified, I tried to get into the house nearest me. But the door was locked and I couldn't get in. I tried another door and another. All doors on Königsteiner Strasse were locked. I heard a horrible crash followed by a flash of blinding light and, in desperation tried yet another door. It gave way and I found myself in a pitch-black hall. Somehow I groped my way to the stairs and down into the air-raid shelter.

In the dim light coming from a blue bulb dangling from the low, beam-supported ceiling, I saw a crowd of people sitting on wooden benches along the walls. I had barely entered when another loud detonation occurred. The change in air pressure was so heavy that it toppled me over and I fell flat on my face on the floor. I decided to stay right there, because this first heavy detonation was followed by a series of others. The whistling of the bombs could be heard as they rained from the sky, increasing in depth and loudness from a high whine to a low grumble and a crash. The light gave out. We were in total darkness. By now it was clear to all of us that Höchst was being attacked. Every moment a bomb could hit us. Again I experienced mortal terror, just as almost a year ago on March 22, 1944. My throat dried out, my heart was hammering and I rolled myself into a ball, numb with fear. All of a sudden a roar as of an approaching train was heard and then an ear-splitting explosion. A tremor went through the foundations of the house, the walls seemed to be shaking and then I felt a heavy impact on my body. "My God, the walls are collapsing!" was my first thought, but then I realized that what had fallen on me was a living human being, not a lifeless stone wall. The person too had been swept off his feet by the air pressure. There was no time for apologies. We just lay still, waiting for .... what? Death? Life? I don't know! I don't even know who that person was, male or female. It didn't matter ... all of a sudden nothing any longer mattered to me .... All of a sudden I no longer felt any fear ... or any hope ... or any wish to survive. All of a sudden there was a vacuum in me, a void, and all my feelings, my emotions had been sucked up into this void. I was no longer I; I had become a hollow shell, just lying there in the dark. It seemed like an eternity, but maybe it was only minutes. I don't know.

Then a flashlight glowed in the dark and I heard a man's voice say, "The attack is over! All is quiet!" It was so. There was a great silence, where there had been an inferno of screaming bombs, staccato gunfire from the FLAK, detonations, the deep humming tones of airplanes. Soon the end of alert was sounded. I heard someone remark: "The bombs fell so close, they surely must have hit houses on Königsteiner Strasse."

I ran out of the shelter, continued to run through the darkness, while a multitude of thoughts raced through my mind: "What has happened at home? Where is Mother? Has our house been hit?" When I got there the house was still standing. Mother was still in our basement air-raid shelter. She too had heard the whistling of the bombs and the horrible noise similar to an approaching train engine.

This noise, our "Bunkerwart" (air-raid warden) told us, was caused by a 300 lb. super-bomb which, fortunately enough, had fallen into the adjoining "Schrebergärten" (vegetable gardens)—in back of our house at a distance of about 400 feet. "If it had fallen on the house only a heap of rubble would have been left," the "Bunkerwart" stated flatly. Nevertheless, the damage to the house due to the immense air pressure is extensive. A huge crack runs from top to bottom on the outer back wall of the six-story building. All windows are smashed, all doors pushed out of their frames. Many inside walls in the apartments have collapsed.

When Mother and I entered our second-story flat about two in the morning and shone a flashlight around, we found the entire floor covered with shattered glass. An icy wind was blowing through the broken windows and to make matters worse, glass splinters stuck needle-like everywhere. It was impossible to sit or lie down.

When dawn came, I put on heavy gloves and started to clear the broken glass away. The worst job was to pull the tiny, needle-sharp splinters one by one out from wallpaper, upholstered furniture, carpets and bedding. This job took me almost all day. I have defied the plant's strict orders that an employee, no matter how heavy the bomb damage to his home may be, has first of all to report to his working place. I stayed home, did not go to my viscometer shack.

It is 8:00 PM now. I'm exhausted, hungry, and half frozen to death. The temperature in the apartment is the same as outdoors:—5°C. Mother is bundled up in bed under heavy blankets with a hot water bottle at her feet. Last night's air raid, horrible as it was, has done one good thing: it has shut up Mother. There is not a complaint, not a nasty remark, not a harsh word out of her!

*February 4, 1945* A new disaster! Starting with today, gas service has been discontinued. Gas had been strictly rationed anyway, but now we can no longer even heat water or prepare hot food. We have no other cooking facilities, only gas. Here we are in ice-cold rooms with the wind blowing about, no hot water and not even a cup of hot tea! What a miserable Sunday this is!

In the afternoon the doorbell rang and much to my surprise Herr Evers stood there, short, skinny and quite timid: "I've come to help you, Fräulein Zarina; I've heard that your house has been badly damaged. Is there anything I can do?" He looked at me with a pleading expression in his dark blue eyes. I was simultaneously annoyed but also touched by Evers' obvious desire to be of assistance. "Come in, Herr Evers. Our main problem is the broken windows. It is frightfully cold in the apartment."

"Oh, we will soon fix that, Fräulein Zarina. I figured something like that had happened, and I brought along strong paper and glue." He ran downstairs and came back with a heavy bundle. Soon Herr Evers was balancing precariously on a chair put on a table top—our apartment has very high ceilings and the windows are equally as high—gluing paper over the empty frames. He also helped to repair the black plastic curtains that serve as "black-out" covers.

In turn, I couldn't even offer Herr Evers a cup of chamomile or peppermint tea—we have not seen Chinese tea in years. All day today we have lived on dry bread and cold water. "Herr Evers," I told him upon parting, "you have been most kind to give up your Sunday afternoon to come and. help me!"

"Oh, don't mention it, Fräulein Zarina, I'd do anything for you!" and Evers bent over my hand and kissed it. What am I going to do with this new problem in my life?

*February 5, 1945* I couldn't bring myself to go back to work, with the prospect of spending most of the day in the bunker, and Herr Evers hovering around me. About 10:00 AM a messenger boy arrived, sent, of all people, by Wernicke, not Dr. Dietrecht, my new boss. Wernicke demanded why I hadn't reported to work this morning and "rattling his sword," concluded the message: "If you don't immediately show up at your working place, I will have to notify the authorities."

Well, well, it's just like in Soviet Latvia. Will they charge me with sabotage, I wonder?

I went.

*February 6, 1945* With so many problems besieging us, I've barely had time to listen to the radio broadcasts. Today I heard that German Forces are defending Budapest against the onslaught of the Red Army. The population, according to the commentator, is "deeply grateful to the German Army for their protection of the Hungarian nation." To me it seems more like a case of choosing the lesser evil. I too, escaping to Nazi Germany in 1941, had to choose between the "frying pan and the fire."

*February 7, 1945* Stepping out of my viscometer shack this noon I saw Mother standing there waiting for me. This was most unusual and one look at her face told me that something dreadful must have happened.

"What is it, Mother?" I exclaimed. "Why are you here?"

Mother burst into tears: "Sven is dead, he died a week ago on Jan 30," and she handed me a letter. I couldn't believe my ears.

"Sven dead? But he just turned fifteen. What happened to him?" Sobbing, Mother translated Uncle Arno's Estonian letter. Sven died on the operating table in a hospital in Jena, minutes after an appendectomy had been performed on him. It all had happened very suddenly. Arno and Meta are heartbroken. Now they only have their little daughter Hiye left. Mother had been right with her morbid prediction of a new tragedy in our family.

*February 8, 1945* Sven's death has added to our emotional burden. We are terribly depressed. The naked truth is that life at this point seems hardly worthwhile fighting for. And yet, and yet—I want to live, I cling to life: life at all costs!

Even Mother is determined to survive. She, whom I remember since my childhood as wailing, "Why didn't I die at age seventeen?" keeps quiet. Now, when life truly is a "vale of tears" I have no longer heard any death wish coming from Mother. She is holding her own, in spite of the cold in the house, no gas, cold food only and no longer even a hot water bottle in bed. She is also the first one in the air-raid shelter and not a bit hesitant to run to the bunker. Could it be that the best cure for people who, living in comparative comfort and security, are forever disenchanted with life, is true hardship, true danger of death? It certainly seems to be working for Mother.

*February 9, 1945* One of the technicians in the Viscometer Shack is a French prisoner of war, a dark-haired pleasant-looking young fellow with rather pink cheeks. I decided to try my recently acquired French from Dr. Torgau's lessons on him: "Pierre, d'où venez-vous?"

Pierre told me that he comes from Marseilles, where he was a schoolteacher and that his young wife and two small children are waiting for him. I assured him in French: "Cheer up, just a short time from now, you will see them again!" Pierre's eyes lit up and smiling happily he replied: "Oh mademoiselle, je serai très heureux de revoir ma famille!" I hope his fervent wish comes true soon.

*February 10, 1945* The Allied. Heads of State are just now meeting at a conference in Yalta in the Crimea. Churchill, Roosevelt and Stalin have got together to decide the future fate of Europe and particularly Germany. As long as England and. the United States are in alliance with the Soviet murderers I simply cannot see any great hopes for a just and peaceful settlement for the European nations involved. The Baltic States will never regain their freedom as long as mustachioed Stalin sits at the conference table.

*February 12, 1945* Today a letter arrived from Berlin. For a moment I thought it might be from Bruno Tann, but it wasn't. It came from Dr. Dehren, the zoologist who early last year was transferred from I.G. Farben Höchst back to Berlin. He writes: "Berlin is preparing for the final storm. The Berliners are presently building barricades and digging ditches. We are in a continuous state of siege. The city is almost uninterruptedly attacked by bombers and strafing airplanes, which every hour on the hour, by day and by night, are raining death and destruction upon us.

"Although I'm considered unfit by the authorities to get married, I'm nevertheless considered fit enough to help build their barricades and consequently fit enough to die on them in the approaching final battle over Berlin!"

Poor luckless Dr. Dehren! For him to have cast all precautions aside, writing such a frankly criticizing letter can mean one thing only—he too has reached a void, but for him it is a permanent void, where he no longer cares what happens to his person!

*February 13, 1945* Scholl is very depressed these days. Kilian tells me that for hours on end he just sits there at his desk staring into space. I'm truly lucky not to have to share an office with him any longer. Today I met him in the I.G. Farben bunker. Rough and unconventional fellow that he is, he quite unexpectedly came up to me and suddenly blurted out, "I'm racking my brains to find a solution to avert the disaster. I'm afraid to think of the future! What will become of my wife and my young children?"

"Dr. Scholl, are you by any chance indicating that the situation is hopeless?"

He gave me a half-dazed stare: "Of course not!" Silence. Then: "But should the Americans really come, I know what I'll do!" he shouted. "I'll shoot myself, but first I'll take half a dozen of them with me!" Having delivered this remarkable threat, he turned on his heels and stalked away, long arms dangling dejectedly at his sides.

*February 14, 1943* Last night wave after wave of bombers—there must have been thousands—flew over our territory in large formations, all going eastwards. A few hours later we heard them coming back, their motors droning above our town and above the bunker in which we sat.

This morning we heard on the radio that the bomber formations had attacked Dresden. The losses of life are incredibly high, preliminary estimates mention 35,000 victims, but the figure could rise as high as 300,000, because Dresden was jammed with refugees from the East. These poor people had crowded into Dresden on their flight from the Soviet Forces. In minutes Dresden was a sea of flames and no escape was possible for the crowds trapped in the railroad station, and in preliminary refugee camps set up in theaters, concert halls, public buildings. They burned to death, suffocated or were torn to pieces by explosive bombs. It is known that many Baltic people had also sought refuge in Dresden. Are Latvian friends among the victims? The thought is unbearable.

The American and the British military commands surely must have been aware of this massing of refugees in Dresden. I can't imagine that their Secret Intelligence could have failed them so badly as not to report this to their superiors. Why then did the Allies commit senseless mass murder, killing innocent people, mostly women and children? Have they no moral and ethical principles left? Are they as evil as the Nazis and the Soviets?

*February 16, 1945* Work at the plant by now has almost become impossible. The sirens begin to howl early in the morning and the alert usually continues for hours. We are lucky if "the sky clears up," i.e. no enemy airplanes are any longer in evidence and we can dash out for our meager lunch at the plant restaurant. But more and more frequently it is just one long session in the bunker from morning till four, five or six o'clock in the afternoon.

Daily life now mostly goes on in the bunker! People try to occupy themselves by reading, studying, knitting, embroidering or just plain talking. Children are playing; their mothers watching them. Babies are being fed and diapered. The families of our I.G. Farben workers have access to the bunker, and by now the bunker for all of us has become a "home away from home," certainly much safer than our apartment buildings.

I frequently visit with Frau Kilian and little Liliane in their favorite bunker niche. The "Kellerassel" is thriving and Papa and Mama Kilian are beaming. Today Dr. Kilian, during my daily bunker visit with them, told me the latest joke about Goebbels:

The Allied Forces have won the War and occupied Berlin. The victory parade is taking its way through the "Brandenburg Gate" and down the street "Unter den Linden." After the sounds of the parade are but a faint echo in the distance and the street is deserted, a sewer lid suddenly lifts up and out pops Goebbels' head, shouting "Und wir siegen doch!" (We shall win, no matter what!) then quickly disappearing again in the sewer.

*February 18, 1945, Sunday* Disaster! Whatever dreams of future happiness I had are broken and shattered. Early this morning the doorbell rang. I opened the door and to my immense surprise saw Ingmar's uncle Edvard standing there. I asked him in; he walked into the living room with slow hesitant steps as though carrying a heavy burden. "What is it, Uncle Edvard?" I asked. He remained standing, not answering, just staring at me in silence. And then I knew. "Oh God, is it Ingmar, is he dead?" I whispered in despair. Edvard only nodded his head. I threw myself at him, sobbing my heart out, while he held me.

"Yes, Ingmar is dead. He was killed in battle at the Russian front. We know no details, only that he is buried in Russian soil," Edvard finally said in a low voice. "Ingmar's mother thought it best if I came to tell you the sad news in person." I lifted my tear-stained face and looked up at Edvard, a tall and slender man, very much like Ingmar, except a generation older.

"Where were you when you got the horrible message?"

"I was with my sister and her husband, Ingmar's father, in a Baltic refugee camp in East Prussia."

"What about Leonid, Ingmar's brother?"

"We have no news about him, but we fear the worst, Irene."

"Dear God, let at least Leonid return safely to his parents!" and I broke out in tears again.

"Irene, your tears won't bring him back," Edvard finally said. "Ingmar loved you very much; he told me so before our final parting in Latvia. He wouldn't want you to break your heart mourning; he would want you to go on living in memory of him and find the happiness that he never had in his short life!" Edvard's voice was cracking. Now it was my turn to comfort him:

"You were his uncle, but you also were his friend. Ingmar was very fond of you. Thank you for always having been so understanding!" and I kissed Edvard on the cheek. Thus we parted. Edvard declined to stay with us: he has Latvian friends in Frankfurt whom he wanted to look up.

I told Mother the news. It did not move her at all. She had never liked Ingmar. I am alone with my sorrow.

*February 19, 1945* Last night held a thousand tortures for me. All through the howling of the sirens, and the droning of the airplanes I could maintain one thought only: Ingmar is dead! Suddenly I remembered a conversation that we had had in 1937, while walking hand in hand through a field of white daisies near the river Gauja in Sigulda. I had laughingly asked him a silly question: "Ingmar, what do you suppose will happen to us ten years from now?"

And like a pistol shot came his answer: "You will be pushing a baby carriage and I will be a dead soldier in foreign soil!" Suddenly a dark shadow fell over our sunlit valley and I felt a cold shiver touching me. The second part of this strange spontaneous prophecy has come true. Will the first part also come true?

I wonder if the ring I gave Ingmar upon parting in 1941 is still on his little finger. The red ruby, that glowed like a fiery spark in its gold setting, a symbol of my love. The Soviets who found his body very likely stripped the ring off his finger. Where is his grave? Somewhere in foreign soil, far away from home!

He is gone, forever gone! His radiant eyes are closed in eternal sleep. The memory of his green eyes haunts me incessantly, those eyes that could express so much without words: love, devotion, joy of life, frustration!

*February 20, 1945* There is no end to the alerts, the howling of the sirens, the droning of the enemy bombers. My senses seem dulled; nothing really frightens me much any longer. My reactions have become automatic: grab your coat, purse and emergency bag and run—to the nearest bunker.

*February 21, 1945* This morning I had an amazing experience. I was on my way to work in the cold gray dawn, pushing my old bicycle, which had developed yet another flat tire, through the rubble of once-proud Höchst. Thinking of all the horrors of this war, my lost friends and family members, most recently my beloved Ingmar, and the uncertainty of my own future existence, I felt myself slipping into utter despair. I remembered my recent diary entry: "Death has now become the daily order and life is the exception." A desperate plea burst out of the darkness of my soul: "My God, hast Thou forsaken me?" And I prayed with the Psalmist: "Out of the depths I cry to Thee, o Lord! Lord, hear my voice!"

Silence! Low hanging clouds! Destruction all around me! No ray of sunshine or hope anywhere! Numb with misery and weak with hunger, I trudged on, dragging my bicycle. Time seemed to tick by endlessly, and then I suddenly caught myself humming a song, a long forgotten melody. "What song is this?" I wondered. What were the words to it? I searched my memory and then, in a flash, it came to me: I was again a pigtailed little girl in German Sunday School in Riga. We were learning a new church hymn:

> Wer nur den lieben Gott lässt walten
> Und hoffet auf Ihn allezeit,
> Den wird Er wunderbar erhalten
> In aller Not und Traurigkeit.

> Allow the Lord to rule your life
> And put your trust in Him alone,
> For then He shall be your salvation
> In all your sorrows and despair.

For a moment I could not comprehend that an extraordinary event had just occurred. The Lord had miraculously answered my cry of despair with a divine promise. Blessed peace and heavenly hope flooded my heart. All fears vanished. At that instant I knew with unshakable clarity that I would survive the war, that I had a future and that the Lord would protect me all the days of my life.

This German hymn, composed by Georg Neumark (who died in 1681) during the terror of the Thirty Years' War (1618-1648) came to the rescue of my soul three hundred years later in another terrible war, and brought me God's message, His comfort and guidance.

*February 22, 1945* Because of the innumerable alerts, food stores are open only when there is no air raid warning. This amounts to a total of two or three hours a day when lines are forming in front of the stores, only to disperse quickly at the first sound of the howling sirens. All movie theaters are closed for good. It sounds ridiculous, but it happens to be true: any kind of social activity or diversion by now can be encountered in the bunker only.

Dr. Torgau has transferred his class to the I.G. Farben bunker. Whenever there is an alert, we meet in a designated spot, practicing our French. Today my friend Veronika commented: "Wouldn't it be smarter, if we polished up our English instead?!" We all laughed, but she is right. The American Forces are moving closer daily. Fortunately for me, my English is quite passable, much better than my French.

*February 23, 1945* Home is no longer much of a home, what with no heat, no hot water, no gas, and paper instead of glass in the window frames! Mother and I are therefore spending most of our time away from our apartment, usually in the bunker. The almost uninterrupted state of siege from enemy bombers crossing overhead doesn't help much either.

I have been able to solve one problem though: we can again prepare hot meals. After the gas was shut off, I remembered that somewhere in our basement storage space we still had our "Primus" kerosene stove, which we had taken with us all the way from Latvia. Kerosene, of course, is nowhere to be had. I knew I could get alcohol at my laboratory for igniting the Primus. But what of the fuel problem?

I finally hit upon the idea of trying some other organic fluid that might burn in the kerosene stove. I investigated the matter and soon found out that an organic waste material—a chlorinated aliphatic compound—was daily dumped down the drain in the Synthetic Research laboratories next door. I asked if I could have the waste matter, and if it was flammable. It was—and it worked in the "Primus." With expressions of joy Mother and I stared at the circular bright blue hissing flame on top of our little stove, and we hastened to put a water kettle on—for hot tea!

It doesn't bother us much that the kerosene substitute while burning, is also forming HCl gas—hydrochloric acid—which irritates our eyes, our nostrils and our lungs. We simply open the kitchen windows wide and leave the room, hoping that the acid will not corrode the metal parts of the Primus. So far the Primus is holding its own, and we again can enjoy hot food!

*February 24, 1945* Today I solved another problem: how to take a bath, shampoo my hair and. wash my clothes! It is now three weeks since these cleansing activities became impossible at home. We have been able to heat up some water on our Primus in an enameled wash bowl and have sponged ourselves off by using gritty non-foaming "Ersatz—soap" (consisting mainly of sand in a mostly unsaponified mixture of solid fatty materials) on a wet washcloth, but hair cannot be shampooed that way, not to mention washing sheets and. towels and clothing.

So, today, I hit upon the idea of taking myself and my laundry to my former Synthetic Rubber Testing Laboratory, to which I still have access. (My move to the Viscometer shack is supposedly "temporary," I have lately learned.) It being a Saturday afternoon, the lab was closed, but I still have the key. I let myself in. Knowing that the hot water lines—maintained by the plant's waste steam—are still functioning, I filled one of the large laboratory sinks, used for dishwashing and dumping of chemicals, with hot water to the brim, added some dish-wash compound, and threw my sheets and towels in. Then I proceeded to scrub them on a board (I took a small wooden shelf off the wall) with a brush that I found under the sink. After the scrubbing was done, I rinsed my laundry a couple of times in clear cold water, wrung it out by hand and then threw it into the huge 105°C oven, which is used for aging rubber samples at high temperatures, simulating climatic conditions which synthetic rubber tires might be undergoing in tropical regions like Africa. (From what I have heard, by the way, German synthetic rubber tires of motorized Army units softened and lost their resilience in the African desert during Rommel's campaign in Africa—one more reason why the battle there was lost.)

Today these heating ovens came in very handy for my laundering project. In about half an hour the wash was dry. I used this time to give myself a bath—also in the laboratory sink—using dish-wash compound. I stripped and hopped in. Sitting there stark naked, I was somewhat worried that the factory watchman, making his hourly rounds, might get the idea of checking the interior of the laboratory building. What would I do then? Splash him with water, as Grandma Amalia did to her French admirer? Get detergent into his eyes, scream, try to run? I wasn't sure! Worse than that was my fear that there might be a serious alert with bombs falling and the FLAK firing. Then I'd really be in trouble.

Fortunately, all remained quiet and I was able to complete my toilette by finally also shampooing my hair—again with dish-wash compound. I must admit, the suds were harsh on the scalp and my hair feels and looks like straw. But better that than three weeks of an oily film forming, containing butyric acid, which is the unfortunate result of the decomposition of sebum, the skin's natural secretion.

I walked home, feeling presentable for the first time in weeks, happily pushing my bicycle, which by now is displaying two flat tires—riding on it is no longer possible—and transporting on it a big laundry bag filled with clean dry wash.

*February 26, 1945* Life goes on, helter-skelter—somehow! My thoughts over and over again go back to Ingmar, to our happy days together. I know that he is no more, but somehow I cannot quite accept his death! To me he is still alive—his memory will always live in my heart! I mourn his passing, but his image will always be a part of my youth, for the rest of my days.

Knowing him was a blessing for me. It enabled me to break out of the rigid cage in which Mother had imprisoned me when still a child. I was not supposed to show any emotions, not supposed to show any pride in my appearance and looks, not supposed to feel any close bonds for anyone except her, not supposed to have ideas of my own, except how to serve and please her.

Ingmar came like the proverbial prince and woke me up from a dream-like, unnatural state, freed me from bondage, instilled in me the courage to express my feelings, to fight for emotional independence. I owe him so much!

*February 28, 1945* The worse the military situation gets, the more the daily press and the broadcasts are extolling the New German Secret Weapon. This weapon, which as far as I can make out, is a long distance rocket, is being directed against England and is supposedly causing terrible damages in London. Headlines in the papers are screaming: "The long awaited German Revenge is in full force! Death toll in England is immense! All of Britain cowering in fear!"

I have not noticed any great exclamations of joy among the German population over this news. Even the Nazi officials seem to have lost some of their usually displayed party-prescribed spunk. Not even Scholl seems to show much excitement. Whenever I meet him in the bunker, he slouches away after a perfunctory greeting, looking quite dejected.

*March 5, 1945* Today came the news that has stirred the people up much more than the Secret Weapon. It is another call to arms: all males born in or after 1929, which means all sixteen-year-olds, will be drafted into the Army and become regular soldiers. The "Volkssturm" also has been reactivated: all men and boys within the prescribed age range, who are not yet at the front, must immediately report to their recruiting stations.

This call has created a tremendous commotion. All our chemists at the plant have to go, Dr. Kilian and Herr Evers have to go, and so have all schoolboys in town sixteen or over. Wives and mothers are crying; everybody is upset. The only persons of my acquaintance who are exempt, as far as I can tell, are Scholl, Lehr, and Wernicke—in other words, all the Nazi bigwigs. They'd rather stay at home and let the others die for them!

*March 6, 1945* Today Dr. Kilian asked me to act as one of two witnesses needed for his last will. He has deeded all his property to his wife. He is leaving in the morning. I said goodbye to him kissing him on the cheek. I do so hope that he may return safely to his family.

In the afternoon there was a timid ring at the door. Upon opening it, I perceived Herr Evers. "I have come to say goodbye to you, Irene!" he said, again looking at me pleadingly with his dark blue eyes. I invited him in. We got as far as the front hall, when he suddenly asked me in a tremulous tone, grabbing my hand, "May I kiss you goodbye, Irene? I adore you! You are my ideal!"

I jerked my hand away and said in a stern voice, "Absolutely not, Herr Evers!" He retreated, jumping backwards. "Good luck to you and all the best, Herr Evers!" I shouted at him, opened the front door and edged him out. I am annoyed—but at the same time I hope that no harm may befall him.

*March 7, 1945* Late this afternoon the doorbell rang. I answered it and saw a skinny, haggard woman before me. "I am Frau Evers," she introduced herself. I politely asked her in, inwardly wondering what the purpose of this visit might be. I noticed, as we entered the living room, that she was even taller than my five feet nine inches, actually looking down upon me. She stood before me with hanging shoulders nervously clutching her handbag. I saw suffering in her face. "Won't you have a seat, Frau Evers?" I said gently to her.

She remained on her feet staring at me, then suddenly blurted out: "Fräulein Zarina, you are standing between my husband and me!"

I couldn't believe my ears. Speechless for once, I felt dumbfounded and stared at her in turn. Then I caught myself: "Where for Heaven's sake, did you ever get that wild idea? Your husband means exactly nothing to me!"

"That is not so! This past year he has continuously been mentioning your name, has been telling me about you, how he has been meeting you daily in the I.G. Farben air-raid shelter. I'm also aware of the fact that he came to your house to help you, after the bombing attack in February had damaged your apartment."

So that was it! The poor woman was driven by jealousy, her emotions intensified by the shock of seeing her husband go off to join the "Volkssturm" the day before. Frau Evers seemed beside herself, in a terribly agitated state. I felt pity for her, although I was also annoyed.

"My dear Frau Evers, try to be reasonable. Why on earth should I take an interest in a married man who is over twenty years my senior and furthermore besides a wife has half a dozen children? What would I want with such a fellow?"

"Fräulein Zarina, Helmut is a fascinating man!"

"I'm glad you as his wife think so! I find nothing attractive in a man who is as bald as a billiard ball, and who is shorter than me!"

"That's just it! Helmut always has been tremendously attracted to tall women, and for a year now he has been constantly raving about your beauty, your Nordic appearance, your intellect, your professional achievements!"

"I'm quite aware of your husband's ideological principles. His main topic of conversation in the air-raid shelter always was: blood and race."

"He considers you the epitome of his ideal of a woman!"

"I'm really not responsible for his opinions nor my looks, furthermore, it seems to me that you yourself represent exactly the fulfillment of all his wishes regarding the ideal 'Nordic woman.' You are even taller than myself, even slimmer, and you are equally as blond and have equally as blue eyes."

Frau Evers smiled for a fleeting moment, and her eyes lit up. "There is some truth to this. When Helmut courted me twenty years ago I was fair and delicate like an apple blossom. I was beautiful then in his eyes. My naiveté, my virginity touched his heart; he wanted to protect me, to hold me in his strong arms, to guide me. I adored him, his radiant blue eyes, his Germanic features, his curly blond hair! I was ecstatic with joy that 'mein deutscher Held—my German Hero'—had asked for my hand in marriage."

I looked at Frau Evers. She was seated by now, hunched in an armchair, listless, sunken eyes looking at me from a pale face, wisps of graying blond hair hanging about her ears, hands, bony and veined, clutching the arm rests. "From what you tell me you must have had a very happy marriage, two people who had each found the ideal partner they had dreamed about!"

"Oh yes, we were happy once, but that is long ago. Helmut progressed in his career, but I stayed at the same level, was nothing but a housewife, had six children in rapid succession. Pretty soon the magic was gone."

"I'm really sorry to hear this, Frau Evers, but you must believe me, I have no interest whatsoever in your husband. The idea is absurd."

Frau Evers cast a doubting eye at me, but her features seemed somewhat less pinched. However, she continued her theme: "Maybe you have no interest in Helmut, but he is wild about you. He has been in love with other women before, but never as badly as this."

I made a gesture of protest but she went on: "I can see why—you are the exception rather than the rule. You are not a mere dull housewife. You are a professional woman, young, attractive and elegant, well dressed and well groomed."

"My dear Frau Evers, the dress I'm wearing I made myself, combining two old garments into one. You can do that too!"

"Oh no, I can't. I can only cook and scrub!"

Nothing I said seemed to have much of an effect on the woman. Finally in exasperation I told her: "You are in a distraught state. Your husband left yesterday to join the 'Volkssturm' and you are naturally worried about his fate. I can imagine how you must be feeling. I have just lost someone who meant a great deal to me for many years!"

Her feminine curiosity was aroused. She looked at me in surprise: "Who was that, Fräulein Zarina?"

I told her about Ingmar and how there had been no news since last November, until I heard about his death in battle just recently. "We planned to be married after the war and were very devoted to each other. I loved him very dearly. Now he is gone forever!" This revelation of mine finally seemed to stir her out of her state of desperation and self-pity.

"I guess I've made a total fool of myself, coming here bothering you with my worries. Forgive me, Fräulein Zarina."

"There is nothing to forgive, Frau Evers. The war has made all of us suffer terribly. We are all in the same boat. It could be worse. We ourselves could be dead. Your children could be dead. At this point, it seems to me, we should be grateful to be alive." Frau Evers thought this over, then she rose, stretched out her hand and clasping mine, shook it in silence, turned and left.

Today's experience with Frau Evers has come as a profound shock to me. The last thing on earth I need is to be considered some kind of "femme fatale" who is wrecking marriages and causing emotional disasters. And all that, while we literally live in the Shadow of Death—every day may be our last. I'm grateful that Mother has no inkling what this discussion with Frau Evers was all about. It would have been oil on her fire. She would have triumphantly used this opportunity to once again point out to me how I had inherited my vivacious Grandma Amalia's "bad blood."

*March 8, 1945* Dr. Kilian is back from the "Volkssturm." He was sent home, being found unfit to handle a gun due to an injury to the index and middle fingers of his right hand. Twenty years ago in a laboratory accident, while still a student of chemistry, he had cut the tendons of both fingers. He cannot bend them, therefore cannot cock a gun. You never know what injuries might be good for! Kilian, of course, was in high spirits and told us some brand-new jokes, referring to the hottest political topic—the "Volkssturm." "Do you know what the only two legitimate excuses are that will get you a leave from the Volkssturm?"

"No, what are they?"

"Your confirmation and your Golden Wedding Anniversary."

I liked the second joke even better: The Lord is holding a council in heaven in order to decide on means to stop the present turmoil on Earth. He asks Methusalem, the oldest, most dignified and wisest of the heavenly inhabitants, to go down to Earth and to bring men to their senses.

Well, Methusalem descends to Earth, but to the great surprise of the heavenly host he is back early the next morning. Fighting, however, is still going on full blast on Earth. "Whatever is the matter with you, Methusalem?" asks St. Peter at the Heavenly Gates. "Why are you coming back without having carried out your given assignment?"

"Oh, I'll tell you what happened, St. Peter. Upon descending from Heaven I landed in Berlin at the Brandenburg Gate. And what do you suppose I saw? Right on that gate was a poster announcing that my age group is presently being drafted! So—I rushed back up here as fast as I could!"

I was still chuckling about poor old Methusalem's plight on my way home, when suddenly I noticed brand new slogans painted in big red letters on house fronts, ruins and pavements: "Der Sturm beginnt, das Volk steht auf!" ("The storm begins, the nation arises!") and: "Lieber tot als Sklave!" ("Better dead than slave!")

The Nazis are still at it: trying to create enthusiasm for a lost and hopeless cause! No one pays the slightest attention to these bombastic phrases.

. . . .

Four years ago today I entered Germany, a country at war. Now the war seems to have come into its final stage. The gains of the Allied Forces at both fronts are increasing rapidly. The Americans have already crossed the Rhine in several places and the Russians have reached German territory in East Prussia. The terror attacks on the civilian population are continuing day and night and all big German cities are in ruins. Berlin, Leipzig and Munich have lately again been severely bombed and even Vienna has been attacked and serious damage inflicted upon this venerable town. The last important city to be destroyed was Dresden.

*March 9, 1945* More tragic news! There seems to be no end to sorrow! Uncle Arno died on March 3, 1945. His wife's letter sounds like Part II of a Greek drama. Part I was Sven's death barely a month ago: "At our son's funeral Arno was so weak and so heartbroken that he could no longer sit up in church. He was lying on a bench next to the coffin holding Svenny's cold hands all during the burial service.

"Shortly thereafter, Arno told me that he had had a dream early this year: He saw himself asleep with Svenny lying at his right side and little Hiye at his left. All three were resting peacefully.

"After he told me this, I knew at once that Arno would soon be joining Svenny in the graveyard. And so it came about. Four weeks after our son's death Arno died and was buried to the left of Svenny. Now I have only little Hiye left, her and two graves." It was amazing to see Mother's reaction. She was deeply moved but remained calm. There was no high drama, like after Father's death.

I too remained calm. When death becomes commonplace, is the order of the day in the outer world as well as in the family, when thousands are dying daily, then the pattern of existence seems reversed: mourning becomes accepted as normal, to be alive becomes the exception. In spite of sorrowing I have the crazy feeling that I should be joyful, because I'm still alive.

*March 10, 1945* A comparatively new plague are the small fighter planes which by now almost continuously circle above the vicinity of Frankfurt and Höchst. No more alert is given when they appear. Their presence has become the rule rather than the exception, with which one has to learn to live. These planes never let us forget that they are dangerous. They may drop a bomb at any moment or all of a sudden descend and machine-gun innocent pedestrians in the streets—many people have been killed that way.

What is particularly upsetting to me are attacks by strafing planes on German farmers working in the fields. What could be more peaceful than tilling the soil and throwing seed into the freshly upturned furrows? And to think that some American fighter pilot, maybe having been raised on a farm himself, has the heart to come swooping down upon an innocent man and his innocent animal pulling the plow, and riddle them with bullets from his machine gun! Is there no more compassion left in this world, no more sanity?

*March 11, 1945* Spring is in the making. It is clear and sunny and the air is balmy. White and blue crocuses are pushing their heads through the soil, the grass is already green, and the buds on bushes and trees are swelling. Dusk was falling last night when I ventured out for a short walk to Unterliederbach, our little farming village nearby. The Taunus hills were still visible at the horizon, but as shadows began to lengthen, their color turned from brownish green to deep purple, and a silvery mist rose in the fields. The sun had already set; the sky was still illuminated by a soft golden light. The evening star started to twinkle first and then to sparkle, sending off rays in a scale of brilliant green hues, hanging like a precious emerald in translucent space.

Suddenly, what was that? I saw a fiery object appearing at the horizon, going into a trajectory, flying higher and higher, closer and closer towards the evening star, it seemed, glowing like a red hot coal, then as it gained height eventually disappearing in the sky. It didn't take me long to figure out that this must be the fabled Secret Weapon on its westward flight to England.

*March 12, 1945* On my way home from work I suddenly heard an awful bang. This sounded like a bomb dropped by a single plane, particularly since no alert had been sounded. I waited for a while and. was about to start walking again, when I heard the staccato of machine-gun fire. Again I waited until all was quiet. Eventually turning into Peter Bied Strasse, I came upon a dreadful scene: the badly mutilated bodies of an old man and a young girl were being removed from the street. They had been killed by the bomb explosion that I had heard. An onlooker in the small crowd which had gathered told me that two strafing planes had suddenly made an appearance, one dropping the bomb, the other descending above the rooftops and shooting at pedestrians who were running to the nearby bunker. "A four-year-old girl has been killed," said the man. "She is still lying in front of the bunker. A seventeen-year-old girl has been badly hurt; both legs have been shot off from under her. She has been rushed to the hospital. It is doubtful whether she will live."

"How ghastly—this is sheer murder!" I whispered, feeling faint.

The man grabbed my arm: "Steady, steady now, Fräulein! This horror can't last much longer! But I'm telling you, I surely hate these American murderers. One of them descended so low into the street that I could see the white of his eyes!" The man gritted his teeth: "To machine-gun an innocent little child—only a damned criminal would be capable of that!"

*March 13, 1945* Today the news reached us at the plant that Dr. Bruno Tann was killed during an air raid in Berlin. No details are known. Another dear and devoted friend gone forever; another excellent, admirable human being senselessly destroyed! Will this carnage never end? In the Middle Ages mankind was being killed off by the bubonic plague, now bombs are killing us off. The Apocalyptic Rider rides again, rides over the Earth, rides high and low, rides on and on and never stops!

*March 15, 1945* But by the grace of God I would now be dead—machine-gunned from a strafing plane. I'm still quite shaken. It is a strange feeling to think that I would be no more, that whatever is immortal in me would have made the transition to another plane leaving its shell, my lifeless body, behind. But I want to live, want to stay right here in the light of our world, don't want to go through the Dark Door of Death!

About lunchtime today, I was on my way to the plant restaurant when I suddenly heard the crash of an explosion and in a split second saw one of our plant's huge gas tanks on fire. Roaring flames came shooting out of it, licking the blue sky with immense orange golden tongues. I turned and started to run towards the bunker, knowing that the adjoining gas tanks, which stand in a row like giant metal-clad sentinels watching over our plant, could catch on fire any second due to the tremendous heat. I didn't get very far; I had barely reached the Arch—famous landmark of I.G. Farben Höchst—spanning the street between two huge buildings, when I heard the humming noise of a descending fighter plane and the "tack-tack" of a machine gun. Suddenly bullets started whistling past me, hitting the walls of the buildings, accompanied by the roaring of the flames in the background.

"Run, run, save yourself!" It was a sharp command from deep down within me. I sprinted forward, reached a door, pushed against it. It opened, and I found myself in the dimly lit, elegantly furnished entrance hall of the Administration Building and in safety, at least from machine-gun fire. There were more bomb explosions, more shooting was going on outside. I heard it as I leaned against the cool stone wall of the hall, my heart racing, breathing hard, staring unseeingly at the multicolored pattern of light on the thick carpet that fell from stained-glass windows.

Eventually the noise subsided; all was quiet and, having somewhat regained my composure, I ventured out again into the beautiful spring day. Little white clouds were busily sailing through a brightly blue sky, a warm wind was blowing, and the sun was at the zenith. But more horrors awaited me. I heard footsteps; three men were approaching me. As they came nearer, I saw that the middle one had blood streaming over his face—it was a Russian worker. Two German sanitary aides were leading him. I stared in shock at all that blood running from a wound in his head.

Turning the corner, I stood again in the little square in front of Zeilsheimer Weg, where I had found myself when the shooting started. The square had been plowed by machine-gun shells. Countless bullet holes were visible in the brick walls of the surrounding buildings. I saw the bodies of two men, one a German, the other a Russian. They lay there, each in his corner, each having pulled up his knees to his face, instinctively trying to protect himself. I know that gesture—I too have rolled myself up into a ball in case of danger. It had not helped them: they were dead, lying in pools of blood. I could think one thing only: "I too could be lying here, dead, with my blood streaming out of me!" and cold horrible fear gripped me.

At that moment two men approached, carrying a stretcher with the dead body of yet another German and in passing I heard scraps of their conversation: ". . . and he said, before dying, 'when you carry me away . . . don't forget to take my leg with me!'" It echoed in my ear like the sound track from some horror movie, ". . . take my leg with me . . . take my leg with me . . . ."

I don't know how I made it back home; my memory is blurred. I only remember walking, walking, walking past rows of houses, through streets, seeing before me images of silent, motionless bodies, blood streaming over a face, a stretcher with nothing but one leg on it, pools of blood.... This, but for the grace of God, could have been me.

. . . .

Tonight, after I had calmed down, I told Mother about my narrow escape from death: Mother gasped in horror, but then she caught herself, remarking lightly, "Unkraut vergeht nicht!—Weeds are hard to kill." It annoyed but also amused me, hearing Mother use this flippant German proverb.

"Thanks, Mother, frankly, I'd rather be a live weed than a dead lily. And that's exactly how I plan to live from now on: be what I want to be, use my time to the fullest, use every day as though it were my last.... For all we know, it might be!" I rose; our stares met and I'm sure Mother must have felt my fierce determination born this noon out of my brush with death: Above all else to be myself!

# CHAPTER THIRTEEN

## Götterdämmerung

*March 16, 1945* This morning I went back to work, as though nothing had happened to me the day before, as though I hadn't almost been wiped out. We all have gotten used to living with danger, just like the soldiers in the trenches—except that they at least have weapons to defend themselves. We civilians don't. I talked about my narrow escape to the people in the viscometer shack. "You were lucky," was their comment, "look what happened to Dr. Raabe—his leg was shot off and he died!"

Hearing this I realized that I had seen Dr. Raabe's corpse on the stretcher, the day before. A long-time research chemist at I.G.Farben, he was the father of one of our female technicians who is working in another section of the Applied Research Department. Dr. Raabe's only son was recently killed at the Russian front. The mother has lost son and husband within a month. Only her daughter Elizabeth is now left—a case very similar to Aunt Meta's tragedy and to thousands of such tragedies all through Germany and Europe.

Tonight, as every Friday night before, I turned the radio on to hear what Dr. Goebbels, the Herr Reichspropagandaminister, might have to say about the worsening situation. True to form, he said only one thing in so many meaningless flowery words: "Und wir siegen doch—and we will win no matter what!" These Goebbels propaganda talks from Berlin every Friday night have been aptly nicknamed by the totally disillusioned population: "Klumpfüsschen's Märchenstunde—Little Clubfoot's fairy tale hour"—referring, of course, to Herr Propagandaminister's, oh so very un-Nordic, un-Nazi-like extremely short height and his badly crippled foot, that he drags behind him with a heavy limp.

I wonder how much longer the Nazi "gods" shall be able to maintain their illusion of all-embracing power, calm sovereignty and august superiority. The shadows are rapidly lengthening, creeping nearer and nearer to their pedestals.

*March 17, 1945* As for Julius Caesar, assassinated on March 15, the "Ides of March" have spelled terrible danger for me also. The End of War seems to be in sight and I have no intention of losing my life at this late stage, a parallel to the unfortunate soldier who gets killed a few hours before armistice goes into effect. My traumatic experience two days ago was a warning, and I will heed that warning. From now on it is every night to the bunker, as soon as dusk falls.

"Mother, do you want to come along with me?" I asked her last evening. "I refuse to spend another night at home." She nodded in agreement.

"Let's take warm blankets, our emergency bag, and let's get going right now!"

So, with wool blankets rolled up under our arms, we trotted off to the bunker. The streets were quiet; no alert had yet been sounded. The noises of the day had vanished. We walked along Königsteinerstrasse under rows of linden trees. The balmy spring weather that we are having has already brought forth little leaves, and the last rays of the setting sun, illuminating the branches, created the effect of green-golden lacy veils against the fading light in the sky.

Suddenly, there came the rolling sound of heavy gunfire. The Western Front is moving nearer daily. It cannot last much longer before the Americans will be in Frankfurt. Having reached the bunker we realized that other people had had the same idea as we. Practically all benches were already occupied, with mostly women and children stretched out on them, rolled up in blankets. We went in search of free places and eventually found some up on the sixth floor. The wooden benches are narrow, hard and cold, but I slept uninterruptedly and peacefully for the first time in months, feeling warm, safe and secure wrapped in my blanket.

Mother woke me about 5:30 AM. She said that there had been several alerts during the night, but all was quiet now. We rose, stretched our limbs, rolled up our blankets and still full of sleep stumbled home through the dawn. After a piece of dark bread with Ersatz-honey and a cup of Ersatz-coffee it was off to work for me—and another day in the bunker, this time the I.G. Farben bunker. We are leading a "bunker existence."

We are like hunted wild rabbits hiding in their dark burrows. But the end is in sight!

*March 18, 1945* Today in the bunker I heard a tale of horror: One of the poor sixteen-year-old boys who had recently been forced to join the Army was sent into battle together with a group of other half-grown lads. The youngster was given a hand grenade and ordered to throw it against an oncoming American tank. Seeing the monstrous war machine coming rolling at him, looming larger and larger, the boy, overcome by fear, panicked and ran, screaming for his mother.

The Nazi military commander in charge spat forth an order: "Knüpft den Verräter am nächsten Baume auf!—Hang the traitor from the nearest tree!" And so it happened. The boy was executed as a warning to other "saboteurs" who might likewise show "cowardice before the enemy."

The people in the I.G. Farben bunker listened to this tale of cruelty, sadism and insanity in silence and remained silent. No one dared to say a word. No one knows, if there might not be another Bernauer—another Nazi spy—lurking in the bunker crowds.

*March 19, 1945* For a number of days it sounded as though the battle noise of cannons firing was coming from all directions, but by now it can be clearly discerned that the heavy rumbling of the guns is concentrated west of us. According to the radio, severe fighting is going on in Mainz, at a distance of thirty kilometers from us, where the Main River meets the Rhine.

The last time I saw Mainz was after a disastrous bombing attack a couple of years ago, and already then the city was in ashes. I can't quite imagine what there might be left in the ruins for the opposing armies to fight over.

*March 20, 1945* Every morning I still go off to my viscometer shack, although no one is doing any work any longer. I wonder what has happened to the recently drafted members of the "Volkssturm." The only one who has returned is Kilian. There is no trace of Evers. No one knows where he or his unit might be and whether they are in actual combat. I hope for the sake of his wife and kids and also for his sake that he survives. Scholl still is around, wandering about the bunker in a half-daze, muttering to himself.

The beautiful spring weather is continuing and the leaves of the linden trees on Königsteinerstrasse are bursting out in green splendor.

This afternoon, on my way home from work I noticed that a cross had been cut into the bark of every other tree. Seeing this, I felt strong apprehensions and a dark foreboding, that something terrible was about to happen to the trees. In anxiety I asked Frau Buchner whom I accidentally met at the entrance to our house: "What is the meaning of these crosses on every other linden tree?"

Frau Buchner stared at me with her big, brown, wide-open eyes and there was contempt in her voice: "Where have you been, Fräulein Zarina; don't you know that our Führer has ordered utmost resistance to the last?"

"I have been at work and in the bunker, Frau Buchner, and what has 'utmost resistance to the last' got to do with our linden trees?"

A superior smile crossed Frau Buchner's features: "You should know better than that, Fraulein Zarina, we shall build barricades with these linden trees!" and she looked at me triumphantly.

I had a sinking feeling in the pit of my stomach: "Oh no, not with these beautiful trees!"

"Oh yes, Fräulein Zarina, our Party Headquarters has ordered ditches dug and barricades built on Königsteinerstrasse, since it is one of the main thoroughfares in Höchst!"

"But Frau Buchner, trees against American tanks?"

I dared say no more. The woman's expression had become rather stern and there was suspicion in her voice: "Don't you think it better to lose the trees and hold up the enemy, than to have the town occupied by American forces?"

In view of the completely hopeless German military situation her answer really shocked me because of its foolishness. Remembering the proverb "Even the gods fight in vain with stupidity" and knowing that this woman was quite capable of having me arrested for "undermining the fighting spirit of the Home Front" I decided to keep my mouth shut. No use provoking fate in these last days before the decline and fall of the Nazi millennium! The American machine guns didn't get me, but the Nazi machinations might yet at the last moment!

*March 21, 1945* Early this morning the sun was shining. On my way to work I stopped before the two old linden trees in front of our house designated to be chopped down by the murderous axe of some crazy Nazi, and I spoke to the trees: "You will not be cut down! I will it! You will be safe! No one will touch you! It will be so!"

And I concentrated my thoughts on the imposing beauty of these trees, which with their wide branches are shading the sidewalk and almost touching our windows on the second floor. "You will continue to grow your leaves and you will bear blossoms in time and you will live!" I whispered touching first one then the other tree. From this moment on I carry within me the conviction that my trees will not be harmed.

*March 22, 1945* On my way home last evening, I came across the first Nazi-built barricades on Königsteinerstrasse. The pavement had been broken up and a ditch about 6 feet deep and 10 feet wide had been dug across the street approximately half a mile from our house. The Nazis were still at it, and lo and behold, whom did I see there? If it wasn't Scholl himself at the bottom of the ditch, digging away, with sweat streaming down his face!

"Hello, Dr. Scholl, fancy seeing you here!" I greeted him cheerfully. "You are doing a great job. Keep it up!" He threw me a hateful stare but didn't respond. It is just as well. No need to taunt the desperate yet still dangerous believers in the "final German victory!"

Turning to go I noticed the desolate stumps of a number of linden trees that already had been chopped down. Further up the street, several Nazi party members, wearing their black swastikas in a white field on a red band around their sleeve, were busily building a fence-like barrier using the cut-off trees. The structure had progressed to the height of about five feet and had an air of utter flimsiness about it.

Two little boys, approximately eight and nine years old, were standing nearby observing the Nazi party members at work. "Fritzchen, look at these barricades. What do you think?" I heard the younger asking the older boy.

"Heini, it won't take the Americans longer than a second to knock them down with their tanks!" And then both children laughed. I'm glad the Nazis didn't overhear this conversation. For all I know, they might have strung up the two little boys from the nearest, spared-by-the axe, linden tree for being "traitors to the cause." From the looks on their faces, it was not hard to tell that the Nazis were in a desperate and ugly mood, capable of any evil deed imaginable.

*March 23, 1945* My linden trees are still standing. Further down the street more trees have been chopped down, more ditches have been dug, more "barricades" built. At noon the telephone rang in our viscometer shack, and much to my surprise I was asked to the phone. "Who would be calling me? No one ever calls me at the shack," I was thinking as I answered the phone.

"Irene, is this you?" I heard a young male voice.

"Yes, who is this?"

"Dr. Werner Schöller from Bayer's Central Rubber Research Laboratory in Leverkusen. I'm in Höchst on my way to Vienna, back to Mother's!" The image of a congenial, blond, brown-eyed young Austrian rose before me, and I remembered the talks I had had with him while training in Leverkusen. It seemed like a lifetime ago, when some semblance of a normal existence had still been possible, when a young man and a girl had still been able to sit together of an evening over a glass of Moselle wine at the Leverkusen plant restaurant, discussing future plans, goals, ideals, hopes. This was only three summers ago, but our world has since then changed so terribly.

"Irene, I have been drafted and ordered to the nearest recruiting station."

"For heaven's sake, don't go, Werner!"

"Of course not, Irene. That's why I'm on my way to Austria. Could I stay this night at your apartment?"

"Anytime, Werner, but it's not safe at home. We sleep in the bunker every night."

"Irene, if you only knew how exhausted I am; I didn't dare to take the train from Cologne. I am considered AWOL, you know. I somehow wound my way here, partly walking, partly being picked up by Army trucks and transported a stretch."

"Weren't you afraid that the military might arrest you?"

"I lied to them, and furthermore, the German soldiers sympathized with me and shielded me from their superiors." And so it came about, that Werner Schoeller will be our guest at the apartment, although the hostesses will be absent.

*March 24, 1945* When I got home last evening, Werner was already waiting for me in front of the house. I showed him my bedroom, apologizing for not being able to give him clean sheets;—there had been no more chance for another laundry session in the Rubber Testing Lab. What was worse, I even had no food to offer him, except a piece of dry black bread and some chamomile tea. Poor Werner was gaunt, pale and covered with dust, with a hungry look in his eyes! All of us are hungry all the time!

I'm glad I was able to fix some hot water on the Primus, so that Werner could at least wash up. The Primus, by the way, has been holding up remarkably well, in spite of the corroding hydrochloric acid gases emanating from it. As dusk was falling, Werner and I said goodbye. We embraced in parting, wishing each other lots of luck. "Make sure you survive the war, Irene," Werner called after me as I was setting out for the bunker with my blanket roll under my arm. Mother, who had briefly met Werner, had already gone ahead.

"The same to you, Werner!" I called back. He is leaving early in the morning. I won't see him again. I'm so glad that he is still alive!

I was a bit worried what Mother's reaction might be to Werner's surprise visit. I dreaded the usual acid-tongued comments, but nothing of that nature happened. Mother said instead, "I hope the poor young fellow has a good night's rest and will be able to make it safely to Vienna."

Could it be that it has finally dawned on her how extremely lucky we have been as compared to most of our friends? We still are alive; we still have a home after four perilous war years. And now the end is in sight! Mother feels it too: "I wish the Americans would hurry up and come!" she mumbled already half asleep, stretched out on the bunker bench in her blanket roll.

*March 25, 1945* I have lived through the wildest, most action-filled, most improbable night of my entire existence, a night that I shall remember for the rest of my days. Contrary to our usual habit of setting out early for the bunker, we decided to wait a while. Rumors were spreading all over town that the Americans had already reached Frankfurt and would shortly arrive in Höchst. But nothing happened. Not even air-raid alerts were given, and neither did enemy airplanes make an appearance.

Dusk fell and slowly a full moon rose above the black silhouette of the Taunus mountains, growing brighter and brighter in a darkening sky, casting its silvery light onto our old town. This night before Palm Sunday could have been a picture of perfect peace on earth, had it not been for the constant drumming of artillery in the south and west. We knew that American forces were approaching, and slowly, as the hours passed, the rumbling sounds became louder and louder.

As Mother and I were finally walking to the bunker, the air seemed filled with tension and expectation. We knew that soon an extraordinary change was going to occur, and I felt scared, but also strangely excited. In the bunker cabin I stretched out on a bench as usual and soon dozed off.

Suddenly, a loud noise awoke me. Glancing at my wristwatch I noticed that it was 11:00 PM. The noise came from the bunker corridor. I heard shrieks and running feet, and then a harsh voice coming from the loudspeaker: "Attention, attention! This is your Air-Raid Warden. The enemy has reached and partially encircled Frankfurt on Main. Our Gauleiter is giving you the following message: No German man, no German woman, no German child shall fall into the hands of the enemy.

Therefore, every inhabitant of Frankfurt and the surrounding outskirts has to obey my orders and must leave town immediately. You are to proceed north and move in the general direction of the city of Kassel! Everyone has to provide himself with food and blankets. Trucks will be waiting at the exits of the town bunkers for women with small children and for the aged!"

The voice stopped; there was a crackling noise in the loudspeaker and then silence. The silence lasted for about two seconds and then bedlam broke loose: shrieking, shouting, crying, lamenting, cursing—a cacophony of voices—and a stampede was heard in the corridor, a stampede to the exits.

But not everybody left. Many were so numb with shock that they seemed to have lost their power of decision. In our cabin sat a young woman with her family, who at first seemed quite calm, then suddenly started to wail loudly, while beating her head with her fists: "What am I going to do? I'm all alone . . . with my three small children . . . and my aged mother . . . and my crippled sister . . . . My husband is at the front . . . he may be dead . . . . Oh God Almighty, I don't have enough strength left . . . I can't even move . . . I can do nothing! I can't help them . . . I can't. I can't. I can't!"

She became increasingly hysterical, continuing to beat her head, and since she was wearing a felt hat, the latter soon was completely ruined, sitting lopsided on her forehead, displaying most unusual newly created peaks and valleys. It was a pitiful sight, but at the same time the comic aspect of her appearance was rather strong. I felt between tears and laughter, while the poor woman's family watched her in terrified silence, her children hanging wide-eyed on their mother's every move.

There was no longer any fear in my own heart. I just knew that the oncoming American troops would not hurt us; I felt it with all my being! Calmly I sat down next to the distraught woman, grabbed both her hands, held them tightly and forced her to look at me: "Now listen to me! The worst is over! No harm will befall you and your children. Stay right here in town. Don't go anywhere!"

The woman stared at me through her tears: "But the Gauleiter has ordered us to leave!"

"My dear lady, try to think! How far would you and your family ever get on foot? Motorized troops certainly move a lot faster and would soon overtake you! This plan of escape is utterly senseless!" She looked at me dubiously. "Calm down, go home and put your kids to bed! You may be certain that there will be no more air raids! Finally you will be able to get a good night's rest!"

"Oh, that's what I need. I'm totally exhausted!" And then, nervously clutching my hand she queried: "Are you sure that the Americans won't hurt us?"

"Yes, quite sure, unless you do something foolish to provoke them!"

A timid smile began to spread over the woman's face: "Thank you, oh thank you so much!" and then turning to her family, who huddling together on the bench had been anxiously awaiting her decision, she said, "Come on, let's go home!"

I watched them troop out, mother in the lead, followed by two little girls and a boy, helping his frail-looking grandma. The woman's sister limped behind. I too went to the exit and stepping out into the night, I almost stumbled over a man who was dejectedly sitting on the steps, head in hands. I heard him sigh, "What am I going to do, what on earth am I going to do?" I did not know the man, but he was obviously in dire distress. He was talking to himself: "I will go home and will take a rope and hang myself!"

"I wouldn't do that, if I were you!" I said to him. "You have been lucky enough to survive the entire war and now when it's ending, you want to kill yourself. Why, what for?"

"The shock of it all! Germany has lost the war! We Germans are the losers! We have lost our place in the world, our power, our pride, our honor, our hope. No proud German can possibly survive this shame, this defeat!"

Mother, coming out of the bunker had caught up with me and heard the man's last words. "Stop blowing soap bubbles!" she told him brusquely in her Baltic German. "Wars have been lost before, but it has not stopped the world from going around! Tirades about lost honor won't change anything for the better!"

"What shall I do, what shall I do?" the fellow started wailing again.

Mother had the answer for him: "Stop pitying yourself and start facing reality!" Slowly the bunker emptied and people hurried home. So did we, only to find another large-scale uproar in our apartment house. The people there had heard the Gauleiter's message on their radios, and wild rumors were rapidly spreading from floor to floor, through all six stories of the house. Our neighbor, Herr Keller, was standing on the stairs leading to the second floor, his listeners gathered below him, entertaining them with horror tales about "the Führer's Secret Weapon." His eyes big and gleaming, his voice dripping with authority, he stated, "I know from reliable sources that our Secret Weapon for strategic reasons has been deliberately held back by our military command, until the proper time should arrive.

"The time is now! The Weapon is hidden right nearby in the surroundings of Frankfurt. The Taunus Mountains are crowded with German troops, who have a special mission. That is the reason why our Gauleiter is ordering everyone to leave town, because the Secret Weapon will completely destroy Frankfurt and with it all American troops. We all must leave instantaneously, in order to escape death!" Herr Keller's audience listened in awe.

Another neighbor broke in: "I heard today that SS troops have been ordered to search all homes for any remaining inhabitants, and to shoot everybody who has not obeyed the Gauleiter's orders and has not left town."

Frau Keller started to weep into her apron, turning to her husband for comfort: "Oh Heinrich, how terrible! Must we really leave our home?"

"Yes, dear, we must!" Herr Keller answered with the grave voice of conviction.

In all this commotion on the stairs it had been overlooked that our Latvian neighbor Dr. Kalns, one of our I.G. Farben chemists, who lives on the third floor, was not in the audience. It was decided to wake him. When Dr. Kalns, who is a widower and lives alone, finally answered the doorbell, he was greeted by a chorus of voices urging him to immediately leave town by government orders. Dr. Kalns, looking very sleepy, first blinked in disbelief and then, suddenly coming wide-awake, shouted: "Impossible! You must be crazy! Don't you realize, that you all are being deceived by enemy agents, who are trying to create disturbances by spreading rumors like this?" Thus spoke Dr. Kalns, slammed the door and went back to bed, to continue his disturbed night's sleep. I wonder what he said, finding out later this morning that the so-called "enemy agents" were the Gauleiter himself.

Mother and I simply could not sleep on a night like this, and we decided to check up on Aunt Erika and little Eva. We knew that they would very likely still be in the bunker nearest to their home. That is, indeed, where we found them. Erika told us that she had watched similar scenes of bewilderment, excitement and despair as we had witnessed in our bunker. Neither she, nor we, nor anyone else ever saw a single one of the Gauleiter's promised trucks for women and children.

It was about 2:00 early this morning, when we left Erika's bunker. The moon was still shining, and it was almost as light as day. By now the streets were filled with people, moving back and forth, some going northeast towards Kassel, some in the opposite direction. Some were pushing wheelbarrows loaded with household goods, others were using baby carriages for the same purpose. The commotion was indescribable. But above it all the moon hung calmly in the sky.

Our adventures weren't yet over! We decided to go and see Dr. Kilian and his family, in order to find out how they were dealing with the situation. On our way to their house we met a group of Russian laborers, whose camp is located in Kilian's part of town. About a hundred of these Russians were led by a couple of SA men in golden-brown uniforms, with swastikas on their sleeves, brandishing guns. From the looks of it, the Nazis were forcing the Russians to leave town. This troop of Russians passed us in complete silence, but in the bright moonlight we could see contempt and hatred written on their faces.

Dr. Kilian's house was dark and silent. We rang the bell, but no one answered. Then it occurred to me that very likely for reasons of safety the family was sleeping downstairs in their basement "hospital" room, where a couple of months ago Liliane the "Kellerassel" had been born. The Kilians probably had not heard anything at all about the uproar in town. We saw light in their neighbors' house and I decided to pay them a visit instead. By this time it was about 4:00 in the morning.

I knew the neighbor slightly. Dr. Ziegler was also a chemist. He served earlier in this war in the German Army with the rank of major and lost one arm in battle. He and his wife were fanatic Nazis, who according to Kilian, up to the last have believed in the final German victory. They would brush away all doubts with one gesture of the hand exclaiming: "Our Führer knows what he is doing!"

I was curious, indeed, to see how this family was facing the new developments. I rang the bell, the major answered, he seemed in terrible shape, extremely upset; he was shaking. "Excuse me, Major, would you know if the Kilians are at home?"

"I have no time to worry about them, I have to pack my bags," the major told me gruffly.

"Where are you planning to go, Major?" I asked him politely.

"Why, young lady, that is obvious, isn't it? I will follow our Gauleiter's orders and go northeast, towards Hanau."

"Where is your family, Major?"

"They have already left; I will catch up with them presently." And then suddenly the weirdness of the situation dawned on him: he, the worthy major and party bigwig was being interrogated at 4:00 in the morning by an overly curious young woman chemist, asking embarrassing questions. He shot a venomous glance at me: "And you, what are you still here for? Haven't you heard the order to leave town?"

"Well, you see, Major, I have no intention of leaving!"

I expected a barrage of accusations, but nothing happened! The major turned and continued packing his bag. He probably no longer considered me, the disobedient, disloyal disbeliever, worthy of his attention. Mother had waited outside. Together we went home through the early dawn. There were fewer people in the streets now. It seemed most of them had made up their minds whether to stay or to leave. At our apartment house, to our surprise, we found all the other inhabitants, including the Kellers, still there. All was quiet and we went to bed.

. . . .

After having slept for a few hours, I woke up to the most beautiful Palm Sunday imaginable. The sun is shining brightly and my linden trees are standing before my open windows in all their springtime glory. The trees have not been harmed: my fervent wish has come true! All that happened last night seems almost like a dream to me, like a dramatic stage performance. As a matter of fact, the tumultuous scenes that I witnessed remind me of the second act in Wagner's opera "Die Meistersinger." There too, is great commotion, turbulence, rapid movement of groups of people and general confusion. Only the music differs: our street scenes last night were accompanied by the rolling of heavy cannon fire.

. . . .

It is now late afternoon. After the Gauleiter's announcement of the previous night, everyone expected the Americans to arrive in a few hours, so all day today, people were standing around on streets, or looking out of windows, and waiting. But nothing happened.

There are all kinds of rumors: that persons here and there have already seen U.S. troops or have met single tanks. But none of them, so far, have proved to be true. The only news is that the Russian laborers are back in town and so are the Germans—looking somewhat shamefaced—who early this morning had set out on foot pushing wheelbarrows and baby carriages towards the north. The Nazi bigwigs all seem to have run away and stayed away. None are in evidence.

We are now completely isolated in Höchst. There is no longer any transportation to and from Frankfurt, and the telephones aren't working. We have no idea what is happening even a few miles away. We understand that German engineers have blown up all bridges across the Main River. The last to go was the Schwanheimer Bridge located only about a mile from the center of Höchst. The heavy artillery fire in the west yesterday must have drowned out the noise of the explosion.

Today the guns are silent. Now and then the sirens will suddenly begin to howl and then stop again. No one pays any attention to them anyway. We are figuring that with U.S. troops already in Frankfurt we should be relatively safe from being bombed. Tonight, for the first time in weeks, we will not go to the bunker, but sleep at home.

*March 26, 1945* Monday morning. Heavy artillery fire woke us. Shells were flying over our town. On first impulse we rushed right down into our basement air-raid shelter. Pretty soon all our neighbors appeared there also.

It is now 9:30 AM and we are still in the shelter, waiting. Waiting for what? For the gunfire to cease, for the Americans to appear? That may take much longer than we expect. The gunfire seems lighter now. I think I'll venture out and investigate what the situation is like in town. After having gone through the terrors of bombing, shooting doesn't frighten me very much, seems relatively harmless.

. . . .

11:30 AM. I'm now in my old office at the Applied Research Department. Kilian and Dr. Heyden are with me. We three seem to be the only employees in our department who have dared to leave their homes and come here. Kilian, noticing me busily scribbling notes in my diary, asked me teasingly, "Have you taken upon yourself to be the chronicler of 'The Last Days of the Millennium' in Höchst?"

"I might as well, or do you believe that I will have many more such opportunities within my lifetime?" I shot back at him. We are all laughing, but this is an uneasy laughter. The gunfire has again increased. Maybe I better get home; I might get cut off and not be able to make it back, if I stay here much longer.

. . . .

2:00 PM. I have lived through more incredibly tumultuous scenes and in the process have helped to loot a German army freight train. Leaving my office, I took the usual route home past the railroad crossing. There I witnessed an extraordinary spectacle. Freight trains were standing in long rows near the railroad station and large crowds of people were busily looting them. Panting and sweating, they were breaking down freight-car doors, crawling in and out, pushing and beating each other, fighting over a bag of flour or a case of canned meat and dragging out as much foodstuff as they possibly could.

I was so immensely surprised to have come upon this totally unexpected scene that I just stood there and stared, while the noise of gunfire filled the air. The looters completely ignored the shooting; all their energies were directed towards one purpose only: grab as much as you can.

It seems the entire population of Höchst was there, from simple factory workers to the most distinguished persons: scientists, doctors, lawyers, as well as their usually extremely well behaved ladies. I recognized Wernicke and Lehr and Frau Lehr and our neighbor Herr Keller plus wife. Frau Lehr, strands of hair blowing in the wind and red in the face from the exertion, was carrying a heavy cardboard carton in her arms, filled with tin cans, I presume. Lehr himself, not far behind his wife, was staggering under the load of two heavy bags, of what looked like flour.

Suddenly, a short, elderly German dressed in a shabby army uniform came up to me and addressed me most unceremoniously in Frankfurter dialect: "Freileinsche, kenne Sie mir helfe?—Could you do me a favor?"

"What is it?"

"I have three bags of flour, and I want to go and fetch my wheelbarrow. I can't leave my three bags alone, or they will be snatched away. Could you stand guard over my bags? For that I'll get you a bag too!"

The little old man looked at me pleadingly. I decided in an instant that this wasn't a bad bargain at all. "All right, I'll do it," I said. He dashed away. I watched his bags, while he got his wheelbarrow and fought for one more bag, which he brought to me. It was very heavy, at least one hundred pounds, and I could scarcely lift it. Somehow, I don't know how, I dragged it home on my bicycle. Once again, I found our apartment house in an uproar. It seems all the neighbors had taken part in the looting, and now they were comparing notes.

"What did you get, Frau Keller?"

"Oh, I got canned meat and butter and sugar!"

"And what about you, Frau Mooth?"

"Robert got hold of some evaporated milk and some lard, and I found white flour and French chocolates and liqueur!" Frau Mooth sang out triumphantly. All neighbors looked at her in envy. I couldn't believe my ears: meat, butter and sugar, not to speak of evaporated milk and chocolates and liqueur! I didn't know that such wonderful things still existed in Germany; I hadn't seen them in years!

"What is this all about anyway, where do these trains come from?" I shouted a question into the general commotion. A chorus of excited voices answered me, and all I could discern is, that these freight trains were supposed to carry supplies to the German troops, but had been cut off by the advancing American forces. The local Nazi command had ordered the trains to be blown up rather than let them fall into the hands of the Americans, but the people in Höchst were too quick and looted them instead. I dragged my bag of flour upstairs to the second floor.

"What have you got there?" Mother greeted me.

"A bag of dark rye flour!" I told her.

"That's all? Couldn't you do better than that? Inefficient as usual!" Mother scolded me. "Everyone else in the house here got hold of meat and butter and other fine things. The Nettlers even have genuine coffee beans, bacon and a bottle of vodka."

"Mother, how can you blame me for something over which I have had no control whatsoever? Be glad that I got this bag of flour!" and I told her about the little man and our strange bargain.

*March 27, 1945* Tuesday morning, 8:00 AM. The firing continues. We are staying most of the time in our basement shelter. That is also the place where one hears the latest news. I understand that several houses in Höchst have been hit by artillery fire and a number of people have been killed. Another bit of information of interest: a bakery at the far end of Königsteiner Strasse has opened up and is selling bread without ration cards on a "first come, first served" basis. I think I'll venture out and try to get to that bakery.

11:00 AM. I'm just back from the bakery. By the time I got there, the bread was sold out. The streets are deserted; the shooting goes on. Once I heard an explosion. I wonder if a cannon shell had hit a house?

2:00 PM. Our neighbors seem to have decided that this siege of Höchst is going to go on indefinitely. This afternoon they all started to move their possessions and even their furniture down into the basement. Some families are setting up their coal stoves right here in the cellar, ready to start cooking their meals. Some bunk beds have also been installed. Our basement is slowly taking on the looks of something between a dormitory, a kitchen and a storehouse. The place is teaming with activity and the confusion is indescribable.

6:00 PM. The firing is still going on, seems to have increased in scope, or maybe it is just the shifting wind that makes it sound louder.

*March 28, 1945* Wednesday morning, 9:00 AM. The artillery fire continues. Where are the Americans? Why aren't they here yet? The suspense is becoming harder and harder to bear.

1:00 PM. From the "news headquarters" in our basement I have just heard what supposedly is going on outside and where all that gunfire is coming from. After having occupied Frankfurt, the Americans are now located south of Höchst across the Main River. North of Höchst one single German SS major with one heavy gun and lots of ammunition on Monday morning took his position on the Autobahn (national highway) and is continuing the fight with only a few of his men left. For three days now this crazy SS guy has been racing back and forth on the Autobahn firing his gun to the south. The Americans are firing back. Höchst just happens to be in between. Fortunately, most of the shells seem to be flying over us, without doing much damage.

9:00 PM. The firing has stopped. All is quiet.

*March 29, 1945* "Gründonnerstag" is dawning—Green Thursday—as the Germans call this religious holiday three days before Easter. The sun has just risen—a fiery ball, rapidly changing into a golden mass of light, evaporating the silvery morning haze hiding the Taunus mountains. I am at my open bedroom window, looking out, listening and watching. All is quiet. What will this Maundy Thursday bring us? It is hard to fathom, that we are in the middle of Holy Week. For us it has been a most Unholy Week, filled with gunfire and tumult.

I am recalling the candlelight services on Maundy Thursday at our cathedral in Riga. The four epistles of the New Testament were read, Holy Communion was celebrated and then we walked home carrying our burning candles through the dark streets, trying to shield them from the wind. Whoever managed to take the blessed candle home without its flame being extinguished was assured of good luck for an entire year. Happy memories!

10:00 AM. Most of our neighbors are in the basement shelter. I will go down and see if there is any further news.

11:00 AM. There is no news. We are crowded together—here in the basement, sitting and waiting.

12:00 noon. All is quiet. Königsteinerstrasse is deserted and nothing is stirring. We are waiting.

1:00 PM. We are waiting.

2:00 PM. We are still waiting.

3:00 PM. A boy just came dashing into our shelter shouting at the top of his lungs: "Die Amerikaner kommen!" and dashed out again. A commotion arose in our crowd. All, it seems, were talking at once. Suddenly, in the midst of this babble of voices a command was heard: "All of you go back to your apartments immediately, raise your window shades and hang out white pieces of cloth, so the Americans won't suspect any kind of resistance!" The speaker was our air-raid warden, who must have come in from the neighboring house. As an afterthought he added: "And don't anyone look out of the windows, because they might shoot at you!"

We followed the warden's advice, concerning the window shades, but I have not seen anyone hanging out a white flag; neither did I. I stood behind the window curtains and looked down on Königsteinerstrasse and there, I finally saw the long-awaited Americans, for the first time in my life. They came in long motorized columns, sitting in jeeps and trucks, in battle dress with helmets, and with guns held across their knees. They looked up at the houses, at the windows and down the street, but as I had expected, they appeared civilized and not at all like killers or savages. Many were smiling.

"Finally the years of fear and danger have come to an end! Now again I can begin to live a normal life, now there is safety and hope for the future!" were my first thoughts. In my elation I hadn't noticed Mother's absence. Turning around I expected to find her standing behind me, but she wasn't there. I went looking for her, but couldn't find her in the apartment. Finally, I found her all alone in the basement shelter, sitting in a dark corner, crying her heart out. I heard her sob: ". . . all our dead . . . our friends . . . our relatives . . . our country lost . . . and for what . . . all in vain, in vain . . . ." and the tears were rolling down her face. I let her cry. Maybe it was for the best; maybe the tears were washing away the tensions of many months of hardship, fear and tragedy. Eventually Mother calmed down and came upstairs with me.

*March 30, 1945* Last night at 10:00 PM there came a supreme moment of bliss: I undressed, put on a nightgown—a nightgown!—what happiness!—and went to sleep in my very own bed, undisturbed by howling sirens. This experience, more than anything else, has spelled the End of War for me. Military action still is going on in Germany, but World War II is over for us.

This morning I turned on the radio and heard a broadcast from Berlin, from the Führer's headquarters there. The news was most interesting: "Terrible fighting is going on in Frankfurt on Main and in the suburbs. The local population is showing utmost resistance, turning each house into a fortress, causing tremendous losses to the enemy." All this, while we in Höchst on this lovely Good Friday morning are quietly recuperating from the ordeal of the last weeks.

Berlin, however, cannot quite deny that at least parts of Frankfurt have been occupied by the Americans, and the Nazi broadcasts therefore are trying to describe life here in the darkest terms. I heard about killings, robberies and rapes, about sudden famine and a terrible epidemic spreading rapidly. These tales of horror do honor to the last efforts of the Nazi propaganda machine.

*March 31, 1945* I took a walk to the railroad station, where the looted trains are still standing in total disarray. The area around them looked like a battlefield covered with debris. I have since heard that the army freight trains had carried not only foodstuffs, but other merchandise as well: coal, leather-wares, army uniforms, furniture and books. Sad remnants of all these things were lying between the railroad tracks: a single shoe, a torn uniform jacket, a broken piece of furniture and dozens of copies of Hitler's "Mein Kampf."

Suddenly my step halted. Something glittered on the ground in the sunlight. I bent down and picked up a "Ritterkreuz—the Knight's Cross"—much-coveted German Army medal for heroism in the face of the enemy. Scores of these crosses lay scattered before me . . . .

It is painful to think of the millions of young soldiers who were ready to die for the honor of receiving such a Ritterkreuz, and now these medals are lying worthless in the dust. It seems to me like a symbol of the tragedy of the deceived German youth. They gave their life, for what? For the glory of the Nazi "gods!" And where are these gods now, where are Hitler, Goebbels, Göring, Himmler et al? They are hiding in their Walhalla, their own "Fortress of the Gods"—the Reich Chancellery in Berlin. Their "Götterdämmerung—twilight of the gods"—is coming to a close. Dusk is falling for them.

# PART 4

## STARS AND STRIPES

# CHAPTER FOURTEEN

## Interregnum

*April 1, 1945* It is Easter Sunday, but no church bells are ringing, calling worshippers to services. In Frankfurt almost all churches are in ruins or heavily damaged. We in Höchst have been more fortunate: St. Justinus's, supposedly built by Charlemagne, St. Joseph's and the Evangelical church are all three unharmed, still standing. However, their doors are locked, and all is quiet. No organ music, no singing of chorales can be heard.

It seems only Nature is celebrating this Easter Day with a bright blue sky, sunshine and springtime glory. I went for a morning walk. The town seems almost paralyzed, with hardly any signs of life anywhere. The people are staying in their houses, the streets are deserted, except for a jeep here and there, filled with American soldiers, who, when seeing me on the sidewalk, would invariably wave at me and shout: "Hi, Blondie!"

I felt uneasy and hastened home. I was also getting hungry. "Mother, what have we got to eat?"

"Three potatoes, two beets and two slices of black bread," was the answer.

"What about the bag of rye flour?"

"Yes, we have that, but we have no yeast to bake bread with it."

"Well, maybe we could make pancakes out of it?"

"We have no oil or fat left."

"Let's fix a porridge then!"

And so it came about, that we celebrated Easter Day with porridge made from dark rye flour. The looks and the taste of the concoction reminded me of carpenters' glue, dark brown and slimy. A sprinkling of salt helped. Sugar would have been better, but we have none left.

It didn't exactly improve our spirits to have enticing odors come wafting in through the open windows from the neighborhood's kitchens. The neighbors were busily preparing sumptuous Easter meals with all those lovely foodstuffs originating from the train looting. If we only had a slice of canned meat or a pat of margarine or a drop of oil! But no one shared even a crumb of cheese or a cookie with us.

Mother looked depressed. "Cheer up," I said, "maybe we are starving, but we are still a lot better off today than we were a week ago. Now at least we know that we have come out of the war alive and unharmed. Tomorrow I'll go and see if and where one may get food with or without ration cards."

*April 2, 1945* I've been all over town looking for food. There is none to be had. The local Wirtschaftsamt is closed. A crowd of people had gathered in front of its locked and bolted doors. From them I heard that for the time being no more food ration cards would be issued, and that the ones still in our possession are no longer valid. At least, no food store is willing to accept them. It looks as if every person is on his or her own. The motto seems to be: "Do the best you can to feed yourself!" I gave Mother the depressing news. "Oh God, what will become of us? We shall starve to death!" she wailed.

"Oh, no, Mother, we will do no such thing! We have 100 pounds of flour, which can sustain us for quite a while. Furthermore, I'll visit my farmer friends in the Taunus Mountains and ask them to sell us some potatoes and vegetables."

"They won't sell you anything! Why should they? What good would our money be to them? They couldn't buy anything with it either!"

"You may be right, Mother, but I could offer them a ring or a bracelet!"

"I wouldn't part with my jewelry for anything! Each piece has too many memories attached to it!"

"Oh yes, you would, Mother, and so would I, if it becomes a matter of being very, very hungry!"

*April 3, 1945* Today I went to the plant to see what was going on there. American military police are guarding the factory. The gates are locked and no one is allowed entrance. I turned and went to Dr. Kilian's home instead, hoping for some information from him. He had none to give me. We don't know whether I.G. Farben will be allowed to continue its operations, and whether we will still have our jobs. We don't know what has happened to our colleagues and our workers since the Americans came in.

On my way home, I suddenly realized that I am facing a totally uncertain future. The I.G. Farben job has been the mainstay of my security in a foreign country at war. What am I going to do without a job? It is true, I have some savings, which should last us through quite a while, but it is equally true that one can no longer buy anything with money, at least not at the present time. However, I should be able to still pay my rent with it. Somehow, I'll manage! The bag of rye flour is a great comfort to me!

*April 5, 1945* Dr. Kilian gave me a bit of oil and some saccharine from unknown sources (i.e. he wouldn't disclose where he got it) in exchange for some of my dark rye flour. The oil has a bitter taste with a hint of castor oil in it, but I was brave enough to use it for pancakes. I'm still alive and my stomach isn't upset either, so, I figure, the oil must be all right. Mother at first refused to eat the pancakes, but seeing that I have survived, she had them today for breakfast. The saccharine is an improvement in the porridge.

*April 6, 1945* In the morning I heard that the I.G. Farben bakery had opened up and was selling loaves of bread on a "first come first served" basis. I dashed up there only to find a long line of people waiting, among them Dr. Scholl, who was sticking out of the crowd, tall, gaunt and hunched more than ever. He too, had recognized me, but avoided my glances. Remembering his boastful outburst of a few weeks ago, how he would shoot himself, but also take at least half a dozen Americans with him, I wondered, why he was still there, standing meekly in a breadline, while American military police were patrolling the street. Had his killer instinct deserted him? He seems to be the only Nazi that has not fled town. I never got the bread. There were far too many people ahead of me.

Walking home I saw another surprising sight. German girls were standing on a street corner and flirting with black American soldiers. One of them had his arm around a blond girl's shoulders and his big hand in her bosom. She squirmed and giggled. I find this amazing. This girl has grown up in Hitler's Germany, being bombarded all her young life by theories of "blood and race." It was impressed upon her daily, that she belonged to a super-race and that all colored races were sub-human. The end effect of years of this indoctrination could be seen here on a street corner.

*April 7, 1945* The Russian laborers are looting the I.G. Farben plant! During the past week their number has swelled from about 500 to several thousand. The Americans have turned the local Russian barracks into an assembly center to which Soviet laborers from other parts of Germany are being brought, with the idea of finally transporting them back to Russia. From what I hear, the Americans have given the Russian laborers free rein. There is no military supervision in their camp. The Soviets can come and go as they please and do as they please. Many of them are armed.

Last night they assembled en masse and under the leadership of our own Russian laborers who are familiar with the plant, broke through the various gates with no one to hold them back. The German gatekeepers have no weapons, and for the Americans the factory territory is "off limits."

This morning I went by the main gate. Two American military policemen were standing there with rifles across their shoulders. I watched thousands of excited Russian laborers streaming into various departments, laboratories, working halls, and office buildings. I saw other thousands streaming out of the gates carrying office furniture, books, instruments, white laboratory coats, bottles filled with chemicals—all totally useless items to this uneducated mob. I got madder and madder watching this senseless looting and finally went up to one of the MP's at the gate. "Why do you not stop these Soviet looters from entering the factory?" I demanded in my halting English.

The MP, a big blond husky guy, gave me a broad grin, smiling down at me, speaking with an unfamiliar twang, "Cain ye blaime thiem, Blondie? They haive suffered a lot at the hainds of you Germans!"

I was annoyed at this answer. "I want you to take note, that I am a Latvian, not a German. The Russians have certainly suffered, but so have we. That does not give us the justification for destruction!" I declared in my best high-school English. The MP just stared at me. Maybe he didn't understand my English. The smile had left his face.

Another MP came up. "Hello, Blondie, won't you join me for lunch? I have some canned meat, some biscuits and some chocolate candy in my office!" And he grinned invitingly. This naive attempt to make contact with a local girl angered me even more. I turned and left abruptly.

*April 8, 1945* The Russians continue their looting and their destructive activities. They surely must be having a heyday. Now they imagine themselves as masters of the situation due to the protection afforded them by the Americans. Now they can prove their power. And how do they prove it? By cavemen tactics, by senseless destruction! And the civilized Americans stand by and don't lift a finger to stop them.

*April 9, 1945* After three days of looting, this morning dawned on a scene of immense and senseless devastation. The huge plant looks as though it had been struck by a tornado. Every building has been ransacked, all over the factory there are broken windows, destroyed machines, damaged apparatus, shattered furniture and laboratory glassware, dumped chemicals, burnt files, scattered books, records and reports. I saw all this as I walked through the plant today about noon. A tense German gatekeeper had warned me not to enter the plant, because a number of Russians were still on the factory grounds. I went anyway. I was determined to go to my office in the Applied Research Department, where I had left my scientific books and my laboratory records and papers. I wanted to see how much damage had been done there.

Upon entering the dimly lit hall of my laboratory building, I made out the shadow of a man at the top of the stairs. At first impulse I shrank back, but the man descended quickly and asked me in German what I wanted. He was of slight build and appeared to be in his fifties. I recognized him at once as a Russian, so I told him in Russian that I used to work in this building: "Zdrastvyte, ya zdes rabotala."

The moment he heard me speak his native tongue he bowed gallantly, and a broad smile spread over his bony face under thinning wisps of sandy-colored hair. Most politely he introduced himself as Feodor Feodorovich and asked for my name and my father's name. After the introduction was completed, he offered to take me on a tour of the building. He escorted me up and down stairs, through halls, laboratories and offices, all the while chatting agreeably, telling me about his stolen goods, while I observed with mounting dismay the complete destruction of everything that could be destroyed. The floors and stairs were covered with broken glass, debris, litter, shattered laboratory equipment, torn laboratory coats, scattered samples, damaged books and files. Even the telephones had been smashed. I stopped to pick up a dictionary. Feodor Feodorovich most gallantly gathered an armful of books and trying to force them upon me, told me in a mood of overflowing kindness, "This all belongs to you, Irina Konstantinovna. You may take it home with you!" He repeated this phrase over and over again, every time he saw me looking at something closely.

Finally we descended into the basement, where our chemicals are stored. I was surprised to find the room in good order so I asked Feodor Feodorovich about it. But he did not seem to listen. His eyes were fixed with a strange gleam on my gold wristwatch, which I had forgotten to take off before venturing out. I heard him whisper in an excited voice: "Where did you get that watch, Irina Konstantinovna? I need one too!" I felt that only quick action could save me from trouble, so I suddenly turned and ran out of the supply room, upstairs and into the open, Feodor Feodorovich following close behind me. When we were outside the building he said in a reproachful voice, "Why are you afraid, Irina Konstantinovna? I would never hurt a friend who speaks Russian!" But I was not at all convinced and quickly left.

The German gatekeeper was very relieved to see me emerge unharmed. From him I heard more details. In the Pharmaceutical Department a great many valuable medicines and tablets fell into the hands of the Russians. In the Analytical Laboratories the looters forced open a safe where platinum catalysts and platinum crucibles, used for ashing of samples, were being kept and stole them. In the Dye Department they poured concentrated sulfuric acid over textiles and wool yarn. The list of senseless destructive activities could go on and on. The gatekeeper asked the same questions that I, Mother and everyone else in Höchst are asking: Why do the Americans not stop these Soviet savages?

When I got home, I told Mother about my encounter with the Russian in our laboratory building. After having given her all the details, I ended by remarking: "There is one thing, though, that puzzles me, Mother! This fellow had such good manners, bowing gallantly, trying to help me up and down the stairs, opening doors for me and stepping aside, letting me enter first. Where, do you suppose, did he get his manners?"

Mother had a quick answer: "Didn't you say he was elderly?"

"Yes, quite so!"

"That explains it. Growing up in pre-revolutionary times, he probably had been able to catch a glimpse of gallant behavior, as practiced then by the middle classes, at a time when good manners were not yet considered a characteristic of the 'capitalists,' the 'enemies of the people.' Some of it must have stuck with Feodor Feodorovich!" Mother laughed.

*April 11, 1945* We seem to be living through an "interregnum," a time without law and order. No food is available. Old ration cards are useless. New ration cards have not been issued. All shops are closed. Nothing at all can be bought. And there is lawlessness in the streets. The Soviets now are turning their wrath upon the population. First it was the plant, now it is the people. They have started to break into houses, looting, raping and robbing. They are threatening and accosting people in the streets. The inhabitants of Höchst are powerless and have no way to protect themselves, except with their bare fists. No one has any weapons. All guns had to be surrendered to the Americans. But no protection for the civilian population is being provided by the American troops.

*April 12, 1945* We here in Höchst have our own private war with the Soviet looters, almost forgetting that big World War II is still going on. The American Forces have since pushed forward into the eastern part of Germany, and today came the news that the US Army under the command of General Patton has crossed the river Elbe and soon will be meeting with the Soviet Forces, which are advancing towards Berlin.

Hitler and his cohorts are still holding out in the Reich Chancellery in Berlin.

*April 13, 1945* The American President Franklin Delano Roosevelt died yesterday of a stroke. Harry Truman is now the new President. Today the Russians have captured Vienna. I wonder what happened to Werner Schöller? Did he make it to Vienna? Did he see his mother again? Is he safe?

*April 14, 1945* We still have no gas and no hot water. We still have no way to do our laundry. Everything is dirty: clothes, underwear, bed sheets, towels, blankets. We aren't the only ones in this predicament, though. All the other tenants in our house have the same problem. So this morning we stuck our heads together, to figure out what to do about the situation. It was decided to put the "Waschküche—the laundry kitchen"—back into working order by joint effort. This mainly means to clean the place and to organize some fuel, either wood or coal, for heating the water kettle.

The communal kitchen is standard equipment for every apartment house in Germany. No such arrangements existed in Latvia. There every family washed their laundry by hand in a tub in their own kitchen. Only large country estates had laundry kitchens. Here in Germany the tenants take turns in the Waschküche. During the past months no laundering activities were possible. One can't wash one's clothes with bombs falling, strafing airplanes on the prowl and no hot water in the kettle.

The men went off in search of wood or coal and the women aired the place, swept the floor, scrubbed the woodwork and polished the huge copper kettle, 3 feet deep and 3 feet in diameter. It was my job to wash the windows and dust the shades. Then we drew lots to determine each family's turn in the Waschküche. We were lucky. Mother and I will be using the kitchen on Monday.

*April 15, 1945* Sunday, but not a very peaceful one! This morning our local Italian workers, brought to Germany during the War by the Nazis, also started to act up. They are now located in the former German Army barracks and there is no love lost between the German population and the Italian "Fremdarbeiter—foreign workers". The Germans call them "Makkaroni-Männchen—little macaroni men") and they frown on any German girl ever seen with one of them.

Early today, the Italians joined forces with the Soviet "displaced persons"—the new name given all foreign nationals in Germany by the Americans—for short "DPs." (I guess I'm a DP too!) Together the Italians and the Russians discovered a food storage vault in one of the I.G. Farben factory buildings that is equipped with a freezing compartment, and proceeded to loot it. When I heard about this from our neighbor Herr Keller, I was very surprised. "Where does all the food come from?" I asked.

"From our I.G. Farben food store. When disorders started, the factory administration had thought it wise to transfer the foodstuffs still in their possession to the basement of one of their plant buildings, rather than leave them in the store," Herr Keller explained, "but the looters got wind of it and now they are dragging out all they can carry." News of this new looting spread fast in our small town, and when I got to the I.G. Farben gates, a crowd had already gathered, watching the ransacking in silence. We saw the Soviets and Italians carry out big bags of white flour, sugar, boxes of canned fat and meat, loaves of bread and packages of frozen vegetables and fruit. I couldn't believe my eyes when I saw all these quantities of normally unavailable food.

All through the war years I had bought our supplies on ration cards in this same "I.G. Farben Kaufhaus—the I.G. Farben Store" and had never seen canned fat or meat there for sale; nor had I seen frozen green peas or frozen grapes. But now the frozen food packages were lying in the streets, where the looters had thrown them, after they began to thaw in the warm April sun.

The Germans stood on street corners in small groups and watched the goings-on. But no one started action against the looters; no one even tried to snatch food away from them. I saw only one German taking part in the looting. She was a girl with long blond curls, and when she came out through the factory gates with a pail filled with sugar, the watching bystanders shouted in unison: "Pfui!" She felt embarrassed and tried to defend herself by declaring that it was better for Germans to get the food instead of foreigners. But nobody seemed to be impressed by that argument.

I saw dozens of dark, short and skinny Italians hurrying to their camp, panting under heavy bags of flour or sugar. One of them approached me and said in broken German, "Madam, do you have cigarettes? Give me two packs and I will carry this bag of sugar straight to your home." I sent the man away and he tried his luck with the next passer-by.

By now cigarettes have become the only valuable commodity. German money is passé; cigarettes have taken its place. Lucky, indeed, are the persons who have some saved up from the "good old times" when German cigarettes were once in a while still issued on ration cards. There also seem to be some Bulgarian cigarettes in circulation, very likely brought in during the past years by German soldiers home on furlough from the Eastern Front.

The sun was climbing higher and higher in the sky; it was getting hotter and hotter. The looting continued. But then, as in a stage performance, the scene abruptly changed and the big surprise came from a rather unexpected side. Suddenly loud yells were heard and the sound of running feet, and down the street they came sprinting: an American Army captain in helmet and battle dress, brandishing a gun high above his head, tall and handsome; behind him two huge black soldiers, to whom he shouted orders.

It looked exactly like a scene from a Western movie, when the dashing hero finally comes to the rescue of the harassed town. The soldiers darted into the crowd of Russians and Italians, grabbing one or the other and wresting their loot away from them. The Germans stood on the sidewalks and cheered. They were so immensely relieved that help had finally come. An old woman grabbed one of the black soldiers by his sleeve and pointing towards one of the looters exclaimed, "Das ist Italiano, da, da, stop, stop!" The soldier ran and by mistake grabbed a German. The old woman, getting rather upset, began to shout,

"Nein, nein, das ist ein Germane, nix Italiano, da, da, stop, stop!" The rest of the crowd began to shout with her, and in the general mix-up that followed, the Italian got away, after having disposed of his bag of flour by throwing it on the street. I saw another Italian with six big loaves of bread, three under each arm, violently resisting the orders of the other black soldier to surrender the bread. Finally the American lost his patience and took the bread by force away from him, at the same time giving him a big kick in the rear, which sent the man flying down the street, accompanied by the laughter of the Germans. These first messengers of good will in the persons of the dashing American captain and the two black soldiers probably endeared themselves forever in the hearts of the German bystanders, and I must admit, in my heart too.

*April 15, 1945* Wonderful, wonderful Monday, on which we finally have gone through a most profound cleansing ritual! We had already soaked our white wash all night long in cold soap water, using the last piece of home-made yellow Latvian soap which Herta and Elsa had sent me a long time ago, and which we had saved for just such an important purpose. This morning, upon entering the Waschküche, we started a coal fire under the copper kettle. It took several hours for the soap water plus laundry to heat up to boiling. We let the wash boil for about 45 minutes and. then transferred it into a large round tub with cold water. There we rinsed each piece by hand, changing the rinse water several times and finally putting the laundry through the mangle to wring out the excess water. This also is a hand-operated job. I feel as if I cranked the mangle for hours. My muscles are still aching.

Meanwhile, the water in the copper kettle had cooled down from boiling to a temperature that our hands could stand. Now we proceeded to wash by hand all colored items: dresses, blouses, sweaters, skirts, even woolen overcoats and last, but not least, our bunker blankets and our heavy, quilted, red comforters. Then followed the triple cold-water rinse, as prescribed by centuries of Latvian and German laundering tradition.

As of this writing, the entire wash is hanging on the line in the back yard, propped up by special two-pronged sticks to keep the clothesline from sagging. The clothesline and the sticks were part of the Waschküche equipment. Hopefully, the colors of the overcoats and the quilted blankets will not run, but I am a bit worried. Hopefully, also, it won't rain tonight, because the quilts will have to hang on the line all through the night and well into the next day, before they can be expected to be dry.

The laundering took all day. When we got through around 7:00 PM, we were exhausted. Our clothes were clean, but we ourselves were still grubby. There was only one thing to do: take a bath in the copper kettle. We drained the wash water out, rinsed the kettle and then poured fresh water in. Again we had to light the coal fire and wait for the water to heat up, but not to boiling this time. When the temperature was right, I pulled the window shades, we stripped and Mother climbed into the kettle first. When she was through, I hopped in.

Oh, what luxury that bath in the gleaming copper kettle was! Even better than the bath I took in my laboratory sink earlier this year. Sitting there in the pleasantly warm water, soaping myself with our yellow Latvian soap that smelled of home, of childhood memories on my grandparents' farm, there came to my mind the delightful story that Grandma Amalia had told me about her bath in a copper kettle in a laundry kitchen lifetimes ago, it seems, when she was young and beautiful, and barely eighteen.

When her mother became a widow at an early age, Amalia, her first child, born in 1852 into serfdom, was taken to live in the castle by the lord of the manor. She was ten years old at the time. It was 1862, the same year that Czar Alexander II, the "Liberator," abolished serfdom in Russia. Grandma Amalia claimed all her life that the lord of the manor was her natural father, and that that was the reason why she was allowed to grow up with his legitimate children. But Amalia was not their equal, only their servant. She was made a chambermaid to the count's daughter, the young "Komtesse." She had to dress and undress her; she had to lace her high boots, lace her stays and put curlers into her hair at night. The curlers were strips of linen soaked in sugar water, so as to give the shoulder-length curls, called "Papillottes," some body. She also had to accompany the Komtesse on all her outings, either on foot or in a carriage drawn by four horses. Amalia, just like her lady, always wore hats and gloves. In summer the hats had wide brims and blue veils to protect the milky-white skin of the girls from even the tiniest ray of sunshine. Besides that, white ruffled parasols were worn as an added protection.

Amalia had a good time, being more a companion than a servant to her presumed half-sister. The years went by and a young man came into Amalia's life. His name was François Dulac and he was the French tutor of the young count, imported straight from Paris. A dreamy expression used to come into Grandma Amalia's eyes when she talked about François. She talked about him often, even in her eighties. He apparently remained her "dream prince." I have the impression that women of former generations, certainly of the Victorian Age, seemed to cling to the idea of the "one great love" of their lives. I saw it in my Mother and also in Amalia. It must have been the fashion then, to languish all your days after the usually no longer obtainable male imbued with superhuman virtues.

"Irene, darling child," Grandma Amalia would intone, "you too would have fallen in love with François, had you ever met him!"

"Oh, what was he like, Grandma?"

"He had dark curly hair and sideburns. His eyes were black and sparkling; he wore a mustache on his upper lip and his cheeks were like red apples."

"Grandma, red cheeks on a man are preposterous! Did you really like him?"

"I loved him passionately. He was so wonderful! We would meet out in the park at dusk, and he would kiss me with such wild passionate kisses, I thought I'd swoon!"

"Did you?"

"No, fainting was the privilege of the upper classes. Servants didn't swoon."

"But weren't you laced also, Grandma?"

"Of course, I was, and a tiny waist I had, much smaller than my lady's. And I wore a striped white and blue dress with huge billowing sleeves and a white ruffled apron and white ruffled cap."

"You must have looked adorable in your chambermaid's outfit, Grandma!"

"I guess I did, at least François said so!"

"What happened then, Grandma?"

"Oh, then, one hot summer's night I was walking past the castle's laundry kitchen, when the thought occurred to me that it would be wonderful to take a bath."

"Grandma, why in the Waschküche? Weren't there any bathrooms in the castle?"

"Darling child, in 1870 no one had ever heard of a bathroom with a tub in it. All we had were wooden tubs that were brought into the bedroom and filled with hot water there. That's how my lady used to take her bath, once a month or so."

"For goodness sakes! And what about you?"

"Servants were not considered to be in need of taking baths. They could go and wash up in the river in summer or go to any of the Latvian farms and use the sauna there."

"Didn't the landlord have a sauna on the castle grounds?"

"What do you think, dear girl? A sauna, where people go in naked in order to sweat, was below the dignity of the German and Russian nobility!"

We both started to laugh, imagining the fat counts and countesses sweating in a steam-filled sauna, getting redder and redder, until they resembled boiled lobsters, and beating each other with fresh, leafy branches from birch trees.

"Grandma, you haven't told me the rest of the story yet!"

"Oh, yes, where was I?"

"You were walking past the laundry kitchen on the castle grounds!"

"Yes, yes, and so I decided to take a bath. I heated some water in the big copper kettle and then took off my clothes and hopped in. I was sitting there with soap bubbles all around me and enjoying myself . . ."

Amalia's thoughts seemed to be trailing off.

"And then what happened, Grandma?"

"Then the door suddenly opened and there stood—François, eyes sparkling!"

"Grandma, what did you do?"

"I didn't know what to do. I watched him come slowly nearer and nearer, until he stood before me. There was no way for me to cover my nakedness. He stood and stared at me and then he said . . ."

Again Amalia's thoughts trailed off.

"What did François say, Grandma?"

"He said, 'You have such beautiful white breasts, Amalia, will you marry me?'"

"Grandma, this is the wildest marriage proposal I have ever heard of! What did you do then, Grandma?"

"I recovered my wits and splashed soap water at him and into his eyes, until he fled in terror!"

"He wasn't much of a hero, was he, Grandma?"

"What do you mean, child? He was wonderful, and I loved him more than ever."

"Then what happened?"

"The next day François went to see the count and asked for my hand in marriage!"

"So, why didn't you marry François, Grandma?"

"The count did not give his permission and we were powerless to do anything about it. Soon thereafter he had François and his sons, the young counts, transferred to another of his estates, and I never saw François again."

"Grandma dear, do you still think of François, do you still love him?"

"Yes, I do, my child, and I will cherish his memory as long as I shall live!"

Did I see a tear glisten in Grandma's eye? Maybe it was my imagination.

*April 17, 1945* The Russians have broken through the German defense lines at the river Oder. This means that the way to Berlin is now open for them. The American radio commentator stated today, that the Nazi empire, which at the height of their power had stretched from the Atlantic to the Caucasus, has now shrunk to a narrow territory about a hundred miles wide in the heart of Germany.

*April 18, 1945* It is fortunate that I am a non-smoker. Today I bartered two packs of German cigarettes still in my possession for two bicycle tubes.

They couldn't be bought anywhere "für Geld und gute Worte—for money or good words" during the last years of the war. Now all of a sudden they can be had—if you have cigarettes. It is a blessing to again have the bicycle in functioning order. Tomorrow I'll ride out to Zeilsheim and try to persuade some farmer to sell me potatoes.

*April 19, 1945* My trip to Zeilsheim almost ended in disaster. Pedaling along on my way to Zeilsheim, I was passing the Soviet DP camp located there, when suddenly a Russian boy, jumping out from behind a bush, grabbed my handlebars and forced me to stop. At that moment a group of tough-looking fellows began to close in on me. They all carried heavy sticks and I could see their leader take a stronger grip on his stick, while glowering at me threateningly from under his brows. I was terrified, but before I could decide what to do, help came from quite unexpected quarters.

Three Russian girls, bedecked in looted finery—long evening frocks not quite appropriate for street wear and strange-looking hats of a decade ago—had been chatting nearby. Now suddenly they rushed over to me, and one of them I recognized as Lydia, my little laboratory-cleaning girl. She was adorned with a wide-brimmed straw hat with a white ostrich plume shading her face. Excitedly she whispered into my ear: "Talk Russian to us, talk in a loud voice, so the boys can hear you. They are after your bicycle!" The girls as upon command formed a protective circle around me, and all three spoke Russian simultaneously—and very audibly too. So did I, and the effect was striking. The sullen expressions of the prospective robbers magically disappeared and broad grins broke out over their faces instead. "Ah Russkaya devushka—a Russian girl" exclaimed the leader greatly pleased, "and we almost hurt you!" My guardian angel was again right there on the spot, when I needed him.

*April 20, 1945* Today is "Führer's Geburtstag—Hitler's birthday". He is 56 years old. Of course, no one here in Höchst cares. Gone are the days when the 20th of April was a state holiday, when the town was decorated with swastikas and the local party leaders made speeches, the Hitler Youth went on parades and the BDM—Bund Deutscher Mädchen (Union of German girls) brightened the festivities with singing and folk-dancing.

*April 21, 1945* I heard today from Kilian that Scholl was recently arrested by the Americans and carted off to a prison camp somewhere on the River Rhine, especially set up for Nazis. His wife and four young kids have now to fend for themselves, just as he predicted.

*April 22, 1945* I still have no news whatsoever from Karen. Mail service has again started and transportation to Frankfurt by streetcar and by train was also re-established a little while ago, but there is no mail for us.

Karen, and Herta and Elsa in Latvia, are the only ones of my dear friends who are not accounted for. I fear the worst, particularly regarding Karen and her babies. She very likely may have fallen into the hands of the Soviets. Being nine months pregnant and having two small children to take care of must have made it extremely difficult, if not impossible, for her to escape from the onslaught of the Red Army.

*April 23, 1945* The Russians, meanwhile, are continuing to terrorize the population. No one any longer dares to pass their camp on Zeilsheimer Weg. What happened to me has happened to many others, except that there was no lucky ending. People have been beaten up and their bicycles have been taken away. Many persons have been seriously hurt, even stabbed and wounded.

The camp by now is holding 13,000 Soviet displaced persons. There is a continuous coming and going. Groups of DPs are daily transported back to Russia while others are newly arriving from the Southern and Western parts of Germany. The camp resembles a beehive. The Russians make a lot of noise, which can be heard for miles around, and every so often they swarm out and advance en masse on the town.

This afternoon, I met Madame Stravatzka, a little old Russian lady, widow of an I.G. Farben chemist, who has been living in Höchst for the last twenty years or so. Madame Stravatzka suffers from a strange incurable condition: her face is covered with dark blue blotches, which give her a very sinister appearance. She told me several years ago what the cause of this discoloration is. She once had been treated with tablets containing a silver salt. For some unknown reason the silver settled in the form of black silver oxide pigmentation in the epidermal layer of the skin on her face and couldn't be removed. For years now she has had to live with this blue face. The poor soul is desperately trying to cover the blotches up with face powder, but nothing helps. The powder just looks like a filmy white veil on a dark blue background. We always speak Russian when meeting.

"Dorogaya—my dear," she exclaimed, "I have gone through the most horrible experience. I am still quite shaken up, Irina Konstantinovna!"

"For goodness' sake, what happened to you, Madame Stravatzka?"

"Last night some Russian looters broke into my apartment and started to ransack the place. They took away my Persian lamb coat and all my jewelry, precious pieces, presents given to me by my dear late husband, which I cherished with all my heart."

"Maria Alexandrovna, dorogaya, I'm terribly sorry to hear that. What a dreadful shock this must have been to you! Couldn't you, speaking Russian, persuade these young hoodlums to leave you and your property alone?"

"I tried, Irina Konstantinovna, but they wouldn't even listen. They called me a capitalist and made fun of me and my 'sinaya morda,—my blue muzzle.'"

"Then what happened, Maria Alexandrovna?"

"They eventually left, taking my precious things with them. Only one boy stayed behind. I said to him: 'Chto ty hochesh, pasholl!—What do you want, get lost!'"

"'I want your earrings, staruha—old woman,' said the fellow. He had noticed my diamond earrings, which I was wearing and which were partially hidden by my hair. 'Davai, ili ya tebya ubyu!—Hand them over, or I'll kill you!' In great fear I removed the earrings and gave them to the lad, who stood before me, stick in one hand and a knife in the other.

"I was crying bitterly. He turned to go. Suddenly an idea struck me. 'Pozhdi,' I told him. 'Wait a moment.' He stopped and looked at me in surprise. 'Do you have a mother?' I asked the boy.

"'Yes, I do!'

"'Do you love your mother?'

"'I do!'

"'What would your mother say if she knew what you have done to me?'

"'I don't know.'

"'But I do, since at my age I could easily be your mother. It would break her heart to know that her son is a thief!' There was a tense silence, then a muscle twitched in the young man's face, tears filled his eyes and with a quick motion he handed me my diamond earrings.

"'Take them back,' he whispered hoarsely, 'and forgive me, matushka!—little mother.' Then he turned abruptly and left."

I looked more closely at Madame Stravatzka. She was wearing her diamond earrings. She moved her head and a sunray struck the precious stones and made them glitter in all colors of the rainbow. I exclaimed, "How beautiful your earrings are, dorogaya!" Madame Stravatzka smiled happily, as a tear rolled over her poor, dark-blue face.

*April 24, 1945* Our main food staple continues to be the rye flour. Today I was fortunate to be able to buy some rhubarb at a vegetable stand. Here and there now fruit and vegetable stands and also food stores are opening up for a few hours to sell some produce. They actually sell it for money, not for cigarettes. I'll make a jam out of rhubarb and saccharine, and it will be a welcome addition to our dark rye gruel and pancakes.

*April 25, 1945* Today American and Soviet troops met for the first time at Torgau on the River Elbe.

*April 26, 1945* Soviet Forces are shelling the Reich Chancellery in Berlin. Hitler and Goebbels, from what is known, are still in their "fortress Berlin." Generalfeldmarschall Goering, fat man with a hundred medals, supposedly has left and is now hidden somewhere in the Bavarian Alps—great hero that he pretended to be.

*April 27, 1945* Another "Klumpfüsschen's Märchenstunde-fairy-tale hour of Little Clubfoot". It is Friday evening and I just heard the news from Berlin.
    And here it was: Goebbels' voice. Today's fairy tale did not deal much with politics or propaganda. He seems to know that it is all over with the "Thousand-Year Reich." He mentioned death: "Wir werden zu sterben wissen!—We shall know how to die!" And then he gave something like a vision of a better German future. He talked about rebuilt cities, busy factories, prosperous farms, green meadows and golden rye fields. But I had the strong feeling that the shadow of death is hovering over Joseph Goebbels. Everyone who today listened to his speech must have sensed the presence of the Dark Avenger.

*April 29, 1945* Today came the startling news that Mussolini was shot yesterday together with his mistress named Clara (I didn't quite catch her last name) on the shore of Lake Como. Their bodies were transported to Milan and hung in a plaza there, apparently not by the neck, but upside down, by their feet. No one here ever had the slightest inkling that the stout old Duce had a young mistress. That makes me dislike him even more.
    I wonder if Hitler may have some female tucked away somewhere. There was talk about a young woman pilot named Hanna Reitsch, and it is known that at the beginning of his career he had a strange emotional relationship with his own niece Angelika, who later committed suicide.
    Right now Hitler is sitting in the bunker under the ruins of the Chancellery in Berlin. No more escape seems possible for him. The Soviets are less than a mile away from the Chancellery.

*April 30, 1945* This morning I looked at myself in the mirror. My cheekbones are standing out, my eyes, although having sunk deeper into their sockets, appear larger than ever and of a darker blue. Whatever curves I possessed have gone by now. There never was much in the first place, as I recall, causing annoyance to at least two SS "super-Germans." The bones at my wrists, elbows, knees and ankles are sticking out, and seem to have increased enormously in size. In other words, I look like a flat, long, narrow, angular board. Not a very flattering description of myself, but unfortunately true. I'm no longer even very hungry: just looking at that sticky dark rye porridge is beginning to turn my stomach. Mother is in equally poor shape, but she is no longer complaining, just apathetic, as though she no longer cared.

I have to do something about the food situation! Yesterday I tried to get some produce from my farmer friends in the Taunus Mountains. Now with my bicycle intact, I can again go there. I got some potatoes, a few carrots and two eggs. These people really have nothing themselves. I'm convinced of that. They sold me the stuff for money. I gave them some cigarettes anyway out of what is left of my meager supply.

*May 1, 1945* Today Admiral Dönitz broadcast from Berlin that "the Führer has died fighting at the head of his troops." Dönitz then went on to declare that the Führer appointed him, Dönitz, to be his successor as President of the Reich, Minister of War and Supreme Commander of the Armed Forces. It was a short broadcast and left us all very puzzled.

The Führer dying fighting at the head of his troops? I don't believe it! If he was so filled with fighting spirit, why didn't he go into battle weeks ago at the Western or the Eastern fronts instead of hiding like a mole in his burrow under the Chancellery?

Dönitz appointed his successor? Why not his closest cronies Goebbels, Göring, Himmler or Bormann? Who has ever heard much of Dönitz? He never was in the public eye! Something is rather strange about this whole sordid business!

*May 2, 1945* This morning I made a decision. "Mother," I said, "I'm going into the Russian DP camp to try and get some food there: fat and canned meat maybe and some sugar!"

"For goodness sakes, Irene, are you out of your mind? They will rape and kill you!" Mother shouted.

"No, they won't! I'll go in the disguise of a Russian peasant girl, pretending to be one of them, a slave laborer from one of the farms around here!"

"Irene, I'll never let you go! It won't work; they'll discover that you're trying to fool them! What if Lydia or Natasha or any of the other Russian girls and boys from your department happens to be around and recognize you? They'll attack you at once!"

"I'm not so sure that Lydia would attack me. Remember, she was the one who saved me from attack, when the Russian guys were after my bicycle."

"Well, she might tell her friends who you really are, and there is no telling what they might do!"

"You're probably right, Mother, but we have gotten to the point where we simply need some fat and protein or else our health will break down rapidly. Remember: 'Wer nicht wagt, gewinnt nicht'—'Nothing ventured, nothing gained!'"

This German proverb seemed to cheer Mother up a bit.

"It might be worth a try! But I must insist on one thing, Irene!"

"What's that, Mother?"

"I'm going with you! I won't let you go alone! I don't want to live without you! I have no one close in the world left but you! If they kill you, they might as well kill me too!"

I looked at Mother. She was determined. I went up to her and kissed her. "All right, Mother, you come along! We must dress in Russian peasant fashion, wearing printed cotton skirts and brightly colored blouses. An apron for you might be appropriate. And not to forget bright kerchiefs for the hair!"

We rummaged through our clothes and found what we wanted: wide skirts reaching to mid-calf, a red and a blue blouse, a white apron for Mother and some cotton kerchiefs in striking prints, which we tied with a knot under our chins. Trying also to imitate the current cosmetic fashions of the Russian girls whom I had recently observed, I painted my eyebrows a striking black, my cheeks an apple red and my lips a glowing orange. We decided that Mother should not wear makeup, assuming that older Russian peasant women weren't as likely to paint themselves up in such a gaudy manner.

About noon today we set out in trepidation on the long trek to the Russian camp on Zeilsheimer Weg, carrying a big cloth shopping bag with us. It is a walk of three miles or more. As we neared the camp my heart began to beat more and more wildly. I could feel the heartbeat even in my throat. Pulling my kerchief deeper over my eyes, I cast furtive glances around. It was the usual "beehive": young men and girls streaming in and out of the gates, chatting gaily and laughing. To our immense relief no one paid much attention to us. So, apparently, we looked to the Russians as though we "belonged." This observation restored my courage somewhat. I whispered to Mother: "We seem to appear authentic enough. I'm so glad that you came along. You speak Russian like a native. And remember, we're supposed to be peasant women."

Up to the camp entrance we marched and then stopped and looked around searchingly. On the other side of the gate was a small wooden structure out of which stepped a young fellow with a pink round face and light-colored eyes under a heavy thatch of blond hair. He was wearing a discarded American GI's uniform.

"Chto vy hotite?—What do you want?" he asked us in a stern voice.

"Tovarishch Ofisér," Mother intoned, "my bedniye ruskiye zhenchini?—Comrade officer, we are poor Russian women!"

The gatekeeper's expression changed from stern to haughty, but at the same time, I could sense how immensely pleased he was to be called an officer. "Chto vy hotite?" he asked again.

"We are looking for food, comrade captain," I answered in a tremulous voice, as though overawed by the young man's appearance.

"There, there, no need for thee to be frightened," said the gatekeeper, addressing me using the familiar "ty" (thou) rather than the formal "vy" (you). A smile appeared on his face as he looked me over. He apparently liked what he saw, which must have been mostly my painted-up face. The rest of me was quite effectively disguised in kerchief, wide skirt and long-sleeved oversized blouse.

With a gesture of his hand our interlocutor invited us to step into the gatehouse, where he seated us on wooden chairs. He himself retreated behind a rickety desk, which maintained a precarious balance standing on three legs only. "What is thy name and father's name?" he asked me, completely ignoring Mother.

"Irina Konstantinovna," I responded, "and this is my Mother Elena Yuryevna." I did the best I could, trying to russify Mother's name Ella and her father's name Georg on the spur of the moment.

"My name is Andrey Ivanovich," said the gatekeeper, leaning back in his chair while continuing to stare at me.

"Ocharovatelno, Andrey Ivanovich—(I'm very charmed)," I said, but then caught myself. That might be rather too good manners. So I suddenly pretended to yawn with my mouth wide open, stretching my legs and arms.

"What is it, are you tired?" asked Andrey Ivanovich.

"Yes, very, I was up all night sewing."
"Sewing what?"
"Oh, rubashki (men's shirts)!"
"You can sew?"
"Yes, and so can my mother. She is a seamstress."
"Ocharovatelno (how great!)" Now it was Andrey's turn to use this word, which has different meanings depending on the context of speech. "Could you sew me some shirts? I need some badly!"

"I'm sure we could, if our farmer boss will let us!" I replied. "You see, we work on a farm, do housekeeping there and sewing. We are hungry: there isn't enough food left for anyone on our farm, and so we came here to see if you would share some of your supplies with us, comrade Kapitan!"

While I was making my little speech, a couple of young men had entered and stood there staring at us. The benevolent smile that Andrey had displayed for me abruptly turned to a grimace and he hissed at them: "Posholl, von!—Get lost, out of here!" The boys obeyed. From this I deduced that Andrey must have some kind of authority around the camp.

"Comrade Kapitan, could you give us some canned meat and fat?" I pleaded, rolling my eyes heavenward and assuming a suffering expression. "We are very, very hungry!"

"What will I get for that, Irina Konstantinovna?" Andrey asked with a honeyed tone in his voice.

"Oh, I'll sew you some shirts, Andrey Ivanovich," I said quickly, "if you can get me the material." I was getting a bit nervous under the stares of this Andrey Ivanovich.

"That's fine, Irochka, but will you also come and see me?"

Now I was really getting flustered. He had called me "Irochka," a pet name derived from the rather stately Greek "Irene" meaning "Goddess of Peace." It is an ancient name: a daughter of Czar Ivan the Terrible was named Irina and that was in the 16th century. I didn't quite know what to reply, when Mother came to my rescue: "Of course, she will come to see you, why shouldn't she come to see a fine young officer like you, Andrey Ivanovich? But give her time! We are very weak from hunger, Andrey Ivanovich!"

"Call me Andryusha," Comrade 'Kapitan' responded. "I'll get you some meat right away!" He jumped up, went to the door, opened it and stuck his head out. We heard him give some orders. Mother and I looked at each other and I winked. Andrey returned and found us both sitting there as before, with demure expressions on our faces.

"Let me give you some good advice," Andrey resumed the conversation. "Why don't you join this camp and ask to be transferred back to your home? Here at least you'll have enough to eat, while you are waiting for transportation, and I'll be here too, Irochka."

Trying to avoid this ticklish subject, I quickly changed the conversation. "You must be an important official, Andryusha," I said, smiling at him.

"Oh yes, I am!" he affirmed with conviction. "Yesterday I talked at length with an American officer!" And Andrey looked at me to see what impression that stupendous fact would create on me.

"You didn't, Andryusha!" I gasped, widening my eyes and staring at him open-mouthed.

"Oh yes, I did, Irochka, and what a conversation that was! We talked about politics and the war and the American colonel agreed with my opinion on all accounts!"

"Really! Did the colonel speak Russian?"

"No!"

"Do you speak English, Andryusha?"

"Oh yes, I do. The colonel was very impressed when I said to him: 'How do you do?' and 'Good morning' and 'O.K.'"

There came a strange coughing sound from Mother. She was holding her hands before her face and sputtering something unintelligible. I had a good idea what this was all about. She was remembering her own efforts at the Hohe Mark sanatorium to say "Good morning" to the British officer, and the comedy of the situation had overwhelmed her. I jumped up and patted Mother on the back, explaining to Andrey, "Moya mamushka ochen prostudilas—my little Mother has a bad cold." Then we settled down again, waiting for the foodstuffs to arrive.

"Come back tomorrow, Irochka, will you? Tomorrow I'll get you several pounds of butter. I know where there is some hidden in the barracks."

"Andryusha, that would be great! Will you be here in this office again tomorrow?"

"No, I won't. We take turns."

"How am I going to find you then, Andryusha?" Andrey thought this over for a while, staring into space. Suddenly he took a tiny notebook out of his pocket, tore out a page, picked up a pencil stump from the desk and got ready to write.

I followed all of his movements with the fascination of the scientifically trained observer. What was this young, ignorant, basically good-natured human being going to do next? I also felt some slight pangs of conscience. In spite of the danger inherent in the situation I was obviously gaining control and misusing Andryusha's trust. But, on the other hand, we were not really hurting anyone by asking for a little food. The Russians had stolen it, taken it by force. They had gorged themselves for weeks on all that good stuff. We were desperately hungry. And I remembered my motto, coined in the last years of the war: "It is survival that counts!"

Andrey hadn't written anything yet. The expression on his face grew increasingly strained; folds appeared on his forehead, he pulled his eyebrows together. Then he started to bite the pencil stump. Finally, his features smoothed out, a smile appeared around his wide mouth and with slow awkward movements he wrote something on that tiny piece of notepaper.

He handed it to me and I read: "Propuskatj v lager—To be let into the camp." That was all. No date, no name, no signature.

Andrey watched me as I was studying the slip of paper. I had a hard time to keep from laughing. I bit my lip, and pretended that something was wrong with my kerchief, adjusting it so as to conceal a smile. At that moment, fortunately, Andryusha's messenger boy arrived carrying some tin cans and a brown paper bag. Andryusha took these items from the boy and handed them to us. "Open up your bag, Irochka," he said. "Here you have some canned meat and some lard and some sugar too!"

"Thank you, Andryusha, you have been very kind to us," I said. "I'll pray for you every night!"

"Do that, do that, Irochka; my mother said to me, when I was parting from her to go to Germany, that she would pray for me every night."

"I'm sure she has, Andryusha."

"She made the sign of the cross over me and she said: "Svyataya deva—the holy Virgin bless you and keep you safe!" and Andrey smiled a forlorn smile.

"Andryusha, don't grieve, you will soon be returning to your matushka," Mother broke in, "but now it is time that we leave," and she stretched out her hand, grabbed Andryusha's and shook it. I followed suit. Andryusha held my hand and smiled, "And you won't forget your promise, will you Irochka? You'll come to see me?"

"Yes, I will," I said, knowing full well that I'd never dare to go into the lions' den again. Andrey accompanied us to the gate and stood there waving, while we hurried away carrying our precious foodstuffs, skirts billowing in the wind and kerchiefs fluttering.

Just now, while I am writing, Mother is preparing a sumptuous meal, consisting of beef and boiled potatoes in a nice fat gravy made of rye flour and lard. For dessert we will have rhubarb fruit sauce sweetened with genuine sugar!

*May 3, 1945* Last night's dinner has made me see life in a more rose-colored hue. I'm sure things will get better again. I gave a fleeting thought to Andryusha: I hope he has a safe trip home to his matushka. Earlier this morning I turned on the radio: "Yesterday Soviet Forces reached the Reich Chancellery in Berlin," I heard the announcer say.

More details followed. There is no trace of Hitler or Bormann but the charred remains of Goebbels and his wife have been found. The Reichspropagandaminister, apparently, after having given poison to his six children, shot his wife and himself on May 1 in the Chancellery garden. His underlings set fire to their bodies, but these were not completely destroyed. The Soviets were able to identify them. Goebbels chose suicide, the coward's way out! Men of courage face their fate head-on!

*May 4, 1945* US Occupation Forces have taken over the entire I.G. Farben plant in Höchst and are using the office buildings as their local headquarters. A lot of new military administration personnel seem to be arriving daily.

It doesn't look as though I.G. Farben is going to start working again. All departments and laboratories are closed. Neither I nor any other employees have received official notification one way or another. There is nothing to do but wait and see what the outcome will be.

*May 5, 1945* "Maybe we should go back to that Russian camp, Irene," Mother mused this morning at breakfast, "Andryusha after all, did promise to give us several pounds of butter."

"Absolutely not, Mother," I said sternly. "One mustn't test one's luck too often."

"But I could go by myself, Irene: some Russians may recognize you, but no one knows me!"

"Mother, forget it! There will be no more excursions into the holdout of these thieves and hooligans. It is much too dangerous!"

"But all that nice butter," Mother said with a sigh that made me laugh, in spite of Mother's wistful expression. The subject, however, was not broached any further.

*May 6, 1945* The mystery surrounding Hitler's death seems to have been solved, at least partially. The Führer apparently committed suicide by shooting himself on April 30 in the underground bunker of the Reich Chancellery. I do not consider this part of the news particularly startling.

I suspected suicide all along. What other choice did a criminal and bloody murderer like Adolf Hitler have?

The thing that really surprises me as well as every one else in Germany is Hitler's marriage on April 29—one day before his death—to some woman named Eva Braun. It was a suicide pact. She died with him on the following day. Their bodies have not been found. There is speculation that faithful attendants incinerated the corpses.

No one in the German population had ever heard of Eva Braun; no one knew that Hitler had a mistress of long standing. This is what Eva Braun was, according to the radio broadcast. This death-chamber marriage is incredibly weird—and quite in tune with the "Götterdämmerung" atmosphere prevailing in the Reich Chancellery.

*May 7, 1945* There is great excitement in town. Over the weekend, a section of Höchst has been taken over by American military personnel. It is the most elegant part of town, where the I.G. Farben chemists and directors have their villas. It is now called the "American Compound" and is off limits to all Germans, except servants who work for the American officers now stationed in these elegant mansions. The houses are in excellent shape: they were never bomb-damaged. All furniture, crystal, china, silverware, paintings, pianos, carpets, rugs, draperies are intact. The houses had to be handed over within an hour's time. The owners were only allowed to take a few personal belongings with them. The Americans made no provisions for new quarters for the evacuated Germans. Each family was on their own and had to find some place to stay before dusk fell. We have a curfew in town: no one is allowed on the streets after dark. Evacuation of German homes will continue, I understand.

*May 8, 1945* World War II has finally come to an end in Europe. Early yesterday morning the Germans—General Jodl and Admiral von Friedeburg—signed the document of unconditional surrender at Rheims in France in the presence of representatives from the Allied Nations: America, Great Britain, the Soviet Union and France.

Today, official word came to the US troops that the war is over. Tonight, as of this writing, the G.I.s are celebrating with singing, dancing, drinking and fireworks in the sky.

*May 9, 1945* I heard from Kilian this afternoon, while visiting with him and his family, that one of the first to be thrown out of their home in the section taken over by the Americans, has been Scholl's wife and their four young children. It seems Scholl's fear of grave trouble for his family, which he expressed to me earlier this spring, has come true.

*May 10, 1945* Walking through town today, I met Dr. Torgau wandering forlornly through the streets. His wife and children are still somewhere in a small village in the Taunus Mountains, where they were evacuated when the bombing terror increased last year. Torgau was unshaven and his clothes looked rather wrinkled. Seeing me, his mournful expression brightened somewhat and a tiny smile lit up his face: "Oh, I'm so glad to see you, Fräulein Zarina. I feel awful, just awful!"

"What happened to you, Dr. Torgau?"

"The Americans yesterday kicked me out of my house and I have nowhere to stay. I spent last night hidden in the city park near the old castle wall."

"But Dr. Torgau, don't you have any friends in town?"

"Oh yes, I do, but they all have already taken in other unfortunates like me and their homes are crowded. What am I going to do?" There were almost tears in Torgau's mild blue eyes and his voice was cracking.

"Come with me, I'll feed you some nice hot gruel made of rye flour with a piece of beef in it, and maybe I'll be able to find you a place to stay!"

Torgau ate my "carpenter's glue" plus beef with much relish. I also fixed some hot water for him, so that he could wash up and shave. Meanwhile, I went to see our four old spinster ladies, the Misses Brettlein, who live on the fourth floor. I told them about Dr. Torgau's plight and asked if they could take him in, since they have a large apartment consisting of ten rooms.

"Oh no, we can't do that." Miss Klara said, "We are very crowded as is!"

"Yes, crowded with soft chairs, chaise-lounges, two pianos and with knickknacks," said I.

Miss Sophie spoke up: "But imagine, Miss Zarina, we are unmarried ladies and for a single man to come and live with us wouldn't do!"

"Come on, now, Miss Sophie, I hardly think you'd have to worry at your age about such matters. Furthermore, Dr. Torgau is married, not single, as you well know!"

"Yes, yes, Miss Zarina," Miss Margot said nervously, "we know that, but we have only one bathroom, and it would be horribly embarrassing for any of us to meet a man at our bathroom door, while we are still in our negligees with curlers in our hair."

"On the contrary, Miss Margot, it should add some gracious stimulation to have a fine gentleman joining your household."

The misses thought this over, then Miss Lucie, the oldest said: "W . . . e . . . e . . . ll, we can't take him into our apartment, but we have an attic room, to which he could move. He could use our bathroom and take meals with us."

And so it was decided that Torgau would make his home in the attic. He was truly elated and thanked me profusely, kissing my hand: "Irene, I'll never forget your help. My very best friends didn't lift a finger for me; only you really tried. Thank you, oh, thank you so much!" I happen to know that the Brettleins have relatives in the country, who provide them with foodstuffs. I do hope that they'll share some of it with poor, timid and hungry Torgau.

*May 11, 1945* The official name of the American occupation forces is "United States Forces European Theater," for short "USFET." USFET headquarters, by the way, will be established in the spacious and well-furnished I.G. Farben Administration building in Frankfurt on Main, which at present is used as a Temporary Camp for Soviet DPs. I wonder if the Americans will still find the place suitable after the Russians have moved out?

*May 12, 1945* Our whole town is in mourning, shocked to the core by the latest and most gruesome misdeed of the Russian DPs. This morning, a German nurse bicycled home from the hospital past the Russian camp on Zeilsheimer Weg. Several young men there apparently saw another good opportunity to get hold of a bicycle. They attacked the girl. She cried for help. Two young boys aged fifteen and sixteen, sons of our local lawyer Dr. Windorf, who were working in the family's little vegetable garden nearby, rushed over to help the nurse. They struggled with the Russian hooligans, but were overpowered and actually clubbed to death. One boy died immediately and his brother a short time later in the hospital.

People are enraged. The murderers have gotten away with no trouble at all. There has been no investigation; there will be no punishment. There seems to be no authority to uphold the law. What is this USFET around for anyway? We are still living in an interregnum.

*May 13, 1945* My name's day, the day of St. Irene! I have no idea where and when this saint lived, but I have always loved this date in May, when my name's day was celebrated in Latvia amidst the first budding of leaves, the first sprouting of grass, the first spring flowers opening their blossoms. Spring comes late to the Baltic States and sometimes there still was ice in the mornings on the pond in the Viestura Garden near our home. However, the swans were out already, sailing along on the pond, causing silvery ripples in the quiet waters, shaded by the first filmy veil of ancient weeping willows growing on the banks.

*May 14, 1945* A letter reached us today from Aunt Meta in Thuringia written on May 4. It had been on its way for ten days, just to cover a distance of a couple of hundred miles. Act III of the Greek tragedy in Meta's life has struck: her little daughter Hiye is dead. Within three months she has lost her entire family: her husband and her two children. Mother and I were horror-struck when we read the shattering news:

". . . I have just come from the funeral of my darling little Hiye. She was killed two days ago by the stray bullet of an American MP.

"Hiye was so excited when the US troops came marching into Rothenstein on the Saale in early April. I too felt a ray of hope, although still crushed by the deaths of my darling Svenny and my Arno. At least I had Hiye; at least I wasn't all alone.

"One month later, on May 2, little Gerda, another eight-year-old, Hiye's good friend, came running to our house shouting, 'The 'Amis' are handing out chocolate candy to the children. Come along, Hiye, so we can get some too!' Hiye dashed out and hand in hand the two little girls ran off. That is the last time I saw my child alive.

"A few minutes later, there was a commotion in the village street and I heard excited voices and then the sirens of the ambulance. I hurried out into the open, just in time to see the ambulance disappearing around the corner. There was a trail of blood in the dust of the street. Someone shouted, 'It is your child, Frau Laane!' I ran as fast as I could, following the trail of blood. I knew then already, that Hiye must have been killed. How could a small child lose that much blood and still live?

"At the hospital I saw my little girl again: she was dead. I collapsed; gentle hands lifted me up. Eventually I was taken home.

"I found out later what had happened: our local Nazis had been arrested and were to be taken to some concentration camp by the US military police. One of the prisoners tried to escape; the MP fired a shot at him, missed and hit Hiye instead. The bullet went right through her left eye. She was killed instantly.

"These last days have been like a bad dream. I still can't perceive it; I can't accept it: my little Hiye can't be dead! She was so alive, such a happy, playful child, always in good spirits, always smiling!

"But yet, I know that she is gone, resting in the cemetery next to her father on his left side, just as Arno saw it in his prophetic dream early this year. I've written you about this dream. He told me about it for the first time after Svenny's funeral. Why didn't it occur to me or to you, that this dream also foretold Hiye's death? Maybe it was a warning: maybe I could have prevented this latest tragedy, if I had understood and heeded this warning!

"But now it is too late, forever too late! All my loved ones are gone and I am totally alone. I don't feel like living! I too want to go to sleep under the rose bush in our cemetery and rest there next to my dear ones."

"Poor, poor Aunt Meta," I said to Mother. "How can she ever get over this triple tragedy?"

"Meta will survive! We Estonians are a tough race, Irene. We have to be, or our small nation would never have survived seven centuries of onslaught, wars and oppression."

"The same goes for the Latvians and the Lithuanians, Mother!"

Mother herself was trying to act the role of a "tough Estonian," but there were tears in her eyes. I have cried all day.

*May 15, 1945* It is a week now since the End of War. The only big change, so far, since the Americans have marched in, has been the end of the blackout. Streets are lighted again at night and dark shades no longer have to be carefully adjusted so that no ray of lamplight may filter through windows and doors. In fact, I removed our black plastic shades on the evening of the 8th of May, rejoicing that never again would I have to worry about committing a "blackout crime." I still vividly remember the time when an overly eager German policeman almost arrested me for that.

Strangely enough, though, I cannot get used to lights at night, particularly my own lighted windows seen from the street. I feel an almost irresistible urge to rush up and turn the lights out or to cover the windows up. In unguarded moments, walking along at dusk and suddenly seeing a light flare up in a window, an irrational fear will grip me, making me relive some horrible moment of the war. I again can hear the sirens howling and the whistling of the bombs, see the street in flames under a dark sky over which searchlights are playing, and listen to the gunfire of the FLAK.

My reason tells me all this horror is now in the past, but my subconscious seems to be living by its own unfathomable laws. It will take a long, long time, I'm afraid, before I'll be able to remember the war years with calmness of mind.

*May 16, 1945* The weather is beautiful; the forsythias are in bloom. Our linden trees by now have big heart-shaped leaves. The white crosses cut into their bark by some desperate Nazi are still visible.

This noon I was looking out of the window admiring the spring scenery, when suddenly I heard a commotion in the entrance hall of our house. A loud conversation was going on, partly in German, partly in English. It had something to do with billets for American soldiers. I opened the front door and looked out. There on the stairs stood our neighbor Frau Keller and a black American lieutenant, who tried in vain to explain to her what he wanted. Frau Keller, not knowing any English, couldn't understand him. Descending several steps, I asked the officer what the matter was.

"I'm so glad that you speak English, Miss. I'm trying to find billets for my company of Army truck drivers and I would like to see the apartments in this house. May I come in?"

My heart sank, as the specter of evacuation rose before my eyes. Where would Mother and I go, where could we go? My hand must have trembled as I motioned the lieutenant to follow me into our apartment. I showed him around; he went through our rooms and seemed very pleased with what he saw.

"That will be just fine for my men," he said, "and very convenient too!" Then facing me he added, "Will you please tell all the tenants in this house to be ready to move out by tomorrow noon? You may take along your clothes and underwear. All other items like furniture, bedding, carpets, kitchen utensils, china, silverware, radios, have to remain in the apartments."

Hearing this I felt even more terrible than before. We have been lucky enough to come through the war with our property intact and now we faced losing it all. There is no telling if we'd ever get any of it back. And what about all the other families living in our house? In the last weeks at least half of the people in Höchst have been ordered to relinquish their homes to members of the American occupation forces. The whole population is now squeezed together in the rest of the town. It seems highly improbable to find any living space at all.

I knew that I had to try my utmost to persuade the American lieutenant not to take over our house for his company. "Lieutenant, will you please consider that in this house live about forty people, several of them political refugees from the Baltic States? My mother and myself are from Latvia and so are Dr. Kalns and his family. His wife is very sick in bed and is not expected to live. Besides that, families in this house have already taken in evacuated persons from other parts of town. Where shall we all go? We all will be out on the streets with nowhere to go! Lieutenant, you can't be so cruel as to impose such great hardship on people who have suffered so much already!"

After having made this speech in the best English I could muster, I looked at him pleadingly. The lieutenant gave me a good-natured smile. "Believe me, Miss, I hate to cause you trouble like this. But on the other hand, I do need billets for my company. Could you name me another apartment house which you think might be suitable for our purposes, and I'll spare you!"

As the full meaning of his words hit me, I knew that I couldn't do it. "I'm sorry, lieutenant, but that I refuse to do. It would be dishonest and mean to wish on others a misery that I am trying to avoid myself. Why don't you take over the high school in Höchst? It is not bomb-damaged and there should be plenty of space."

"Thank you, Miss, for the advice. I'll think it over and I'll give you my final decision by tomorrow noon. But be prepared to move out if necessary, and give this message to all the other tenants as well." The lieutenant smiled, gave me a military salute and left.

During our conversation the news of a possible evacuation had spread from floor to floor. As I stepped out of my apartment, most of my neighbors were already waiting outside for me. "What did he say? Do we have to leave? What did you talk about?" I heard a barrage of questions fired at me. I gave them the lieutenant's message. Now all that is left to do is to wait for his decision.

*May 17, 1945* 8:00 AM. Mother and I spent a restless and sad night. It may be our last day in our home. Do we again have to leave most of our belongings behind? We went through this once already in Latvia in 1941.

10:00 AM. Our clothes are packed. I hope they let us take our personal belongings, our documents and our jewelry with us.

2:00 PM. The lieutenant appeared on the stroke of 12:00 noon. He brought his sergeant with him, a Hawaiian with light brown skin and the most enormous brown eyes I have ever seen. Both came straight to my apartment. I asked them into my living room, where they remained standing, smiling at me.

"What is your decision, Lieutenant?" I asked tensely.

"You may stay in your house, Miss," the officer said and smiled some more.

"Oh thank you, thank you, Lieutenant, I'm so happy!" and I almost danced with joy.

"And do you know why I came to this decision, Miss?" the American asked.

"No, why?"

"I liked your attitude. You did not send me off to some other apartment house like the people in your neighborhood, who sent me to this place yesterday, in order to get rid of us. And do you know where we will move in? We will move right into their house!" And a mischievous grin spread over the lieutenant's face. The Hawaiian sergeant grinned with him, flashing magnificent white teeth.

The lieutenant turned to go; the sergeant stayed behind and suddenly approached me, behind his superior's back: "I'd like to learn German. Will you teach me?" I was stunned, but only for a moment. I didn't dare say no, for fear, the sergeant might induce the lieutenant to reverse his decision, so I simply nodded my head. The Hawaiian gave me the sweetest of smiles, rolled his eyes, while whispering into my ear, "I'll come when it grows dark!" whereupon he left, catching up with his boss.

Meanwhile, word had spread that the Americans had arrived and a crowd of people from our house was gathering in front of the lieutenant's jeep outside. His driver, big as a mountain and as black and shiny as ebony, was sitting in the vehicle waiting for his superior, and like the Hawaiian, also flashing his snowy white teeth. The Germans on the sidewalk seemed fascinated by the driver's unusual and impressive appearance. I noticed that the four Misses Brettlein were there, Frau Nüssler, fiftyish and graying, from the fifth floor, and also Dr. Torgau; all people who speak English. None of these persons knew yet that the lieutenant had already informed me of his decision, and as he was coming out of the house ready to enter his jeep, Dr. Torgau, disheveled in appearance as usual these days, with one of his shirt-tails hanging out of his pants, stopped the American, hurriedly delivering a prepared speech in English, while the rest of the group joined in, all at the same time.

This created quite a turmoil, with everyone talking and gesticulating at once. It was rather amusing to watch the smiling calmness of the Americans in contrast. Finally the lieutenant managed to make himself heard and announced to the group that our house would not be evacuated.

*May 18, 1945* Last night, as it was growing dark I became increasingly scared that the Hawaiian sergeant would indeed make an appearance. Fortunately, he didn't come.

Today the story is all over town, how our house was spared from being occupied by a US Army black soldiers' company due to the persuasive efforts of one person or another. I've heard a number of versions: it's either Dr. Torgau who saved the house, or any of the four Misses Brettlein, or Frau Nüssler from the fifth floor—anyone but me! Only Frau Keller came today to our apartment carrying a bunch of forsythia branches. Handing them to me she said, "This is my thanks to you, Irene, for having saved us from being thrown out of our homes. I gathered the branches in our backyard. No store is open where one could buy flowers, but I wanted to do something to show my appreciation. If it weren't for you, we'd all be now on the street without a place to stay!" I took the flowers and thanked her kindly.

*May 19, 1945* This afternoon the Hawaiian sergeant suddenly appeared quite unexpectedly and announced that he would have no time to take German lessons. I feel greatly relieved. I also believe the true reason to be the "anti-fraternization law" enforced among the US occupation forces. No friendly contact with the German population, and especially the women, is allowed. German homes are off limits to Americans. Fortunately for me, the Hawaiian doesn't know that I'm a Latvian.

*May 21, 1945* I've heard horror tales about the open field between Höchst and Bad Soden, where now garbage from the American compound is dumped daily. Quite a few hungry Germans, apparently, make it their regular job every day to inspect this place. I decided to go and see for myself. Hopping on my bicycle I took off around noon today. After a trip of about two miles, I reached the spot.

It was quite a sight: sweating black soldiers carrying and emptying garbage cans, which they had brought in trucks, and Germans—women and children of all ages—waiting close by like hungry birds. As soon as the soldiers left, the Germans swarmed all over the place and began to dig around feverishly in the smelling heaps of garbage, looking for crusts of bread or bits of fat in tin cans or for occasional crumbs of chocolate in crumpled paper. Nearby in the tall grass, some black soldiers could be seen enjoying the charms of their newly acquired German girl friends. They don't seem concerned by the "Anti-fraternization Law."

From what I hear, these girls are being paid with chocolate candy bars, canned meat, lard and American cigarettes. I've also heard that some Germans specialize in collecting enough lard from the garbage dump in the period of a week or two so as to fill an entire one-pound can. This they then sell for an exorbitant price to their financially better situated compatriots. Some way of making a living! But it also proves to me that the food situation in town is desperate indeed.

*May 22, 1945* By now the US Occupation Forces are taking care to ship the Soviet DPs home as quickly as possible. Within the last week the

Americans have finally stopped the Russians from looting and generally misbehaving. Knowing that their time is up, the wretched Russians can think of nothing better to do than to demolish their own camp on Zeilsheimer Weg. They have broken the windows, their bunks and have defecated on the floors. What is even worse, not being allowed to take their stolen foodstuff with them, they have set out to destroy anything edible left behind.

After parts of the barracks last week were cleared of DPs, the American found there a large food storage area all in shambles: the sugar had been mixed with sand, hydrochloric acid had been poured over butter and lard and the Russians had urinated into the flour.

*May 24, 1945* Today I had a strangely unnerving experience. I had taken a walk and gone as far as to the suburb of Nied, when I suddenly heard a streetcar approaching. It went around a curve and, braking, came to a halt with a long screech. Suddenly I had the howling of sirens in my ear, this horrible swelling and diminishing screeching sound indicating danger. I again felt icy fear grip me; I had the strong impulse to duck, run and hide. I started to tremble and then broke out in tears, standing there on the sidewalk, amidst crowds of people in broad daylight.

I was powerless against this irrational, ominous, dark fear, powerless against these shattering memories! I don't know how long I stood there, motionless, with tears streaming down my face. Eventually, I caught myself and came home.

*May 26, 1945* The Russian DPs have been cleared out of the I.G. Farben Administration building in Frankfurt. The USFET military personnel intended to move in. The Americans have taken one look and retreated in shock. They have found an unbelievable mess. All windows are smashed, doors and furniture are broken, upholstered chairs and sofas cut wide open, the fillings torn out, carpets burned full of holes, oil paintings slashed to pieces, telephones smashed, light bulbs shattered, toilets stuck and overflowing. Many rooms look as though fires had been built on the parquet floors, most floors have been defecated on, and the heavy Persian rugs have apparently been especially popular for urinating on.

Herr Mooth, from the sixth floor of our house, has found a job with the Americans, helping to clean up these Soviet-style Aegean stables there in Frankfurt. He is my source of first-hand information. The whole building has to be repaired, all rooms cleaned and repainted, new telephones and lamps have to be installed, new furnishings brought in.

The damage goes into hundreds of thousands of marks. Quite some fine allies the Americans seem to have in their Soviet friends!

*May 27, 1945* There is no word yet from Karen, Something dreadful must have happened to her, or else she would write. I know she would! She and her babies probably fell into the hands of the Red Army, suffering a horrible fate. Unbearable thought!

*May 29, 1945* Word has come that Scholl has died in prison camp. Kilian today told me the news. Scholl died of typhoid fever contracted in camp. The starvation diets on which the Allies keep the Nazi prisoners didn't help either, I'm sure. I'm not sorry for Scholl. He got his just reward: he was crushed just as he crushed the little sparrow one year ago.

*May 30, 1945* This afternoon the doorbell rang, and to my immense surprise and slight shock the black American lieutenant stood there and smiled. "What does he want now?" shot through my brain. "Maybe he needs more billets for more soldiers? What am I going to do?" I asked him in, waiting in trepidation for what he would say.

Still smiling, he seated himself and then pulled out a copy of a small-format magazine. It looked well worn, the corners bent and fingerprints all over the front cover. He handed me the copy. I looked at it and read the title: The Reader's Digest. "What kind of a magazine is that, Lieutenant?" I asked.

"It is quite popular in America, Miss" he replied. "I thought maybe you'd like to read it, to see how we live in the States, and how we think and feel!"

I looked at him in surprise. Did this American really care what I knew about the United States and its people? Was it important to him to provide me with some information about his country? I studied his face. He was serious now and hoping that I would accept his gift. "You are very kind, Lieutenant, to come here and bring me this magazine. I will read it and translate what I don't understand with the help of a dictionary."

The lieutenant was again smiling. "Back home I am a school teacher, you know," he said, "and it is my business to spread information." He rose; I extended my hand in European fashion. He seemed a bit surprised, then took it and we shook hands. A final salute and he was gone.

*May 31, 1945* It is the last day of May. Some semblance of order is slowly coming into our lives. My future is still totally uncertain, but for the time being we still can pay our rent, we haven't been driven out of our home yet, and we still have some rye flour left, some sugar, lard and one or two cans of beef. We ought to be able to survive for another month or so. And who knows, some good fortune may be waiting just around the corner!

# CHAPTER FIFTEEN

## Yankee Doodle Dandy

*June 3, 1945* It has been two months now since American forces marched into town, two hungry and tension-filled months, but no longer fraught with bombing terror and daily death scares. We have very little to eat and I have no job, but the worst is over.

*June 5, 1945* Today it was announced that the Allies have come to an "Agreement for Control of Germany." Four occupation zones have been established in Germany under the supreme command of the Allied Control Council located in Berlin. Berlin itself will be administered jointly by the four Powers. Frankfurt and surroundings have now officially become part of the American Occupation Zone.

*June 7, 1945* The most shocking, most incredible news has come through! In the wake of the "Control Agreement," American Forces are withdrawing from territory occupied by them in Saxonia, in order to let the Red Army take over all of Eastern Germany. Berlin, which is located in this Eastern Zone, has been divided into four parts, into three western and one eastern sector. The dividing line between east and west is going straight through the center of town.

The German population is extremely upset over these decisions. This morning I saw some German citizens standing on street corners gesticulating wildly and I heard fragments of conversations: "Es ist zum Haareausraufen! Diese Idioten—It is enough to make you tear out your hair! These idiots!."

"Dem Russen freiwillig Land abzutreten—To hand territory over to the Russians, just like that! . . . . Der Stalin hält sich den Bauch vor Lachen!—Stalin must be laughing so hard, he has to hold his belly!"

I cannot help but agree with the popular opinion. To divide the capital of Germany is a very strange solution. And worse yet, to voluntarily hand German territory over to the Soviets, for which they never did a stroke of fighting, seems to me to be military and diplomatic nearsightedness. Haven't the forces in power considered the consequences of such a move? The Russians never give anything back that they once have grabbed. Who knows that better than we, the Baltic people! It appears now, that the only true winners in this Second World War have been the Soviets—only they have permanently gained large territories, only they are in sole control of all of Eastern Europe, from the Baltic to the Mediterranean. Peter the Great's imperial dreams of Russia as a World Power have finally come true.

*June 10, 1945* I went walking this morning when to my great surprise I met two young Dutchmen, whom I had known as technicians at I.G. Farben, and with whom I had occasionally chatted during my lunch hour at the plant restaurant. Pieter and Jan would join me at my table and we would talk about our respective homelands—Holland and Latvia—and compare notes.

I hardly recognized them. They looked well clothed and extremely well fed. I stopped them: "Pieter and Jan, I didn't think you were still in Germany! How nice to see you again! You seem to be in fine shape, judging from your looks."

"Oh, we are, Irene, we are working for the Americans and are being fed daily!" Pieter informed me with a joyful grin.

"How lucky you are! Mother and I are starving half to death."

"Oh, we know, Irene, life in Germany right now is pretty miserable, and so is life in Holland. That's why we decided to stay right here with the Americans."

Suddenly an exciting idea struck me: "Listen, the two of you! Do you suppose I also could get a job with the Occupation Forces?"

"Why not, Irene? Come to see us tomorrow at our office. Maybe we could arrange something for you!"

"Where do you work?"

"We work for the USFET in their local employment office in Höchst. Come to Room 103 of the former I.G. Farben Administration building. You will find us there, Irene." We shook hands and parted. I have an appointment at the USFET Employment Office for tomorrow morning at ten.

*June 11, 1945* I dressed with care, wearing a white skirt and a blouse that I had made out of my old light-blue taffeta pajamas. I appeared in Room 103 on the stroke of ten o'clock. Pieter filled out a form, asking me whether I could type (which I can, thank goodness! I always knew that typing would come in handy some day!) what languages I could speak, whether I could read and write English, whether I had ever belonged to the Nazi Party (which of course, I haven't) etc. Then he picked up a phone and I heard him make a brief statement: "Colonel Maughan, I have found a secretary for you. The young lady speaks five languages and can type. Her English is very good. Shall I bring her over?"

The answer must have been affirmative, because Pieter turned to me and simply said, "Let's go, Irene!" I walked out of the office behind him, followed him across a factory backyard, entered a small building and stumbled up a flight of dark stairs. Pieter pushed open a door, I found myself in a low-ceilinged room furnished with a desk, a chair and a typewriter. Another door opened and in walked a tall, stately man in uniform, who appeared to be in his mid-fifties. Piercing blue eyes under bushy brows in a tanned face framed with steel-gray hair looked me over, as Pieter was introducing me. "Colonel Maughan, this is Miss Irene Zarina, your new secretary."

I felt truly over-awed. Never before in my life had I spoken to an American of high military rank, and now I was to work for one without having any secretarial training. But I pulled myself together, smiled and said: "How do you do, Colonel?" with the best English pronunciation I could muster. I'm afraid it may have sounded like a cross between Oxford English, Latvian and Baltic German.

"How do you do, young lady?" the colonel said in a jovial tone. "Please be seated. This will be your desk. I understand you can type. Have you ever typed in English?"

"No, I haven't, Colonel, but it seems to me, if you can type in German, you can also type in English."

"Well, well, we shall soon see, Miss. Here is a letter for you to type. Bring it to my office when you're done. My office is next door to yours." The colonel turned and left. I was alone. It was now 10:20 AM. In twenty minutes my fate had taken an exciting new turn.

I typed the letter with much care. It looked pretty good to me. The colonel seemed pleased also: "Fine job, Miss!" Then he looked at his wristwatch: "Almost time for lunch. Has it been explained to you at the Employment Office that with this job you get one meal a day in addition to your salary?"

"Yes, I have been told about it, Colonel."

"Excellent, excellent! And when are you starting your meals, Miss?"

"I believe tomorrow, Colonel, as soon as I get my employee identification card."

"Very good, Miss. See you later!"

Again I was left alone. I wished I too could go out for lunch, but I had nowhere to go. I stayed in the office, practicing some English typing. With all the excitement I didn't seem to notice how hungry I really was.

In the afternoon the phone rang. I lifted up the receiver and heard something like: "Wa, wah rah . . . mm . . . ar . . . ?" I didn't understand a word. What was I to do? I realized, of course, that my main trouble was with the American pronunciation of English, which seems so much broader and somehow lazier than the clipped Oxford English that I was taught in high school. When talking to an American directly, I could do some lip-reading, but over the phone I did not seem to be able to get the meaning. While the "wa, wah—rah-" continued on the phone I did some quick thinking and then said, "Excuse me, Sir, but could you speak more slowly and distinctly? I am not used to American English and cannot understand you very well!"

I heard some male laugh at the other end of the line and then some words were spoken slowly and came through very clearly: "Tell . . . Colonel . . . Maughan . . . that . . . Bob . . . would . . . like . . . to . . . talk . . . to him." I used the same technique of dealing with phone calls all through the afternoon and it worked very well.

Mother is pleased that I have found a job with the Americans, mainly for one reason: it means a tremendous improvement in our food situation. Starting with this June, new food ration cards have been issued and Mother will be able to utilize some of my rations while I eat at the American Mess.

*June 12, 1945* The big event of the day was my first meal at the G.I. Mess Hall. This morning I received my employee identification card and promptly at noon went to the Soldier's Mess, which is set up across the street from the I.G. Farben restaurant in one of the factory buildings.

Upon entering I found myself in a crowd of G.I.s who were quickly forming a line—"chow-line" I heard it being called. I followed suit; stood in line; picked up a tray, just as the soldier in front of me did, and advanced towards a long serving table, behind which stood half a dozen cooks with white jackets and high white hats, ladling out pea soup, ground meat with mashed potatoes and carrots, gravy and a green salad. Then followed a heaping dish with vanilla ice cream, a big piece of snowy white bread with a pat of butter on it, and finally a mug of genuine coffee with cream and sugar. I looked in exultation at all this lovely wonderful food on my tray, and in such quantities too!

I sat down on a long wooden bench in front of a long wooden table. I was alone only for about one minute. The spaces next to me and across the table filled rapidly with American soldiers, who started to eat straight from their trays. So did I. Grabbing my spoon, I quickly emptied my soup bowl, then delved into the delicious mountain of meat and whipped potatoes. I ate and ate and ate; I must have really gobbled my food in an outrageous manner, because suddenly there was silence at my table, where there had been the din of fast-flowing conversation before. I lifted my face from my plate and saw all eyes of my tablemates on me, staring at me in silence and apparently also in disbelief. "Do you really like this chow, Honey?" I heard my neighbor ask me.

"I do, very much indeed! It tastes so good!" said I.

"Can you eat all that, Blondie?" the fellow from across the table queried.

"Oh yes, I can! I'm terribly hungry!" And I continued to gobble the meat and vegetables. Then came the ice cream and finally the coffee, while the G.I.s watched me in fascination.

Finally I was done. Every crumb of food and every drop of coffee was gone. I stood up, sighed happily, smiled at my tablemates and left, accompanied by a chorus of male voices: "See you tomorrow, Blondie!"

The afternoon went by rather fast with typing and with telephone calls. I couldn't wait to get home and to tell Mother about my fabulous meal. And to think that tomorrow I'll be served another equally wonderful meal!

*June 13, 1945* I awoke this morning with a tummy ache. In the office it got worse and worse, the pain became excruciating, and pretty soon I had a full-fledged case of diarrhea. Noontime arrived but I couldn't even think of food. My colonel noticed that something was wrong with me: "Don't you feel well, Miss? You look rather shaky."

"I am feeling sick, and I don't know what to do about it!"

"Why don't you go to the Dispensary? The doctor there will give you some medication," Colonel Maughan advised me. That is what I did. In the doctor's office I came face to face with a dark-haired, dark-eyed young man in uniform with the serpent of Aesculapius on his sleeve. It was the physician on duty.

"What is your complaint?" he asked me. I told him my tale of woe. "What did you eat yesterday?" he wanted to know. I told him about my fabulous meal. He started to laugh. "You Germans come to this Dispensary by the dozens, all with the same complaint: an upset stomach. Don't you realize that the sudden intake of high protein, high fat-containing food has a disastrous effect on your digestive systems, which no longer are used to this kind of highly nutritious diet? It will take you several weeks before you will be able to tolerate good food."

I looked at the doctor in astonishment, but only for a moment. Then I remembered my bout with the meat, fatty gravies and whipped cream I had had during my visit to Latvia in 1943. Of course, that is it! How stupid of me not to remember that digestive systems used to starvation diets cannot suddenly be switched over to high calorie intakes. "Here are some tablets for you, Miss," the doctor said. "Come back tomorrow if they don't help."

*June 14, 1945* The tablets have helped some, but I can't eat much. However, today I again went to the G.I. Mess Hall. I had a small serving of whipped potatoes and some soup, but no meat and no fatty gravy or butter.

*June 15, 1945* Colonel Maughan's staff consists of two persons besides me, both Germans: a Dr. Lederer and a Fräulein Rainer. Dr. Lederer has just recently returned from Argentina, where he worked as chemist for a subsidiary of I.G. Farben. His English is first-rate. Emmi Rainer is a refugee from East Prussia, a very quiet, nondescript girl, who is in mourning. She lost her only brother at the Russian front a few weeks before the War ended. We three get along splendidly. There is only one problem: not enough work for all three of us.

*June 16, 1945* Today I had a most unexpected visitor at my office. Dr. Haller, my first I.G. Farben boss, appeared out of the blue at my desk. "Dr. Haller, what a surprise! I have not seen you in years. Aren't you any longer in Berlin? What are you doing here in Höchst?"

"I'm getting myself and my family ready to go to America."

"What!! I can't believe it! You are actually leaving Germany and going to America? How did you manage that?"

"You remember, don't you, Fräulein Zarina, that during the war I was ordered to go to Berlin to serve as intermediary between I. G. Farben and a research group in Peenemünde? The Americans are transferring this group to the States, where rocket research will continue under the same group leader, our Wernher von Braun."

"So that's where the V2 rocket—Hitler's famous 'secret weapon'—originated?"

"Yes, that was it!"

"Dr. Haller, you are very lucky to have your future cut out for you in such an exciting way!"

"And you, Fräulein Zarina, are very lucky to have found a job with the Americans. Your colleagues, our I.G. Farben chemists, are all starving. There are no jobs in Germany, neither is there sufficient food." We shook hands. Haller is leaving in a few days. I probably will never see him again. I gave him a pack of American cigarettes as a farewell present, which I had accidentally found in the G.I. Mess. Haller seemed highly pleased.

After Haller left, I experienced another surprise, but this time unpleasant! Our colonel announced that American WACs (Women's Army Corps) will be arriving in a few days and will take over our jobs, at which time all Europeans will be dismissed. We three—Lederer, Emmi and I—are quite depressed. We all have been here a very short time only, we all have been most happy to have our wonderful one meal a day, and now we must leave again. How sad!

*June 18, 1945* The town is suddenly swarming with WACs. On my way home I saw one sitting in uniform on the stone railing of the small bridge that crosses the Liederbach near the entrance to the American Compound. An American soldier stood before her and was kissing her. This public display of affection in broad daylight with both parties in uniform seems most peculiar to me.

Today is Monday, the beginning of the week, but it was my last day in Colonel Maughan's office, and also my last meal at the G.I. Mess. I was employed for one week only. What am I going to do now?

*June 19, 1945* I have figured out what to do! I'll go to see the American lieutenant in charge of the U.S. Officers' Mess located at the former I.G. Farben restaurant. I'll offer him my services as secretary or interpreter or both. Only one day without a decent meal—namely today—has convinced me that I must make every effort possible to continue working for the Americans.

*June 20, 1945* I again donned my white skirt and my blue taffeta blouse of pajama origin and went to look for a job. Not knowing anyone at the Officers' Mess, I went straight to the boss, Lt. Downwood. I knocked on the door, entered the office and found myself in front of a tall, slim, dark-haired man in uniform. He seemed rather surprised to see me: "Can I help you?" he said looking at me with dark eyes, which sat at somewhat tilted angle in his sallow face.

"Oh yes, you can, Lieutenant!" I exclaimed, "I need a job!"

"But this is not the employment office, Miss!" Lt. Downwood declared coolly.

"I know that, Sir, but I have already worked for one week for Colonel Maughan at Group CC Headquarters Command. I had to leave there because the WACs took over."

"Why have you come here then looking for a job, Miss?"

"I speak five languages and it seems to me, Lieutenant, that in the Officers' Mess, where you have visitors of many different nationalities, you might need an interpreter," said I, looking at him hopefully.

The lieutenant remained silent, pondering the issue. Then he asked, "Do you speak Polish?"

"No, I don't, but I speak Russian very well, and all Poles can understand some Russian, even if they can't speak it and vice versa."

"How is that, Miss?"

"Russian and Polish are both Slavic languages and have many words in common."

"You mean to say, Miss, if you spoke Russian, the Poles would understand you?"

"Yes, they would! Not every detail, but they would get the idea!"

"I see, Miss! What is your name?"

"Irene Zarina."

"O.K., Irene, you are hired. You will be our hostess, and you also will be in charge of our Polish waitresses, who don't understand a word of English. They are all new here and we are having a lot of trouble trying to explain to them what we want them to do. Do you think, Irene, that you could manage this bunch of silly girls?"

I could sense how intensely Lt. Downwood disliked his new waitresses. "They just need training, Lieutenant. Once they understand what is expected of them, they will be all right. I will do my best, Lieutenant."

"O.K. Irene, go to see Mr. Halfpap. He is our headwaiter. He will give you further instructions." The interview was over and I had a job.

Mr. Halfpap was a funny-looking little man, no more than five feet tall with curly black hair, sparkling eyes and pink cheeks. His somewhat rotund figure was squeezed into black pants and an oversized tailcoat, with which he wore a white shirtfront and black tie. The tails of the tailcoat almost reached to his ankles. He reminded me of a dignified penguin.

Judging from the name, I expected Mr. Halfpap to be an American, but he was German. The Polish waitresses address him as Herr Halfpap. His wife, Frau Halfpap, was the opposite of him, at least in looks—tall, skinny and very pale. The couple struck me as being very kind and very polite. The first thing Frau Halfpap said to me was, "Have you already had lunch, Fräulein Irene?"

"No, I have not!"

"Let me fix you something. What would you like? Here is today's menu."

I explained to Frau Halfpap that I had to be very careful with my diet. She understood: "It is happening to all the local people who work here." She also said, "Do you know, Fräulein Irene, that as a member of our staff you are entitled to three meals a day here at the Officers' Mess?"

"No, I didn't know that, Frau Halfpap, how lovely!" I exclaimed joyfully. "Where does the staff eat?"

"In a big room adjoining the kitchens. I'll show you where it is."

"No, my dear," said Herr Halfpap to his wife, "there is no time now. First I have to give Fräulein Irene her instructions regarding her job." I looked expectantly at him.

"Do you have a dark dress and a white apron, Fräulein Irene?" he queried.

"Yes, I do, but why do I need that kind of outfit, Herr Halfpap?"

"You will be in charge of the waitresses and that's what they are wearing."

"Herr Halfpap, I was hired as hostess and interpreter."

"Let me check with Lt. Downwood!" and out dashed Herr Halfpap. Soon he was back again. "Yes, yes, you are right, Fräulein Irene! Excuse me, please: I misunderstood. Do you know what a 'hostess' is?"

"I have a vague idea, but I'm really not sure."

"Yes, yes, I know, Fräulein Irene. We have no 'hostesses' in restaurants in Germany. They are unknown here. Do you have some nice dresses, the Sunday-afternoon tea-time kind?"

"I do indeed, Herr Halfpap!"

"Very good, Fräulein Irene. You will always be nicely dressed and waiting at the entrance to our dining room for guests to arrive. You will smile pleasantly, greet them politely and take them to their table, first checking with me, the headwaiter. I will assign tables to your guests. You will also have to interpret the guests' orders to the Polish waitresses, in case they don't understand. You will work during all meal hours, during breakfast, lunch and dinner. In between meals your time is your own, Fräulein Irene. You'll start tonight at 6:00 PM."

Still hungry, I left the plant restaurant, where for four years I have taken my daily lunch as one of the three hundred chemists employed at I.G. Farben. Now I will be working there as a servant. "Mother, I said when I got home, "I've found another job with the. Americans, I will be a 'hostess'."

"What kind of a job is that?" asked Mother. I gave her the details as far as I could make them out.

"Sounds like a combination between a receptionist and a headwaiter," said Mother.

"Something like that, Mother! It truly bothers me. What a step down from being a 'Fräulein Diplom-Ingenieur,' a professional woman, to a servant's position! I find it hard to take, Mother!"

"Nonsense, Irene, remember your Aunt Cecilia, who married a Russian nobleman and was presented at the Imperial Court? After the Revolution in 1917 she and her husband, the high and mighty Vladimir Michailovich, had to flee Russia and landed in Paris doing menial jobs."

"I know all about it, Mother! Aunt Cecilia worked as a seamstress in a boutique and Uncle Volodya waited on tables."

"Well, how do you feel about that, Irene? Do you believe that these jobs impaired their dignity?"

"Of course not, but it must have been hard for them to take!"

"No doubt that was so, but there were thousands of Russian aristocrats stranded in Western Europe who went through the same tribulations, having to make a living somehow. Don't you think you're an awful lot better off than they were, Irene?"

"You're right, Mother! I just have to get over this feeling of hurt pride. I worked so hard for my chemical engineering degree and now it is of no use whatsoever."

"Don't be silly, Irene! No one can take your education away from you. Furthermore, your life isn't over yet. How do you know what the future might bring? Some day you will again be a chemist, Irene."

"Mother, I can't believe it, you have turned into an optimist!" I went over and kissed her.

"Maybe I too have learned something in this war!" was Mother's reply.

*June 21, 1945* I appeared yesterday evening at the Officers' Mess. Herr Halfpap looked me over and seemed pleased: "I like your dress. It looks very dignified. Your hairdo is nice too. You make a good impression!" and he smiled up at me. I was wearing my dark green peau de soie Sunday-afternoon best and my shoulder-length hair was brushed back with front curls above my forehead. "Now, Fräulein Irene, take your position here in the vestibule between the double stairs leading up to the landing. Greet the guests with a smile and conduct them to the dining room!"

I stationed myself near the railing, where the vestibule forms a kind of balcony between the big winding double stairs. Across the vestibule opposite the railing a huge mirror is hanging between two marble columns, which in turn are flanked by potted palms. The floor is inlaid with black and white marble tile. Amazingly enough, in four years at I.G. Farben, being a daily guest in the plant restaurant, I had never consciously taken in all these details. The lights in the crystal chandelier flared up, suddenly brightening the dim entrance hall. The mirror reflected my image. I saw myself standing at the black wrought-iron railing looking rather skinny and tall in my long-sleeved, high-buttoned dress.

The first guests started to arrive. They were all in uniform: lieutenants, captains, majors, lieutenant colonels and full colonels. Full colonels are granted the privilege of a private dining room, should they desire one. We have a number of "chambres separées" furnished with red velvet drapery, held by golden cords and tassels, all in very ornate, highly Victorian style. I never knew before that such private rooms existed at the I.G. Farben restaurant.

The guests are predominantly male: only occasionally a woman in uniform will make an appearance. I understand that these few ladies are high-ranking members of the nursing corps or else are executive secretaries. Ordinary WACs, like common soldiers, are not permitted into the Officers' Mess.

We offer only one menu per meal. There is no choice. The officers can either take it or leave it. The price per meal is fifty cents, paid in conscription dollars, which are valid only in the American Occupation Zone. The officers pay when leaving the dining room. A cash register is set up for that purpose, with a Mess sergeant in charge of it. The menu is typed on a small piece of paper, one for each table. All went well; Herr Halfpap was very pleased with me.

The Mess stopped serving at 8:00 PM. After that the staff was served in their own dining room. No elegance here, only long wooden benches and plain wooden tables. We had to fetch our food ourselves, using the "chow line" system. A cook dealt out the foodstuff, just as in the G.I. Mess Hall. But what does it matter? The food is excellent! I'm still very careful, though, about my intake.

*June 25, 1945* I am supposed to work every day, seven days a week. Communicating with the Polish waitresses has worked out as I expected. They mostly understand my Russian; I understand some of their Polish, and one of them, Bronya, is fluent in both languages and can interpret when necessary.

I will never have a day off, because I'm the only hostess and my presence, according to the American system, is required at every meal. I really don't mind at all. Every day at the Officers' Mess means three wonderful meals. I'm being paid a pittance in German marks, but who cares, anyway! One can buy next to nothing for money. The only currency that nowadays counts is American cigarettes. The local people are after every butt they can find on the streets. They collect the butts, remove the remaining tobacco and roll new cigarettes out of this refuse. One pack of American cigarettes represents an impressive bartering value. One can get one pound of butter for it or five loaves of bread or one silk blouse. There exist endless bartering possibilities.

*June 27, 1945* I have gained some weight: my body is beginning to fill out, the bones in my arms and legs no longer seem to be so prominent. My face too looks rounder and smoother. This job is a blessing! Mother also is beginning to feel and look better. She now has the full use of my food rations. Once in a while I even manage to sneak a piece of cake, a sandwich or some fresh fruit out of the Mess in order to bring it to Mother. This is strictly forbidden, but every member of the staff is doing it. They all have family members at home to whom such tidbits are precious gifts.

*July 20, 1945* Last night I gained a glimpse into the "inner workings" of the American Army, and I am truly amazed! It was after 8:00 PM. The Mess was closed and our Mess Sergeant Jack appeared on the scene, flawlessly groomed as ever. He nonchalantly sauntered into the dining room and informed me in his pleasant voice that he wished to take his dinner in one of the "chambres separés" reserved exclusively for the Commandant of Höchst and the latter's guests. I gave orders to the waitresses to bring up the food from the kitchens. Sergeant Jack had just seated himself at the table and was starting to eat. I stood at the window, giving Jack the requested account of the day's happenings.

Suddenly the heavy red velvet curtain hiding the entrance was shoved aside and—in walked the Commandant in full uniform, golden colonel's eagles glistening on his shoulder straps. With him were two of his aides, both majors. I stood mortified. What was going to happen to Jack? What severe disciplinary action would be taken against the little sergeant intruding into the realm of the almighty Commandant?

The Commandant stopped in his tracks. Jack slowly and gracefully rose from the table and smiling most pleasantly, greeted the Commandant with a polite "Good evening, Sir!"

The Commandant frowned and then asked with a severe tone in his voice, "What are you doing at my table, Sergeant?"

Completely unruffled Jack replied calmly. "Sir, you are late! I did not expect you anymore. The Mess is already closed, and so, for a change, I decided to have my dinner in this room."

To me Jack's words sounded like incredible effrontery and utmost insubordination against his military superior. Behavior like that, of a soldier in the presence of a high officer, would have been unthinkable in the German army, or for that matter in any European army. I expected a terrible outburst of wrath, but nothing violent at all happened. The Commandant only smiled: "You are right, Sergeant! I am late, and so we might as well all have dinner together!" And to my tremendous amazement the colonel and the majors sat down with a mere sergeant at the same table and had their dinner together, all four of them chatting amiably, and all four of them in high spirits.

*July 29, 1945* The "Bride in Black," whose wedding I attended such a short time ago, is dead. Barbara Herzelt, our custodian's daughter-in-law living on the top floor of our apartment building, died yesterday at the hospital where she had been a patient for several weeks. Tuberculosis had ravaged and finally killed her.

The last time I saw Barbara, the once beautiful girl was only a shadow of her former self, her body racked by terrible coughing fits, dark eyes burning feverishly in a deathly pale face. The horrors of the War years, the hunger and deprivations had taken their toll of this young life. My premonition of disaster, felt strongly on Barbara's wedding day, has come true.

*July 30, 1945* "Der Schnitter Tod"—the Grim Reaper Death—has passed me by, while leaving in his wake hecatombs of victims, cutting off my dearest friends, mostly in the prime of youth, and taking away many of my closest relatives. I mourn their loss, but this feeling of sadness shall not prevent me from seeing life as the Great Adventure, or to put it in scientific terms, as the Great Experiment, to be observed and participated in, feeling the excitement of challenge and discovery and very likely defeat also, as long as the Experiment lasts....

*August 3, 1945* Today is Father's birthday. He has been dead for six years. Mother and I were talking about him this morning, when the mailman arrived with a letter from Aunt Meta. She is at present in Holland, having joined her youngest sister there. We were in for more sad news:

"We all assumed that your cousin Elra was killed in the fall of 1943, when trying to escape by boat from Estonia to Sweden. As you recall, Soviet fliers bombed many boats crossing the Baltic at that time. I have just received information from Estonian friends that Elra never made it to the boat, that the Soviets caught her, separated her from her husband, and that she has been deported to Siberia . . . . How will this fragile young girl, grown up in luxury, be able to stand the ravages of slave labor camps? She will perish like her mother and father before her . . . ."

Memories of Elra keep flooding my mind. The last time I saw her was on her wedding day. She was such a beautiful bride.

*August 4, 1945* Besides the Americans and the British, more and more frequently now, officers of many different nationalities are visiting the Canteen: Canadians, French, Irish, Polish and very rarely even the Soviets.

The Polish are quite a large group and always occupy the same tables. Our waitresses, of course, are beaming, hearing orders given in their own native tongue. I've come to know the Polish guests quite well, especially a short, stocky, blond girl in uniform who holds the rank of lieutenant in the Polish Army. Today she told me about the Insurrection of Warsaw against the Nazis during the months of August through October, 1944, and how she took part in the fighting just like a man: "I shot with machine guns, I threw hand grenades . . . the house in which I had found shelter was hit by an artillery bomb and collapsed . . . I was buried under rubble and dust, but luckily I escaped death and continued to fight . . . until the Germans overpowered the Polish resistance . . . Warsaw was all in ruins."

The leader of the group, a major, had watched the young woman telling me her story, which he, no doubt, had heard many times. He looked at her with pride, his eyes shining: "Lieutenant," he said, "you are an inspiring example to all Polish patriots, who love their country, who, like you, are willing to die for Poland's freedom!" and he bowed deeply before her, clicking his heels. The fierce patriotism of the Polish is legendary. Today I had an illustration of it.

*August 6, 1945* A horrible explosion took place today in Japan in a town called Hiroshima. The description given by the radio broadcast was shocking: a single American plane appeared and dropped a single bomb. There was a blinding light and fiery heat waves as if of a thousand suns, and then a huge black mushroom cloud began to form high above the center of the explosion. In an instant many thousand persons were killed and whole city blocks evaporated, simply disappeared. The outskirts of Hiroshima are in ruins and the fate of any surviving victims is unknown.

This was no ordinary explosive bomb; this was an "atomic bomb," based on the principle of nuclear fission, a bomb never before used in this war, a bomb to end all wars. That's what the radio commentator said. No one in Germany, or for that matter, in the entire world, knew that the United States had developed such a bomb. It came as an incredible shock to all nations on earth. Japan is still at war with the United States. Will Japan continue to fight?

*August 7, 1945* This afternoon I had the pleasure of meeting two gentlemen, representatives of the Latvian Red Cross, who are now in charge of the Latvian DP camp in Esslingen near Stuttgart. They had heard about me and came to see me. From them I heard about the fate of a good many of my Latvian friends, some of whom have been deported to Siberia, some of whom are now living in Esslingen. These Latvian representatives know a lot about the present conditions in Latvia. They are watching the international press and if ever any news finds its way out from behind the Iron Curtain, they are aware of it.

They informed me that a commission has been set up in the American Occupied Zone of Germany for the express purpose of reinstating lost citizenships to peoples of the Baltic States. They advised me to regain my Latvian citizenship. I will do so.

They also told me that all Latvians in Germany firmly hope and believe that the great injustice done to the Baltic States will not last forever, that the governments of the United States and of Great Britain will intervene, as soon "as the time is ripe." Their belief is based upon the Declaration of the United States immediately after the invasion of the Baltic countries by the Soviet Union in 1940. I asked for a copy of this important document. It reads in part:

"From the day, when the peoples of these Republics first gained their independent and democratic form of government, the people of the United States have watched their admirable progress in self-government with deep and sympathetic interest. The people of the United States are opposed to any form of intervention on the part of one state, however powerful, in the domestic concerns of any sovereign state, however weak. The United States will continue to stand by these principles." (Department of State Bulletin, July 27, 1940, Vol. III, #57, p. 48)

This was of course formulated before the USSR became an ally of the US against Hitler. Still, the United States are our only hope in our longing for freedom!

*August 9, 1945* Today the Americans dropped the second atomic bomb on Japan, on a seaport called Nagasaki. The explosion was equally as awesome and equally as disastrous as in Hiroshima. Many thousands were killed; the city was destroyed.

*August 14, 1945* Japan today accepted the Allied terms of surrender.

*August 21, 1945* True to their promise, my Latvian compatriots from the DP camp in Esslingen sent me a clipping from a Swiss paper with the latest news about conditions in Latvia. On Aug. 15, 1945 the "Baseler Nachrichten" printed the following article under the heading:
Deportation of Balts by Soviet Government
"Stockholm, A.G. "Aftonbladet" reports, that according to statements made by Estonian refugees, the Russian element is now predominating in the population of the Estonian capital. Large numbers of Russian soldiers, sailors and civilians have been settled there. For Riga the situation is similar. Large groups of Balts, on the other hand, have been transported to the Interior of Russia. Thousands of Estonians and Latvians are reported to be working in factories in the inner parts of Russia. Near those plants, reportedly, are located more than 140 camps for Baltic people, with 1500 persons in each of them. Karelians and Ingermanlanders (Finns) have been settled in the region of Saratov, where they are working under military guard. Balts have been mostly relocated to the region of Kalinin."

Once more, I can only say, there, but for the grace of God, go I! I wonder if my cousin Elra is somewhere near Kalinin.

*September 1, 1945* My post-war life is slowly becoming routine. The first excitements and the first disappointments are over. I've gotten used to the fact that I'm the wrong girl in the wrong job. Neither by training nor by inclination would I ever have chosen such a type of work, but fate decided for me. Under the circumstances, it was the best thing that could have happened.

By now I'm beginning to long for the time when I'll be out of the Officers' Mess and again working as a chemist. At present, with Germany's industry down and out, with her factories being dismantled, my chances for a chemist's job are equal to zero. And, of course, I can't return to Latvia!

*September 2, 1945* Japan has formally surrendered. World War II has finally come to an end in the Pacific Theater also.

*September 5, 1945* It has been a long time since I last talked to Dr. Kilian. I accidentally met him today. He is still out of a job and living on his savings. It is hard on him because he has a family to support. He asked me if I knew that our former technical director, the high and mighty Dr. Lehr, is clearing rubble in the streets of Frankfurt. The U.S. Occupation Forces have ordered the former high-ranking Nazi Party member to make amends by doing this kind of humble, backbreaking work. On top of that, Lehr and wife were forced at the beginning of this summer to evacuate their home in Höchst, which is now part of the American compound. "How is our former technical director Wernicke?" I asked.

"He is in great shape, Irene: he was smart enough never to join the Nazi Party and is now claiming that the Nazis forced him to 'toot in their horn.' It seems Wernicke will get off scot-free!"

"Who would ever have thought that the disagreeable little fellow had that much brains, Dr. Kilian!"

"Well, he does, Irene!"

"Do you know anything about Herr Evers?"

"His wife has had word from him. He is alive, but in an American Prisoner of War camp. It will be a while, before he will be released, having been most devoted to the Nazi cause."

*September 15, 1945* I have followed the advice of my Latvian compatriots and regained my Latvian citizenship. It was quite a simple procedure. Some representatives of the American Commission in charge of such matters had come to Höchst. I went to see them, brought along my documents proving my Latvian origin and have now a note in my German passport stating that I am a Latvian citizen.

I don't quite understand Mother. She prefers to keep her German citizenship. When pressed for the reason she answered, "I am an Estonian, I don't even speak Latvian. What good would it do me to be a Latvian citizen living in Germany? We can't return to Latvia, as long as it is part of the Soviet Union!" Well, maybe she has a point there!

*October 3, 1945* It is October already. Time seems to be flying, without accomplishing much of anything, at least not for me. I see no prospects of a change anywhere. There is no way for me to return to conditions that I would consider normal—a life as it used to be in Latvia before the war.

*October 29, 1945* Today finally, finally, I had news from my best friend Karen, whom I had given up for dead. It was a post-card with only a few words scribbled on it: "Have survived, but have gone through hell. Am now in a refugee camp in Bodenfelde near Hannover. Will write you a letter as soon as I feel calmer. Will then give you all the sad details. God have mercy on us and on the souls of our departed. Your friend, Karen"

I'm deeply troubled. Something horrible must have happened. Someone must have died: her husband, a child perhaps? I will write to her immediately.

*November 15, 1945* This afternoon our Mess Sergeant Jack offered me an office job. He knows that I don't particularly care for my hostess's activities. I will be in charge of distributing C-rations. I have gladly accepted.

*November 17, 1945* In my new job I wear a black uniform with a white collar. I don't like it, but at least I continue to get lunch and dinner with the other employees at the Officer's Mess.

*December 2, 1945* The first Sunday in Advent. I still can't quite fathom it that this coming Christmas season, after six years of war, will no longer be darkened by the threatening shadow of a murderous time.

*December 12, 1945* It is very cold. The central heating system in our apartment is still not in operation. I don't know what we'd do if we didn't have the little black coal stove which the custodian Herr Herzelt installed a few days ago in our living room. Mother and I have set up our beds in there, and brought all our plants in from the other rooms, where the temperature is below freezing. It is almost as though we were camping in our own parlor.

*December 18, 1945* Today Karen's letter came, filled with suffering, tragedy and grief. It reads like a nightmare. Shortly before the Soviets occupied Posen last January, Karen managed to get out of town with her two little boys. It took them two weeks, partly moving on foot, in terribly cold weather to get to Binz on the Island of Rügen in the Baltic, where according to Nazi sources, a home for refugee mothers-to-be had supposedly been set up. There was no such home.

Karen had barely arrived in Binz when she went into labor. In the middle of the night she had to walk all alone by herself to the hospital where her third son was born a few hours later. Some refugees meanwhile took care of the two older boys. In a day or two Karen was ordered to leave the hospital. "Wearily, I trudged back through the ice-cold streets to my cold room carrying my newborn. I was very weak but had to go out and try to collect some wood for the stove."

On May 8 the War was over, and Soviet troops moved into town. There was no more electricity, no more water or fresh food supply, because the Rügendamm, the only bridge from island to shore, had been blown up. Karen could get no more milk for the children. German farmers had tried to bring some milk from their dairies in the interior of the island to their little town. Soviet soldiers seized the cans and poured the milk out on the street.

Besides terrorizing the population, the Soviets looted to their hearts' content, carrying off not only watches, jewelry, china and silverware, but also furniture, pianos, rugs, paintings and even bath-tubs, toilets and kitchen sinks. The goods were loaded into trucks and shipped to Russia. Soviet soldiers would force their way into homes in broad daylight, drag out young girls and old women—any female they could get hold of— and rape them. Karen lived in constant terror of such an attack.

By the end of June the Soviet administration of Binz ordered her to leave town and to return to Posen, "where she belonged." No passenger train service existed. A Soviet guard in the railroad station told her to try to find some space on a freight train that was going east. It turned out to be a train carrying German reparations to Russia. Huge harvest machines sat loaded on open platforms, on two sides supported by twelve-foot high walls. Multitudes of refugees were swarming like ants over machines and platforms: men, women, children, everyone trying to find a little space, somewhere to settle down for the trip east. Karen, holding the baby, and her little boys sat 10 feet high on top of one of the huge machines. From her high perch Karen witnessed a heartbreaking scene:

"The train started to pull out, when suddenly I heard a horrible scream: 'My child, my baby!' and a tall, blond woman bent far over the twelve foot high side wall, stretching out her arms in despair, getting ready to jump. We held her back by force. She would have killed herself if she had attempted to leap from the moving freight car. On the platform stood a tiny, blond girl, arms uplifted, tears running over her little face, whimpering: 'Mutti, Mutti, nimm mich mit!—Mummy, take me with you!'"

After several days of travel eastwards, Karen heard at a railroad station where the train had stopped, that the Polish border was closed to all German citizens and that it was futile for her to try to go back to Posen. She and her children joined the crowds waiting for a train back to the west. "No one knew when the next train might come. It could be days! I went begging for food to nearby farmhouses, with my baby in my arms, so tiny and undernourished, gray in the face, with blue shadows under his eyes. The farmers felt sorry for me and gave me some milk. After the baby's birth I had tried to nurse him myself, but had not been able to. Now his life hung on a thin thread, depending on the pity and charity of strangers."

They had to wait for the next train for two days and two nights, camping between the railroad tracks. Then, in the dark of night, the train came rolling along. The refugees threw themselves onto doors and windows. Somehow Karen and her children managed to get in.

They made it back to the Island of Rügen where Karen found work on the fields of a large German country estate. The German manager told her that all his Polish laborers had left him at War's end. It was already July and the clover had not yet been cut on the meadows, which stretched all the way to the horizon. Soon the rye also had to be cut. Karen worked very hard, getting up at sunrise and helping with the harvesting of the grain.

In return, she received enough food for all four of them: milk, potatoes, fruit and sometimes even meat. Once she received some pork from a pig that had died of Erysipelas. Karen was told to cook the meat most thoroughly, in order to avoid infection. A few days later she noticed a big painful red spot on her right hand, which spread rapidly. She had caught the disease, which has a high rate of fatality—in pigs as well as humans.

Karen was lucky and recovered. But soon thereafter tragedy struck. She had been so happy, that she now was able to get good milk for her little baby, but it was too late: the months of inadequate nutrition, the many tribulations, the cold and the unsanitary conditions, had undermined the baby's resistance. He developed a severe diarrhea, cried for two days and two nights and then death ended his suffering. "I was numb with pain, no tears came. I walked to the nearby village, bought a tiny coffin, and carried it home on my shoulder. The rest was like a bad dream: the ride with the little coffin to the cemetery in an old dilapidated field wagon, the women refugees who accompanied me, the minister's words at the small grave and the lonely walk home through the fields of rye swaying in the summer breezes."

Two weeks later on a Sunday, Karen's three-year-old got sick. Karen put Wölfchen into a small wheel-cart and transported him six miles to the hospital, where she had to leave him. In a week Karen went back to visit her child. Wölfchen was in an oxygen tent. He had diphtheria and was deathly sick. On two more Sundays she made the long walk to town and back, always barefoot. Her only shoes had long since gone to pieces.

On the fourth Sunday the doctor told Karen to take Wölfchen home. There was no more hope for him. Wölfchen recognized Karen as his mother, but could no longer speak. She tried to feed him, but he couldn't swallow. Horrible coughing fits racked his weak little body.

His breathing became increasingly labored, frequently he seemed near suffocation. Then Karen would grab him and run to the open window for fresh air: "I could see that my child was in agonies of suffering and fear, and I was totally helpless. Death came one afternoon in August. Wölfchen suffocated before my very eyes, after a torturous death struggle. I tried in vain to blow air into his lungs by mouth-to-mouth resuscitation. I held my child in my arms and saw him die. A blue shadow crossed his lips, I heard a last sigh, and Wölfchen was no more."

Again, Karen had to go through the procedure of ordering the coffin and making funeral arrangements. The minister recognized her immediately. Only six weeks had passed since she had buried her youngest child. Again she carried a coffin home on her shoulder; again a child of hers was lying in state in an empty room of their workers' barracks. "I decorated Wölfchen's coffin with flowers from the fields: daisies, cornflowers, wild carnations. I held a lonely wake for my dead little son all through the night, gazing at him by the light of flickering candles. His face was pale as wax, his features stern and remote. He seemed to have stretched in death, appeared taller than in life. Suddenly I thought: he lies there like a soldier! All that the little fellow had had were three short years! He had always been so full of joy and laughter!

"The next morning came, and another terrible walk to the cemetery. I was totally alone among all the strangers surrounding me at the grave."

By the end of the summer the grain was harvested, the fruits were picked and potatoes and vegetables stored in the cellars of the big country house. Early one morning, a troop of Soviet soldiers on horses appeared in the center yard of the estate. Without any preliminaries they started to loot the living quarters, the storage houses and the cellars. Nothing but empty walls remained. The owners were arrested as "enemies of the people" and "capitalists" and were taken away.

"The next move of the Russians was to gallop on horses into our village, order the people out of their homes, and then chase us to the nearest town for registration. We had to run on foot, while the Soviet soldiers sat on horses and cracked their whips. Just as in the 'good old days' in Czarist Russia, when the Cossacks were sent out to chastise a village!"

Through the Refugee Center, Karen in late September received a message from her husband, who had been a pilot in the German Air

Force. He had found shelter in a village near Hannover. She set out with Bernd, age 6, to join him. Karen's trip to Hannover led over Berlin and Leipzig: "Berlin is in ruins. Huge city blocks for miles and miles are nothing but rubble. The Tiergarten, famous park in the center of town, consists only of burnt tree stumps and naked soil."

At the Anhalter Station, an immense crowd was waiting for trains to Leipzig. Whenever a train arrived, the people would rush forward, trying to squeeze through a narrow ramp leading to the trains. Karen, holding little Bernd by the hand, stood there for two days and two nights moving at a snail's pace. Heat and thirst tortured them. Bernd was totally exhausted and kept on whimpering softly.

At dawn on the morning of the third day they finally made it to the exit. People were storming the train that was coming in. British soldiers stood on guard with bayonets uncovered. Ever so often, they would fire a shot into the air, trying to control the mad rush to the train. People stood outside of the compartments on doorsteps and even sat on wagon rooftops.

In Leipzig Karen found her sister and her parents, even her old grandmother, Madame Vishnevsky. All had reached Leipzig on foot from the Warthegau. The Nazis had forced Karen's elderly father to join the "Volkssturm," with the result that he contracted TB. He is very sick. After several days in Leipzig, Karen continued her trek, leaving the Eastern Soviet-controlled zone of Germany, crossing the border at Friedland into Western Germany and then on to Bodenfelde, where she was reunited with her husband. "We again are a family, but my heart is broken. I can never forget my sweet babies . . . and two lonely wooden crosses on two little graves."

*December 19, 1945* I gave Mother Karen's letter to read. "Do you now see how lucky we were not to have settled in the Warthegau?" I asked her. She remained silent.

*December 24, 1945* Holy Night! We went to church and I thought of Karen and the terrible tragedy that she has had to live through. How blessed I am!

*December 31, 1945* New Year's Eve! I spent a quiet evening alone with Mother. At midnight I laid out the cards, trying to cast a glance into the future. "Mother," I said, "look at this combination of the Six and Ace of Hearts next to my card—the Queen of Diamonds. And here we have the King of Diamonds on the other side of me."

"What does it mean, Irene?"

"Well, it indicates marriage!"

"What nonsense, Irene! Where did you pick up these fortune-telling tricks?"

"Grandma Amalia taught me, and she learned it from an old gypsy, when she was a young girl."

"Where did your grandmother ever meet a gypsy?"

"She met her in the deep, dark woods of Russia almost a century ago."

"She wasn't even born then, Irene."

"All right, Mother, it was three quarters of a century ago, then."

"I don't believe a word of what you're telling me, Irene!"

But I just smiled.

*January 1, 1946* For the first time since 1940 New Year's Day is no longer the beginning of more months of suffering, terror, and destruction. Within a few short months the pendulum of my fate has swung the other way: where there was fear of death, there now is joy of life, where there was starvation there now is abundance, where there was loneliness and despair, there are now new acquaintances and there is new hope. It is true, Europe is still in ruins and our country is still lost, but we, the survivors, again have a future: the outlook is no longer death.

*January 7, 1946* A number of changes have occurred in the Officers' Mess. Lt. Downwood is gone and has been replaced by a new Mess officer, who, however, has brought along an assistant Mess officer—I'm not sure what for. It is my impression that Sergeant Jack is running the place. As a result of the administrative change, the entire restaurant is being redecorated, new wall paint, new curtains, new tablecloths, a new color scheme.

*January 15, 1946* I see new faces daily in my little office. It is as though I were looking through a kaleidoscope. This morning a jovial, mustachioed, middle-aged Frenchman came in, a major in the French Army. After receiving his traveler's rations, he complacently sat down in my visitor's chair and stayed for hours, talking.

My French is not good enough and his English is equally poor, so we talked in German, which he knows quite well. He talked about conditions in France, which are just as bad as in Germany, about his family, his civilian job. He is a chemist from the province of Languedoc in the southeast of France. At present he works in the French Control Office of the former

I.G. Farben Plan in Ludwigshafen, where in 1941 I had attended a course, and where in 1944, stepping out the train I had found a field of ruins. When finally leaving, the old fat major suddenly grabbed my hand and planted a big, wet kiss on it, his long moustache brushing my skin.

*February 6, 1946* Not much new is going on in the Officers' Mess except that some Russian DP's have been hired to do cleaning jobs.

*February 15, 1946* This afternoon, the door to my office opened and in walked—a Soviet officer. We don't see many of them in our Mess, but this certainly was an outstanding specimen. He was over six feet tall, much above the average height of the Russian males that I had encountered in Latvia. Furthermore, he was exceedingly good-looking with flashing blue eyes in an aristocratic face and with well-groomed dark hair. Clad in an elegant black uniform, big gold epaulettes glittering on his shoulders and brass buttons shining, he approached my desk with long elastic strides, asking for directions to the American Headquarters in Frankfurt. He spoke politely in excellent English, although with a haughty expression on his face. All I could think of was that the Soviets are probably sending their elite officers to Western Germany in order to properly impress the Americans and their other allies, the British and the French, with the superiority of their Red Army leaders. He was a tremendous contrast to the Soviet military personnel that I had encountered in Latvia six years ago: short, thick-set fellows, wearing shabby uniforms—frequently only quilted jackets—with no elegance whatsoever.

For a moment I stared at the Soviet officer in a state of shock, but then I pulled myself together and gave him the requested information in English, suddenly, upon impulse, switching to Russian. Now it was the officer's turn to appear surprised. "Why didn't you talk to me in Russian in the first place, comrade? Why did you let me break my tongue with this accursed English language?" he asked in an insolent tone, speaking Russian.

I had only waited for some such reaction: "I'm not your comrade; I'm not a Russian, I'm a Latvian. We don't want to be part of the Soviet Union: we want to be free . . . ." The officer stared at me in shocked disbelief, but I continued to shout in Russian, "Do you know what freedom means? Freedom—svoboda!"

Retreating a few steps the colonel watched me in silence, his blue eyes burning with suppressed fury. Then he turned abruptly and left. I'm still quite shaken up.

*March 12, 1946* This morning a short, stocky bow-legged man in British uniform marched into my office. Alert, darting eyes looked at me from a round face with protruding cheekbones. "Is this the place in charge of K & C rations, Miss?" he asked haughtily.

"This is correct. May I see your travel orders, Sir?"

"I haven't any, Miss."

"Then you'll have to come back later, after you have obtained them, Sir."

"I don't believe in ridiculous bureaucratic regulations. They are an invention of the capitalists!" the Britisher burst out.

I looked at him in surprise: "I don't quite follow your train of thought, Sir."

"Oh you don't, do you? Let me tell you, capitalism is the root of all evil." And he went into a harangue very familiar to me from my year under the "Sun of Stalin's Constitution" in Latvia.

"I've heard these theories before . . . in Soviet Latvia."

"Oh you have, have you? So you know all about Communism, eh?"

"Yes, I do!"

"And you don't approve, eh, Miss?"

"No, most certainly not!"

"Now let me tell you one thing, Miss: if you had grown up in a coal mining district you would think differently. I am a mining engineer, but my father was a coal miner in Wales and I grew up in abject poverty. Communism was our only hope. Only Communism promises equality and equal distribution of wealth and power. Communism is the only effective solution to all problems of life!"

"Maybe in theory, but not when it comes to its practical day-by-day application . . . . I have lived through almost a year of it and it was terror and disaster . . . ."

The Welsh mining engineer became increasingly agitated as our discussion continued, until he finally shouted at me, "How could I ever expect you to sympathize with Communism? You simply don't fit in with us laborers and workers. If you were ugly like me and short and bowlegged, then you would know what it is like to be the underdog, to belong to the oppressed, unwanted. But you, all you've got to do is smile, and success is yours!" Casting a last furious glance at me, he dashed out, slamming the door behind him.

*April 10, 1946* This afternoon before my very eyes, a "Cops and Robbers" game was being played out in the Officers' Mess. The door to my office opened and in walked a Polish captain, asking for travel rations. He was an older man, heavy-set, coarse-looking, with beady eyes and a fleshy nose. "May I see your travel orders, Sir?"

"I haven't any, but I need the rations. What shall I do?" I sent him to see the Mess Officer.

Three minutes later two young MPs burst into my office, in helmets, holding guns: "Hey Miss, have you seen a Polish captain, an older guy, chunky, with a ruddy face?"

"Yes I have. I just sent him to the Mess Officer."

"Where is he?"

"Through the bar next door and then left."

"Thanks Miss!" and out dashed the two MPs.

"Now, what is all that about?" I wondered, and peeked out of my office. All was quiet in the hall in front of me. Suddenly the double doors leading to the bar burst open, and out raced the two military policemen brandishing their guns.

"You leave through the front entrance; I'll take the back: this way we'll trap him in the back yard," I heard one of them shout. They sprinted by me and then went off in different directions. Greatly curious now, I ran to the Main Office and found everyone there very agitated, talking all at once, standing at a broken window. The Polish captain was gone.

"What happened? Where is the Polish fellow?"

"Why, he hurled himself out through the closed window, breaking the glass!"

"Where is he? Lying on the walk below?" I shuddered, imagining the man stunned and bleeding from cuts caused by broken glass. He couldn't very well have been killed, as the window is only eight feet above ground.

"Gosh no, Irene! He landed on his feet and got away. The police are after him."

"What a wild guy!" the Mess Officer said.

"What has he done? Why is he on the run?" I wanted to know.

"He has stolen some important documents and is trying to reach Berlin. That's why he came here for travel rations."

"Could he be a Soviet spy and no Polish captain at all?"

"Who know, Irene, everything is possible!" Later I heard that he got away. The MPs failed to catch him.

*April 30, 1946* Jack the Mess Sergeant and I were talking in the office when in walked two Soviet officers. One was an ordinary-looking fellow, but the other's appearance was rather unusual. He was tall and heavy-set, probably in his early forties. His bald, round head, unadorned by even a single hair, shone like a polished pink billiard ball. His eyes gleamed with a cruel green light, and oddly, he had painted two thick black stripes in place of nonexistent eyebrows, slanting them upward toward his temples. This gave him a truly devilish look, so I inwardly nicknamed him "Mephisto" after the famous satanic character of the "Faust" saga.

I wondered what business brought these two Soviets to our Mess hall, when Mephisto turned to Jack and informed him haughtily and in fluent English that he was a representative of the Soviet Repatriation Commission and had come to talk to the Russian employees of the Officers' Mess. Jack sent for our Russian DP workers, of whom there are about half a dozen.

After several minutes in walked just one small figure. It was Konstantin—"Kostya" for short—our 17-year-old Russian cleaning boy. I busied myself at my typewriter to dissimulate my interest in the proceedings as well as the fact that, knowing Russian, I could follow the remarkable interview that ensued between "Mephisto" and Kostya.

Mephisto asked gruffly, "Do you want to go back to Russia?"

"Nyet!"

"Why?"

"Because I don't care to live under your Soviet government."

"You are a traitor!"

Pale blond Kostya shot a furious glance at his accuser: "No, I am not. I love my country, but I hate Stalin and his gang."

"What is your name?"

"Eto nye vashe dyelo. (That is none of your business.)"

"Where were you born?"

"That is none of your business."

The second Soviet officer just stood listening, without uttering a word. Mephisto glared at the young Russian boy: "Why don't you want to give your name and birthplace?"

"Because I wish to protect my family who still live in Russia from your persecution."

"Aren't you longing to see your family again? Come on now, we will forget what you said, and Russia will receive you with open arms!"

"Sure, as soon as I am safely behind the Iron Curtain you will take excellent care of me by hanging me from the nearest tree."

"Why do you consider us such villains?"

"Very simply because you are."

The second officer still said nothing. Mephisto started again: "Now stop fooling and let's be friends. We only want what's best for you."

"If you consider a mass grave in Siberia's slave labor camps my best, then you may be right."

That was too much for Mephisto. He exploded, "Proklaty durak—you damned fool, leave this room immediately!"

Kostya remained very calm, looking Mephisto straight in the eye, while a mocking smile slowly spread across his face: "Stop shouting, Comrade. Here you have nothing to say!" And Kostya remained in the office.

White with fury, Mephisto turned to Jack: "Where are the other Russians?"

"They refuse to see you, sir."

"Order them to come here immediately!"

"I can give them orders regarding their work only. We Americans respect freedom of will, and if they don't want to meet you, sir, there is nothing I can do."

Mephisto stared at Jack, green eyes blazing. Then abruptly, he turned to his fellow officer, speaking in Russian: "'Prokladniye Amerikantsy—these damned Americans' Very embarrassing situation! We will only appear ridiculous if we go on insisting. I guess we better leave this damned place." And thrusting their caps on the heads, the Soviets, without taking their leave, directed their steps towards the door. There Mephisto suddenly stopped and casting an infuriated glance at Sergeant Jack, shouted, "And you want to be an American soldier? I am very sorry that our American Allies have such fools as you in their army!"

Jack turned white and for a moment I thought that he would throw himself onto the insolent brute, but then, gaining control, he stated calmly, "Your anger only emphasizes the failure of your mission, sir. Good day, sir!"

As soon as Mephisto and cohort had disappeared behind the door, Kostya rushed up to Jack. "Why didn't you punch that scoundrel in the nose, Sergeant? I would have helped you beat him up."

"We don't want to start an international incident, do we, Kostya?" was Jack's smiling reply.

I broke in: "Jack, you've missed your calling, you should be a diplomat!"

"Thanks, Irene. I'm glad you were here and able to understand their language. Will you please make a written report about this Soviet visit?"

Kostya is being celebrated as a hero throughout the Officers' Mess by Russians and Americans alike, because he had dared to speak his mind to the Soviet commissioner.

*May 5, 1946* I have been ordered to move to the Main Office. Starting in two weeks I will be the chief secretary, head cashier, main bookkeeper and interpreter—in other words "das Mädchen für alles" as the Germans would call it—"maid for all purposes."

*May 10, 1946* It was cloudy this morning when I started work at my office. About 10:00 AM the door opened and in walked an American officer all blond and bespectacled. From the insignia on his uniform I saw that he had the rank of a US Army colonel. On his sleeve was a sign saying "Scientific Consultant." The young man asked me for directions to the Mess Officer's quarters, which I gave him. He left and about ten minutes later he was back. To my surprise, he walked up to my desk, stopped in front of it and said, "It is raining today."

"It rains very often in the Rhine-Main valley," I responded. Silence, and then we started a conversation. In the midst of it I suddenly heard an inner voice: "This is your future husband." It seems so silly! I have no idea who this man is—nothing about him—his age, his background, his family. Is he married? I burst out laughing. "Why are you laughing?" he demanded.

"Oh, a very funny thought just struck me!" I answered. Thank goodness he did not ask me what that thought was! Then he told me his name: Merit White, and asked if he might come again and visit me at my office. I agreed and he left. An interesting fellow! Will I see him again?

*May 15, 1946* Since I work in the Main Office, I now have Sundays off. Also, for the first time, I have a chance to observe the two Mess Officers more closely. It is as I suspected, they do nothing all day long. They sit with their feet on their desks, occasionally answering the phone, either chatting or reading the "Stars and Stripes," chuckling over the comics' section. In the afternoons their lady friends come to visit, both cute American girls. Today, to my surprise, these young ladies also put their feet up on their boyfriends' desks, claiming that "in this hot weather it is much more comfortable to sit with your feet up."

I'm not sure what I find more peculiar: feet on desks or ladies on gentlemen's laps during working hours. Yesterday the girls placed themselves on our Mess Officers' laps and remained seated there, while visitors were moving in and out of the office. No one seemed to mind—I was probably the only one who felt slightly shocked. Then I decided, "Well, these are probably American customs!"

*May 23, 1946* Mother's words are still reverberating in my mind: "I wish we could return home!" We have come a long way, starting from the shores of the Baltic Sea, crossing the continent from north to south, living in turmoil under a string of different governments. Mr. Maximoff, the old high school teacher, back in Latvia seven years ago, was right when he predicted that the outbreak of the war would greatly change all our lives, that it would be similar to "living on a volcano." It was!

One big chapter in my life—the War—has ended; a new one is beginning. What will it bring? Like an echo out of the past, I seem to be hearing Father's advice, always given with a twinkle in the eye: "Just wait, my girl: you'll yet see wonders blossom!"

# EPILOGUE

The "inner voice" announcing I had met my future husband was right! So were the fortune-telling cards which on New Year's Eve predicted my imminent marriage. Less than a year later, I married the young American scientist who had appeared in my office on May 10. In fact we were married three times due to the confusing regulations of the occupying forces in the first post war years: First by a Latvian minister in a refugee camp, then in a civil ceremony in the town hall, and finally a church wedding.

My oldest daughter was born in Frankfurt on Main in 1947. I remembered Ingmar's fateful prediction: "In ten years . . . you will be pushing a baby carriage . . . ."

In November of 1949, we arrived in the United States, and made our home in a New England college community where my husband was engaged in teaching as well as research for the government.

On November 18, 1950, I attended a celebration to commemorate the founding of our Latvian Republic thirty-two years ago. We met in Boston, where many Latvian-Americans had gathered. There, to my great surprise, I came upon Dr. Arturs Dinbergs, my former boss in Riga, where as a young chemical engineer I had worked under him in my first job. I had last seen Dinbergs during the Soviet Occupation in February of 1941, shortly before I fled to Germany.

Dr. Dinbergs greeted me joyfully: "Irene, I never thought I'd ever meet you again! Do you know that you were incredibly lucky to leave Riga when you did?"

I was quite startled: "Why, what do you mean?"

"Irene, two weeks after your departure, two Soviet Commissars came to our plant asking for 'Comrade Zarina.' I suspect they wanted to arrest you for 'traitorous' anti-Soviet activities."

I stood transfixed in shock: "My God, what happened then?"

An expression of satisfaction spread over Dr. Dinbergs' face. "I told them, 'Comrades, you come too late. Miss Zarina has left for Germany.'"

Old fears rose. I realized immediately what fate would have awaited me, had I fallen into the hands of the Soviet extermination machine: deportation to far-away Siberia, cruel work in a slave labor camp, and most likely, in the end, a mass grave. Quite shaken, half crying, half laughing, I threw my arms around my dignified silver-haired Latvian friend: "I was saved by the grace of God against overwhelming odds, not even knowing it until this moment. How strange and how wonderful!"

After this memorable meeting I soon took up professional activities. I taught physics for a number of years at a women's college. After my third and youngest daughter was born I switched to research in the chemical industry. In 1967 I again returned to the academic field, teaching biochemistry at a university. That same year, following a lifelong interest, I went back to school and studied literature in my spare time. In 1970 I acquired another Master's Degree, this time in the Arts, not Sciences.

Mother followed me to the United States, where she enjoyed her granddaughters and lived to be 85.

I stayed in touch with my friends and relatives who had escaped from behind the Iron Curtain of Soviet domination. Aunt Meta, who had lost her entire family in the first three months of 1945, joined her sister in Holland, where she eventually remarried and lived the rest of her life in a quiet suburb of Den Haag. My friend Karen, whose two youngest boys died of deprivation during her flight from the Soviet forces, settled in Hamburg with her surviving son Bernd, who grew up to become an engineer for Lufthansa. My Aunt Erika and Cousin Eva immigrated to Australia. Aunt Erika visited me in America in the late 1970's with her third Latvian husband.

I never heard again from Dr. Dehren, forbidden to marry by the Nazi genetic ideologists. I fear he died on the Berlin barricades, which he had mentioned in his last postcard to me. I do not know either if Walter of the German Foreign Service in Berlin survived the war. My admirer Herr Evers was released from the American prisoner of war camp in the late 1940's. I ran into him a few years later when I visited Höchst. I stayed in touch with Dr. Thorgau, our amiable French teacher, who went back to work for Höchst Farbwerke (the successor company of I.G. Farben). Dr. Ķilian likewise went back to work for Höchst Farbwerke, as did his two sons. The Kilians' much younger daughter, Liliane the "Cellar-bug," grew into a beautiful girl, became a teacher, married and had two sons.

I was particularly saddened to learn, years after the war, of the fate of my Jewish friends after the Nazi occupation of the Baltic States. The parents of Gabriel, my first dancing-school partner, committed suicide in July 1941, when German troops were approaching Latvia. They took potassium cyanide together with Gabriel's younger brother, no doubt in order to escape any possible Nazi persecution, even though they had converted to Lutheranism. When this news reached Gabriel in Switzerland, he shot himself to death.

My neighbor Kreina, also Jewish, could have been saved if her Latvian boyfriend had married her. But he didn't, and she perished in a concentration camp.

In 1991 a miracle occurred; the unbelievable happened: the Soviet Union broke up, and after 50 years of destructive oppression the three Baltic States regained their lost freedom. I had never ever dared to hope that this momentous event would occur during my lifetime. But it did!

I could now write to friends still living in Riga. Many have disappeared or have since died. Herta, who insisted on returning to Soviet-occupied Latvia, died shortly after the war. So did my friend Elsa. I found out that my cousin Elra had remarried in Siberia and had a son. She had finally returned to Estonia, but died before I could see her again. My daughters are now in contact with her son and grandson, the only surviving members of my family in the Baltic States.

I visited Latvia and Estonia with my eldest daughter in 1997, for the first time in 54 years. I had the impression that every third adult we met had spent time in Soviet prison camps. We saw many people, particularly old people, begging, often with only rags on their feet instead of shoes. Russians represent about 30% of the population, with an even greater concentration in the capital cities.

It was a joy to meet old friends and discover their children and grandchildren. I visited Sigulda in hopes of finding Ingmar's family, and indeed, still living in the familiar house I found his younger brother Leonid, who up to that time I believed had also been killed in the war. We fell into each other's arms, weeping.

In 2004 Latvia and Estonia were among ten new member nations admitted to the European Union.

Looking back upon my life since my childhood and youth in Latvia, the terrible war years in Germany as a young professional, and finally my family life and career in my new home, America, I am reminded of a sinus curve, a never-ending sequence of ups and downs and new adventures.

Westerly, Rhode Island<br>June 2005

Made in the USA
Middletown, DE
22 April 2016